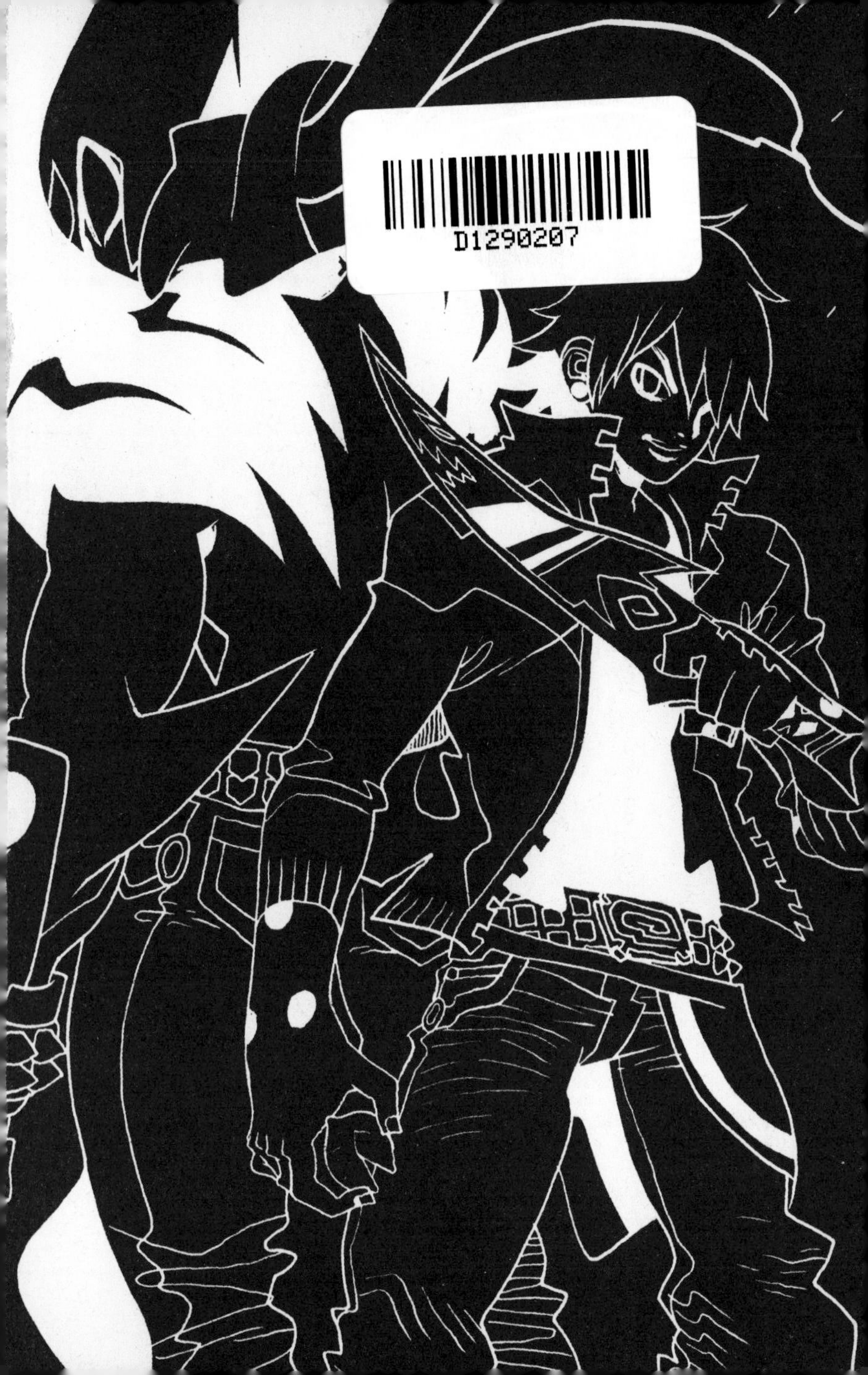

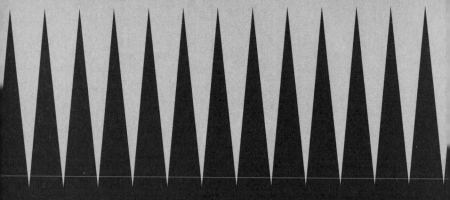

STORY + ART BY
COREY S. LEWIS REYYY

GRAYTONES BY
DAN CIURCZAK
+REYYY

Published By Oni Press, Inc.
JOE NOZEMACK *Publisher*
JAMES LUCAS JONES *Editor in Chief*
GEORGE ROHAC *Operations Director*
CORY CASONI *Marketing Director*
KEITH WOOD *Art Director*
JILL BEATON *Editor*
CHARLIE CHU *Editor*
TROY LOOK *Digital Prepress Lead*

ONI PRESS, INC.
1305 SE Martin Luther King Jr. Blvd.
Suite A
Portland, OR 97214
USA

www.onipress.com
www.reyyy.com

First Edition: March 2012
ISBN 978-1-932664-27-0

1 3 5 7 9 10 8 6 4 2

PRINTED IN THE U.S.A. at Lakebook Manufacturing

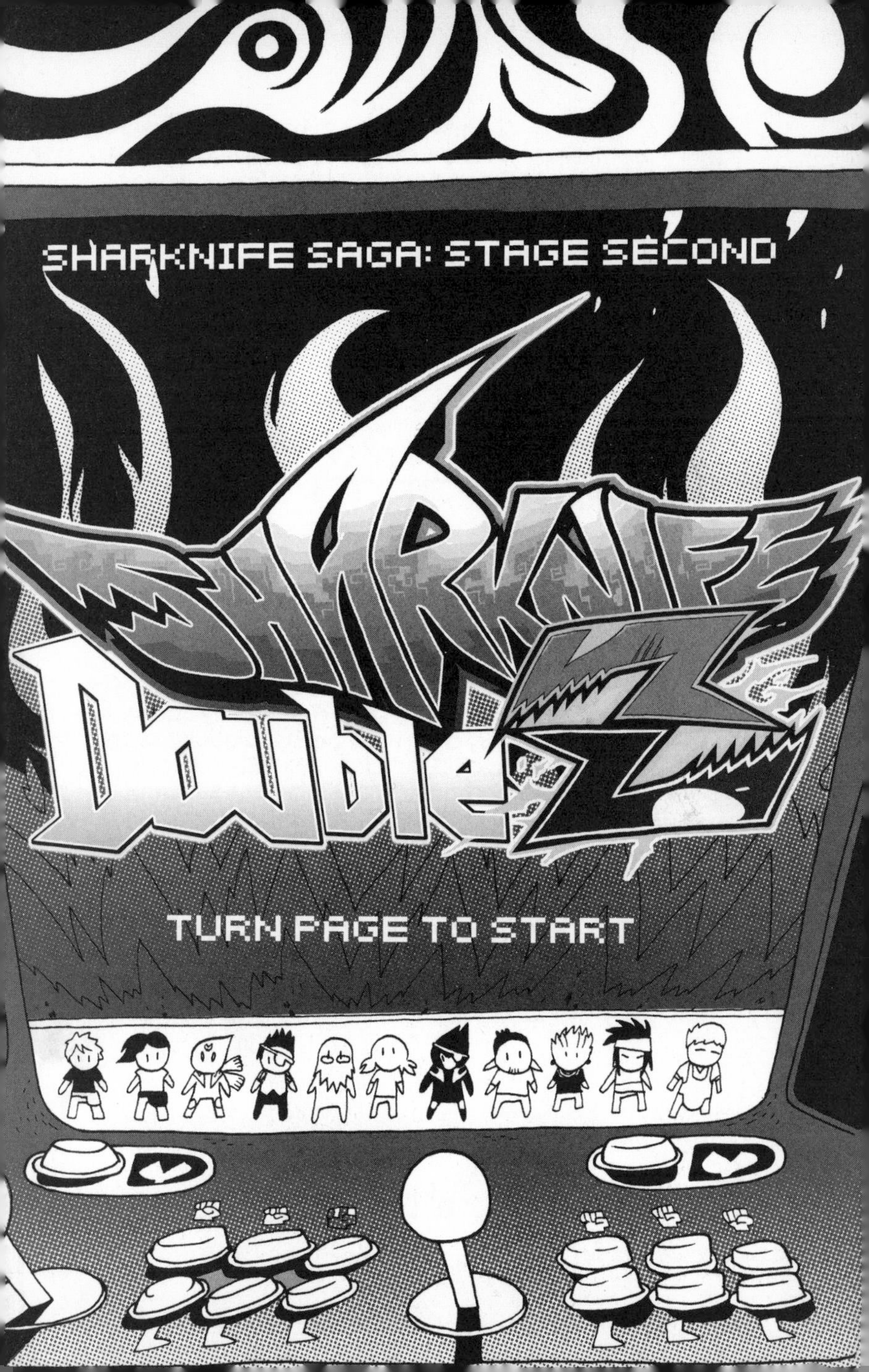
SHARKNIFE SAGA: STAGE SECOND
SHARKNIFE
DOUBLE Z
TURN PAGE TO START

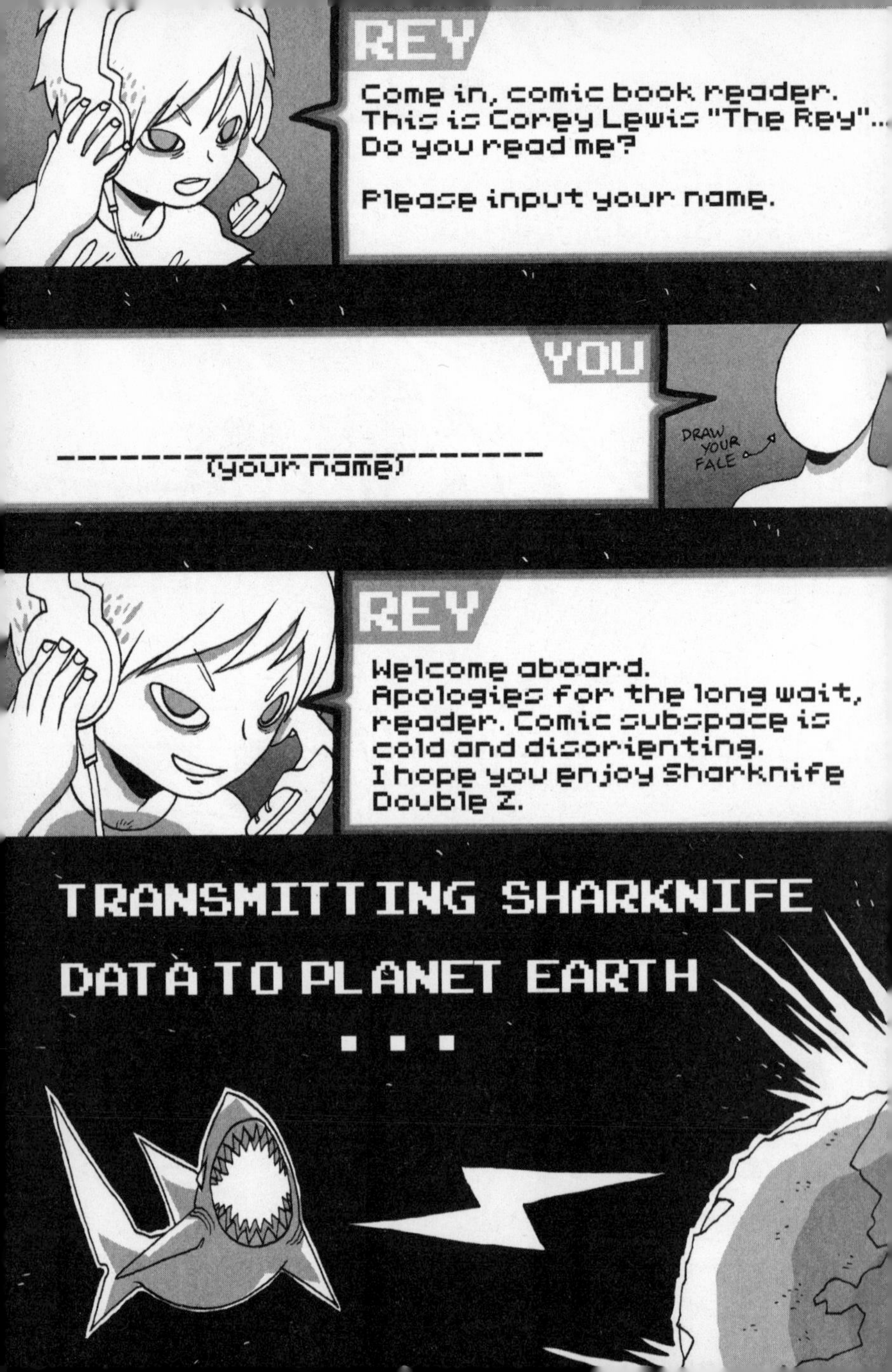
REY
Come in, comic book reader. This is Corey Lewis "The Rey"... Do you read me?
Please input your name.
YOU
(your name)
DRAW YOUR FACE
REY
Welcome aboard. Apologies for the long wait, reader. Comic subspace is cold and disorienting. I hope you enjoy Sharknife Double Z.
TRANSMITTING SHARKNIFE DATA TO PLANET EARTH
...

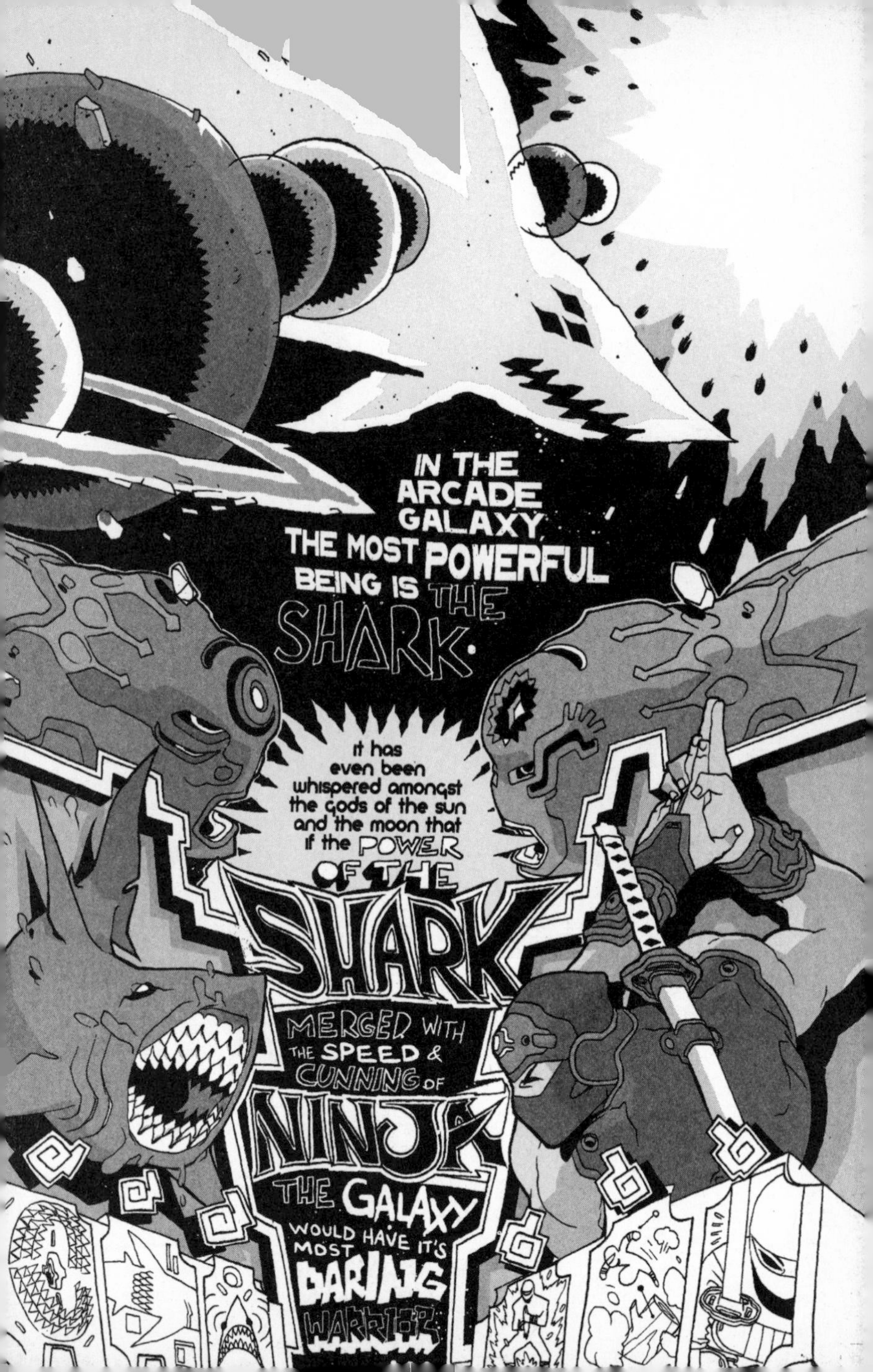
IN THE ARCADE GALAXY, THE MOST POWERFUL BEING IS THE SHARK.
it has even been whispered amongst the gods of the sun and the moon that if the POWER OF THE SHARK MERGED WITH THE SPEED & CUNNING OF NINJA THE GALAXY WOULD HAVE IT'S MOST DARING WARRIOR

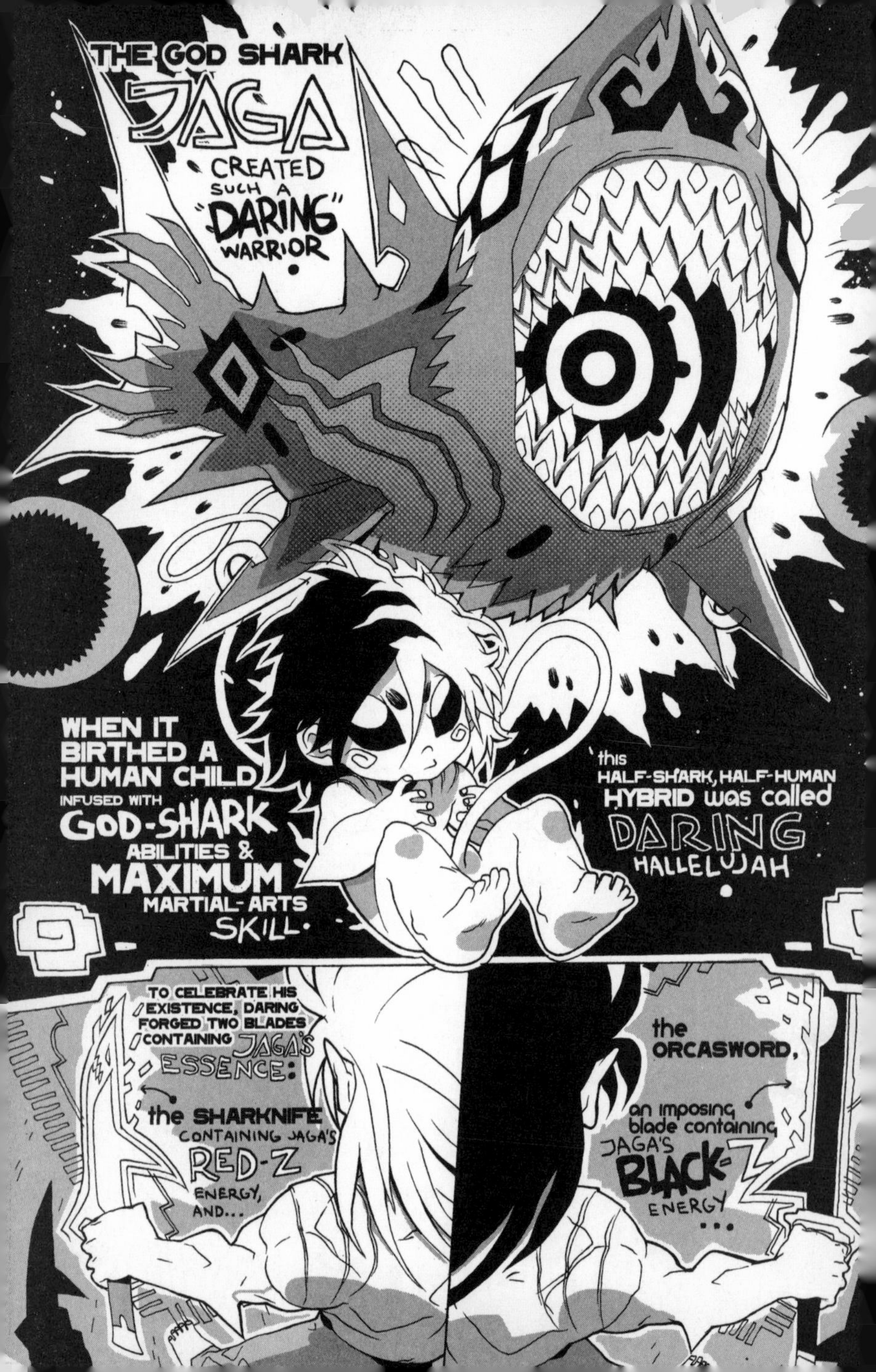
THE GOD SHARK
JAGA
CREATED SUCH A "DARING" WARRIOR.
WHEN IT BIRTHED A HUMAN CHILD INFUSED WITH GOD-SHARK ABILITIES & MAXIMUM MARTIAL-ARTS SKILL.
this HALF-SHARK, HALF-HUMAN HYBRID was called
DARING
HALLELUJAH.
TO CELEBRATE HIS EXISTENCE, DARING FORGED TWO BLADES CONTAINING JAGA'S ESSENCE:
the SHARKNIFE CONTAINING JAGA'S RED-Z ENERGY, AND...
the ORCASWORD,
an imposing blade containing JAGA'S BLACK-Z ENERGY...

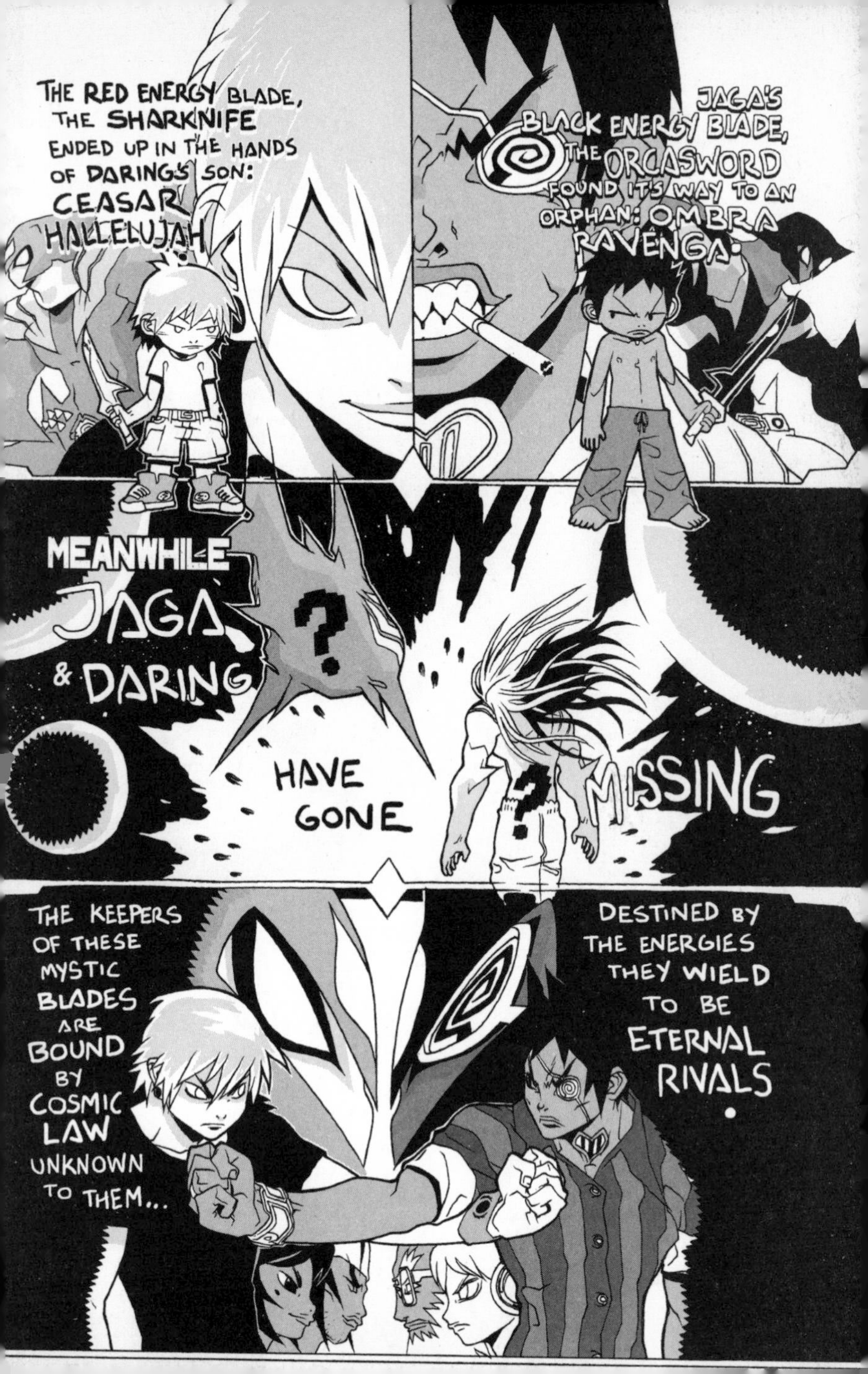

THE RED ENERGY BLADE, THE SHARKNIFE ENDED UP IN THE HANDS OF DARING'S SON: CEASAR HALLELUJAH
JAGA'S BLACK ENERGY BLADE, THE ORCASWORD FOUND IT'S WAY TO AN ORPHAN: OMBRA RAVENGA.
MEANWHILE JAGA & DARING
HAVE GONE
MISSING
THE KEEPERS OF THESE MYSTIC BLADES ARE BOUND BY COSMIC LAW UNKNOWN TO THEM...
DESTINED BY THE ENERGIES THEY WIELD TO BE ETERNAL RIVALS.

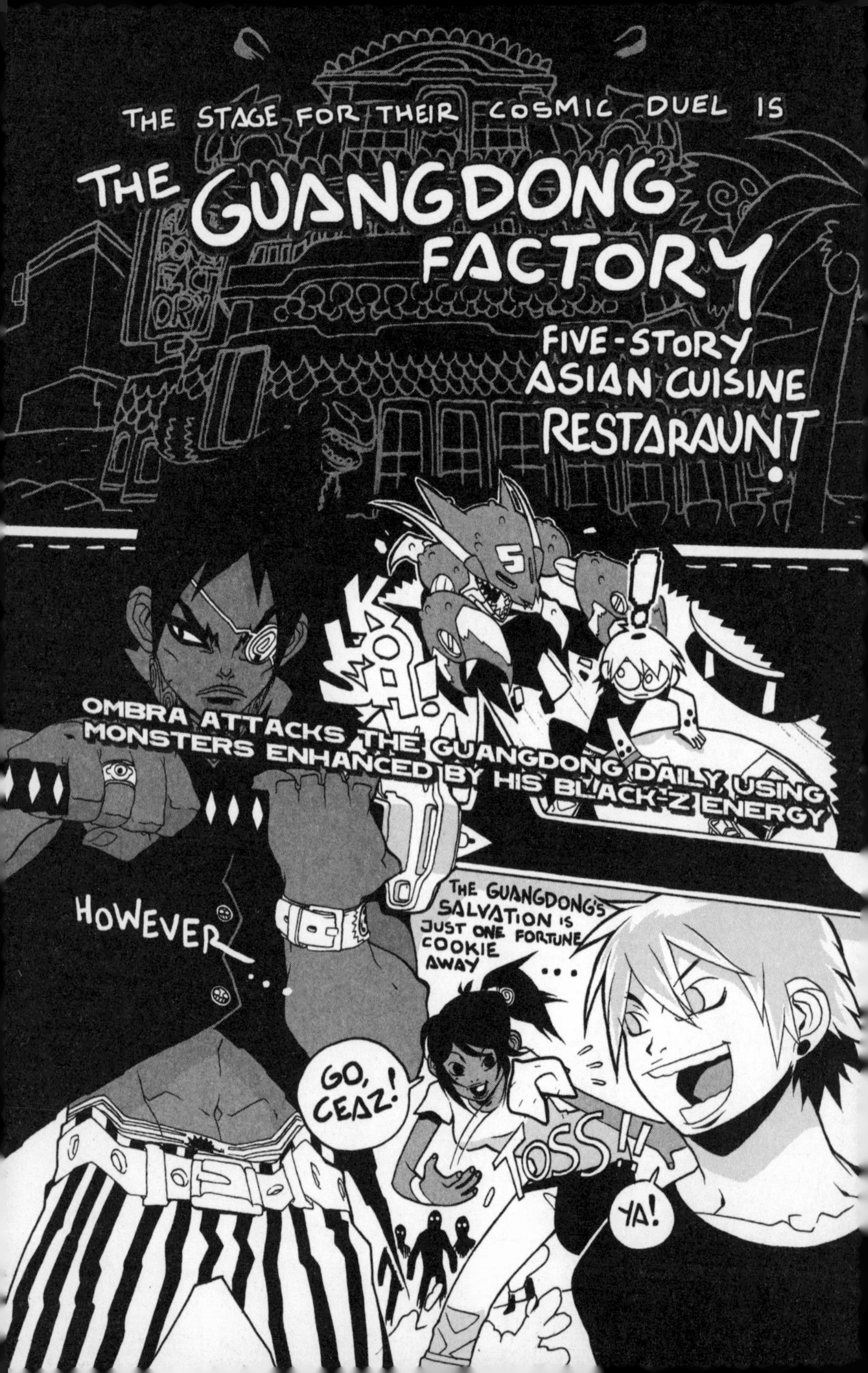
THE STAGE FOR THEIR COSMIC DUEL IS
THE GUANGDONG FACTORY
FIVE-STORY ASIAN CUISINE RESTARAUNT!
OMBRA ATTACKS THE GUANGDONG DAILY USING MONSTERS ENHANCED BY HIS BLACK-Z ENERGY
HOWEVER...
THE GUANGDONG'S SALVATION IS JUST ONE FORTUNE COOKIE AWAY
...
GO, CEAZ!
TOSS!!
YA!

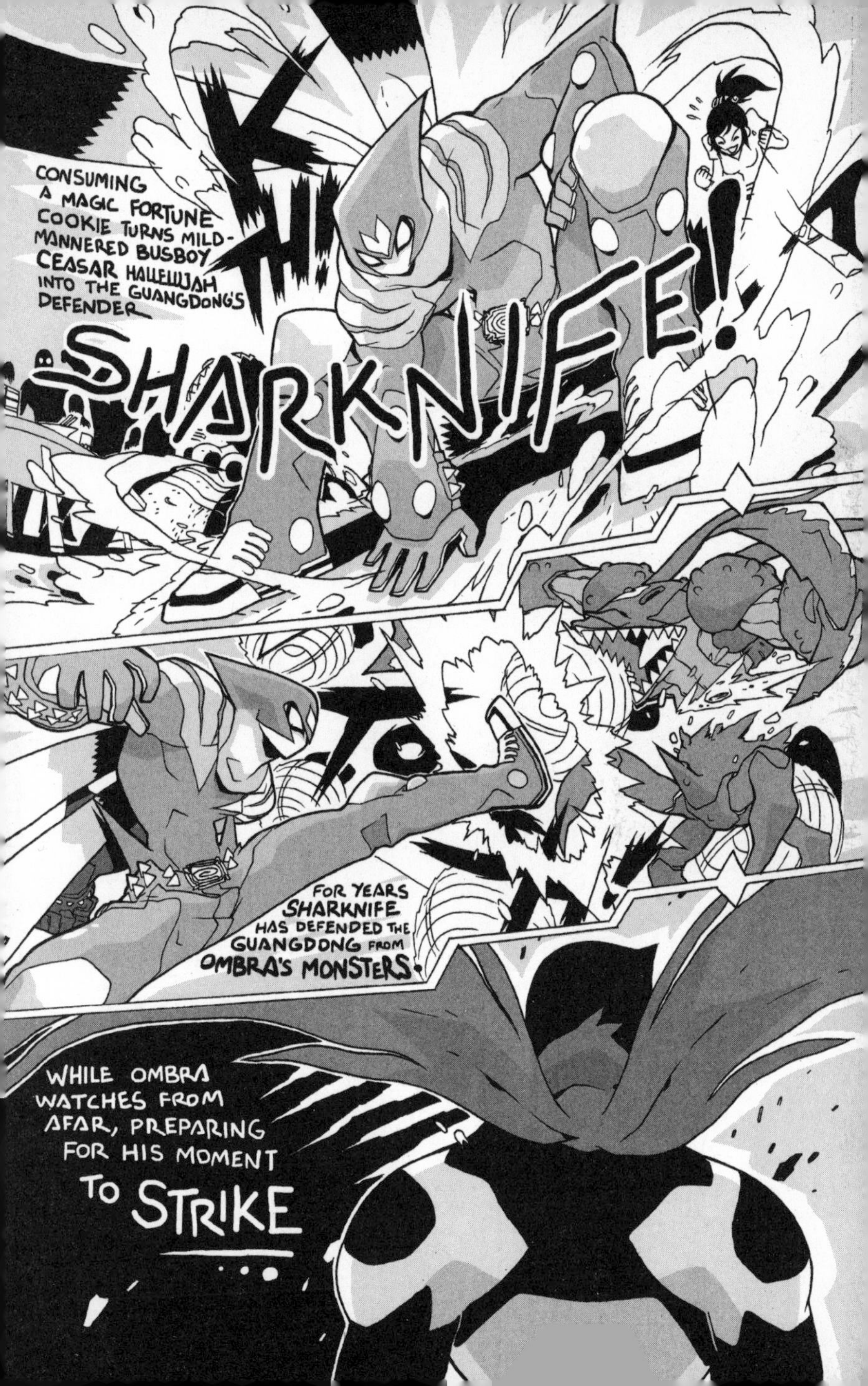
CONSUMING A MAGIC FORTUNE COOKIE TURNS MILD-MANNERED BUSBOY CEASAR HALLELUJAH INTO THE GUANGDONG'S DEFENDER
SHARKNIFE!!
FOR YEARS SHARKNIFE HAS DEFENDED THE GUANGDONG FROM OMBRA'S MONSTERS.
WHILE OMBRA WATCHES FROM AFAR, PREPARING FOR HIS MOMENT TO STRIKE
...

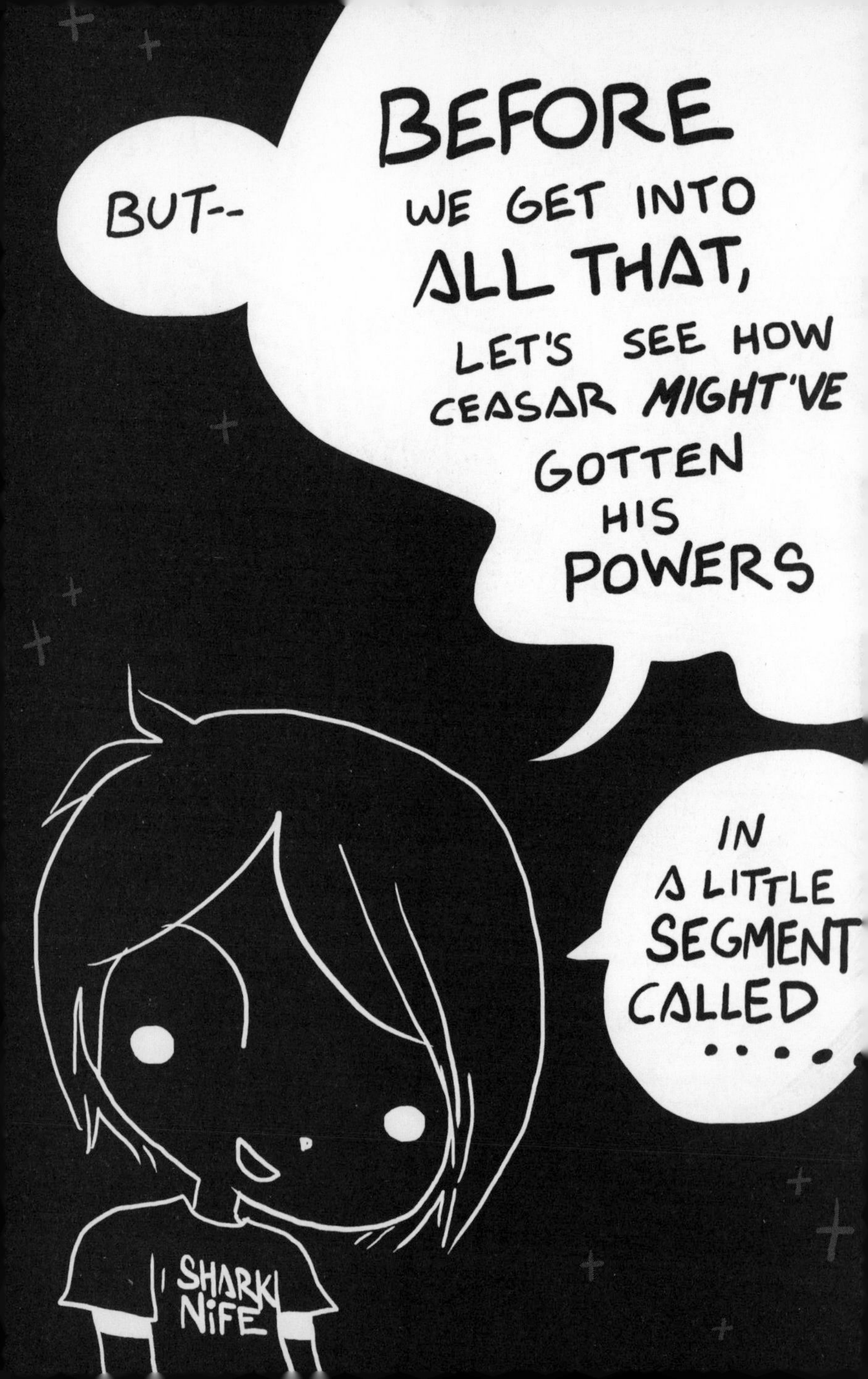
BUT--
BEFORE WE GET INTO ALL THAT, LET'S SEE HOW CEASAR MIGHT'VE GOTTEN HIS POWERS
IN A LITTLE SEGMENT CALLED ....
SHARK NiFE

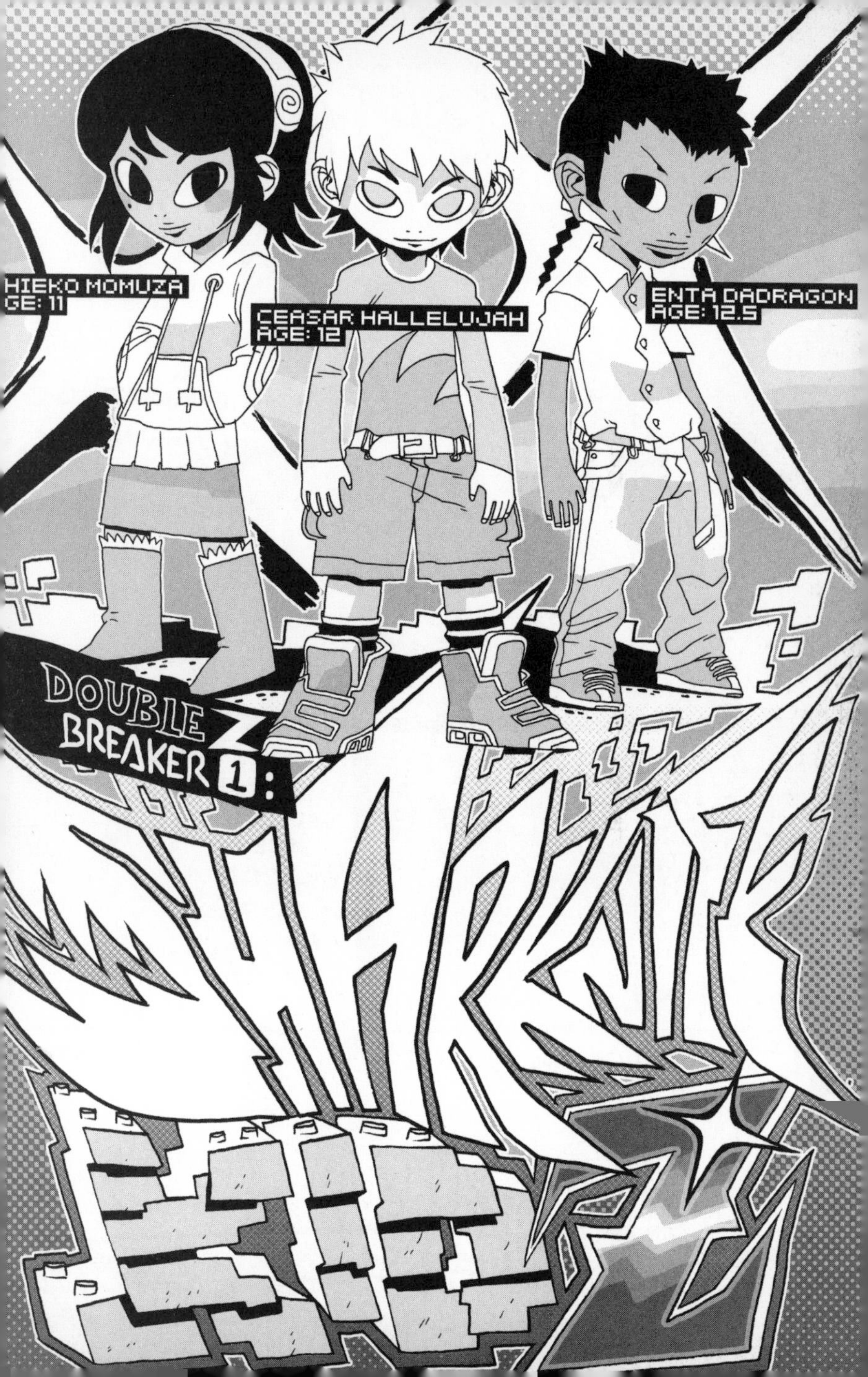
HIEKO MOMUZA
GE: 11
CEASAR HALLELUJAH
AGE: 12
ENTA DADRAGON
AGE: 12.5
DOUBLE BREAKER 1:

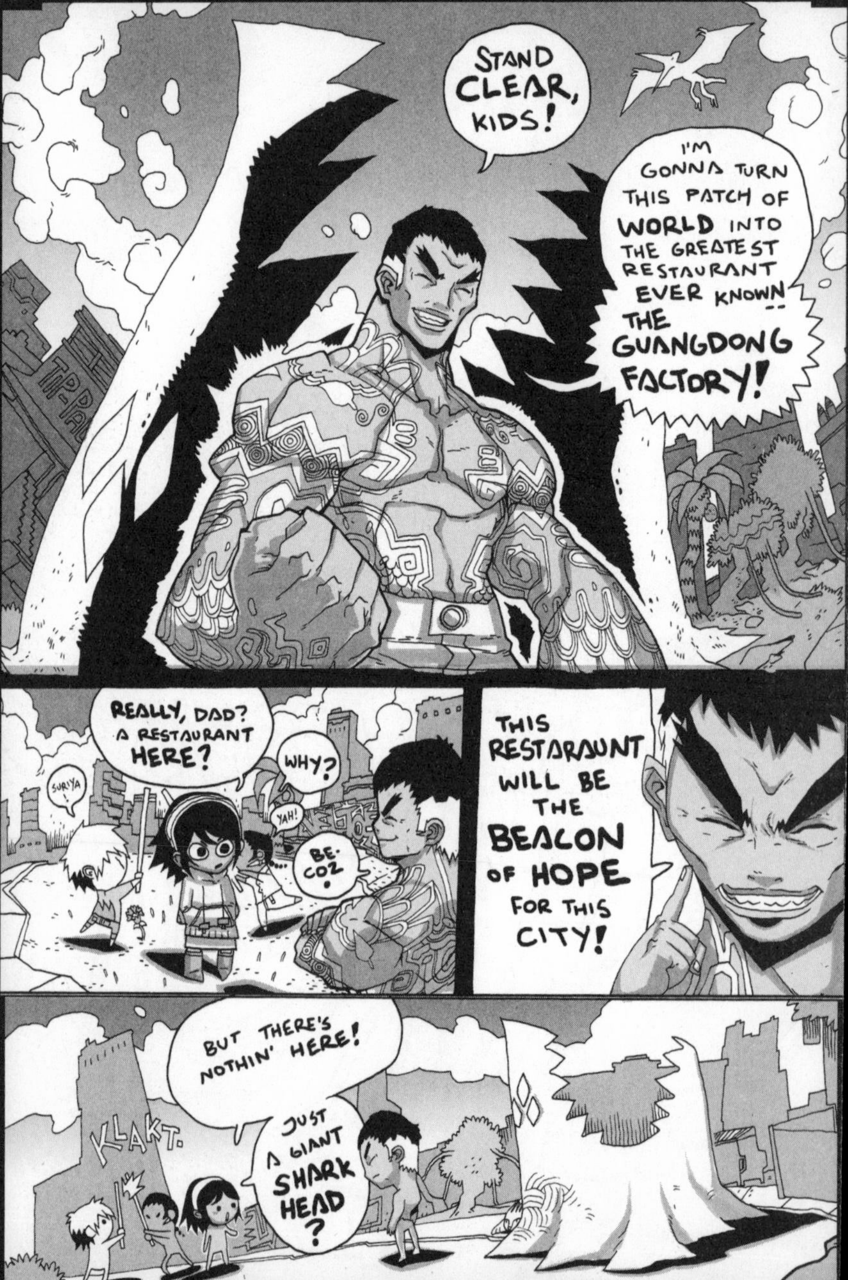
STAND CLEAR, KIDS!
I'M GONNA TURN THIS PATCH OF WORLD INTO THE GREATEST RESTAURANT EVER KNOWN -- THE GUANGDONG FACTORY!
SURIYA!
REALLY, DAD? A RESTAURANT HERE?
WHY?
YAH!
BE. COZ.
THIS RESTARAUNT WILL BE THE BEACON OF HOPE FOR THIS CITY!
KLAKT.
BUT THERE'S NOTHIN' HERE!
JUST A GIANT SHARK HEAD?

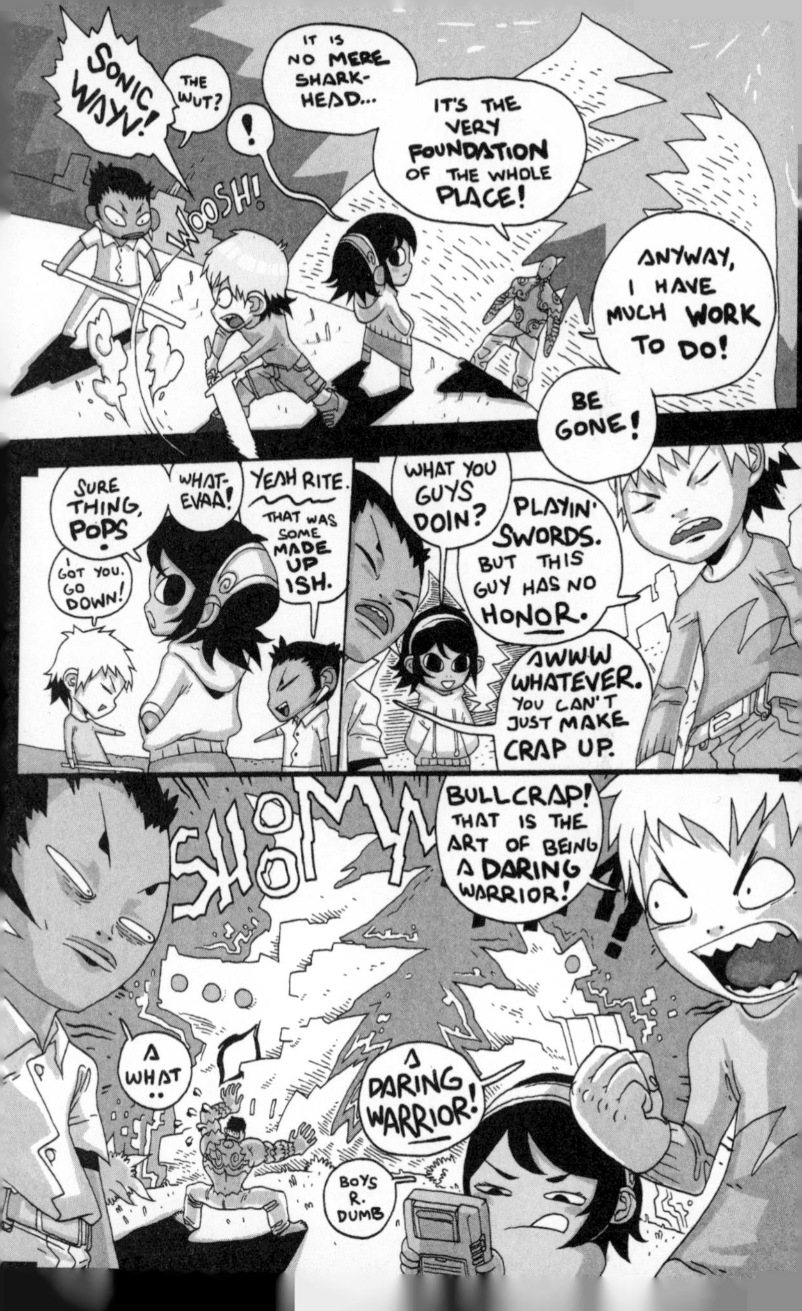
SONIC WAYV!
THE WUT?
!
IT IS NO MERE SHARK-HEAD...
IT'S THE VERY FOUNDATION OF THE WHOLE PLACE!
WOOSH!
ANYWAY, I HAVE MUCH WORK TO DO!
BE GONE!
SURE THING, POPS.
WHAT-EVAA!
YEAH RITE.
THAT WAS SOME MADE UP ISH.
I GOT YOU. GO DOWN!
WHAT YOU GUYS DOIN?
PLAYIN' SWORDS. BUT THIS GUY HAS NO HONOR.
AWWW WHATEVER. YOU CAN'T JUST MAKE CRAP UP.
SHOOM
BULLCRAP! THAT IS THE ART OF BEING A DARING WARRIOR!
!!
...
A WHAT..
A DARING WARRIOR!
BOYS R. DUMB

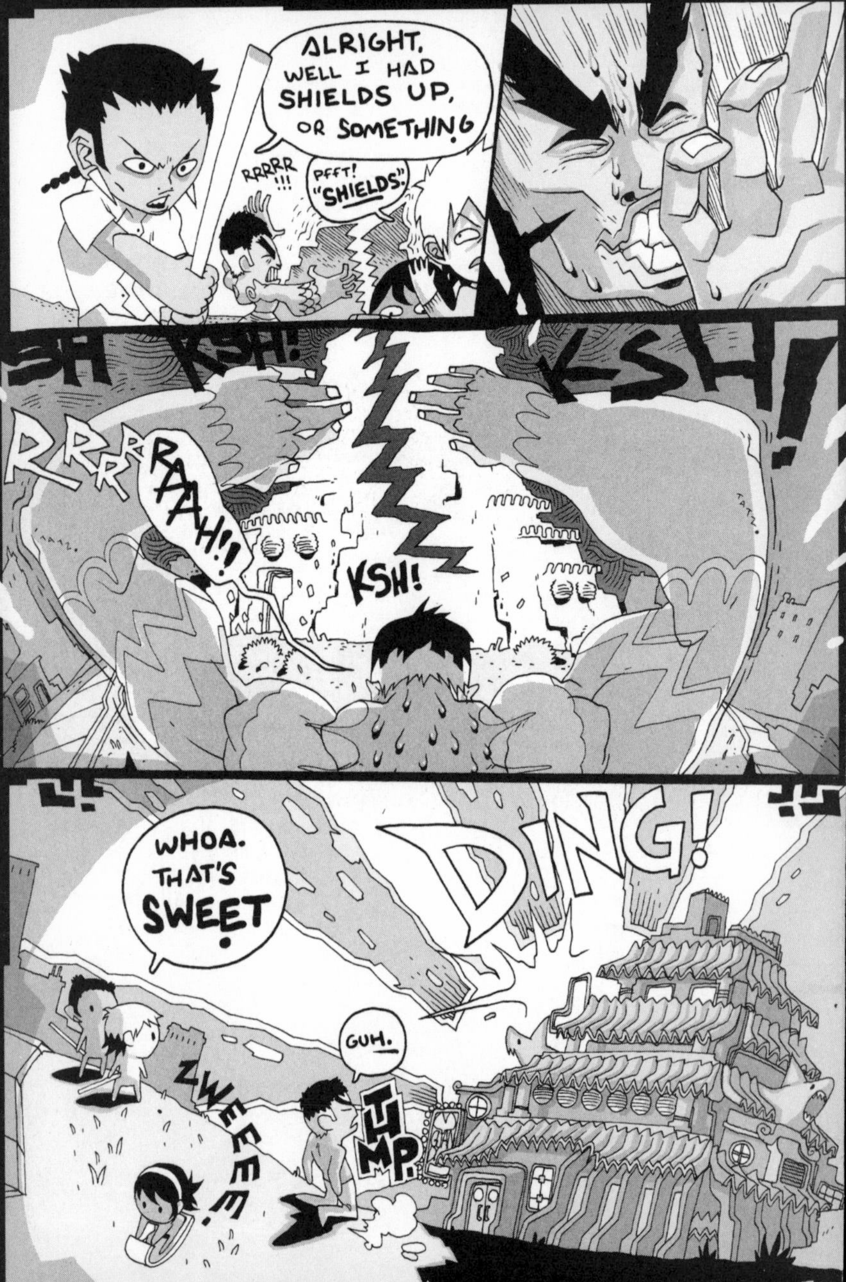
ALRIGHT. WELL I HAD SHIELDS UP, OR SOMETHING.
RRRRR !!!
PFFT! "SHIELDS."
SH KSH!
KSH!
RRRRRAAAH!!
KSH!
WHOA. THAT'S SWEET.
DING!
GUH.
ZWEEEEE!
THUMP.

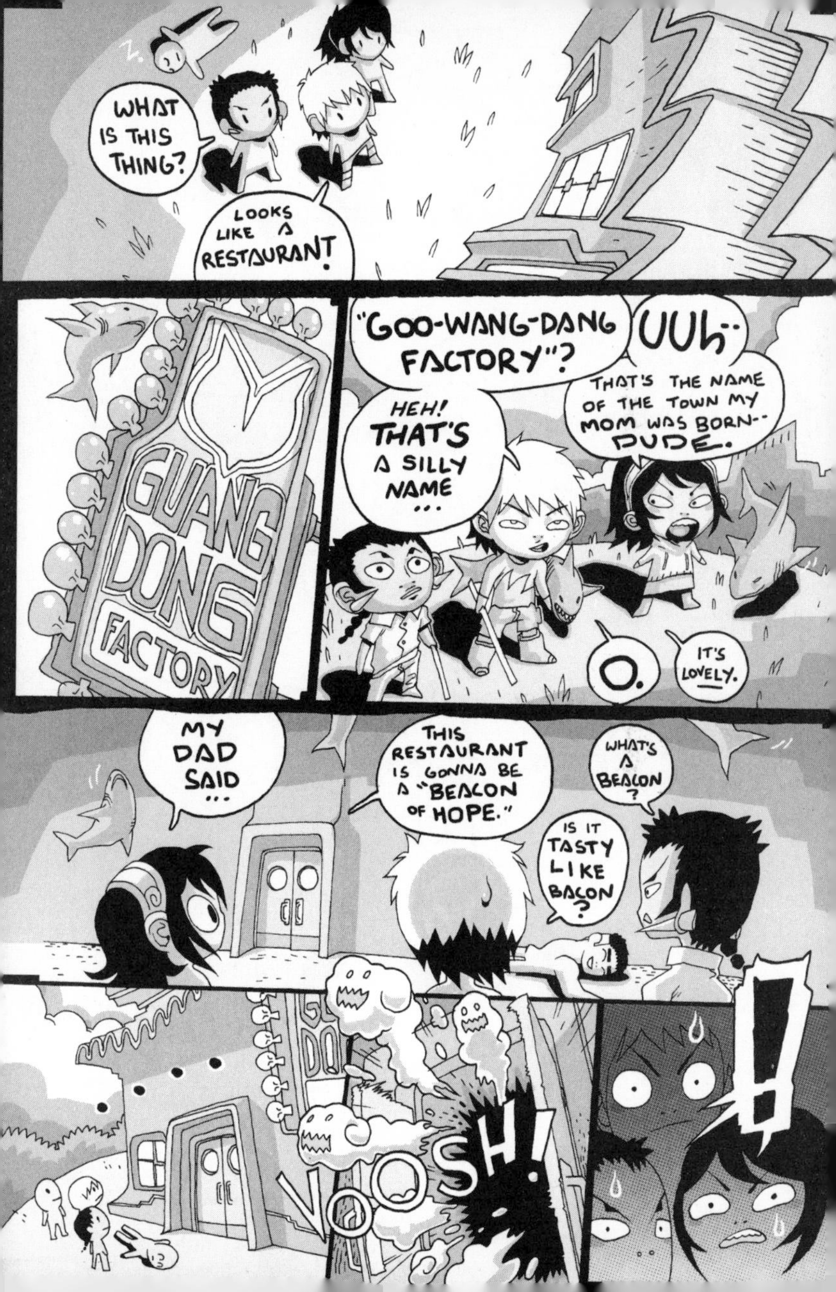
Z
WHAT IS THIS THING?
LOOKS LIKE A RESTAURANT!
GUANG DONG FACTORY
"GOO-WANG-DANG FACTORY"?
HEH! THAT'S A SILLY NAME...
UUh..
THAT'S THE NAME OF THE TOWN MY MOM WAS BORN-- DUDE.
O.
IT'S LOVELY.
MY DAD SAID...
THIS RESTAURANT IS GONNA BE A "BEACON OF HOPE."
WHAT'S A BEACON?
IS IT TASTY LIKE BACON?
VOOOSH!
!

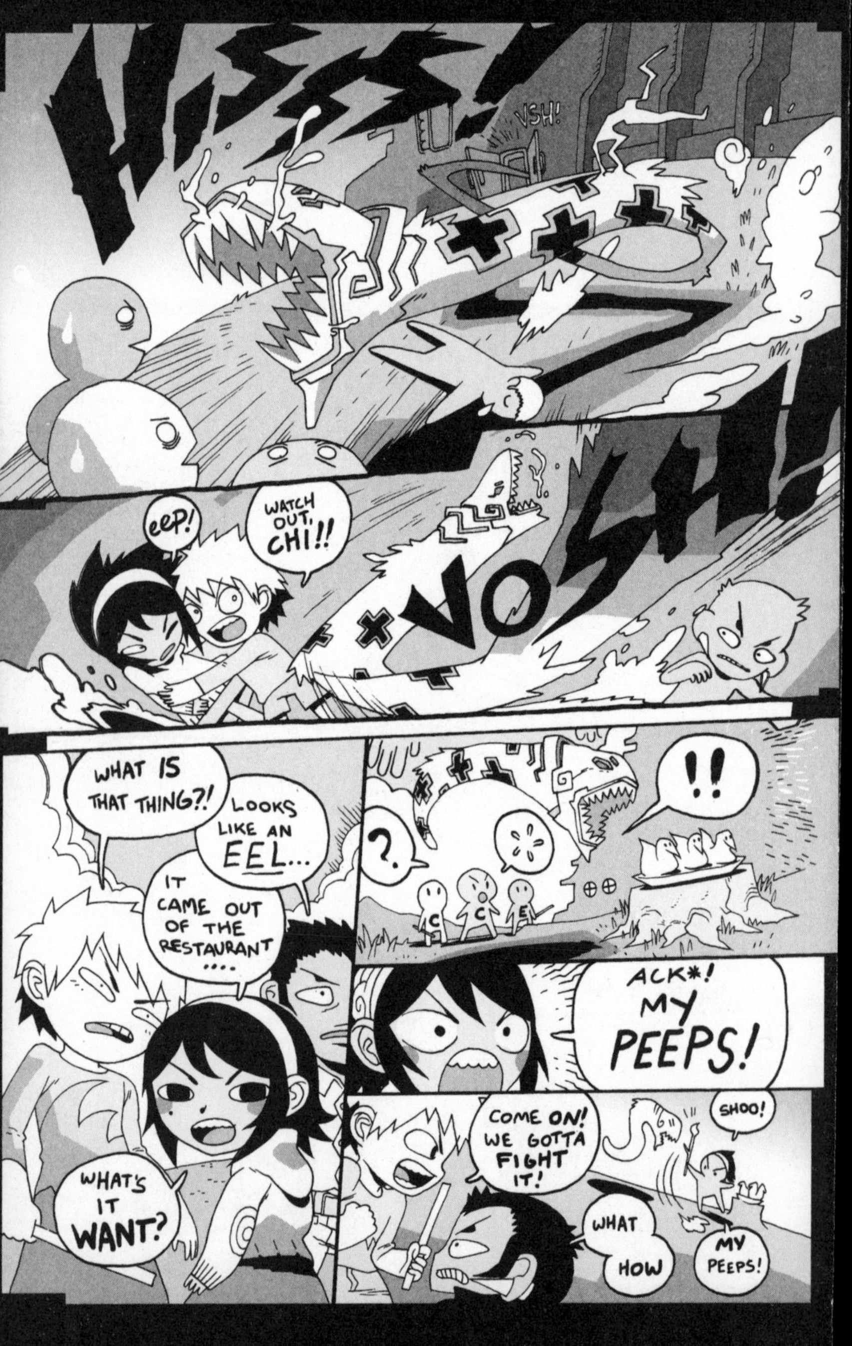
HISS!
VSH!
VOSH!
eep!
WATCH OUT, CHI!!
WHAT IS THAT THING?!
LOOKS LIKE AN EEL...
IT CAME OUT OF THE RESTAURANT ....
WHAT'S IT WANT?
?
!!
ACK*! MY PEEPS!
COME ON! WE GOTTA FIGHT IT!
SHOO!
WHAT
HOW
MY PEEPS!

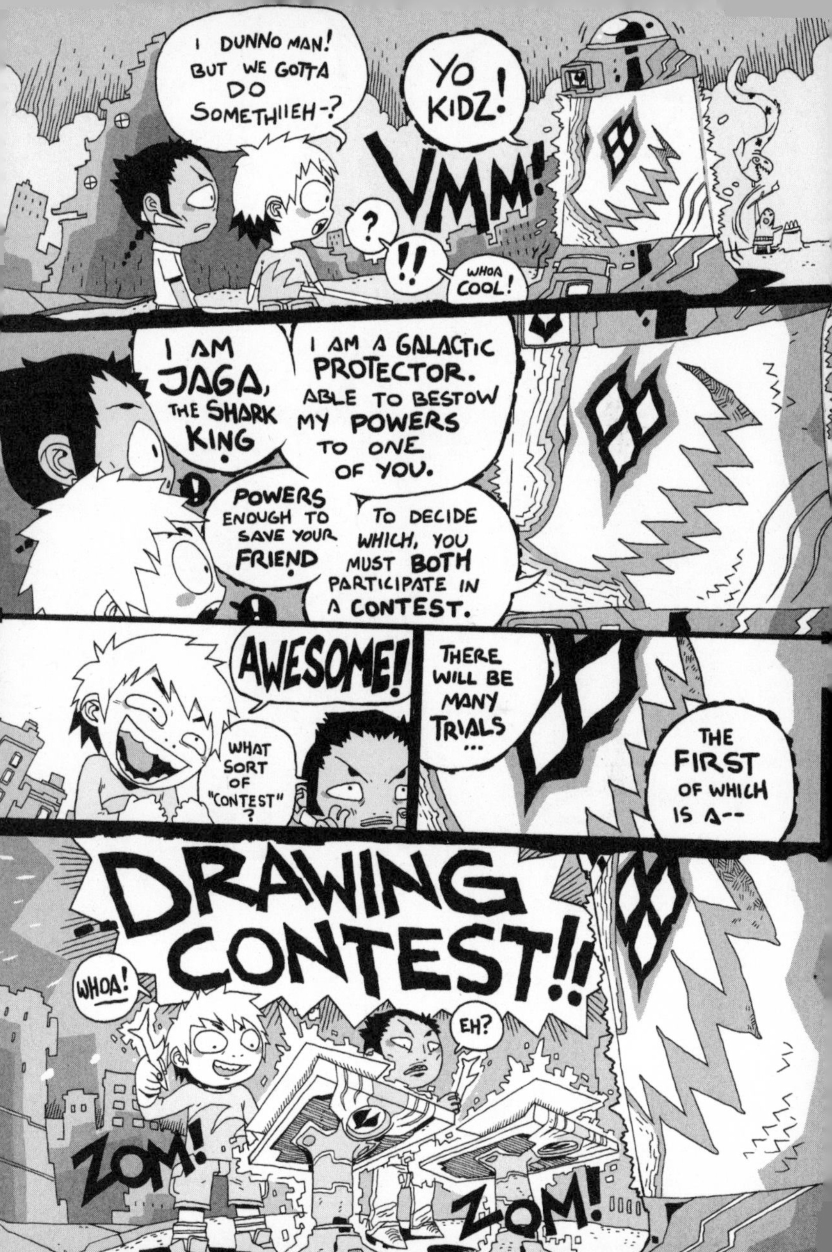
I DUNNO MAN! BUT WE GOTTA DO SOMETHIIEH-?
YO KIDZ!
VMM!
?
!!
WHOA COOL!
I AM JAGA, THE SHARK KING.
I AM A GALACTIC PROTECTOR. ABLE TO BESTOW MY POWERS TO ONE OF YOU.
POWERS ENOUGH TO SAVE YOUR FRIEND.
TO DECIDE WHICH, YOU MUST BOTH PARTICIPATE IN A CONTEST.
AWESOME!
WHAT SORT OF "CONTEST"?
THERE WILL BE MANY TRIALS...
THE FIRST OF WHICH IS A--
DRAWING CONTEST!!
WHOA!
EH?
ZOM!
ZOM!

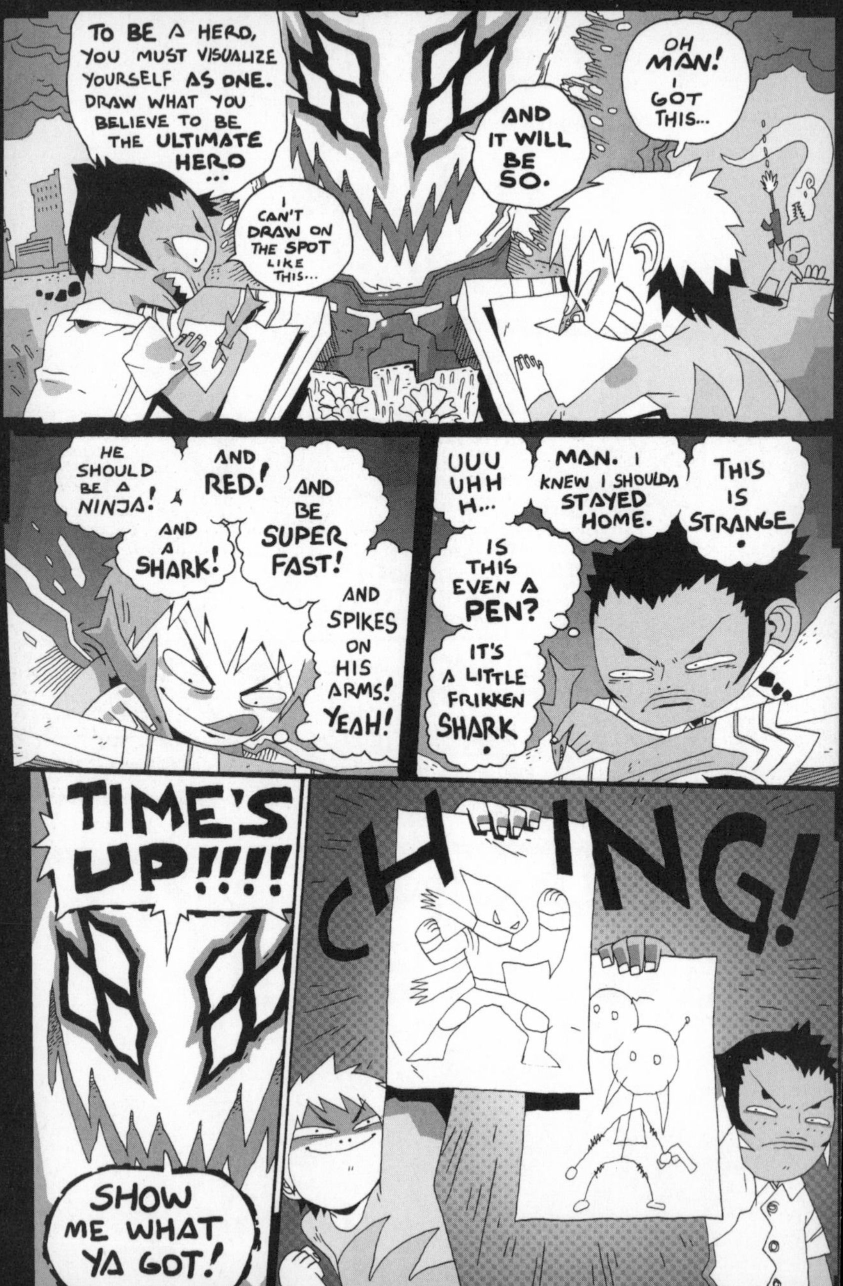
TO BE A HERO, YOU MUST VISUALIZE YOURSELF AS ONE. DRAW WHAT YOU BELIEVE TO BE THE ULTIMATE HERO...
I CAN'T DRAW ON THE SPOT LIKE THIS...
AND IT WILL BE SO.
OH MAN! I GOT THIS...
HE SHOULD BE A NINJA!
AND RED!
AND A SHARK!
AND BE SUPER FAST!
AND SPIKES ON HIS ARMS! YEAH!
UUUUHHH...
MAN. I KNEW I SHOULDA STAYED HOME.
THIS IS STRANGE.
IS THIS EVEN A PEN?
IT'S A LITTLE FRIKKEN SHARK.
TIME'S UP!!!!
CHING!
SHOW ME WHAT YA GOT!

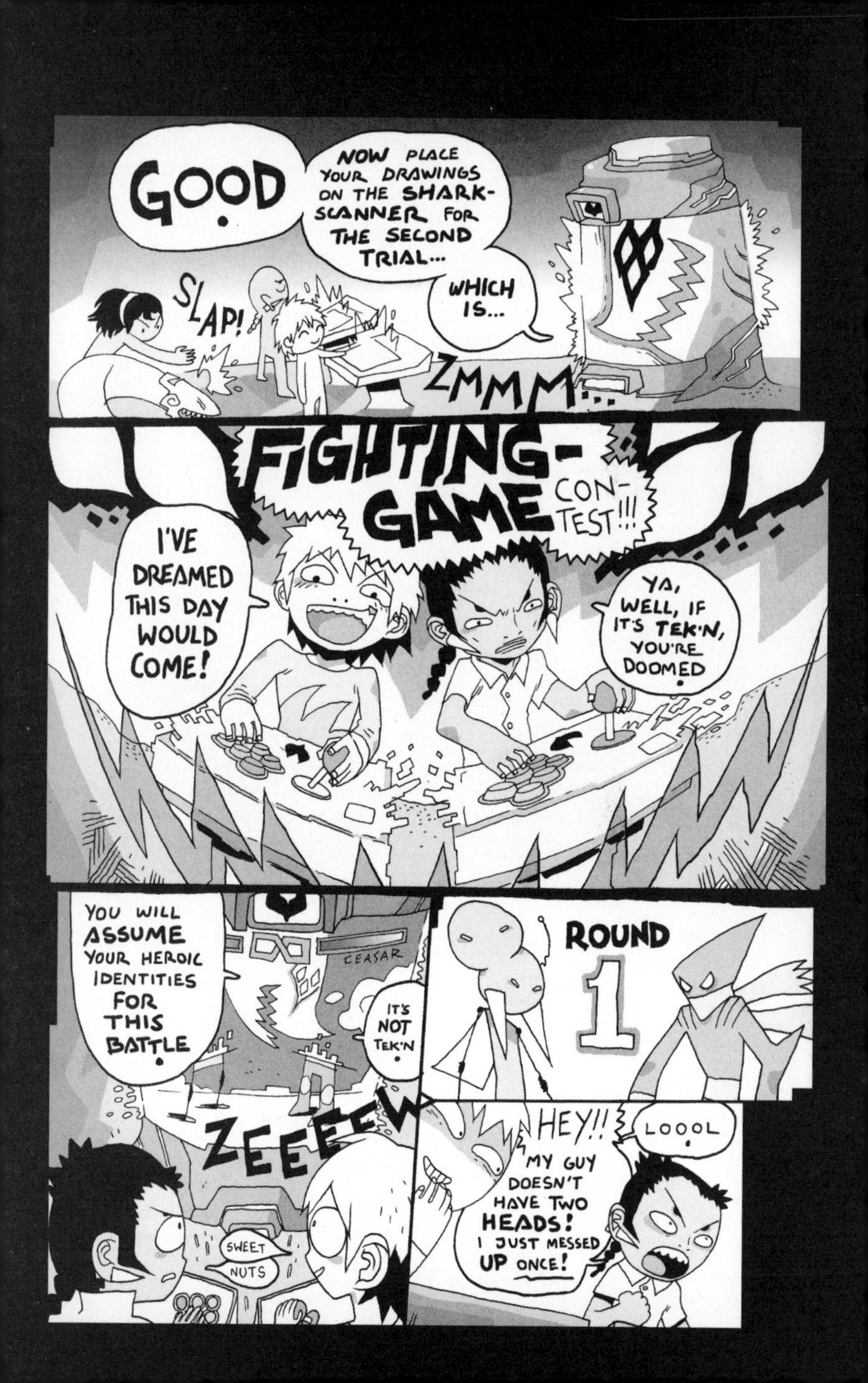
GOOD.
NOW PLACE YOUR DRAWINGS ON THE SHARK-SCANNER FOR THE SECOND TRIAL...
WHICH IS...
SLAP!
ZMMM...
FIGHTING-GAME CON-TEST!!!
I'VE DREAMED THIS DAY WOULD COME!
YA, WELL, IF IT'S TEK'N, YOU'RE DOOMED.
YOU WILL ASSUME YOUR HEROIC IDENTITIES FOR THIS BATTLE.
CEASAR
IT'S NOT TEK'N
ROUND 1
ZEEEEEW
SWEET
NUTS
HEY!!
LOOOL.
MY GUY DOESN'T HAVE TWO HEADS! I JUST MESSED UP ONCE!

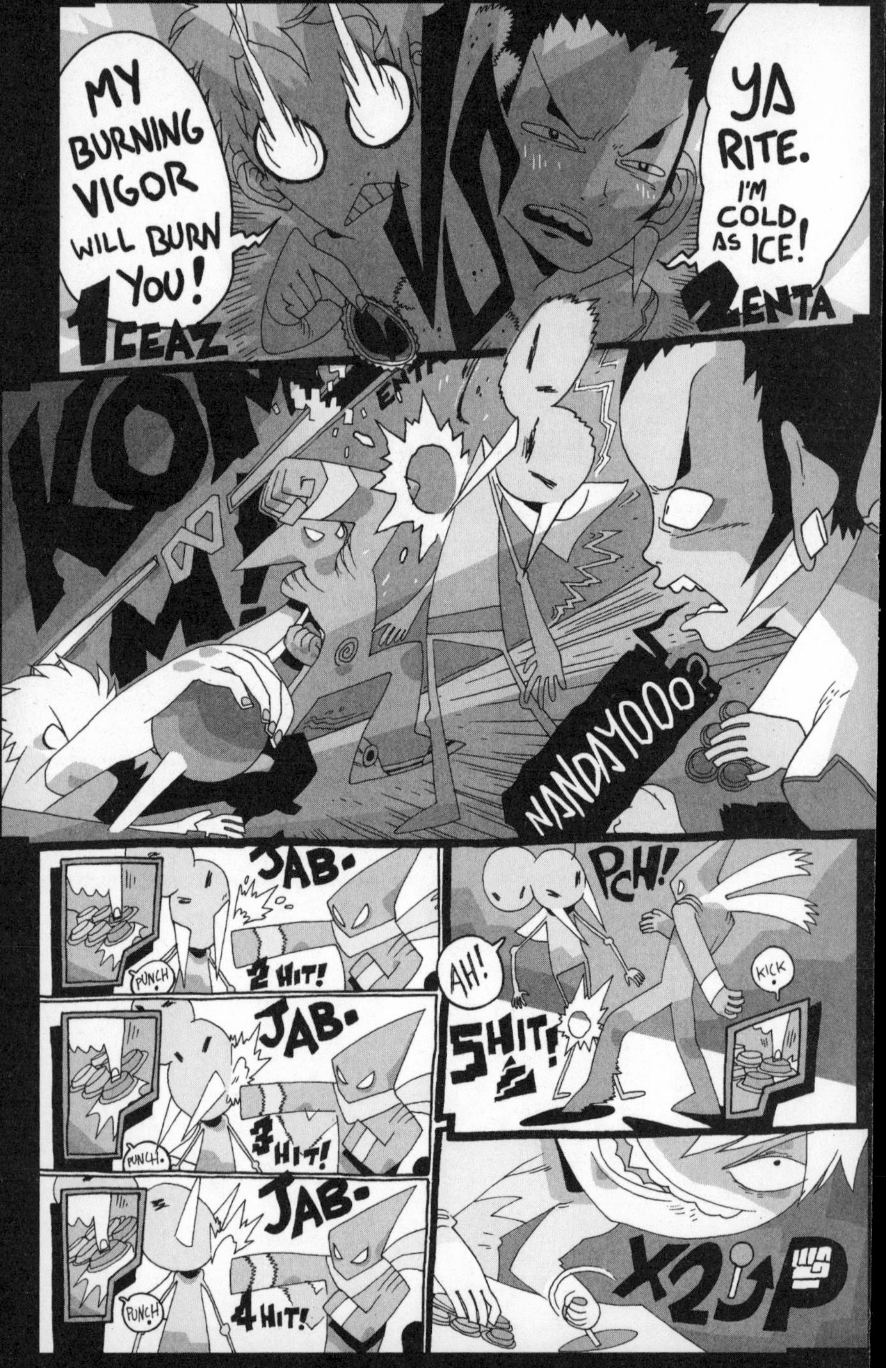

MY BURNING VIGOR WILL BURN YOU!
1CEAZ
VS
YA RITE. I'M COLD AS ICE!
2ENTA
NANDAYOOO?
JAB.
PUNCH
2 HIT!
JAB.
PUNCH.
3 HIT!
JAB.
PUNCH
4 HIT!
PCH!
AH!
KICK
5HIT!
X2

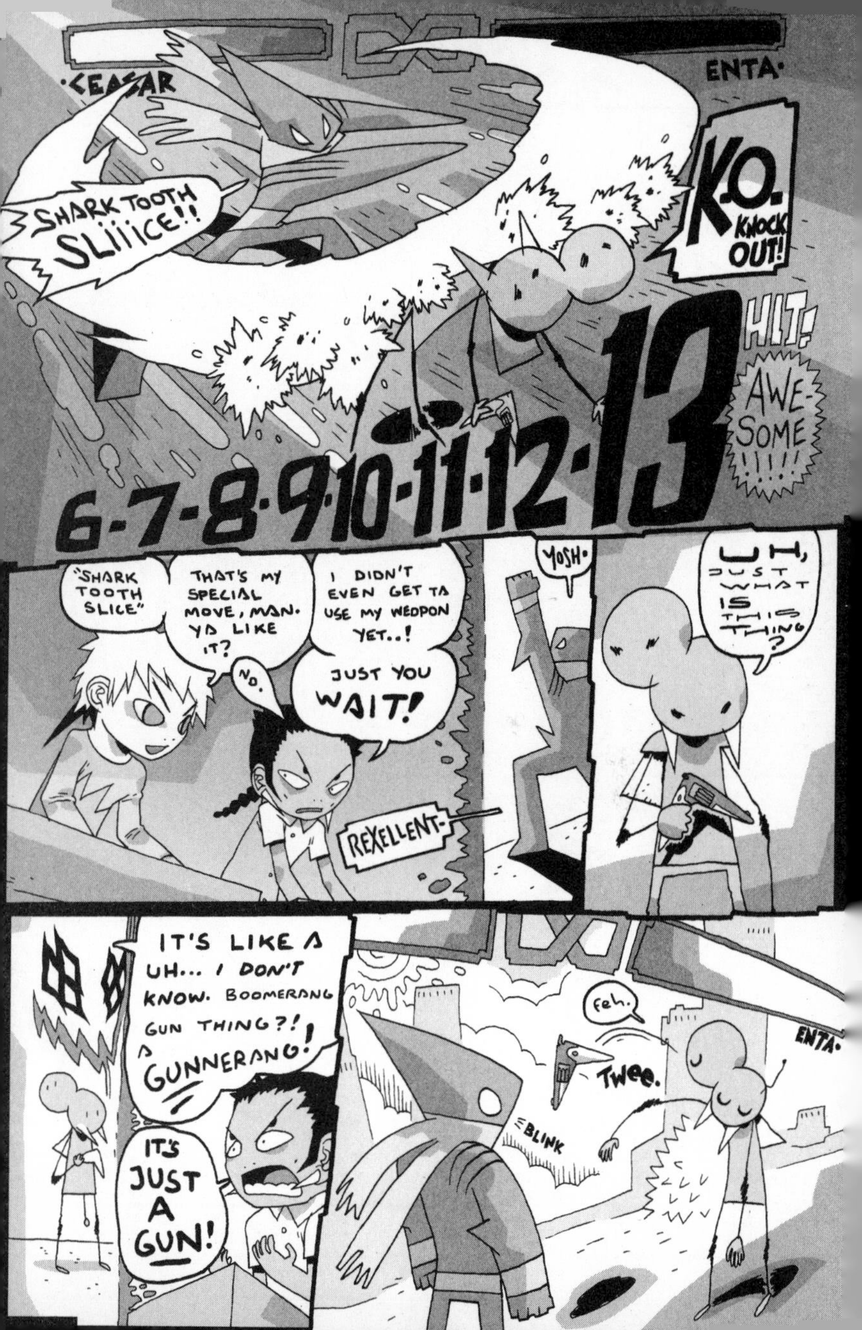

CEASAR
ENTA
SHARK TOOTH SLIIICE!!
K.O. KNOCK OUT!
6-7-8-9-10-11-12-13 HIT!
AWESOME!!!!!
"SHARK TOOTH SLICE"
THAT'S MY SPECIAL MOVE, MAN. YA LIKE IT?
NO.
I DIDN'T EVEN GET TA USE MY WEAPON YET..!
JUST YOU WAIT!
REXELLENT
YOSH.
UH, JUST WHAT IS THIS THING?
IT'S LIKE A UH... I DON'T KNOW. BOOMERANG GUN THING?! A GUNNERANG!
IT'S JUST A GUN!
feh.
ENTA
TWEE.
BLINK

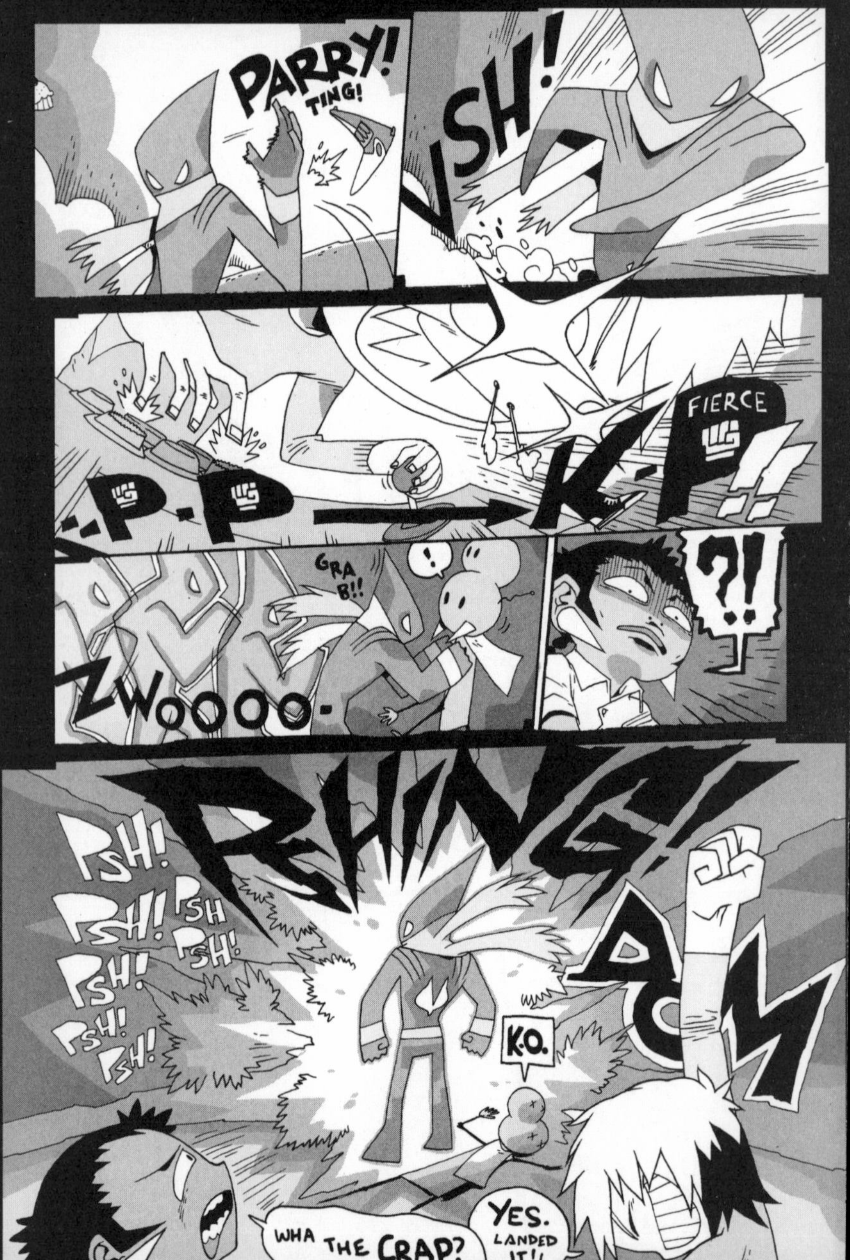
PARRY!
TING!
VSH!
FIERCE
P P K P!!
GRAB!!
!
?!
ZWOOOO-
RSHING!!
PSH! PSH! PSH PSH! PSH! PSH! PSH!
BOOM
K.O.
WHA THE CRAP?
YES. LANDED IT!!

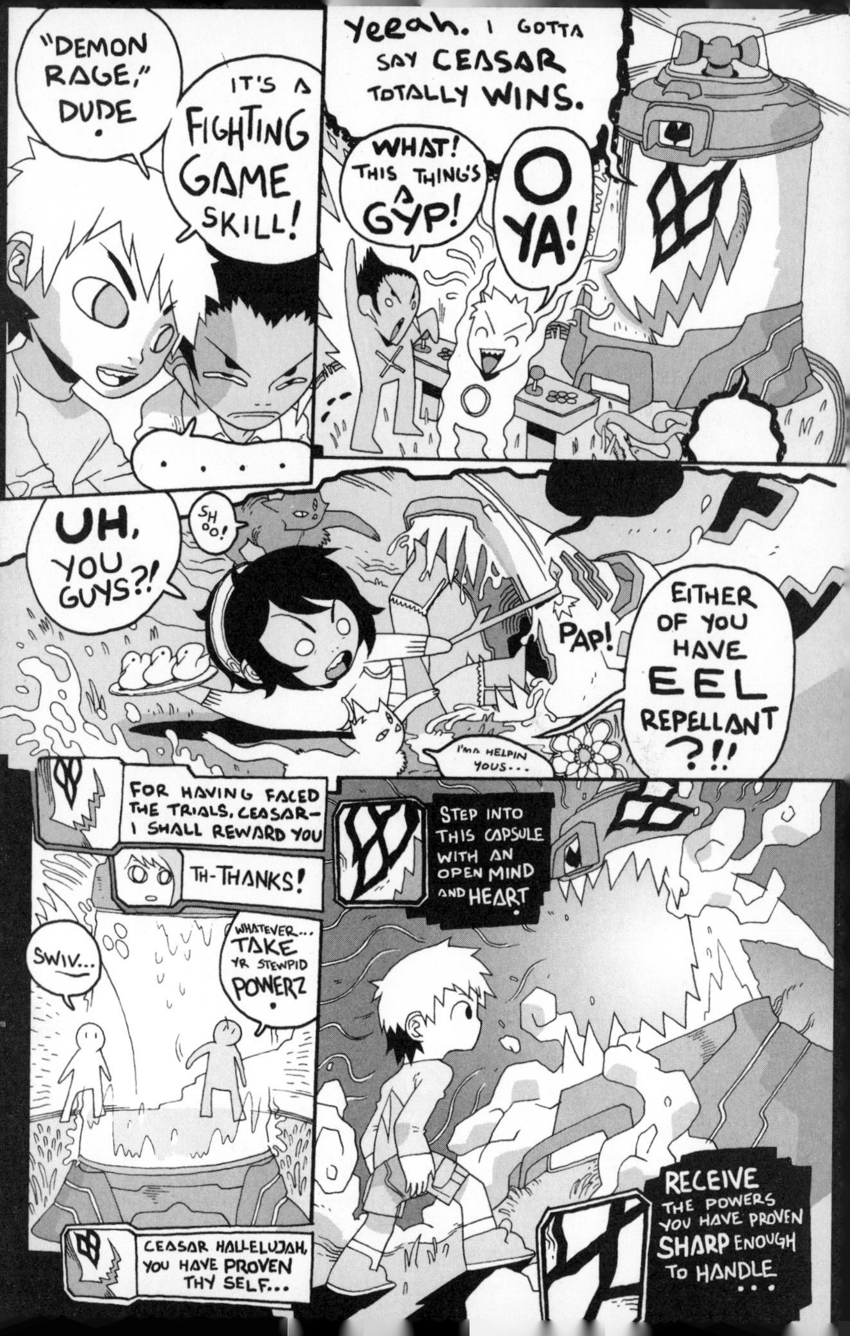
"DEMON RAGE," DUDE.
IT'S A FIGHTING GAME SKILL!
. . . . .
Yeeah. I GOTTA SAY CEASAR TOTALLY WINS.
WHAT! THIS THING'S A GYP!
O YA!
UH, YOU GUYS?!
SHOO!
PAP!
EITHER OF YOU HAVE EEL REPELLANT?!!
I'MA HELPIN YOUS...
FOR HAVING FACED THE TRIALS, CEASAR- I SHALL REWARD YOU
TH-THANKS!
STEP INTO THIS CAPSULE WITH AN OPEN MIND AND HEART.
SWIV...
WHATEVER... TAKE YR STEWPID POWERZ.
CEASAR HALLELUJAH, YOU HAVE PROVEN THY SELF...
RECEIVE THE POWERS YOU HAVE PROVEN SHARP ENOUGH TO HANDLE...

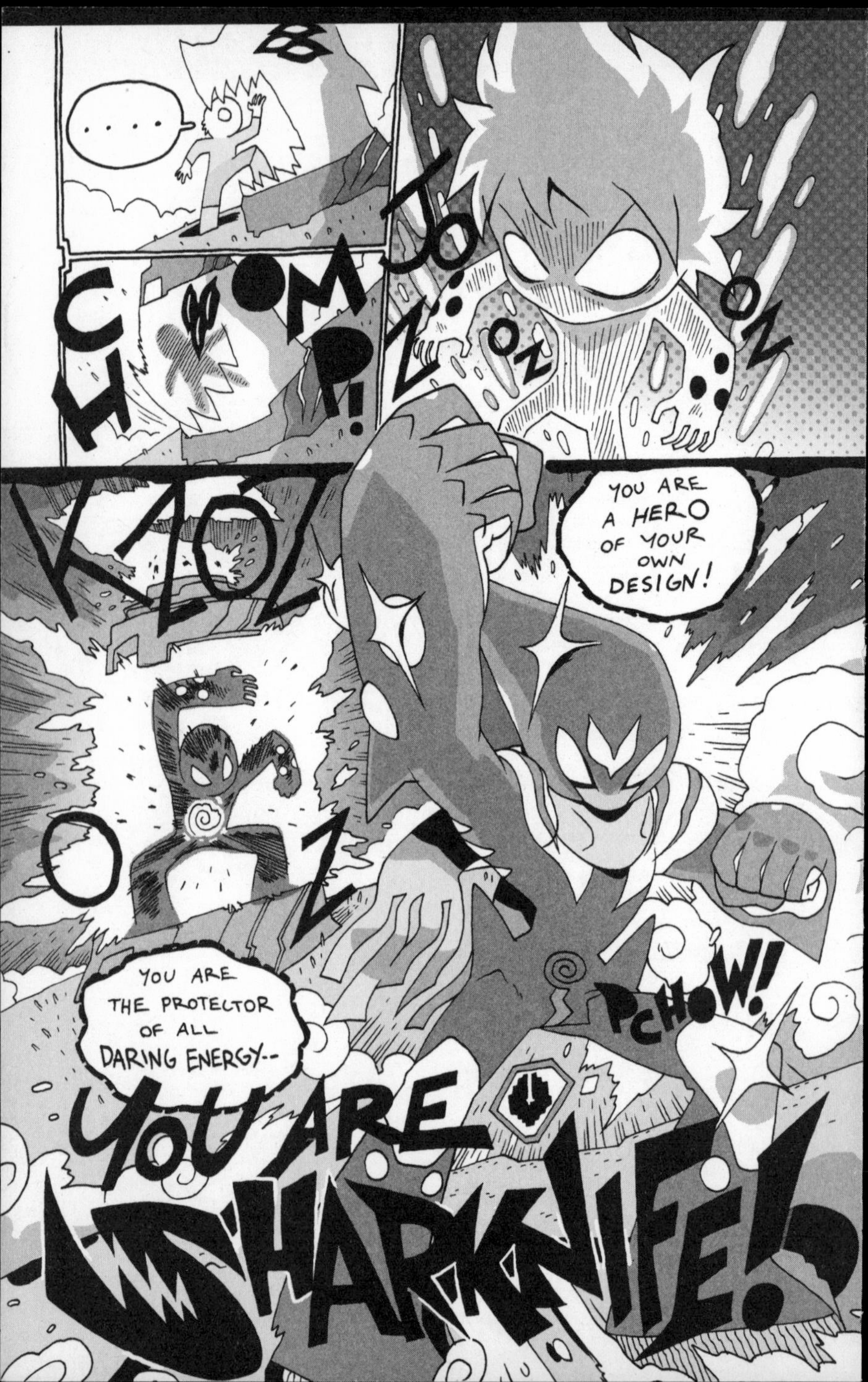
.....
CHOMP!
YOU ARE A HERO OF YOUR OWN DESIGN!
YOU ARE THE PROTECTOR OF ALL DARING ENERGY--
PCHOW!
YOU ARE SHARKNIFE!

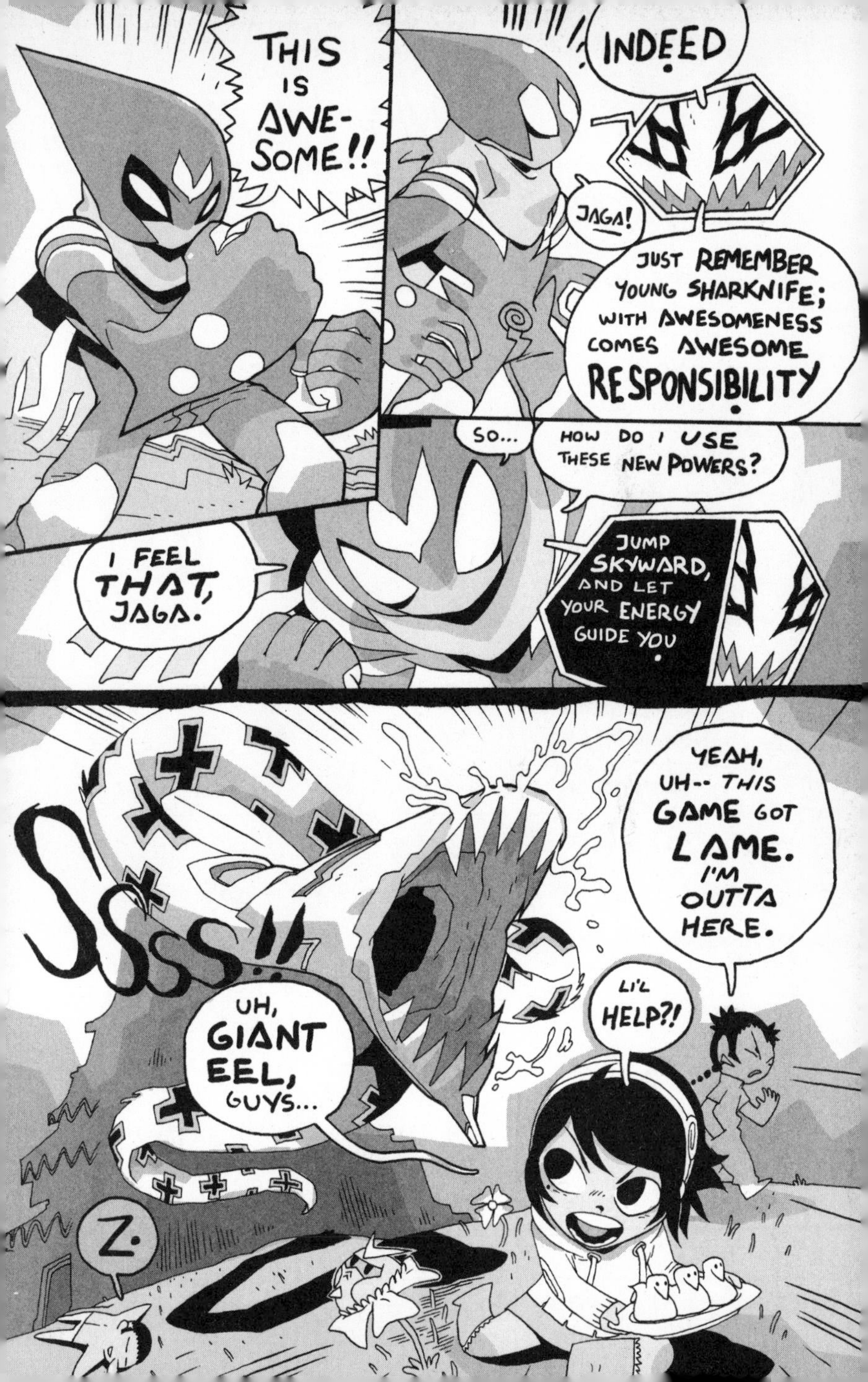
THIS IS AWE-SOME!!
INDEED.
JAGA!
JUST REMEMBER YOUNG SHARKNIFE; WITH AWESOMENESS COMES AWESOME RESPONSIBILITY.
SO...
HOW DO I USE THESE NEW POWERS?
I FEEL THAT, JAGA.
JUMP SKYWARD, AND LET YOUR ENERGY GUIDE YOU.
SSSS!!
YEAH, UH-- THIS GAME GOT LAME. I'M OUTTA HERE.
UH, GIANT EEL, GUYS...
LI'L HELP?!
Z.

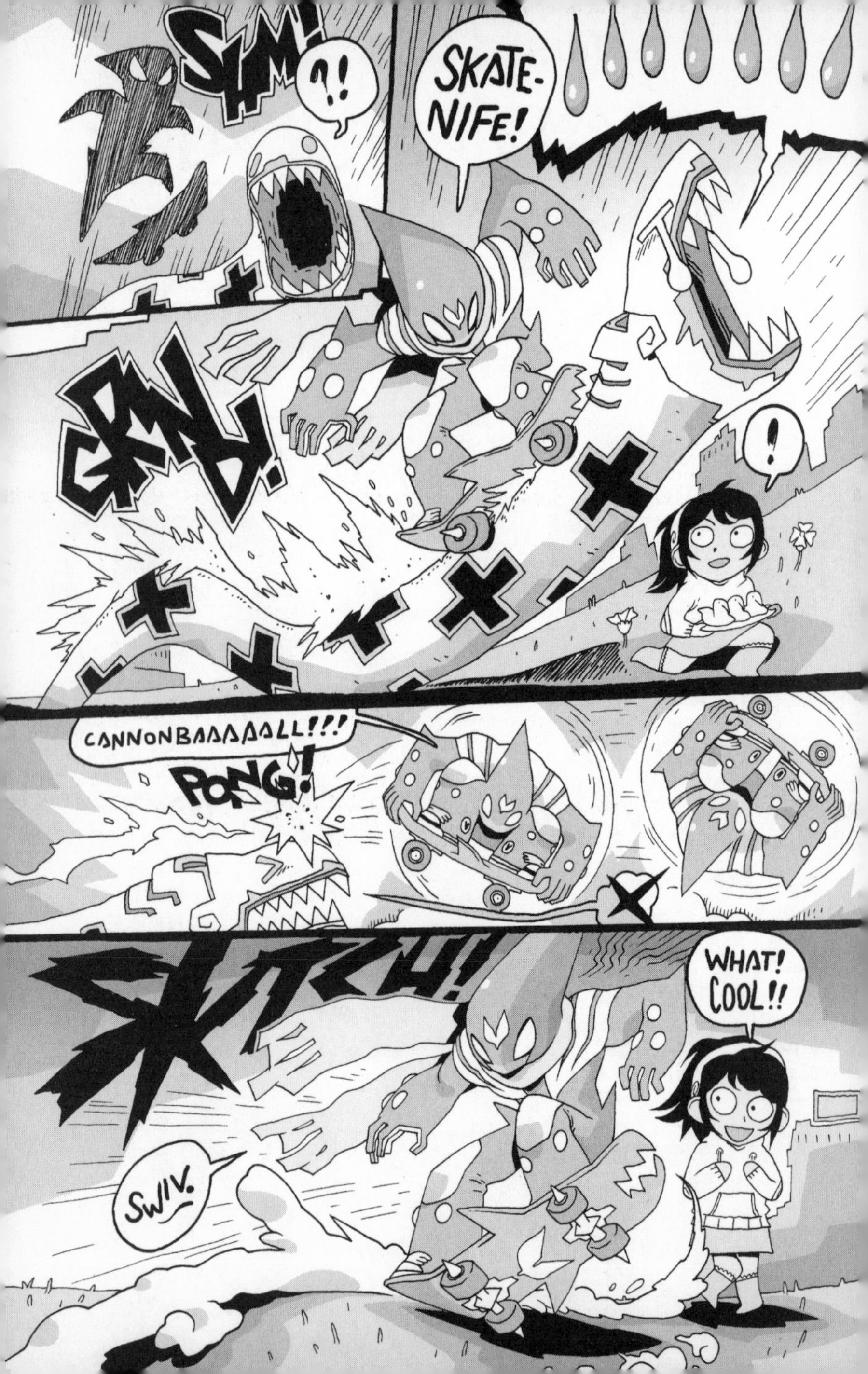
SLAM!
?!
SKATE-NIFE!
CRUNCH!
!
CANNONBAAAAALL!?!
PONG!
WHAT! COOL!!
SWIV.

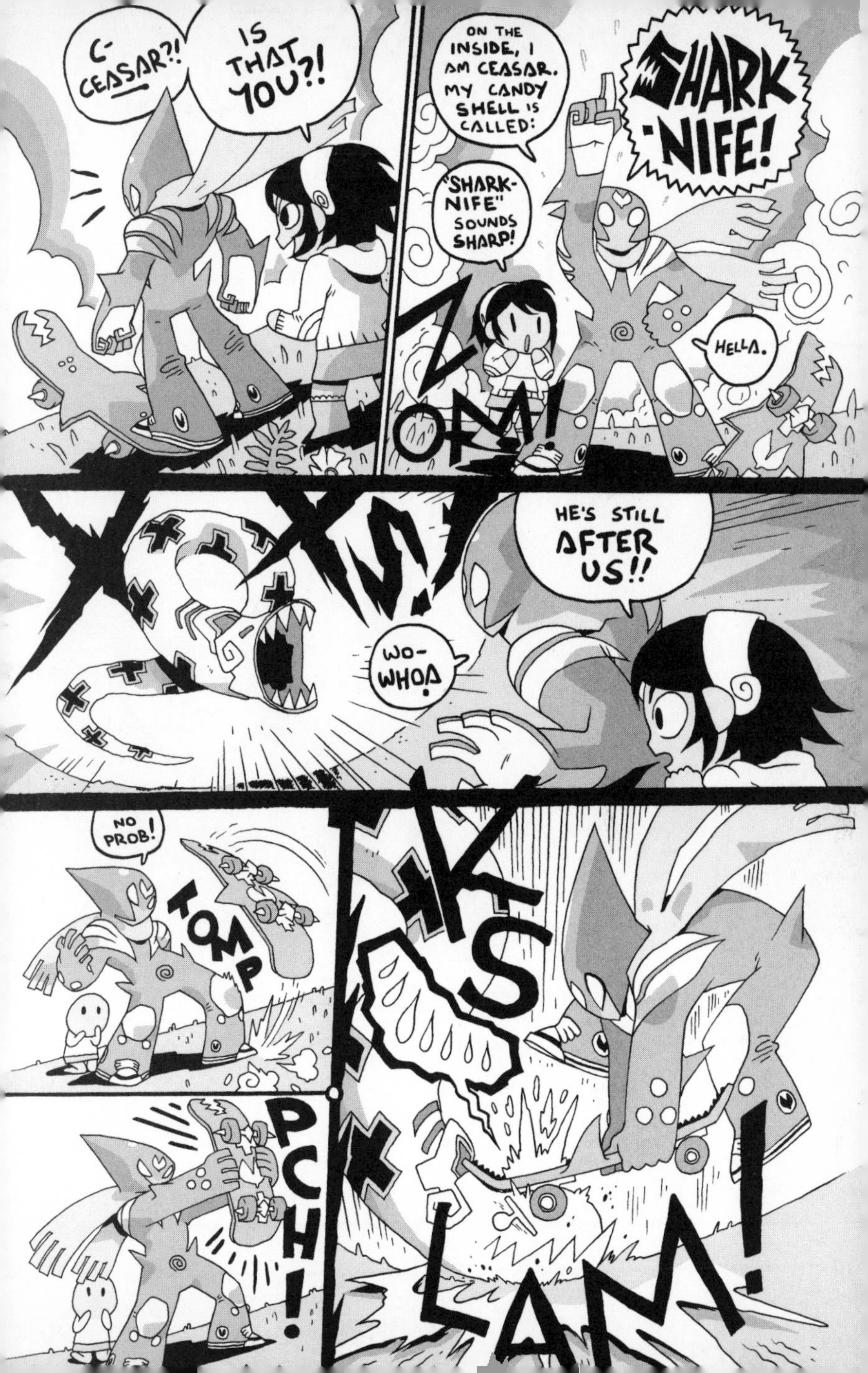
C-CEASAR?!
IS THAT YOU?!
ON THE INSIDE, I AM CEASAR. MY CANDY SHELL IS CALLED:
SHARK-NIFE!
"SHARK-NIFE" SOUNDS SHARP!
HELLA.
ZOOM!
XXSSH!
HE'S STILL AFTER US!!
WO-WHOA!
NO PROB!
TOMP
PCHI!
KSSLAM!

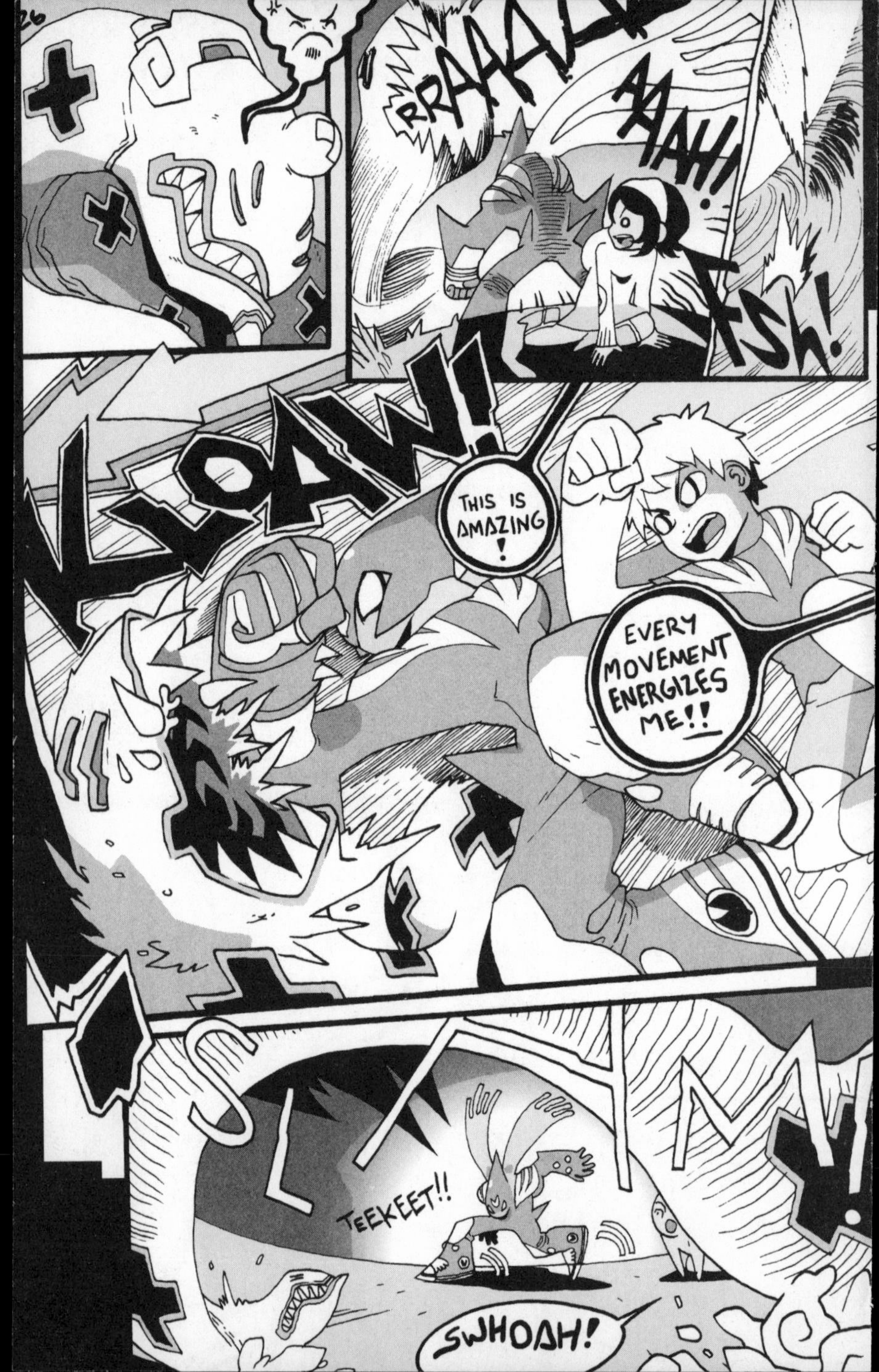
RRAAAA
AAAH!
FSH!
KLOAW!
THIS IS AMAZING!
EVERY MOVEMENT ENERGIZES ME!!
SLAM!
TEEKEET!!
SWHOAH!

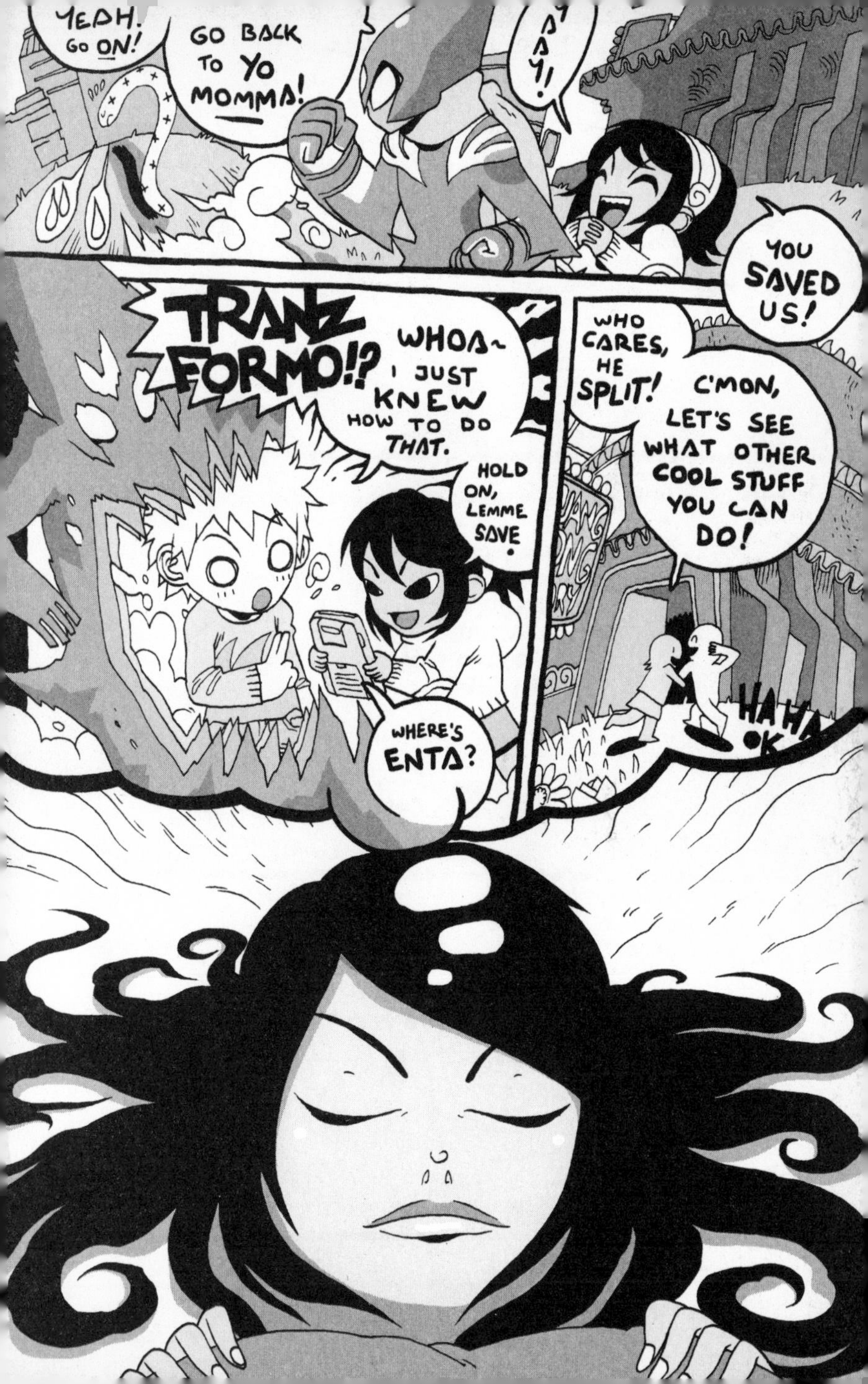
YEAH. GO ON!
GO BACK TO YO MOMMA!
YAAY!!
YOU SAVED US!
TRANZ FORMO!?
WHOA~ I JUST KNEW HOW TO DO THAT.
HOLD ON, LEMME SAVE.
WHERE'S ENTA?
WHO CARES, HE SPLIT!
C'MON, LET'S SEE WHAT OTHER COOL STUFF YOU CAN DO!
HAHA OK

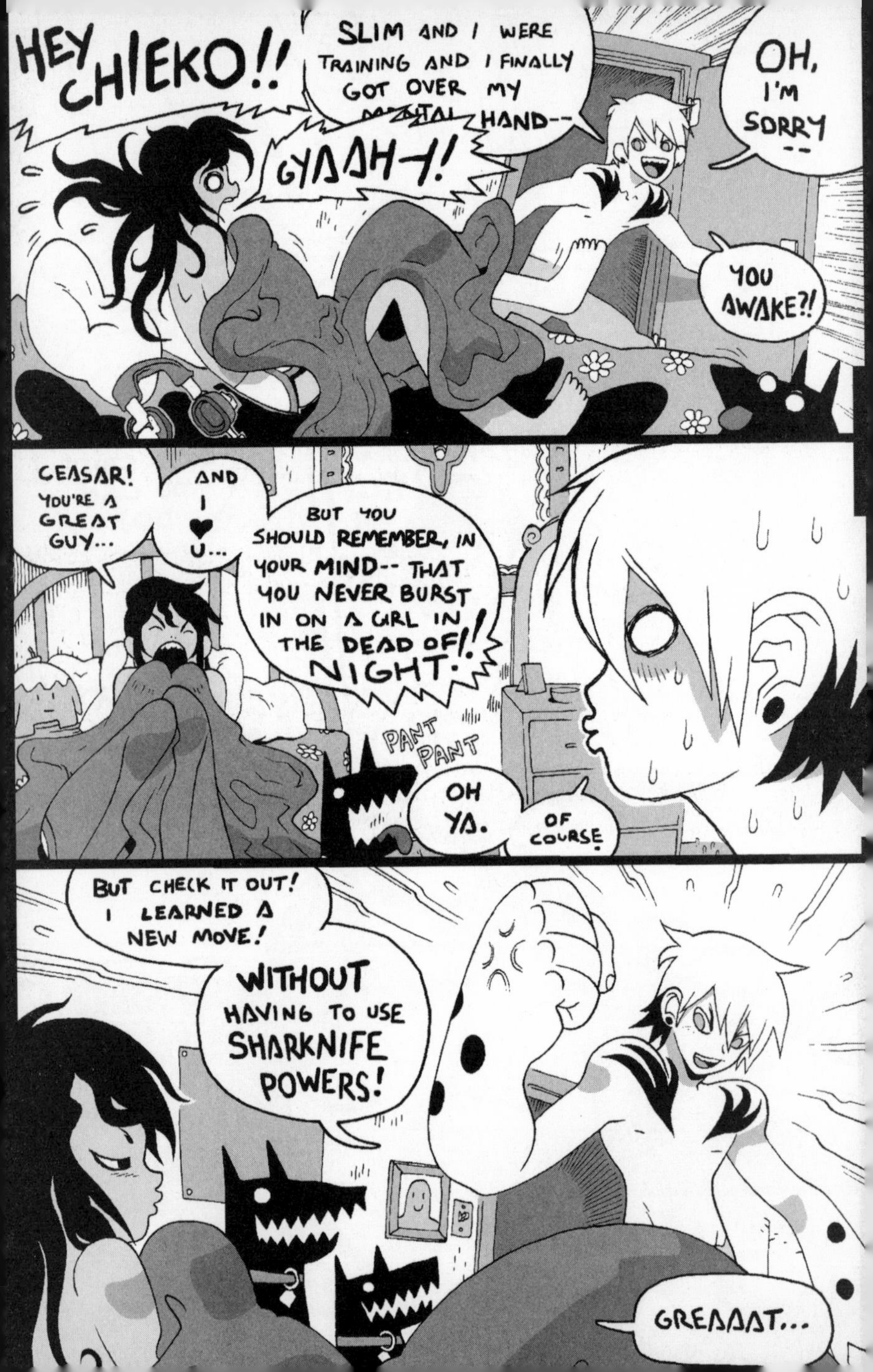
HEY CHIEKO!!
SLIM AND I WERE TRAINING AND I FINALLY GOT OVER MY HAND--
GYAAH-!
OH, I'M SORRY --
YOU AWAKE?!
CEASAR! YOU'RE A GREAT GUY...
AND I ♥ U...
BUT YOU SHOULD REMEMBER, IN YOUR MIND-- THAT YOU NEVER BURST IN ON A GIRL IN THE DEAD OF NIGHT.
PANT PANT
OH YA.
OF COURSE.
BUT CHECK IT OUT! I LEARNED A NEW MOVE!
WITHOUT HAVING TO USE SHARKNIFE POWERS!
GREAAAT...

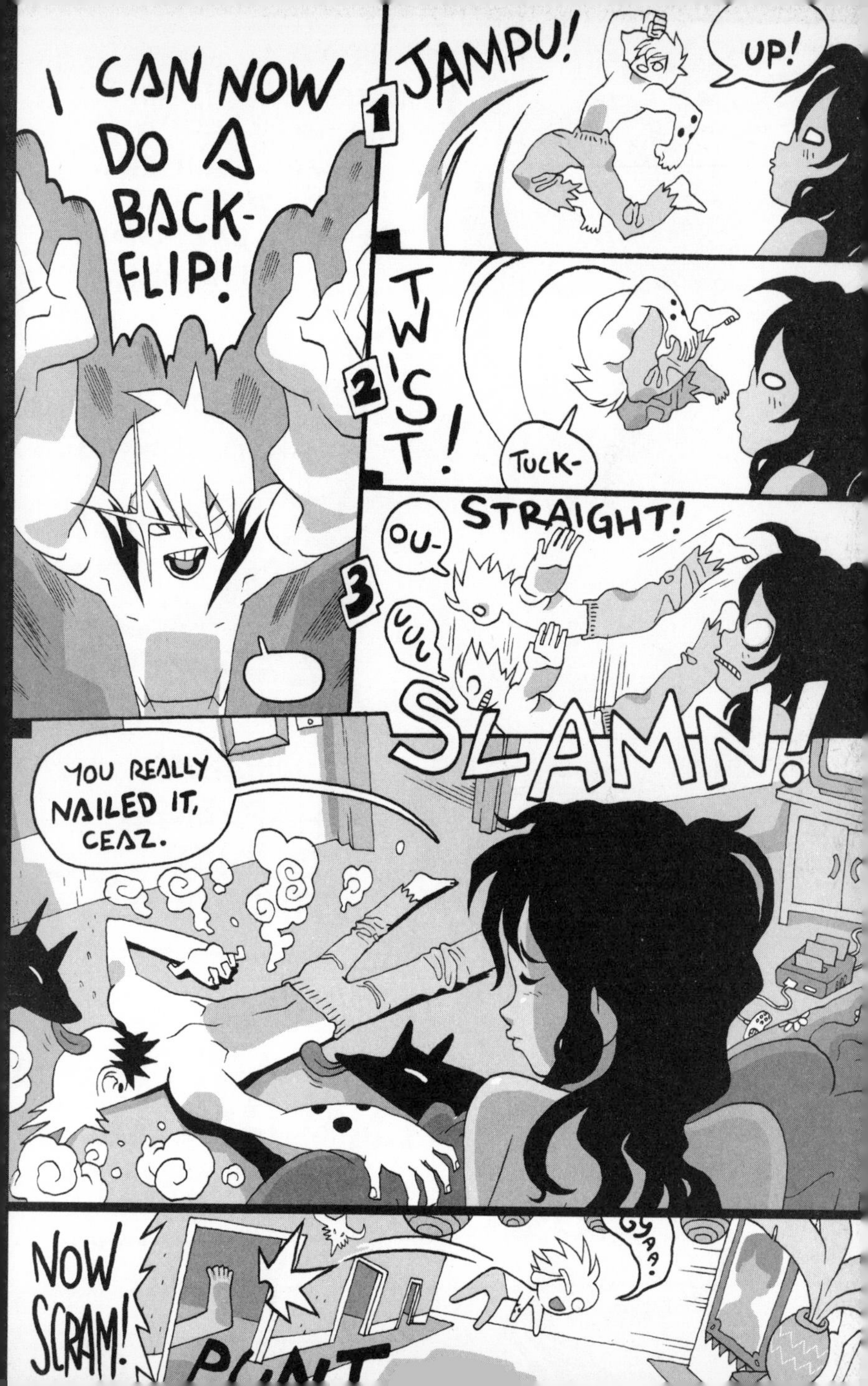
I CAN NOW DO A BACK-FLIP!
1
JAMPU!
UP!
2
TWIST!
TUCK-
3
STRAIGHT!
OU-
UUU
SLAMN!
YOU REALLY NAILED IT, CEAZ.
NOW SCRAM!
GYAA.

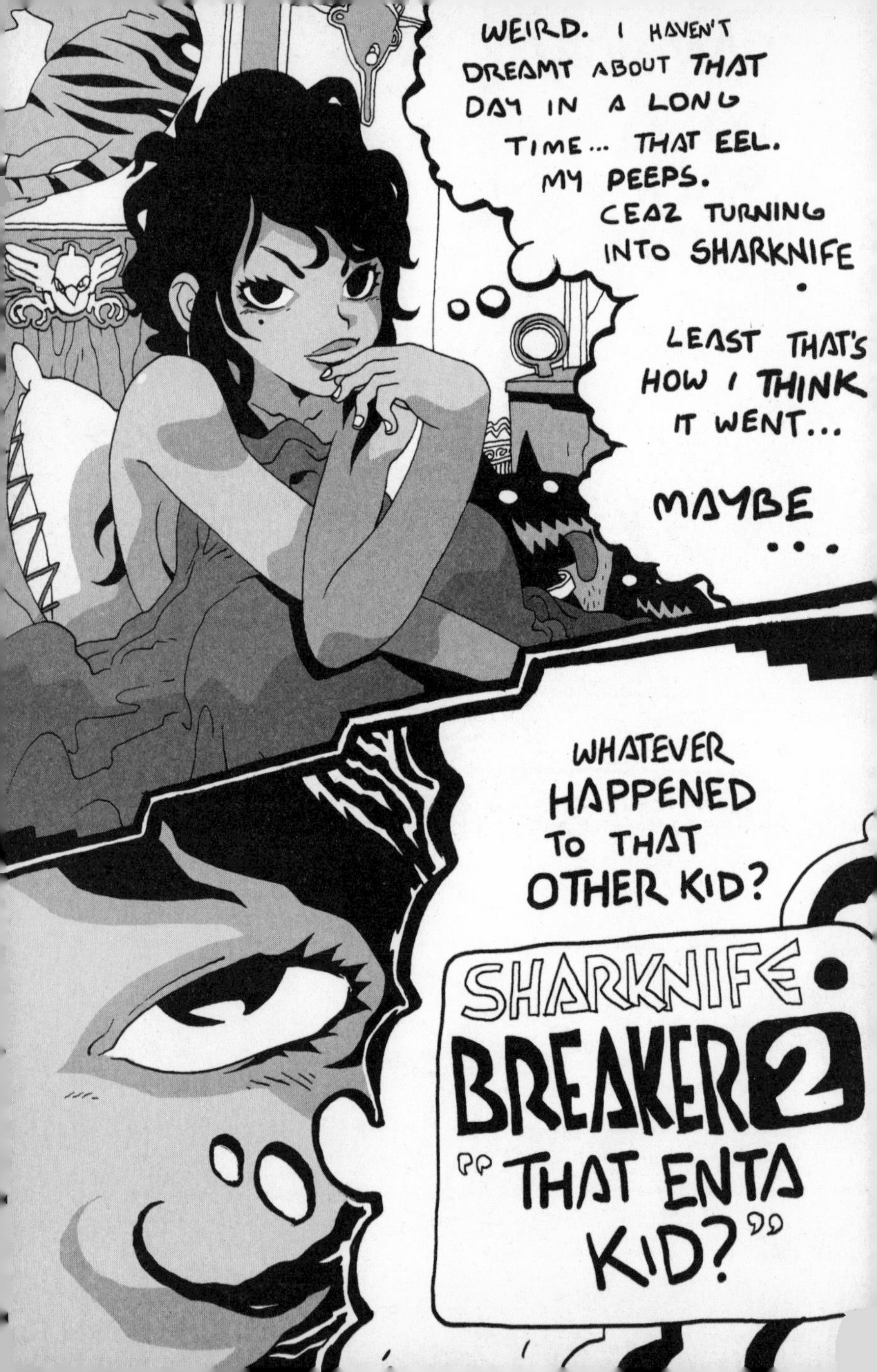
WEIRD. I HAVEN'T DREAMT ABOUT THAT DAY IN A LONG TIME... THAT EEL. MY PEEPS. CEAZ TURNING INTO SHARKNIFE.
LEAST THAT'S HOW I THINK IT WENT...
MAYBE...
WHATEVER HAPPENED TO THAT OTHER KID?
SHARKNIFE: BREAKER 2
"THAT ENTA KID?"

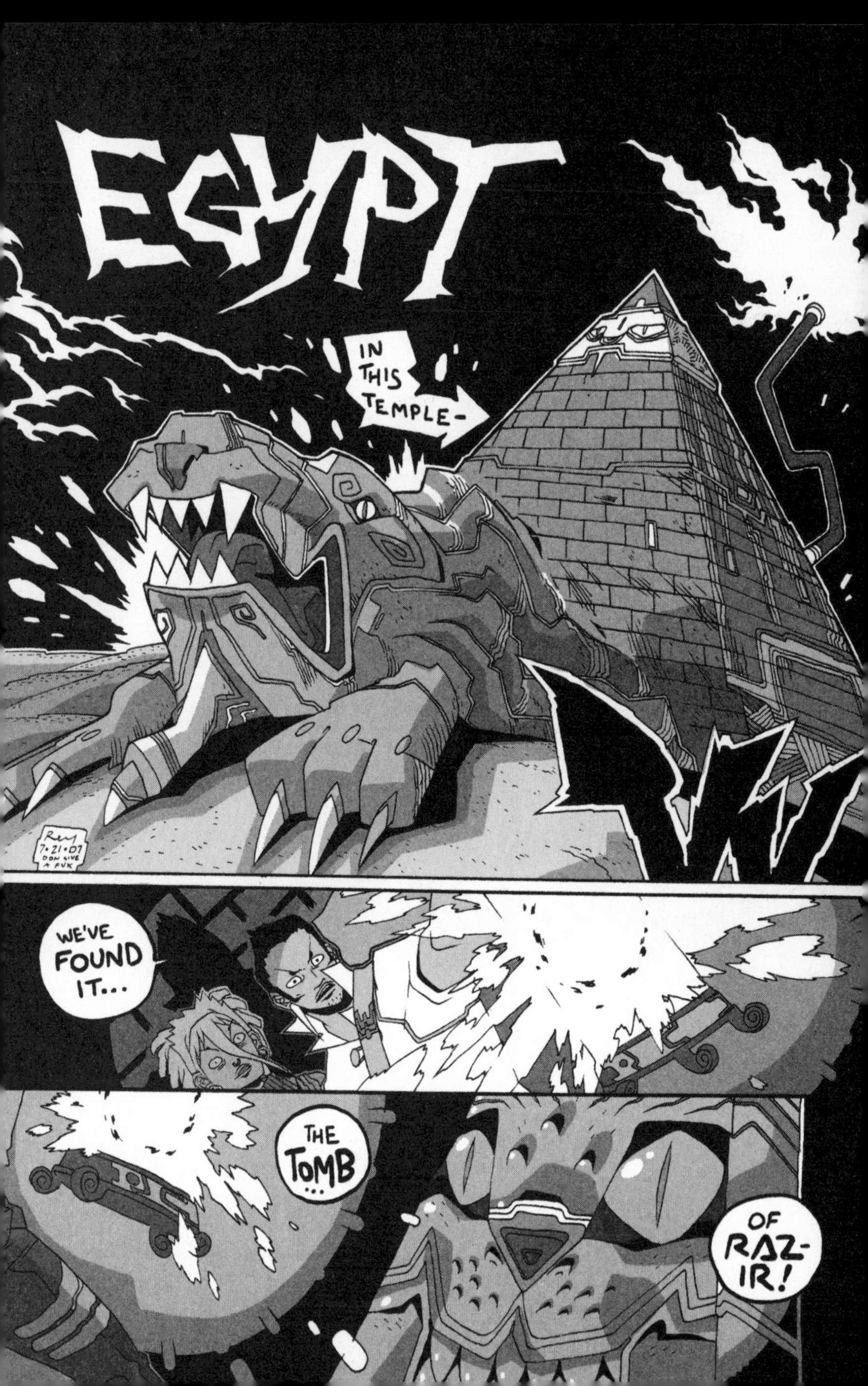
EGYPT
IN THIS TEMPLE-
WE'VE FOUND IT...
THE TOMB...
OF RAZ-IR!

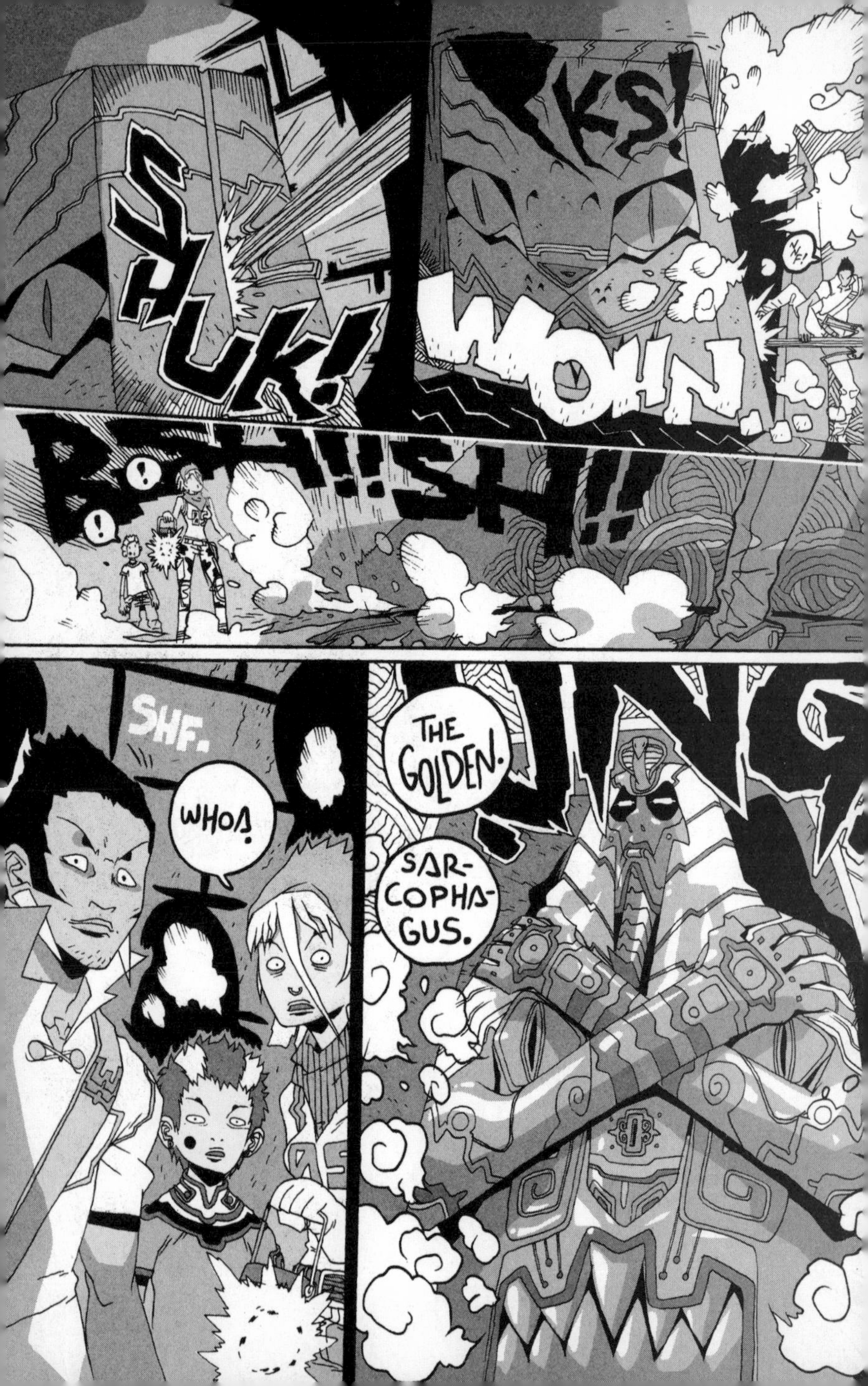
SHUK!
KS!
NNF!
WOHN
!
!
SHF.
WHOA!
THE GOLDEN.
SAR-COPHA-GUS.

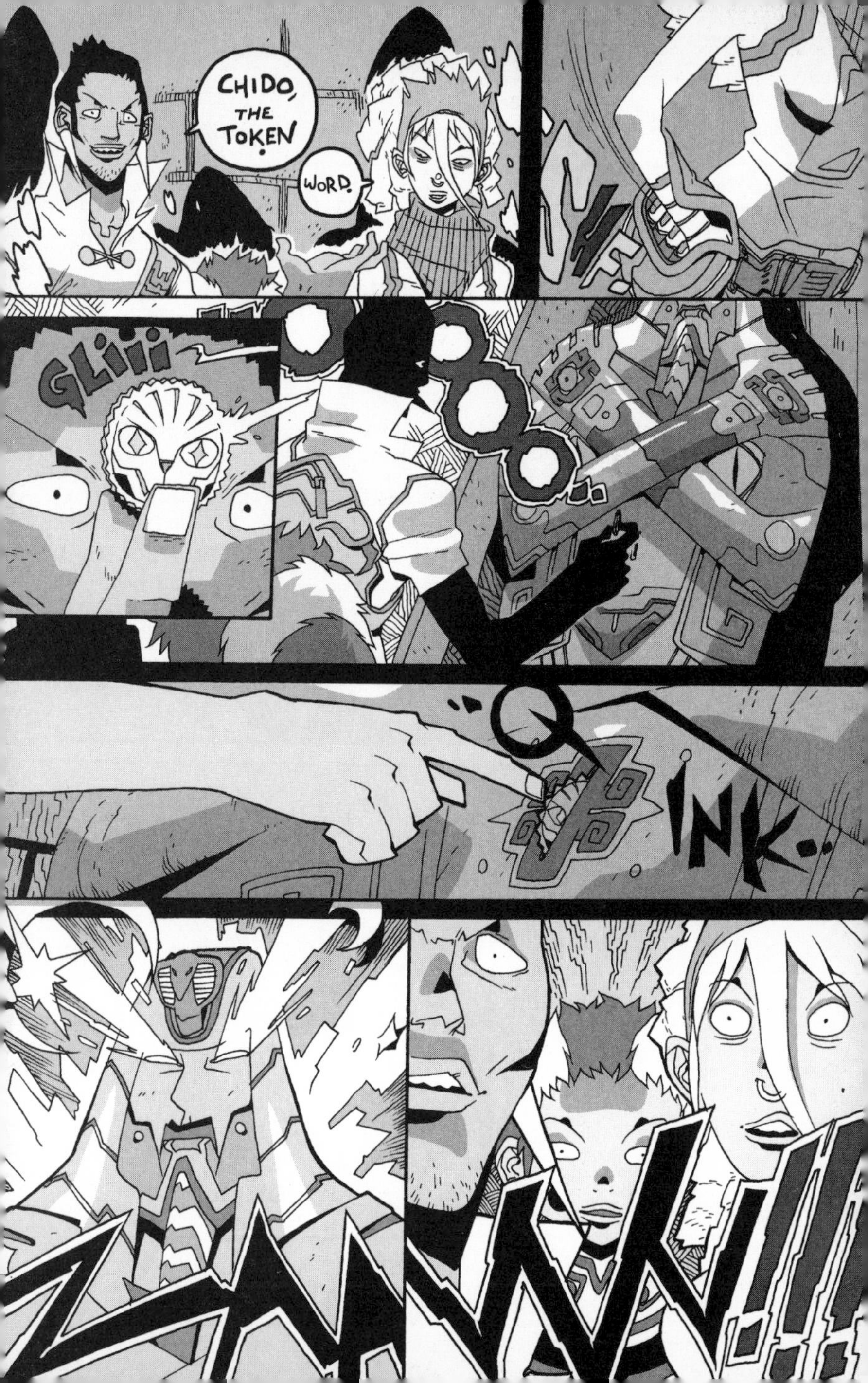

CHIDO, THE TOKEN.
WORD.
GLIII
INK..

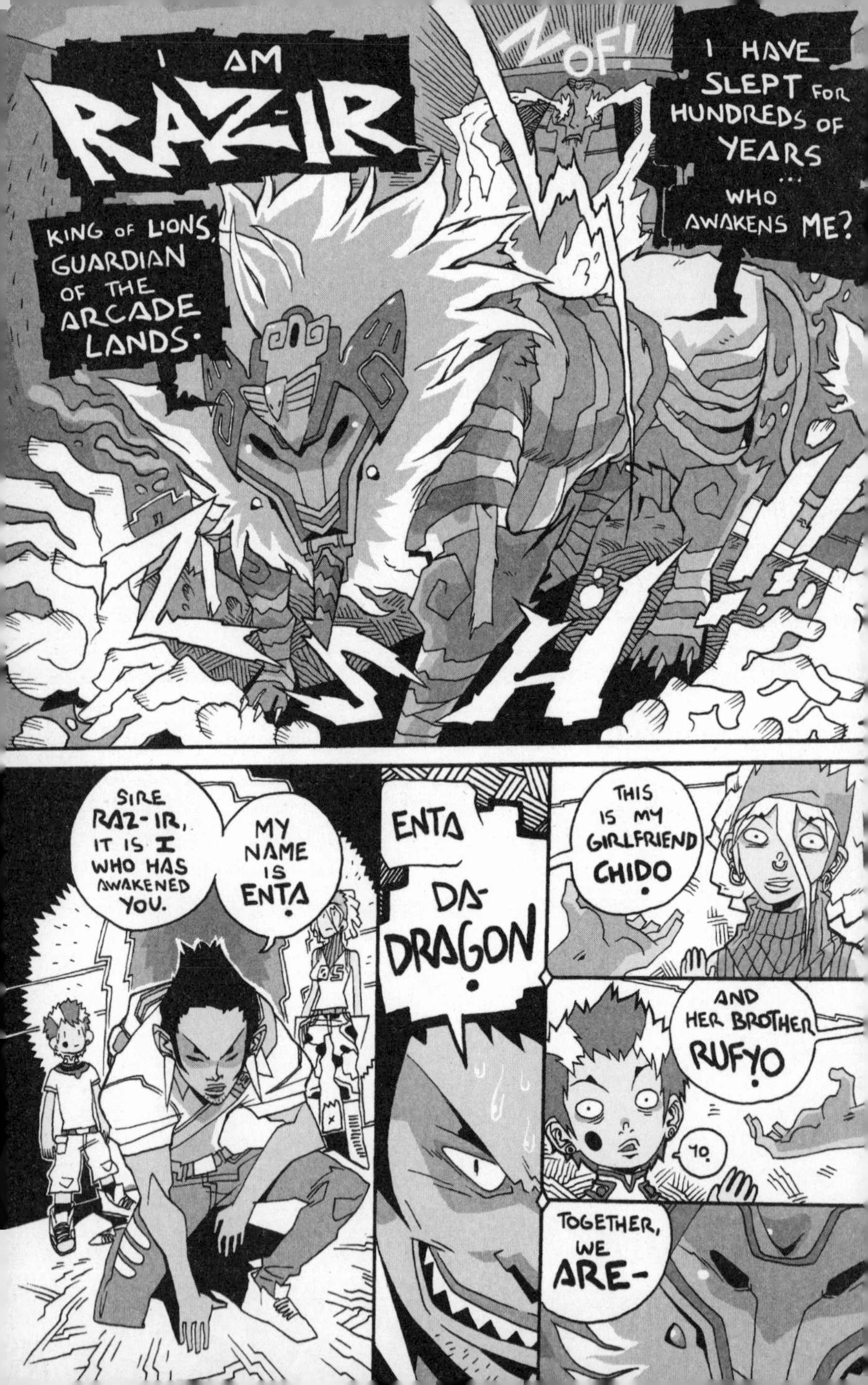
I AM RAZ-IR
KING OF LIONS, GUARDIAN OF THE ARCADE LANDS.
NOF!
I HAVE SLEPT FOR HUNDREDS OF YEARS...
WHO AWAKENS ME?
SIRE RAZ-IR, IT IS I WHO HAS AWAKENED YOU.
MY NAME IS ENTA.
ENTA
DA-DRAGON.
THIS IS MY GIRLFRIEND CHIDO.
AND HER BROTHER RUFYO.
YO.
TOGETHER, WE ARE-

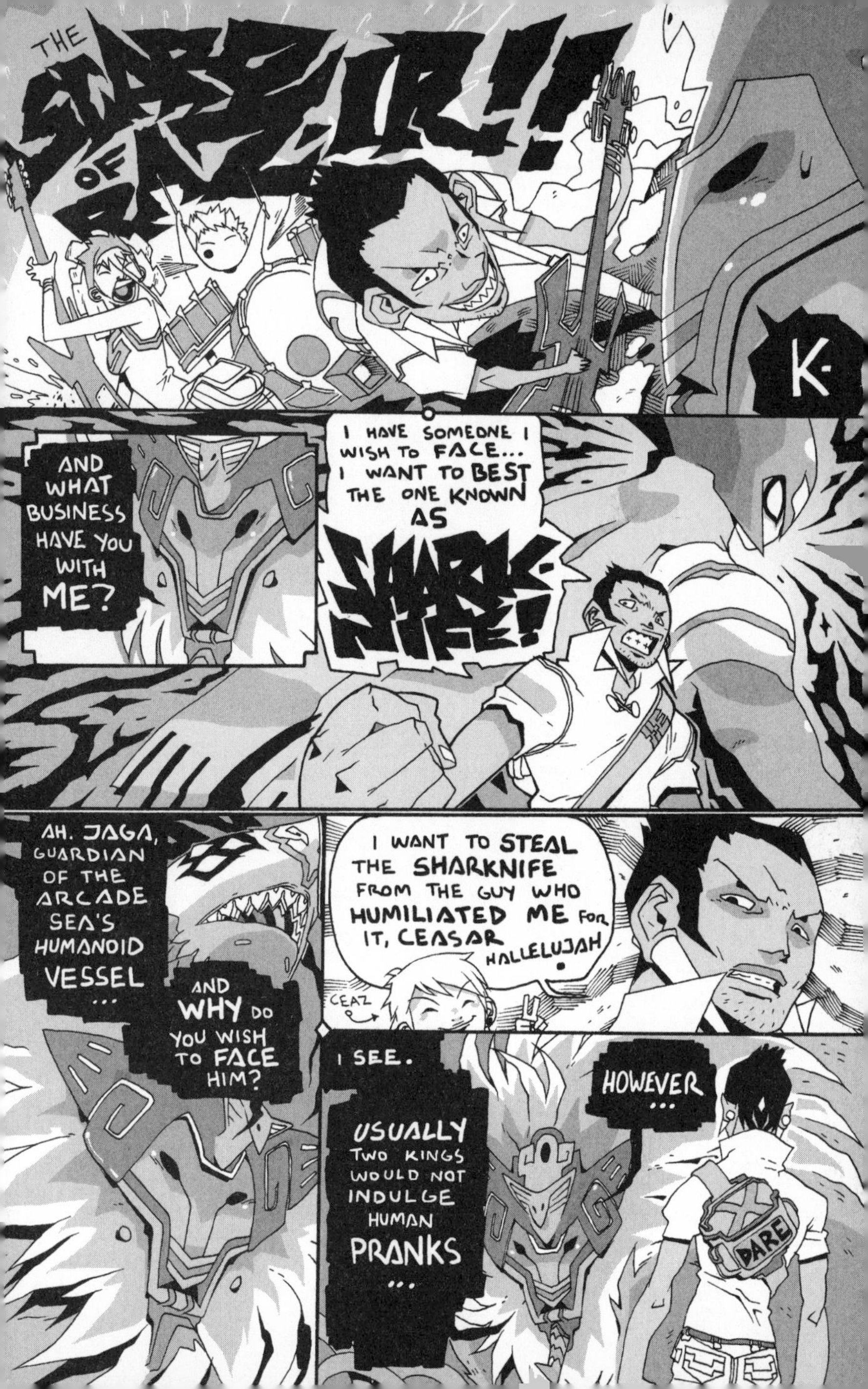
THE
OF
K-
AND WHAT BUSINESS HAVE YOU WITH ME?
I HAVE SOMEONE I WISH TO FACE... I WANT TO BEST THE ONE KNOWN AS
SHARK-NIFE!
AH. JAGA, GUARDIAN OF THE ARCADE SEA'S HUMANOID VESSEL ...
AND WHY DO YOU WISH TO FACE HIM?
I WANT TO STEAL THE SHARKNIFE FROM THE GUY WHO HUMILIATED ME FOR IT, CEASAR HALLELUJAH.
CEAZ
I SEE.
USUALLY TWO KINGS WOULD NOT INDULGE HUMAN PRANKS ...
HOWEVER ...
DARE

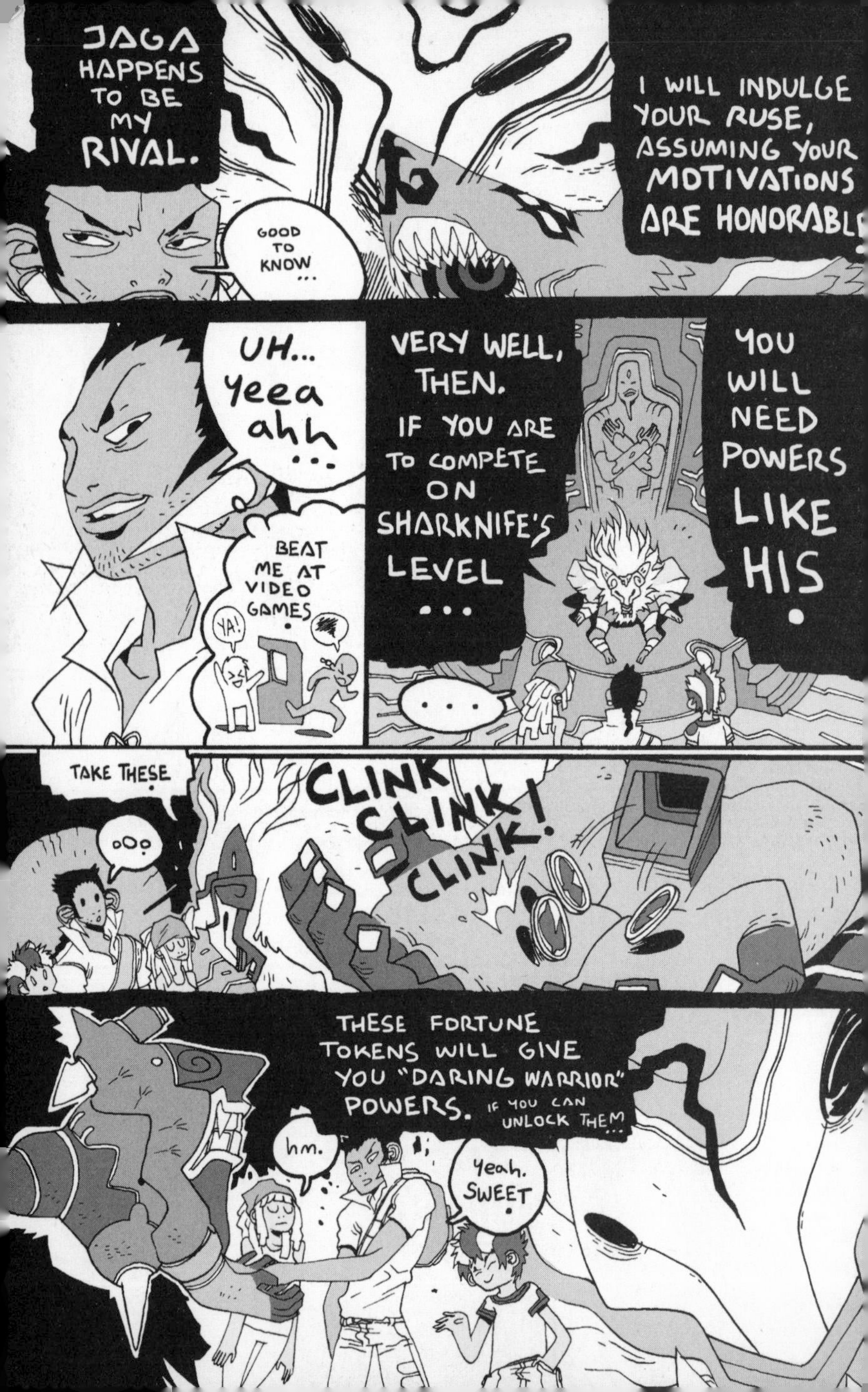
JAGA HAPPENS TO BE MY RIVAL.
I WILL INDULGE YOUR RUSE, ASSUMING YOUR MOTIVATIONS ARE HONORABLE.
GOOD TO KNOW...
UH... yeea ahh...
BEAT ME AT VIDEO GAMES.
YA!
VERY WELL, THEN.
IF YOU ARE TO COMPETE ON SHARKNIFE'S LEVEL...
YOU WILL NEED POWERS LIKE HIS.
...
TAKE THESE.
ooo
CLINK CLINK! CLINK CLINK!
THESE FORTUNE TOKENS WILL GIVE YOU "DARING WARRIOR" POWERS. IF YOU CAN UNLOCK THEM...
hm.
yeah. SWEET.

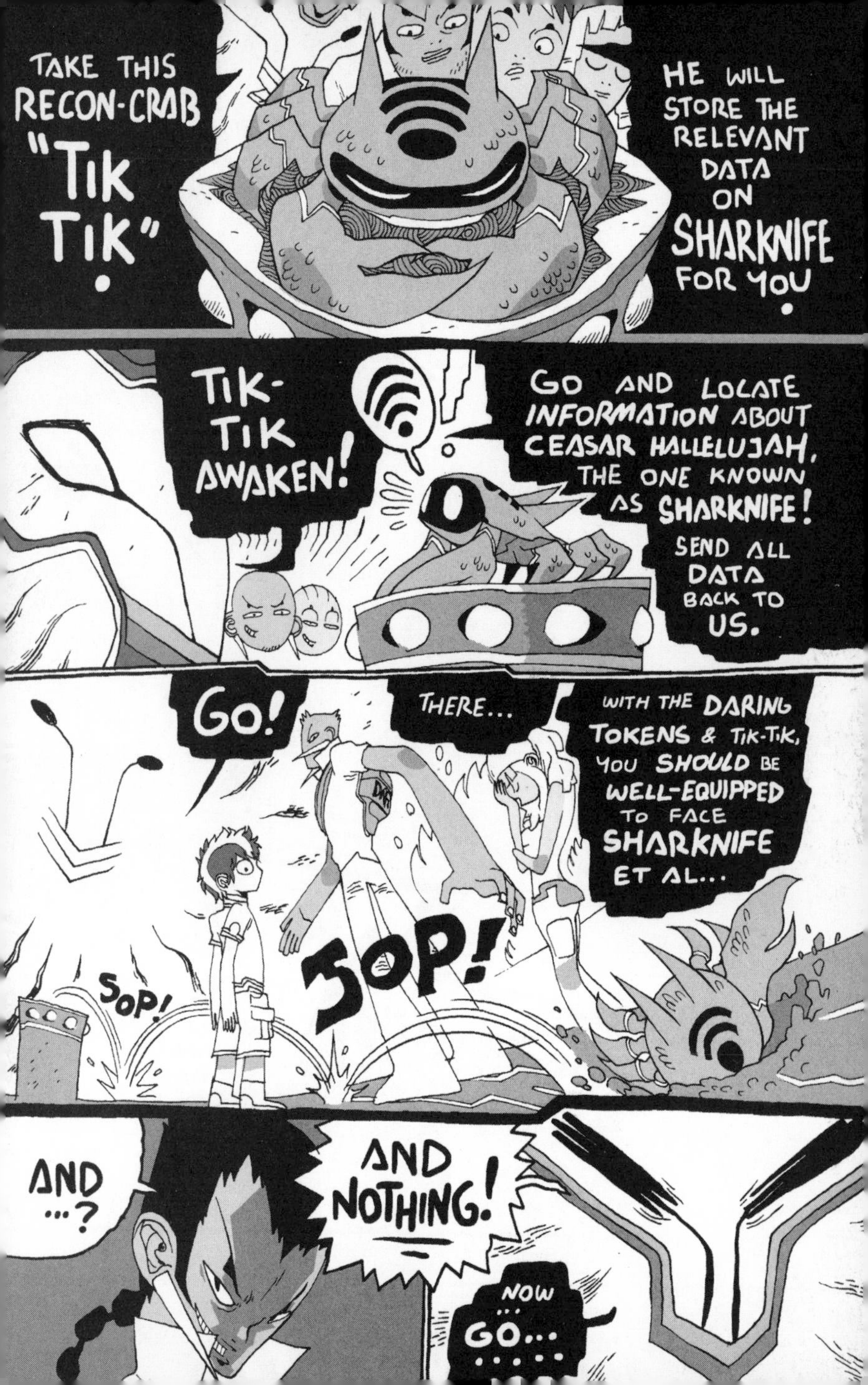
TAKE THIS RECON-CRAB "TIK TIK"!
HE WILL STORE THE RELEVANT DATA ON SHARKNIFE FOR YOU!
TIK-TIK AWAKEN!
GO AND LOCATE INFORMATION ABOUT CEASAR HALLELUJAH, THE ONE KNOWN AS SHARKNIFE!
SEND ALL DATA BACK TO US.
GO!
THERE...
WITH THE DARING TOKENS & TIK-TIK, YOU SHOULD BE WELL-EQUIPPED TO FACE SHARKNIFE ET AL...
SOP!
SOP!
AND ...?
AND NOTHING!
NOW ... GO... .....

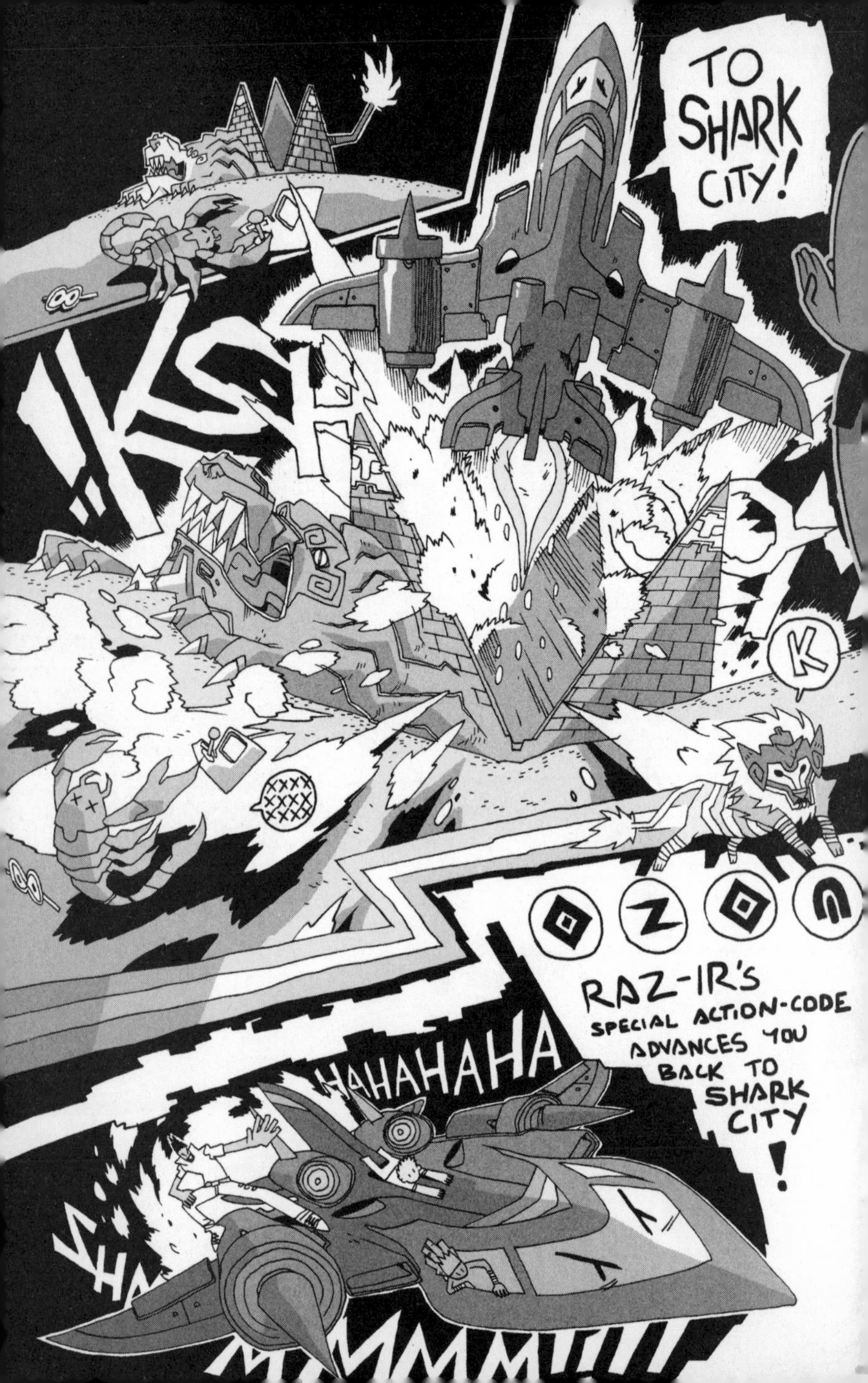
TO SHARK CITY!
K
OZON
RAZ-IR's SPECIAL ACTION-CODE ADVANCES YOU BACK TO SHARK CITY!
HAHAHAHAHA
MMMMM

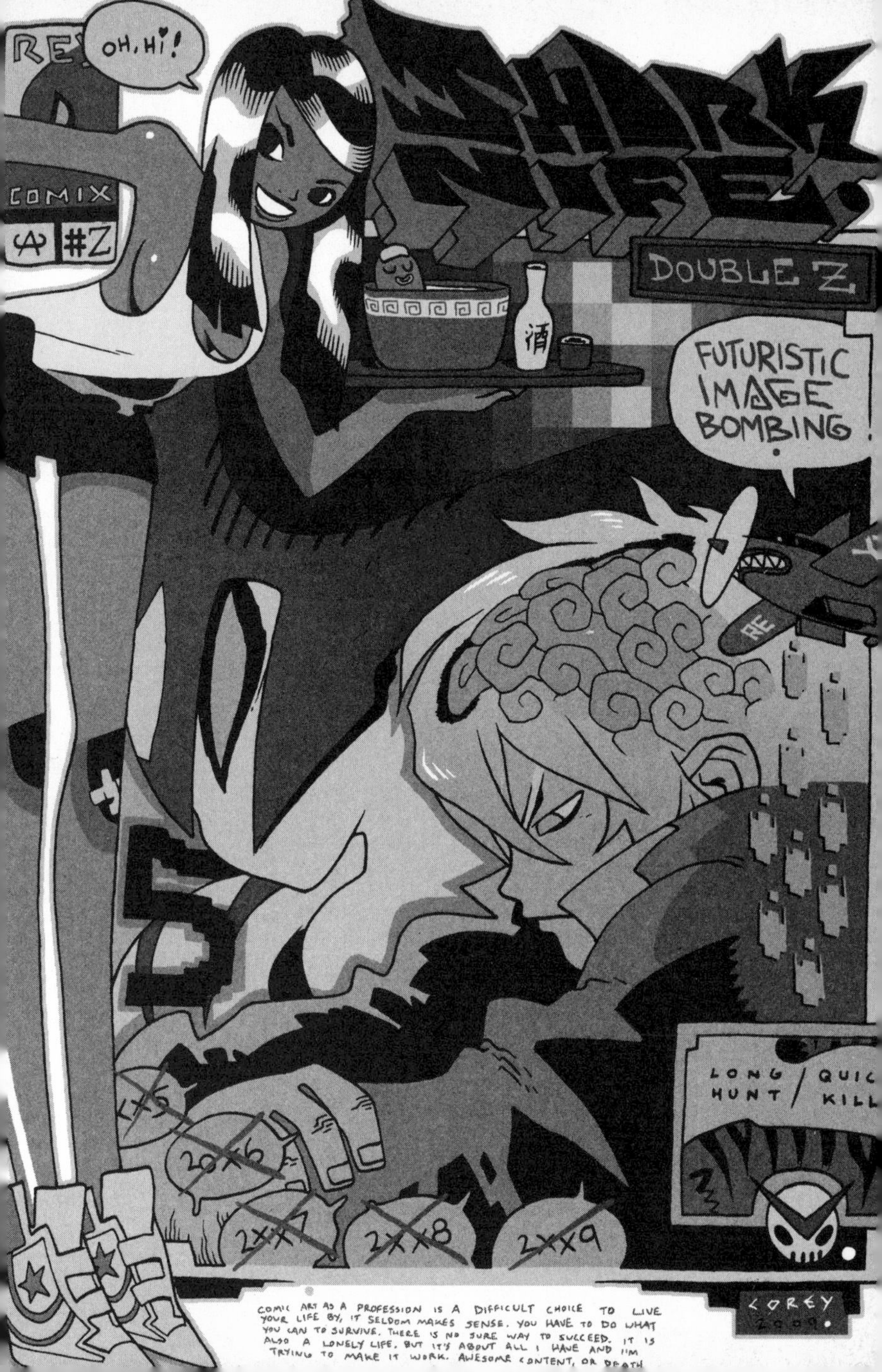

OH, HI!
COMIX
#Z
DOUBLE Z
FUTURISTIC IMAGE BOMBING!
LONG HUNT / QUIC KILL
2XX8
2XX9
COREY
COMIC ART AS A PROFESSION IS A DIFFICULT CHOICE TO LIVE YOUR LIFE BY, IT SELDOM MAKES SENSE. YOU HAVE TO DO WHAT YOU CAN TO SURVIVE. THERE IS NO SURE WAY TO SUCCEED. IT IS ALSO A LONELY LIFE. BUT IT'S ABOUT ALL I HAVE AND I'M TRYING TO MAKE IT WORK. AWESOME CONTENT, OR DEATH

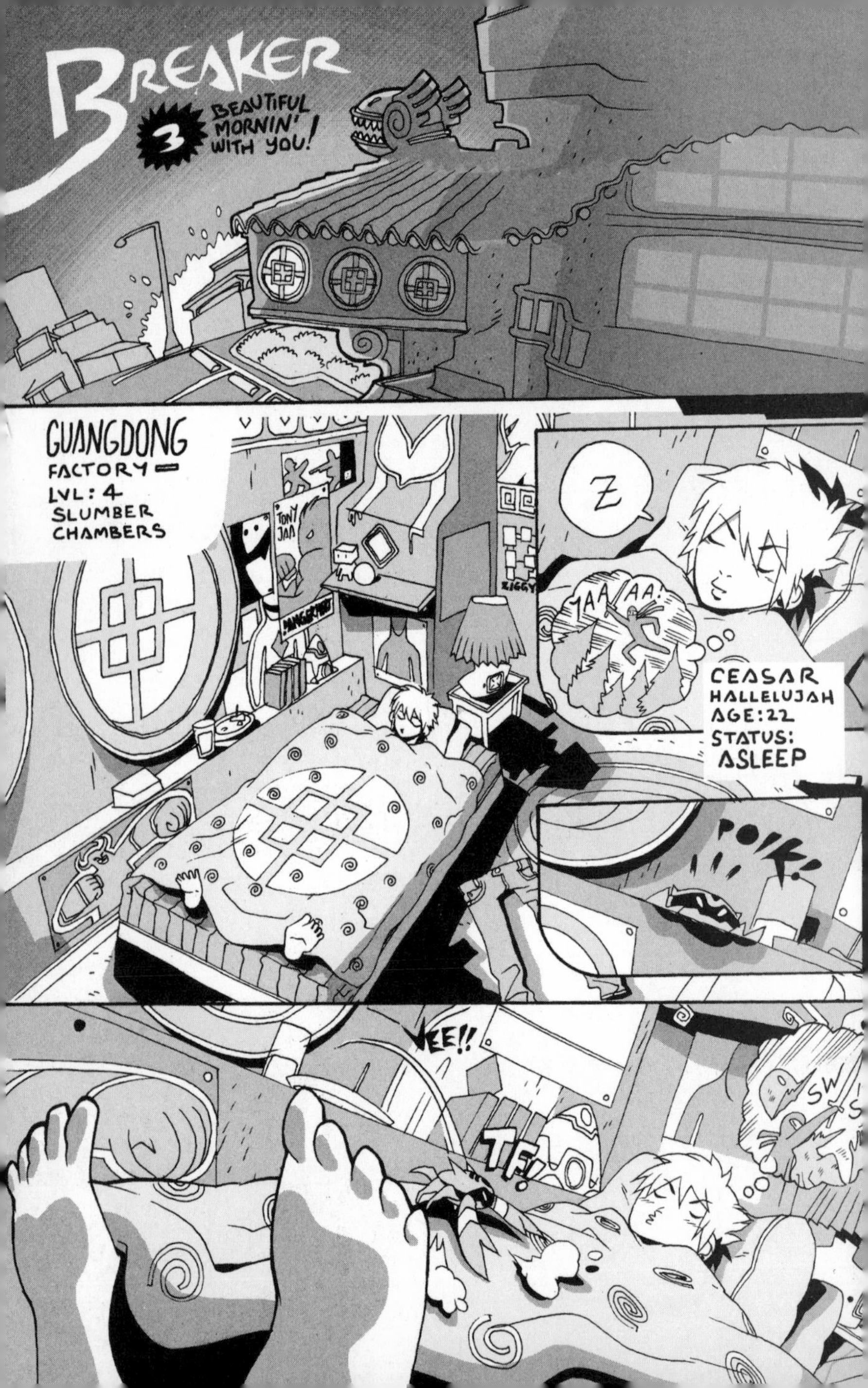
BREAKER
3
BEAUTIFUL MORNIN' WITH YOU!
GUANGDONG FACTORY — LVL: 4 SLUMBER CHAMBERS
TONY JAA
ZIGGY
Z
YAA AA!
CEASAR HALLELUJAH AGE: 22 STATUS: ASLEEP
POIK!
VEE!!
TF!
SW

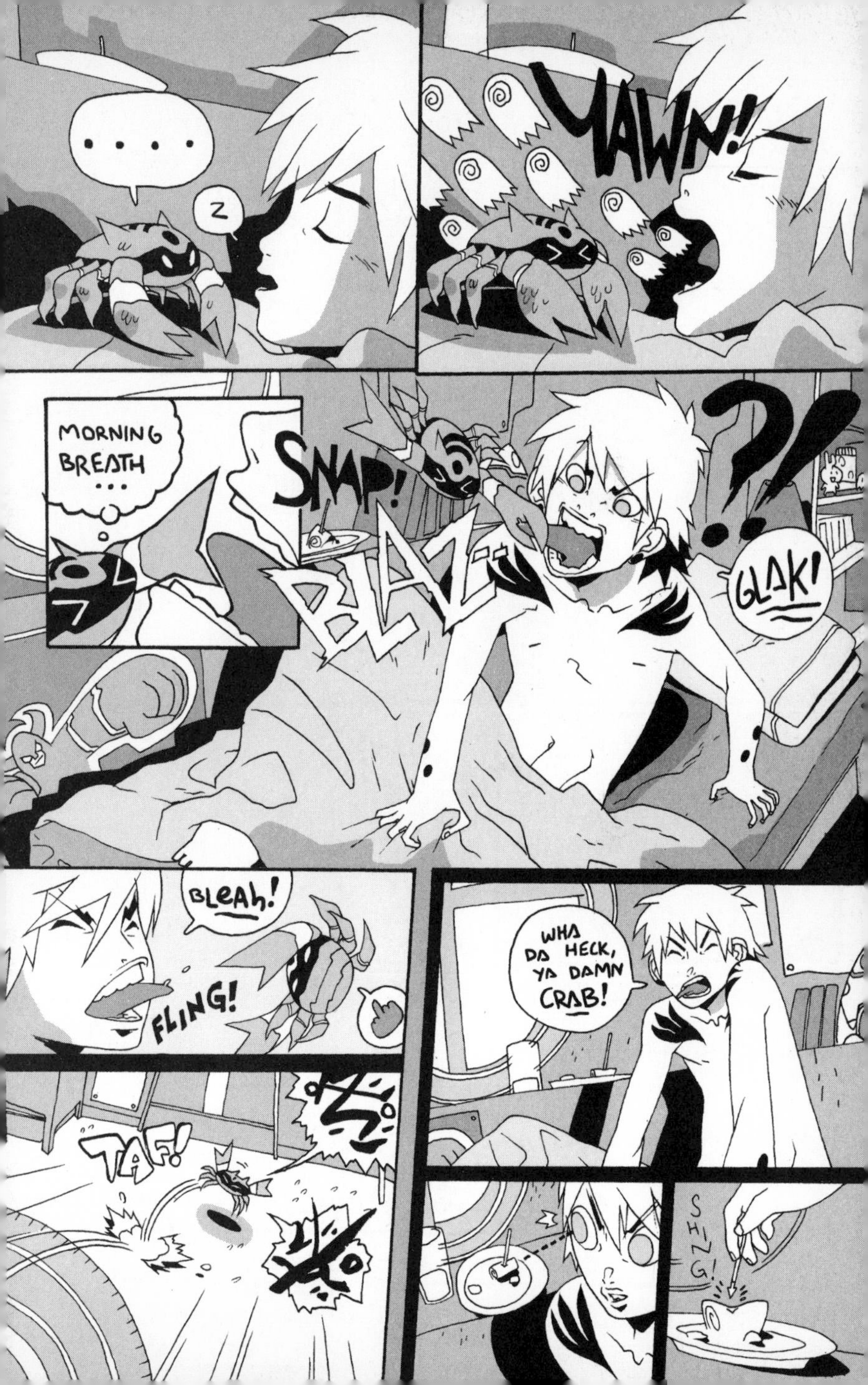

. . . .
Z
YAWN!
MORNING BREATH ...
SNAP!
BLAZ
??!!
GLAK!
BLEAH!
FLING!
WHA DA HECK, YA DAMN CRAB!
TAF!
SHING!

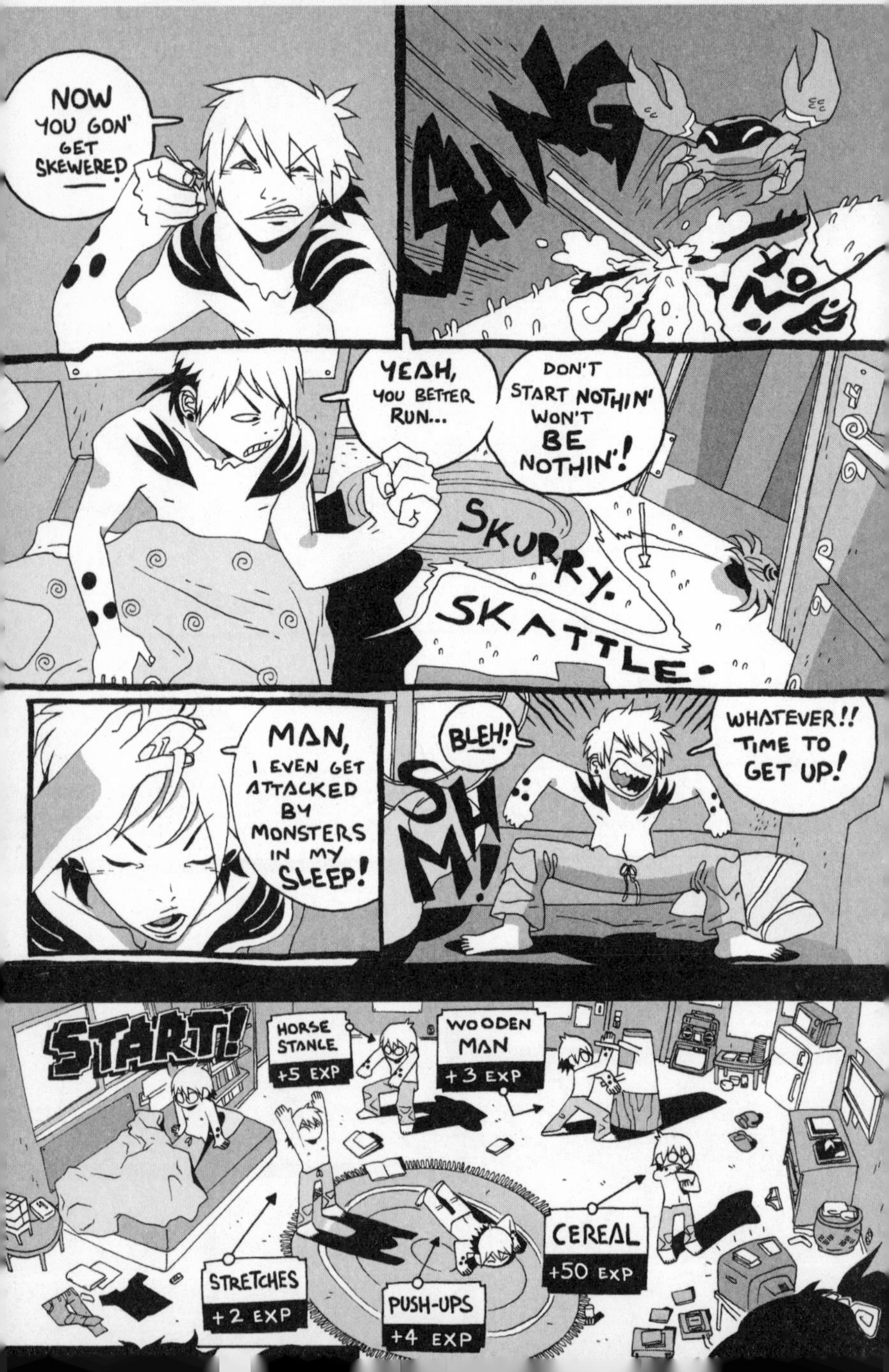
NOW YOU GON' GET SKEWERED
YEAH, YOU BETTER RUN...
DON'T START NOTHIN' WON'T BE NOTHIN'!
SKURRY.
SKATTLE.
MAN, I EVEN GET ATTACKED BY MONSTERS IN MY SLEEP!
BLEH!
WHATEVER!! TIME TO GET UP!
START!
HORSE STANCE
+5 EXP
WOODEN MAN
+3 EXP
STRETCHES
+2 EXP
PUSH-UPS
+4 EXP
CEREAL
+50 EXP

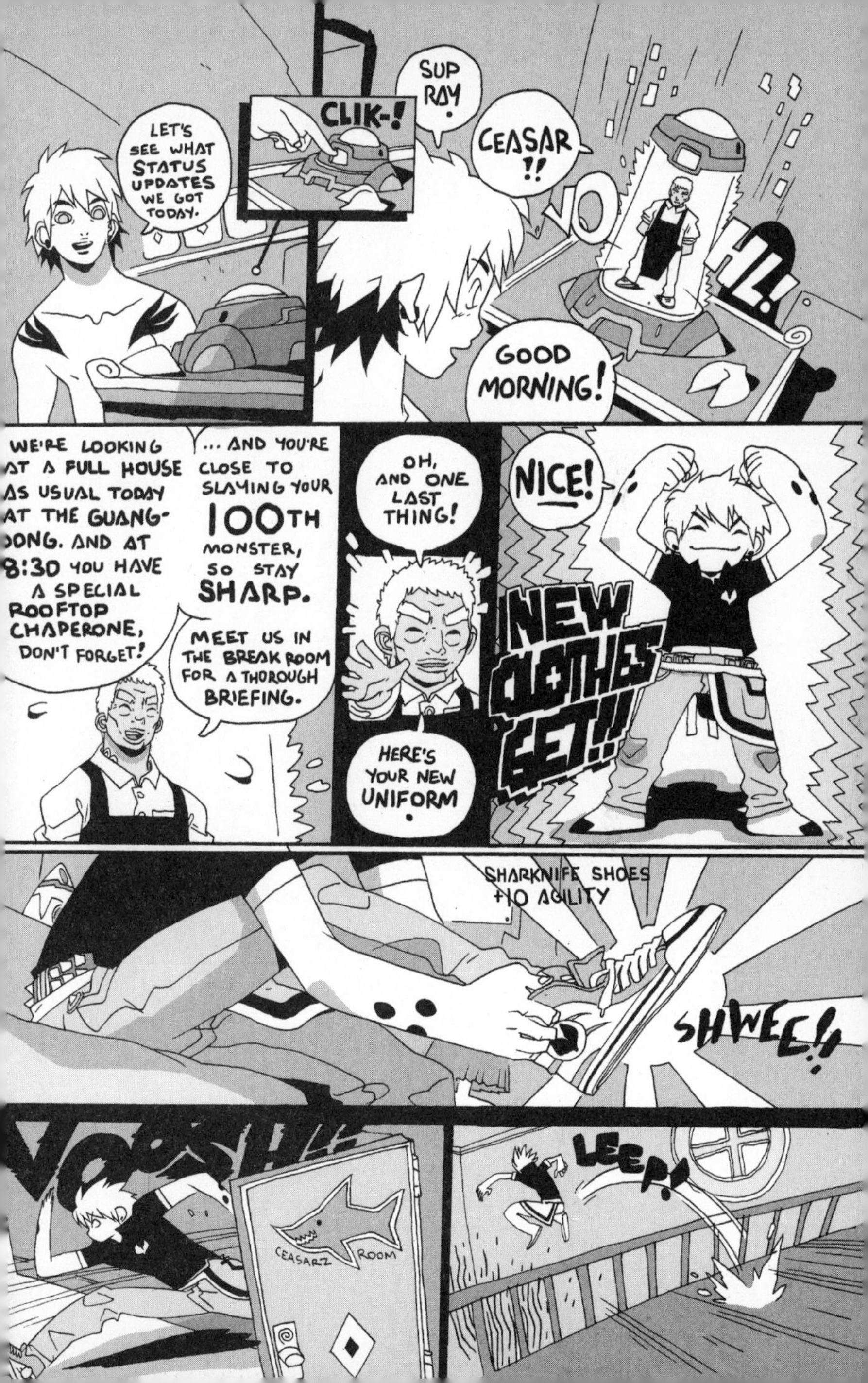
LET'S SEE WHAT STATUS UPDATES WE GOT TODAY.
CLIK-!
SUP RAY.
CEASAR!!
VOOSH!!
GOOD MORNING!
WE'RE LOOKING AT A FULL HOUSE AS USUAL TODAY AT THE GUANG-DONG. AND AT 8:30 YOU HAVE A SPECIAL ROOFTOP CHAPERONE, DON'T FORGET!
... AND YOU'RE CLOSE TO SLAYING YOUR 100TH MONSTER, SO STAY SHARP.
MEET US IN THE BREAK ROOM FOR A THOROUGH BRIEFING.
OH, AND ONE LAST THING!
HERE'S YOUR NEW UNIFORM.
NICE!
NEW CLOTHES GET!!
SHARKNIFE SHOES +10 AGILITY
SHWEE!!
CEASARZ ROOM
LEEP!!

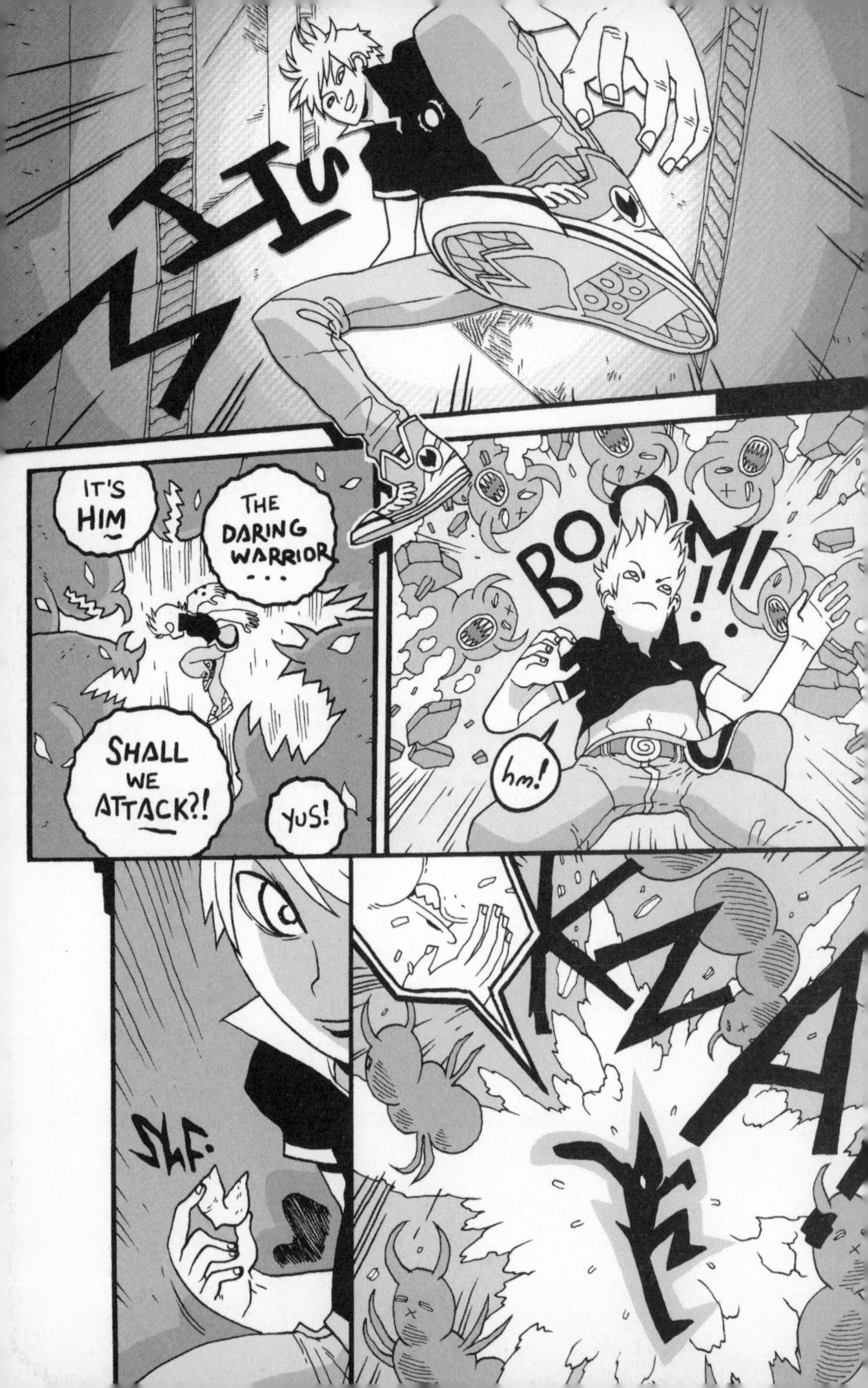
SHIT
IT'S HIM
THE DARING WARRIOR ...
SHALL WE ATTACK?!
YUS!
BOOM!!
hm!
SHF.
KAA!

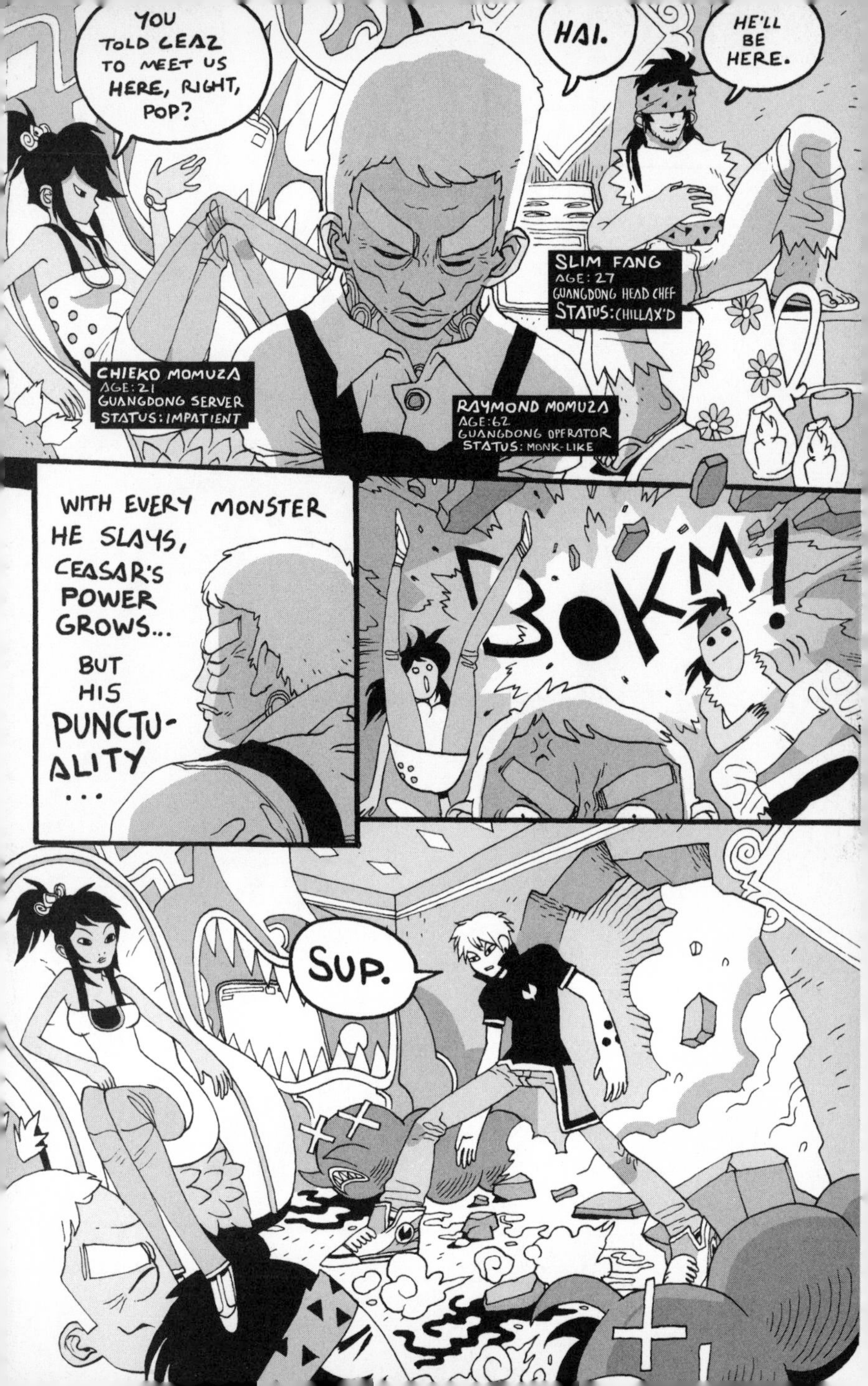
YOU TOLD CEAZ TO MEET US HERE, RIGHT, POP?
HAI.
HE'LL BE HERE.
SLIM FANG
AGE: 27
GUANGDONG HEAD CHEF
STATUS: CHILLAX'D
CHIEKO MOMUZA
AGE: 21
GUANGDONG SERVER
STATUS: IMPATIENT
RAYMOND MOMUZA
AGE: 62
GUANGDONG OPERATOR
STATUS: MONK-LIKE
WITH EVERY MONSTER HE SLAYS, CEASAR'S POWER GROWS...
BUT HIS PUNCTU-ALITY ...
BOKM!
SUP.

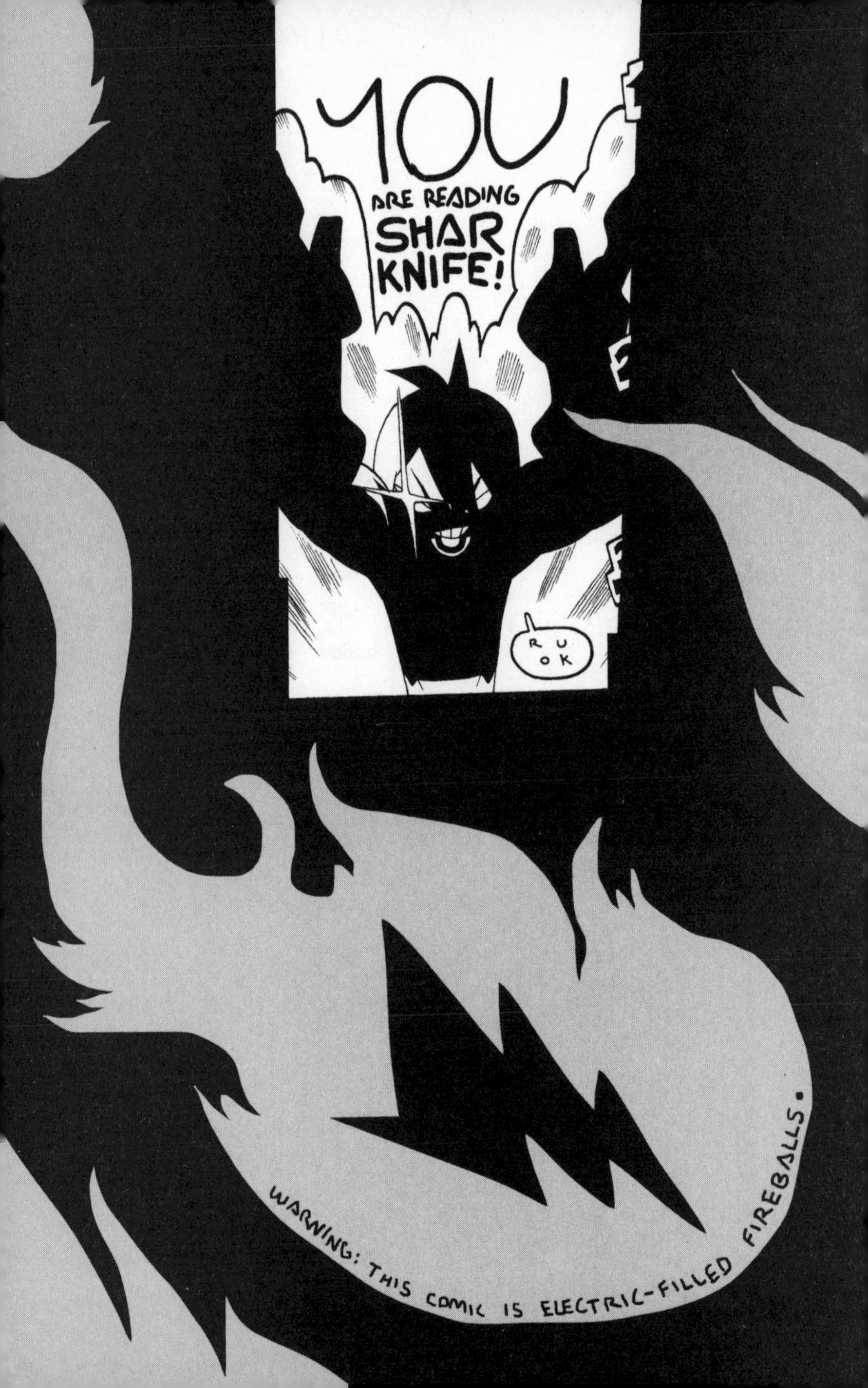
YOU
ARE READING
SHAR
KNIFE!
R U
OK
WARNING: THIS COMIC IS ELECTRIC-FILLED FIREBALLS.

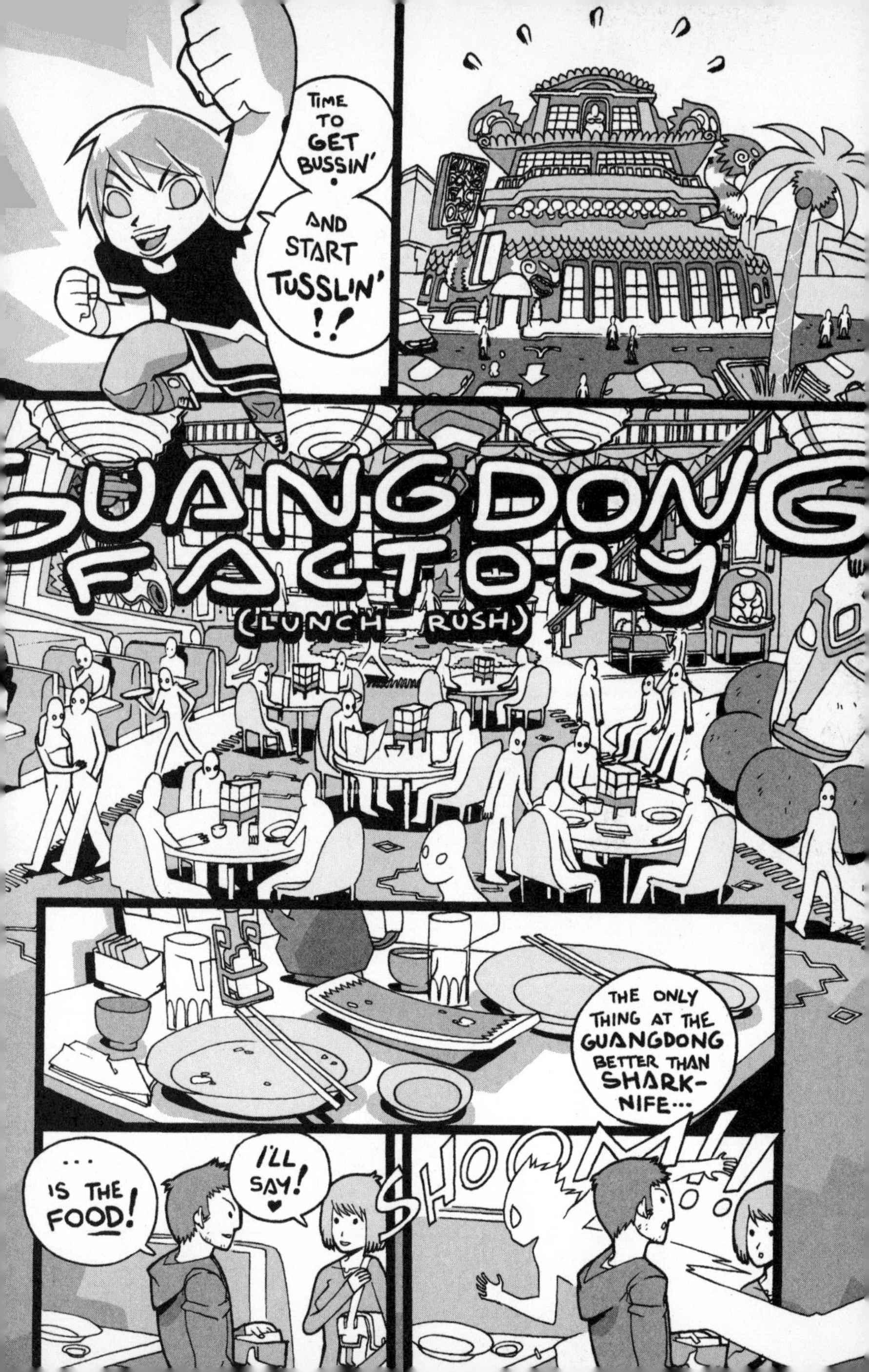
TIME TO GET BUSSIN' •
AND START TUSSLIN' !!
GUANGDONG FACTORY
(LUNCH RUSH)
THE ONLY THING AT THE GUANGDONG BETTER THAN SHARK-NIFE...
... IS THE FOOD!
I'LL SAY! ♥
SHOOM!!

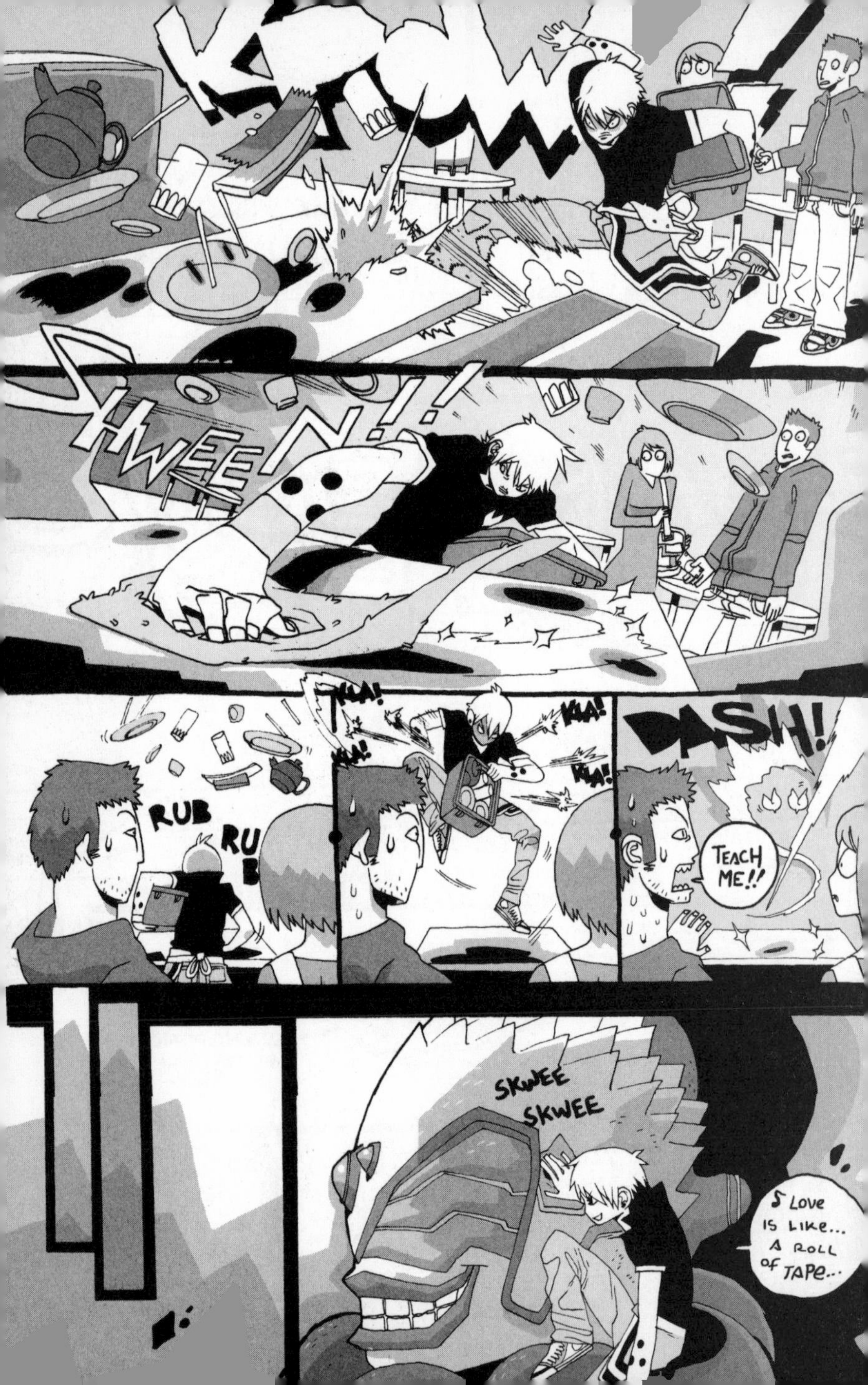
KA-POW
SHWEEN!!
RUB
RUB
KLA!
KLA!
KLA!
KLA!
DASH!
TEACH ME!!
SKWEE
SKWEE
♪ Love is like... a roll of tape...

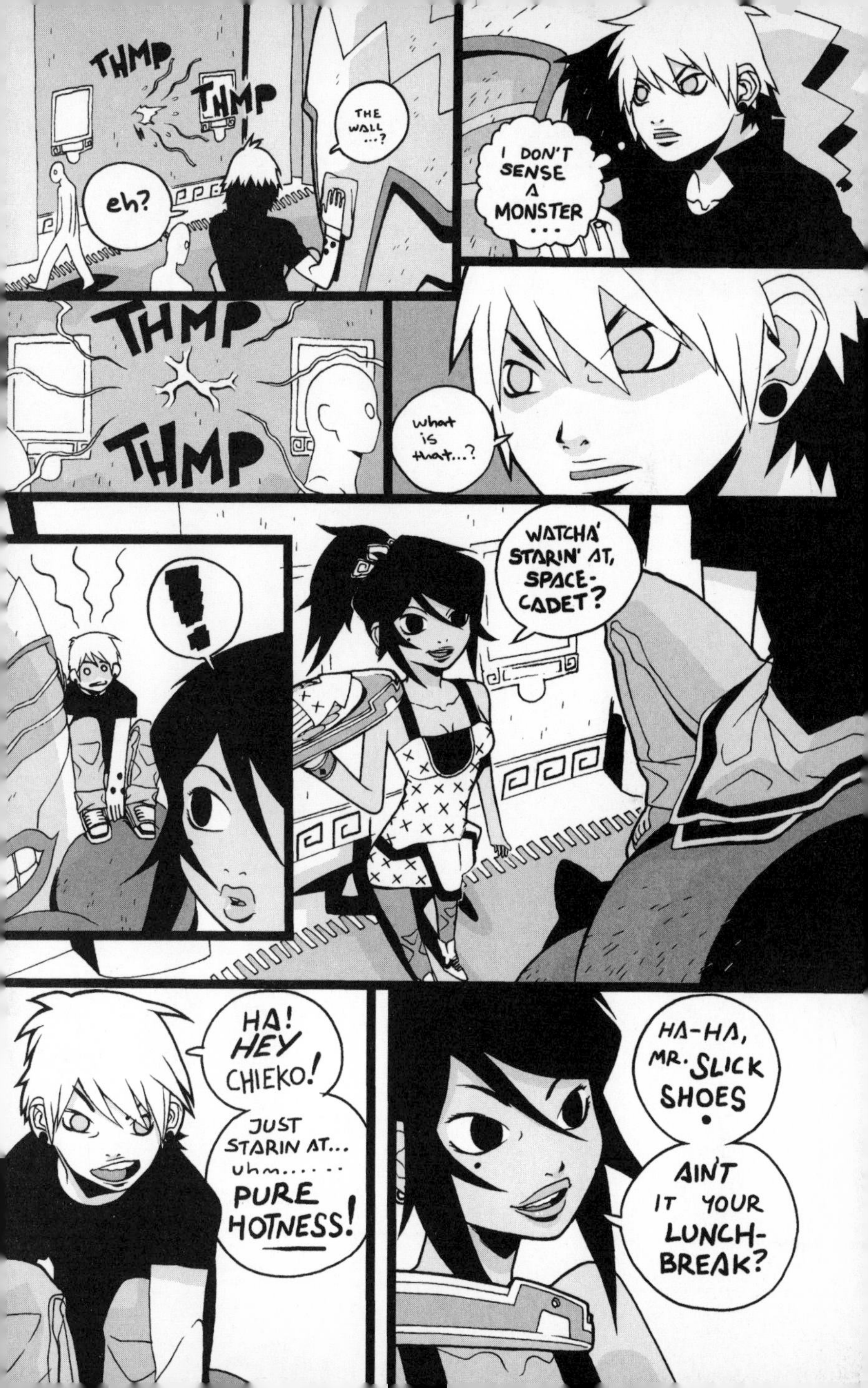
THMP
THMP
eh?
THE WALL ...?
I DON'T SENSE A MONSTER ...
THMP
THMP
what is that...?
!
WATCHA' STARIN' AT, SPACE-CADET?
HA! HEY CHIEKO!
JUST STARIN AT... uhm...... PURE HOTNESS!
HA-HA, MR. SLICK SHOES.
AIN'T IT YOUR LUNCH-BREAK?

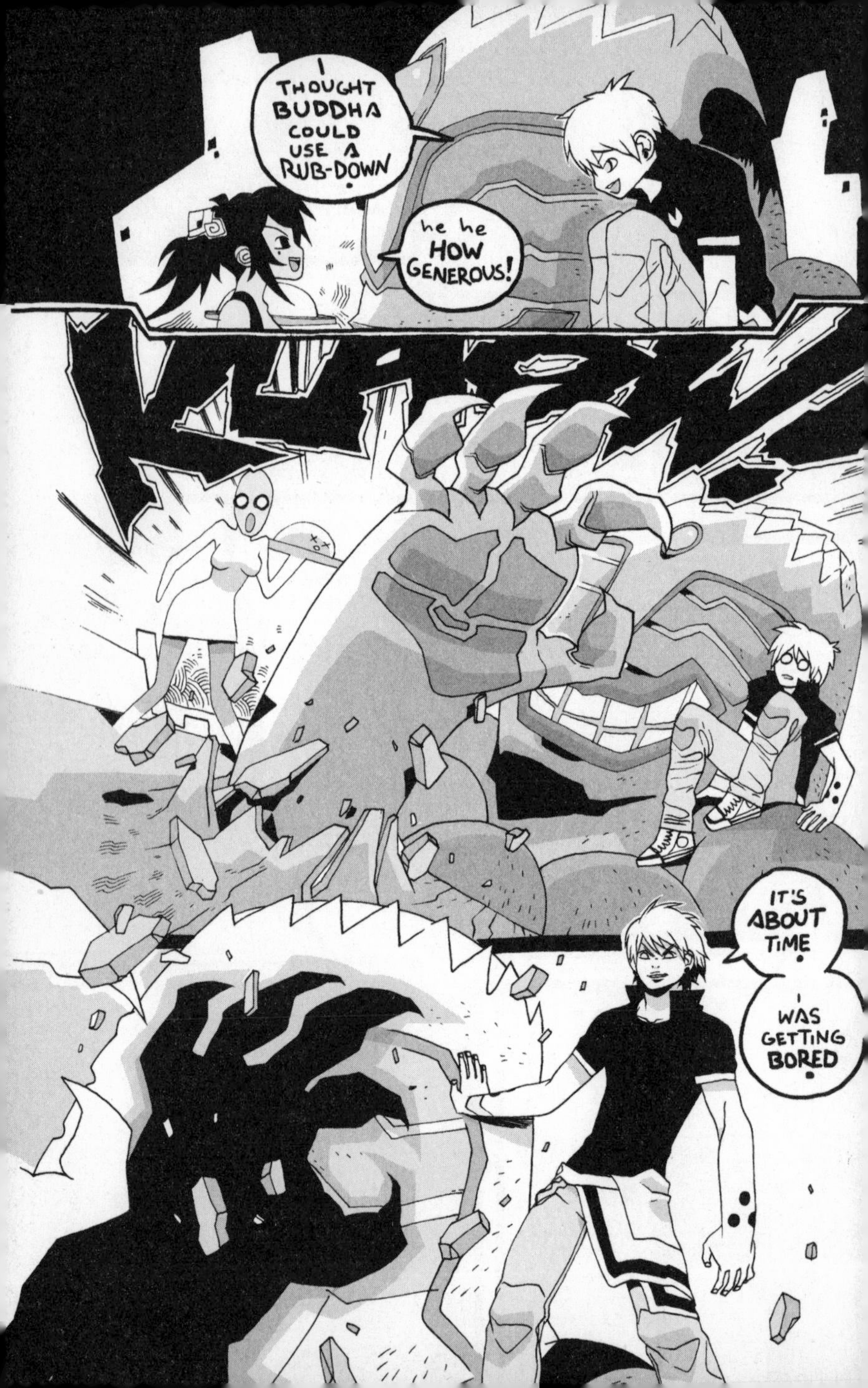
I THOUGHT BUDDHA COULD USE A RUB-DOWN.
he he HOW GENEROUS!
IT'S ABOUT TIME.
I WAS GETTING BORED.

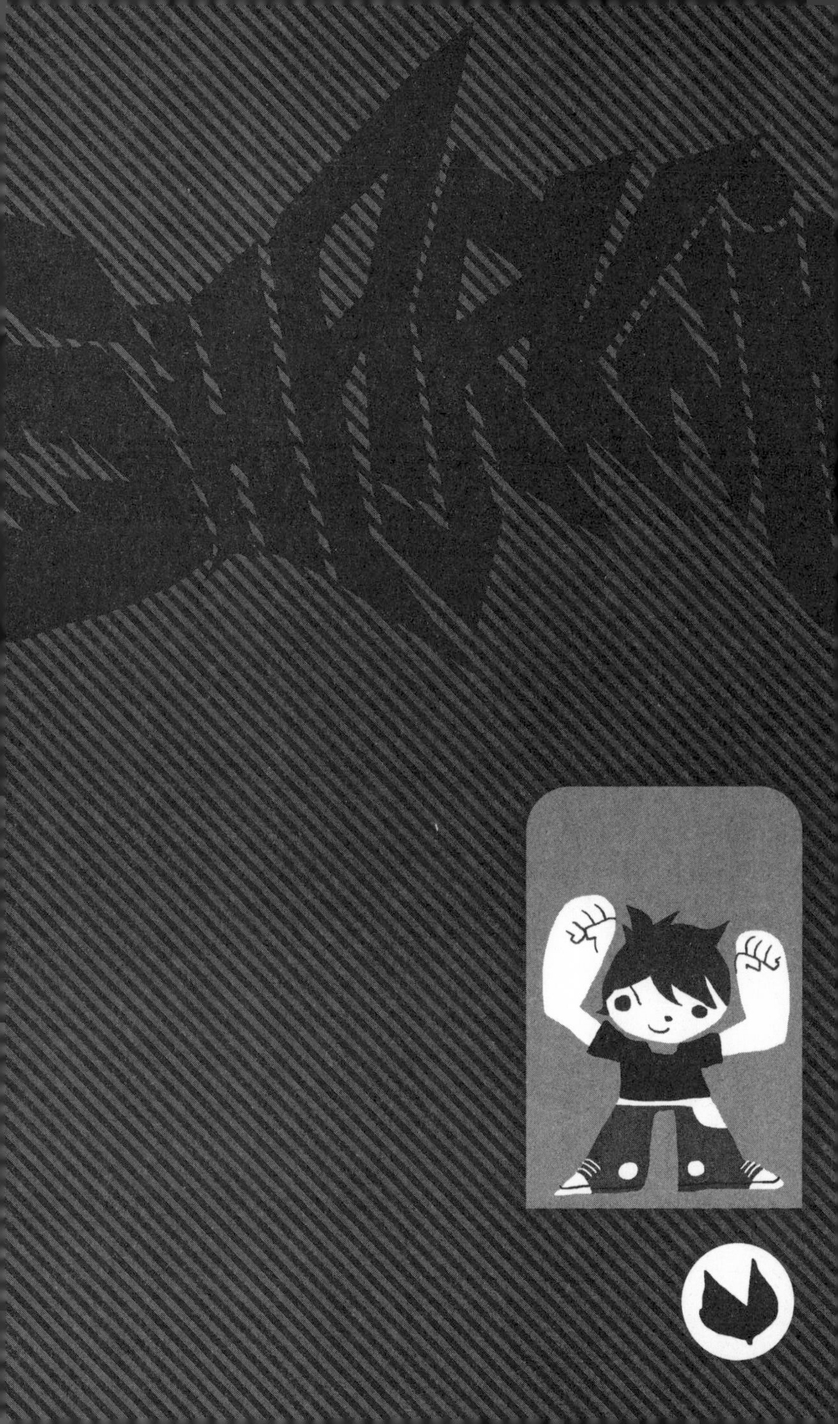

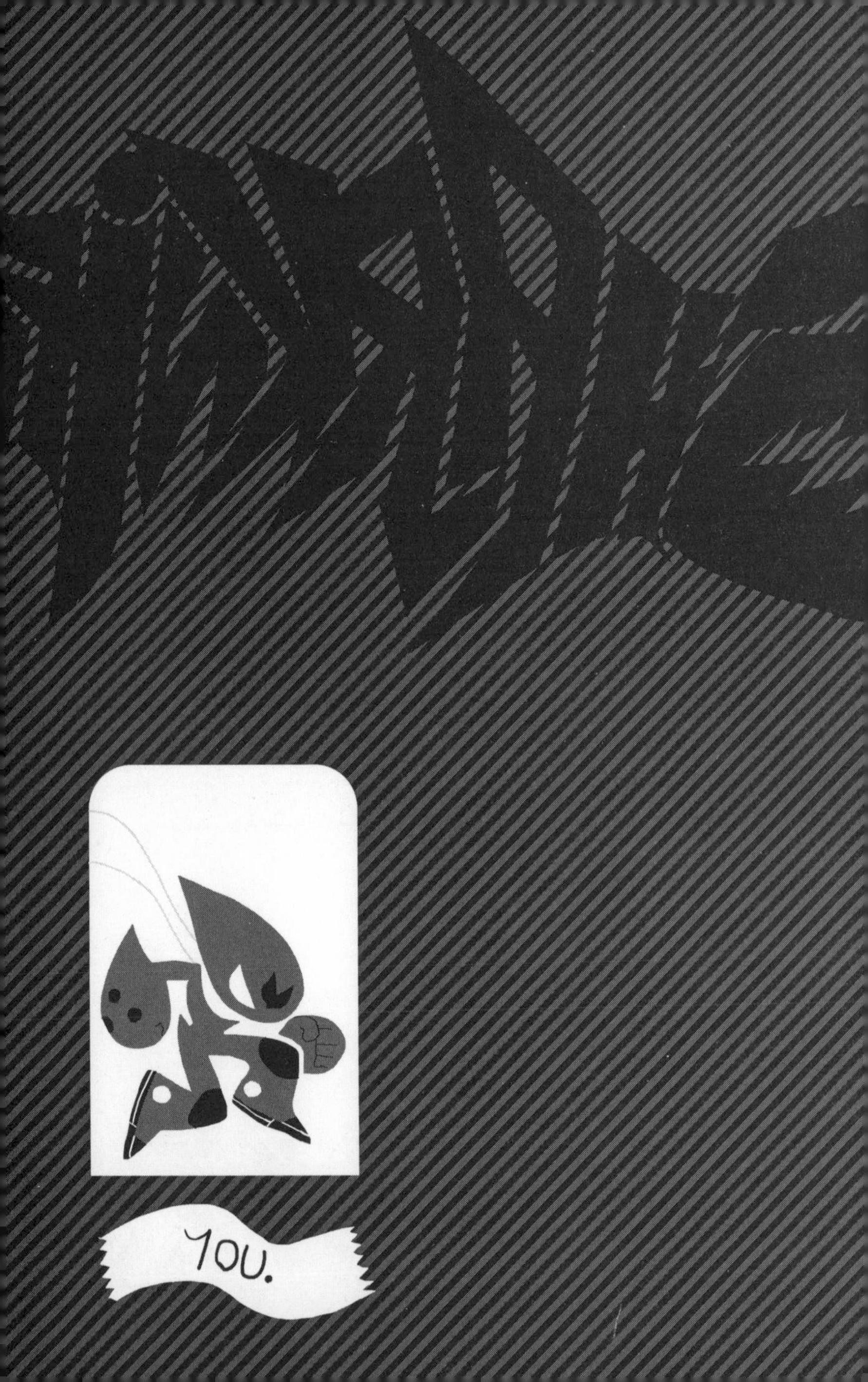
YOU.

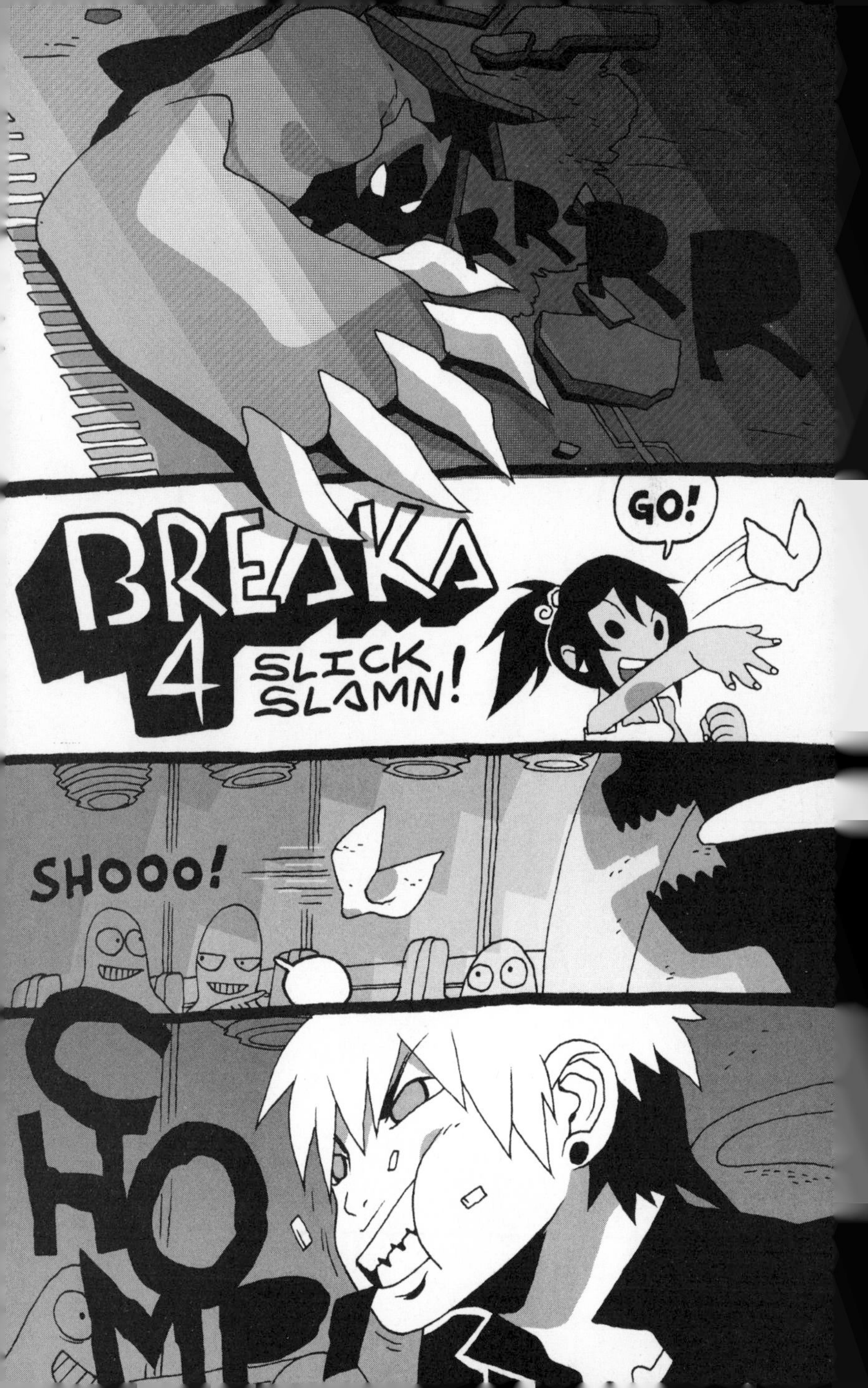
GO!
BREAKA 4
SLICK SLAMN!
SHOOO!

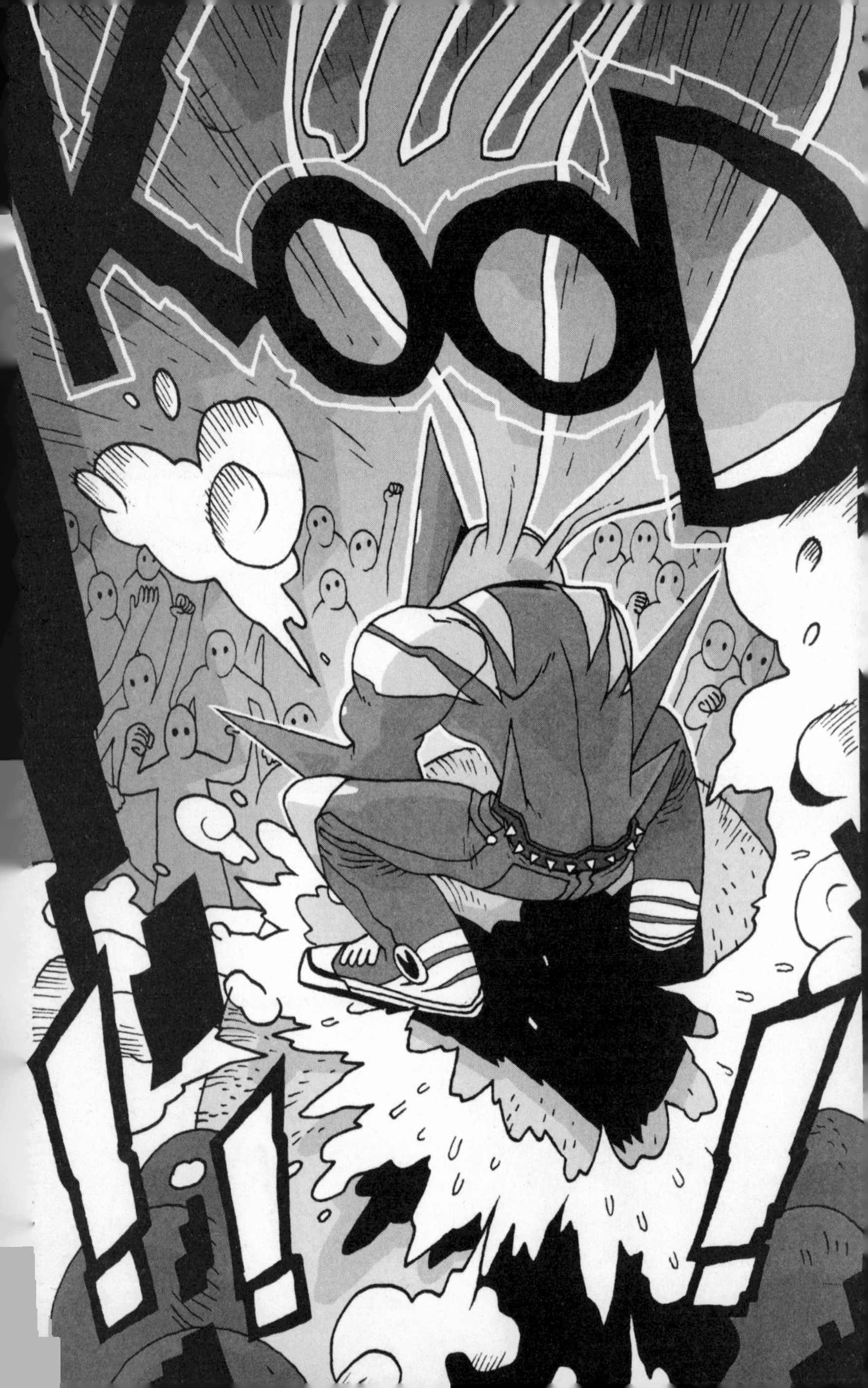
KOOD!!!

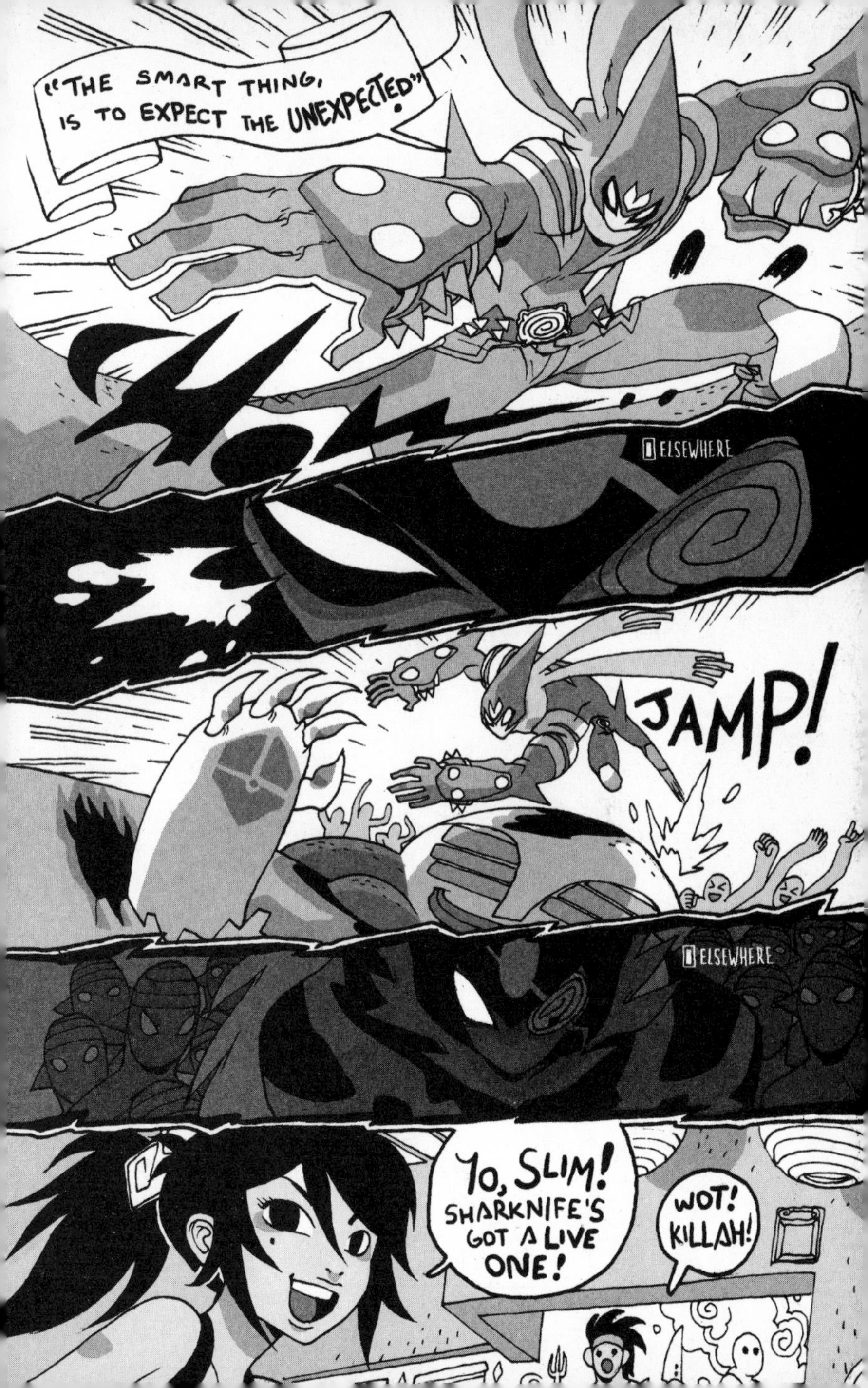
"THE SMART THING, IS TO EXPECT THE UNEXPECTED".
ELSEWHERE
JAMP!
ELSEWHERE
Yo, SLIM! SHARKNIFE'S GOT A LIVE ONE!
WOT! KILLAH!

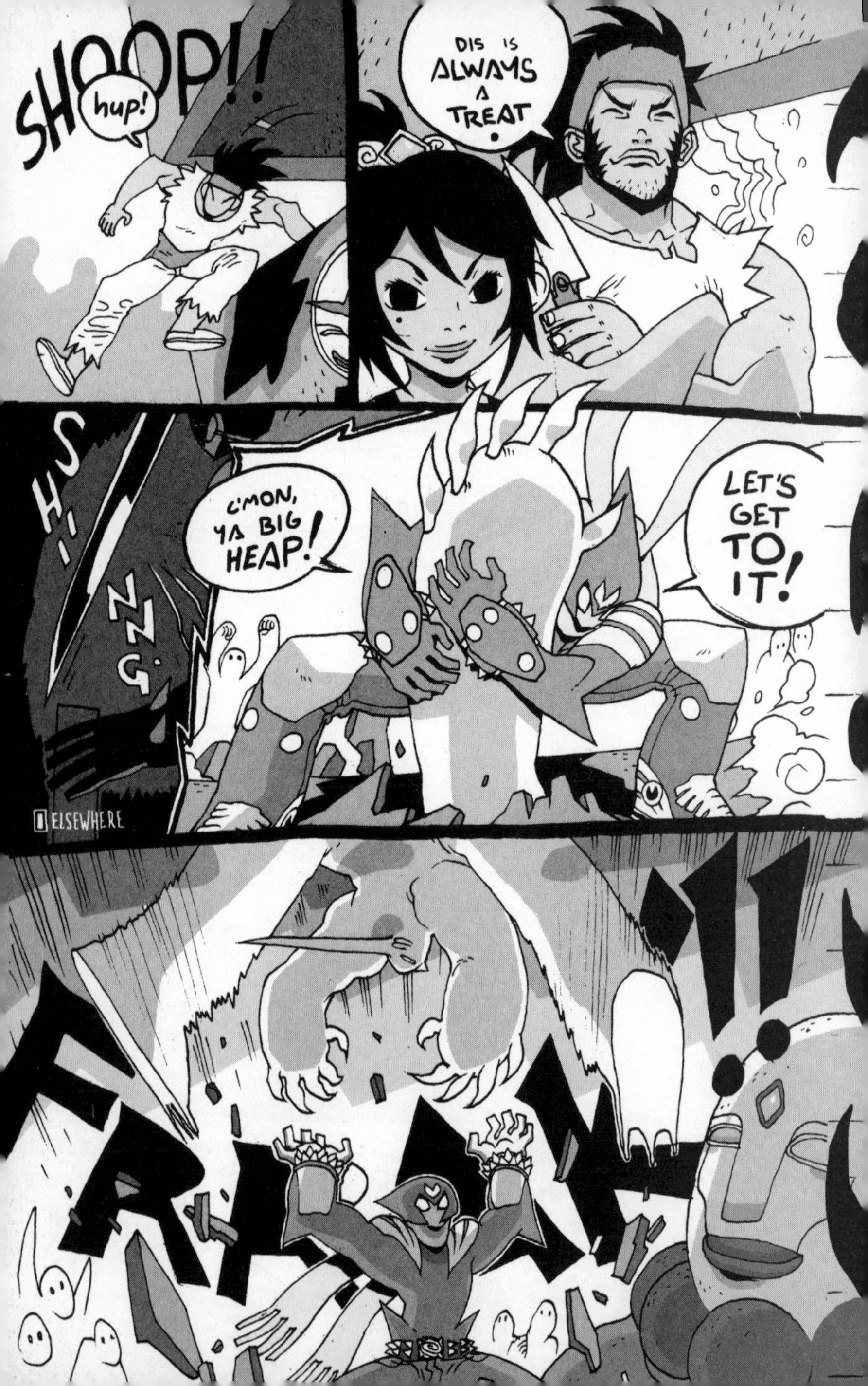
SHOOP!!
hup!
DIS IS ALWAYS A TREAT.
SHING
C'MON, YA BIG HEAP!
LET'S GET TO IT!
ELSEWHERE

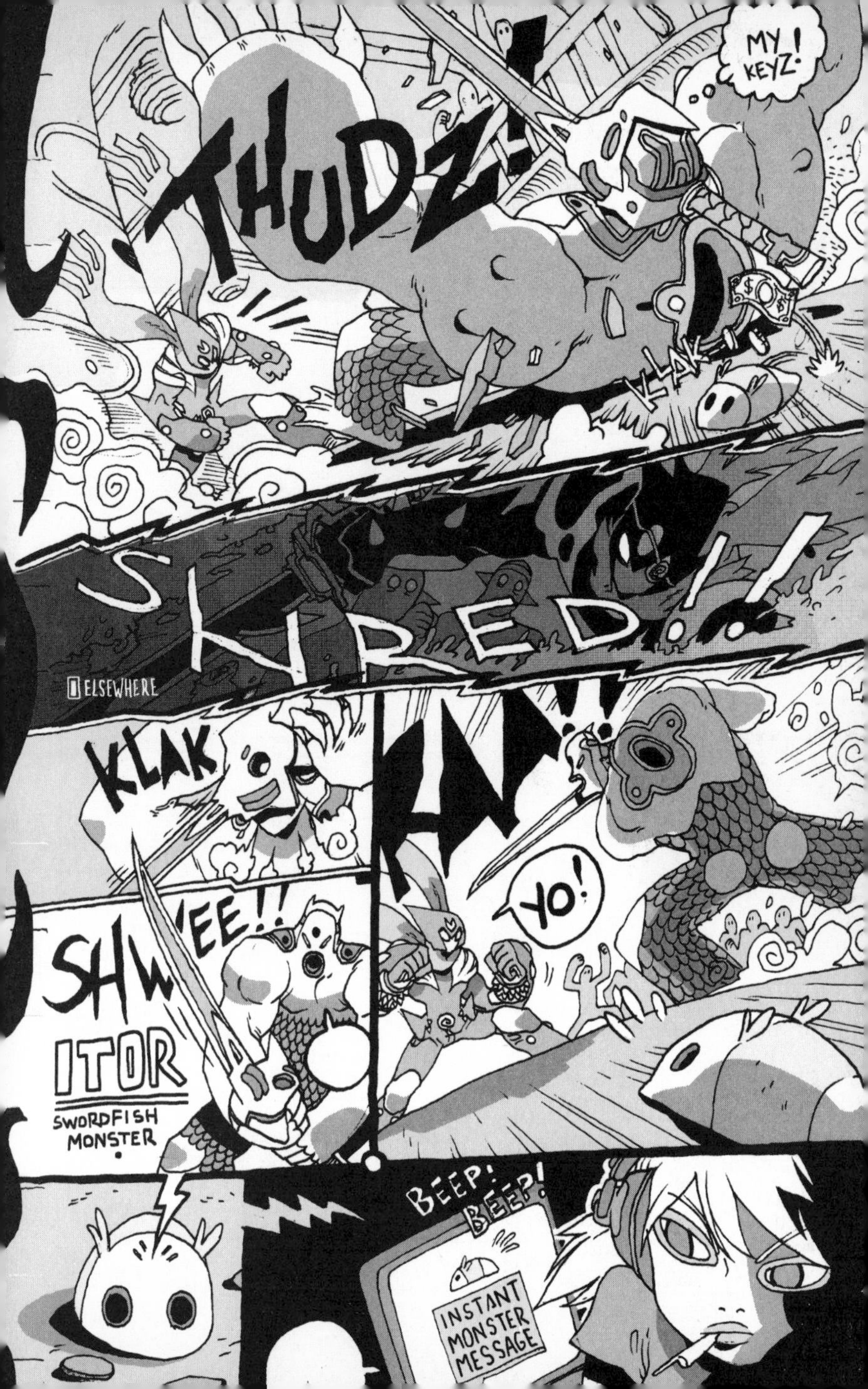
MY KEYZ!
THUDZ!
KLAK
SHRED!!
ELSEWHERE
KLAK
KRAK!!
SHWEE!!
ITOR
SWORDFISH MONSTER
YO!
BEEP! BEEP!
INSTANT MONSTER MESSAGE

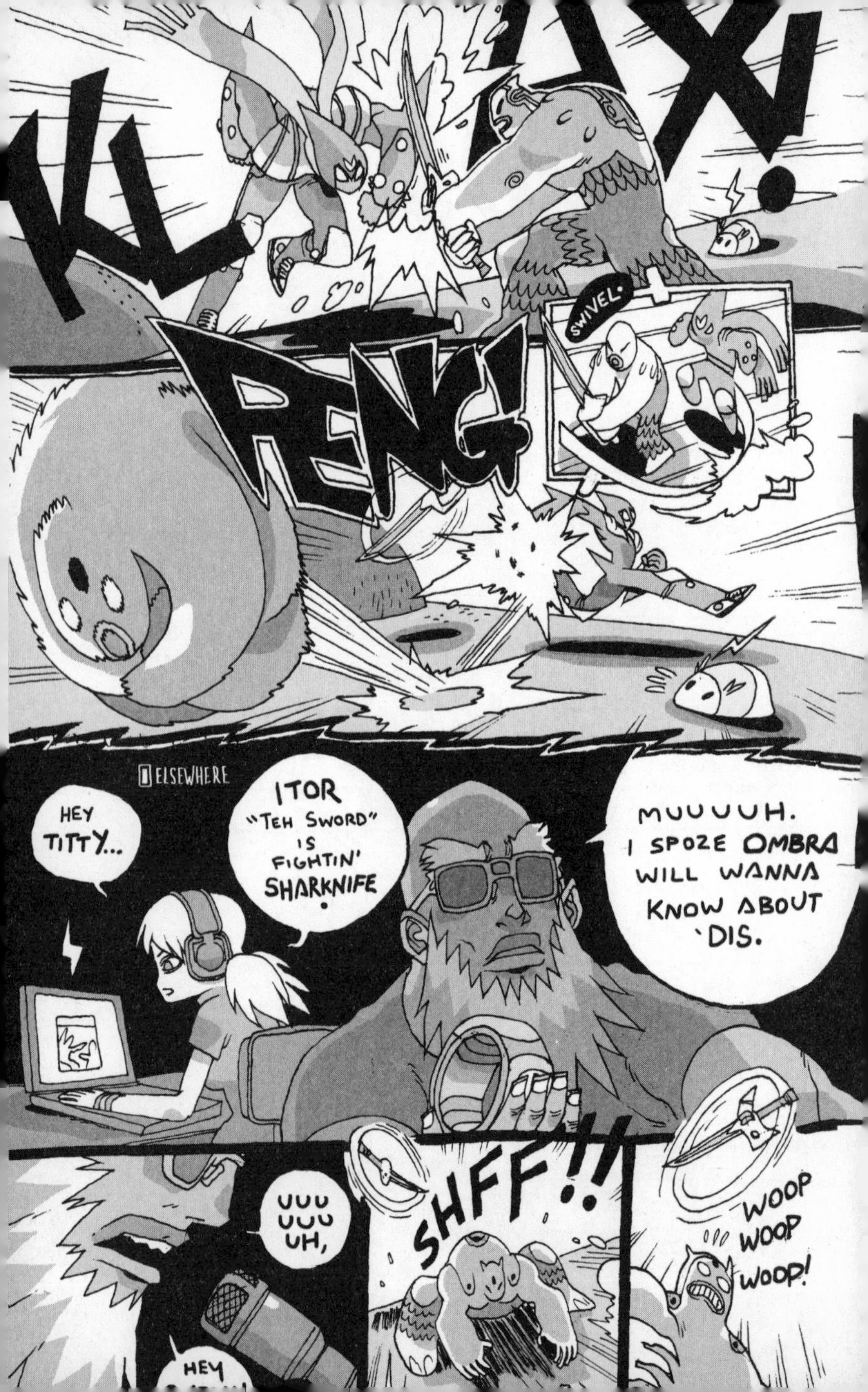
KLAX!
SWIVEL
PENG!
ELSEWHERE
HEY TITTY...
ITOR "TEH SWORD" IS FIGHTIN' SHARKNIFE.
MUUUUH. I SPOZE OMBRA WILL WANNA KNOW ABOUT 'DIS.
UUU UUU UH,
HEY
SHFF!!!
WOOP WOOP WOOP!

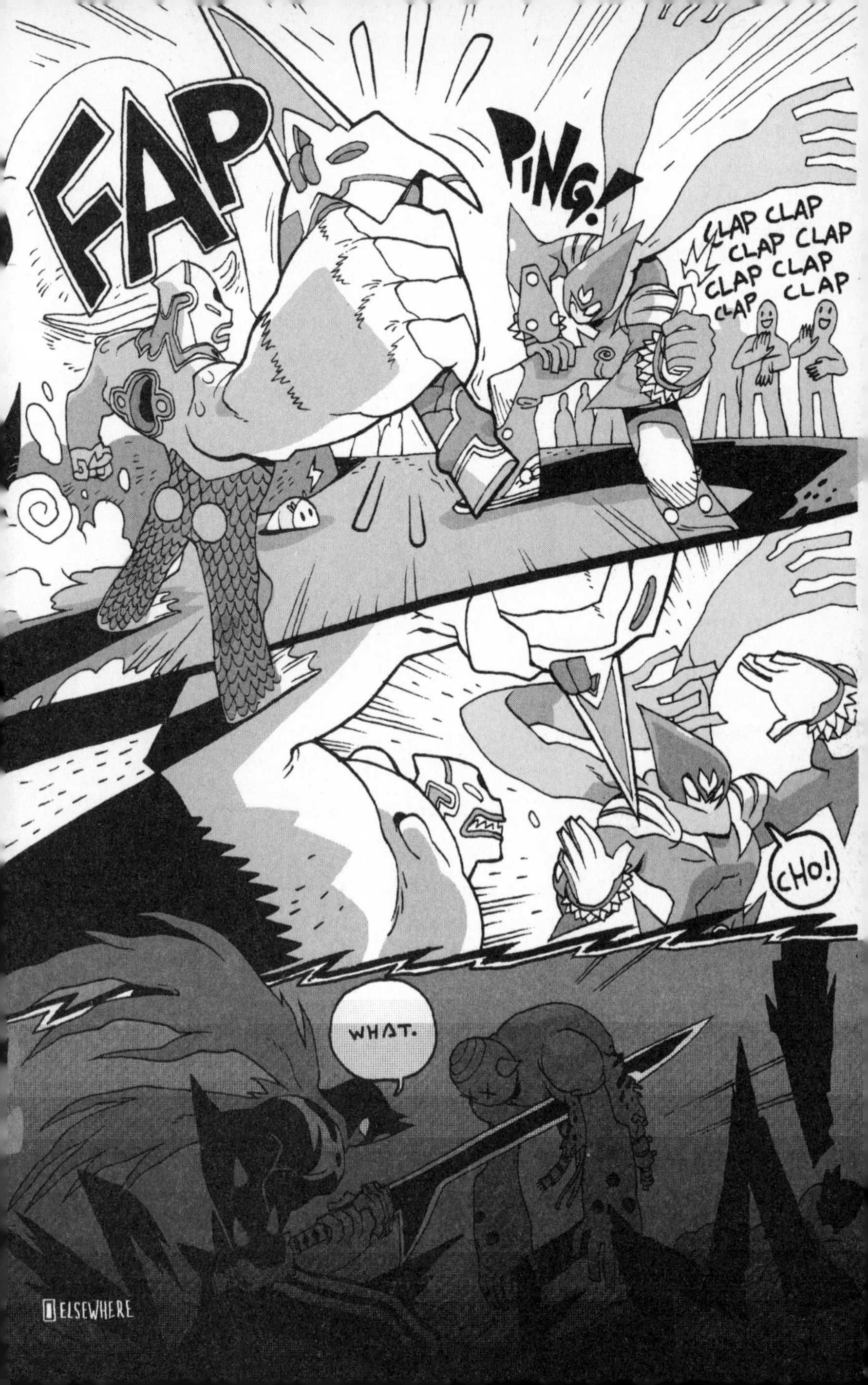
FAP
PING!
CLAP CLAP
CLAP CLAP
CLAP CLAP
CLAP CLAP
CHO!
WHAT.
ELSEWHERE

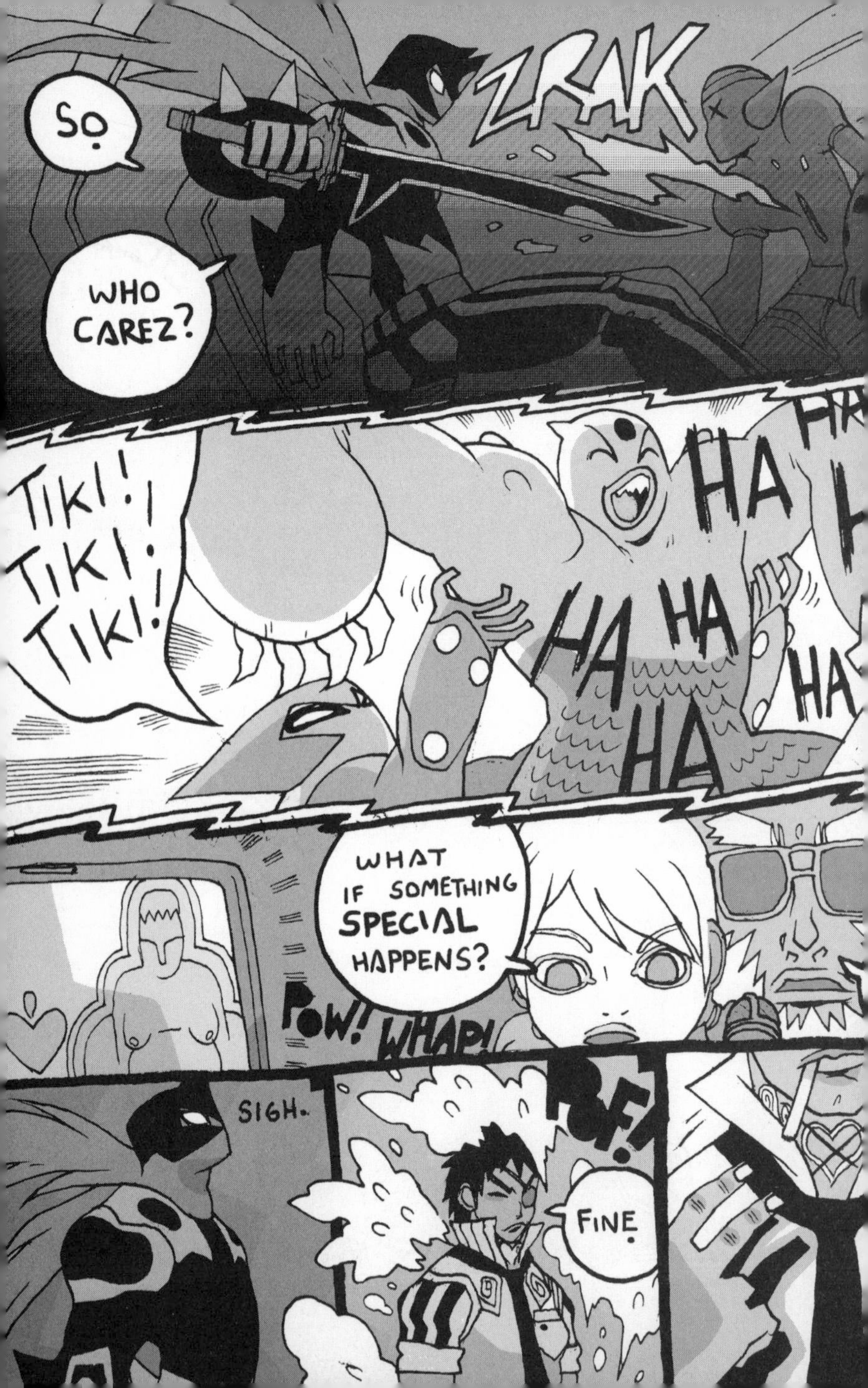
SO.
ZRAK
WHO CAREZ?
TIKI! TIKI! TIKI!
HA HA HA HA HA HA HA HA
WHAT IF SOMETHING SPECIAL HAPPENS?
POW! WHAP!
SIGH..
FINE.

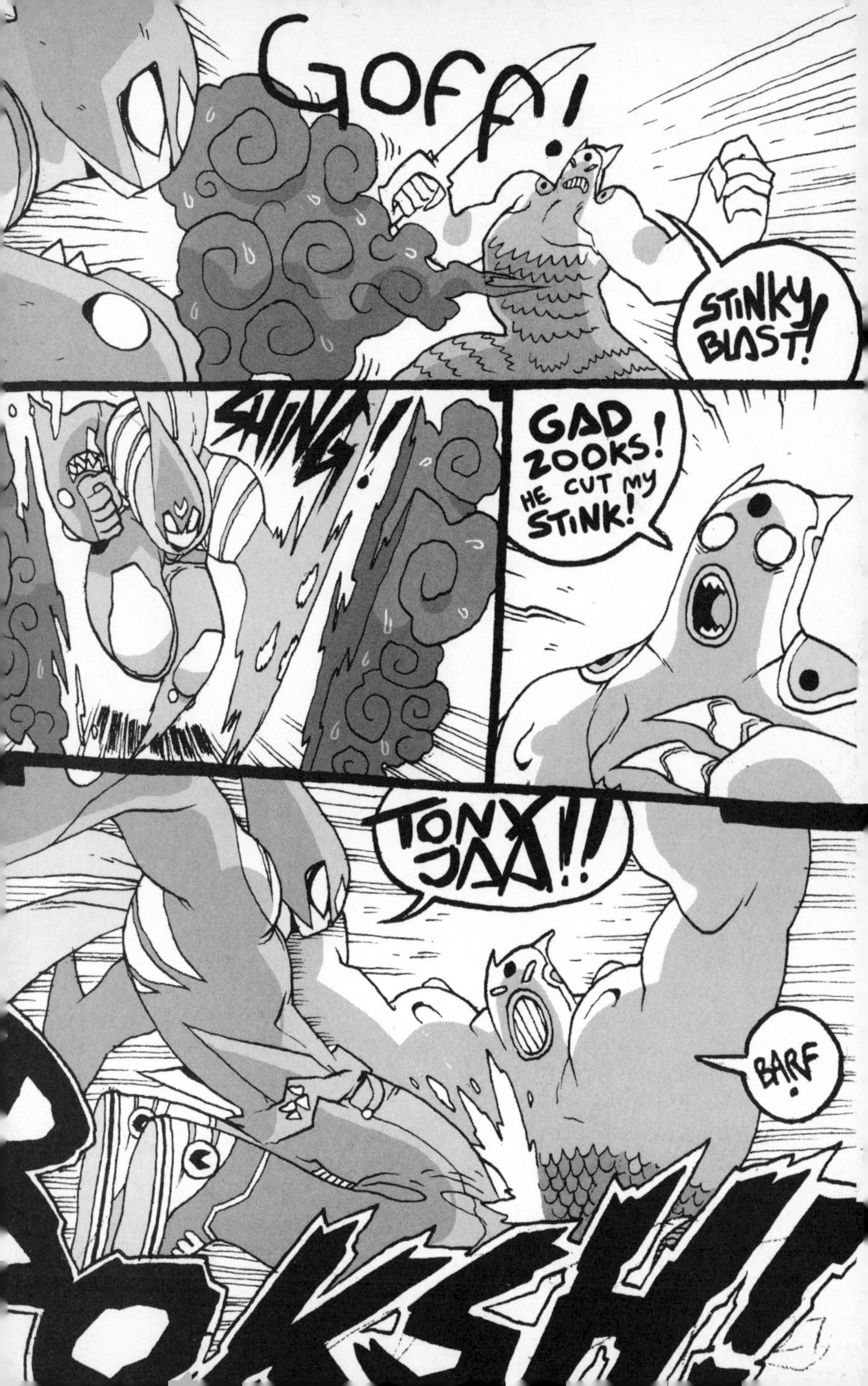
GOFF!
STINKY BLAST!
SHING!
GAD ZOOKS! HE CUT MY STINK!
TONY JAA!!
BARF
BOKSH!!

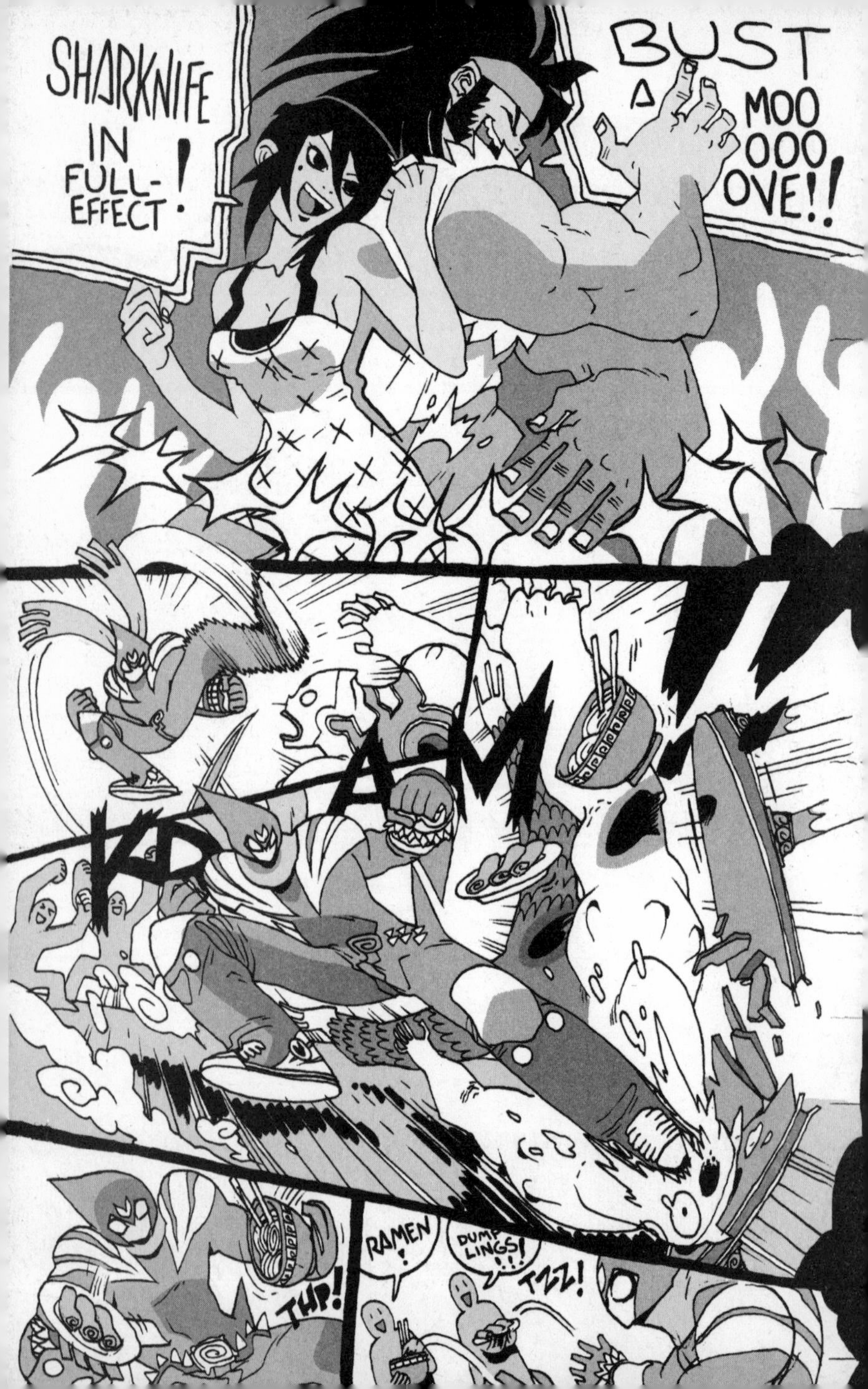
SHARKNIFE IN FULL-EFFECT!
BUST A MOOOOOOVE!!
KA-BAM!
THP!
RAMEN!
DUMPLINGS!!!
TZZ!

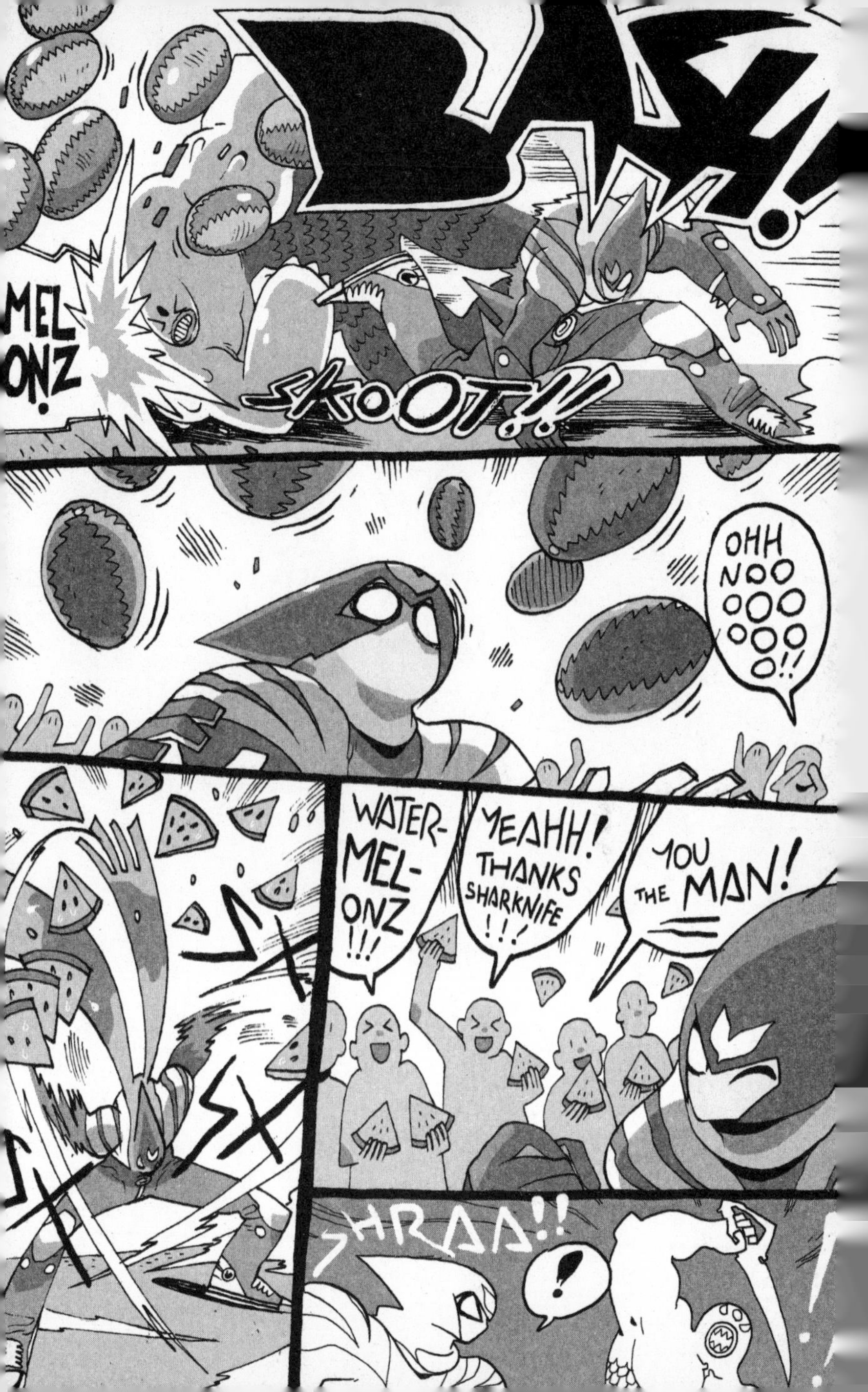
MELONZ!
SKOOT!!
OHH NOOOOOOOOOOOOOO!!
WATER-MEL-ONZ!!!
YEAHH! THANKS SHARKNIFE!!!
YOU THE MAN!
SHRAA!!
!

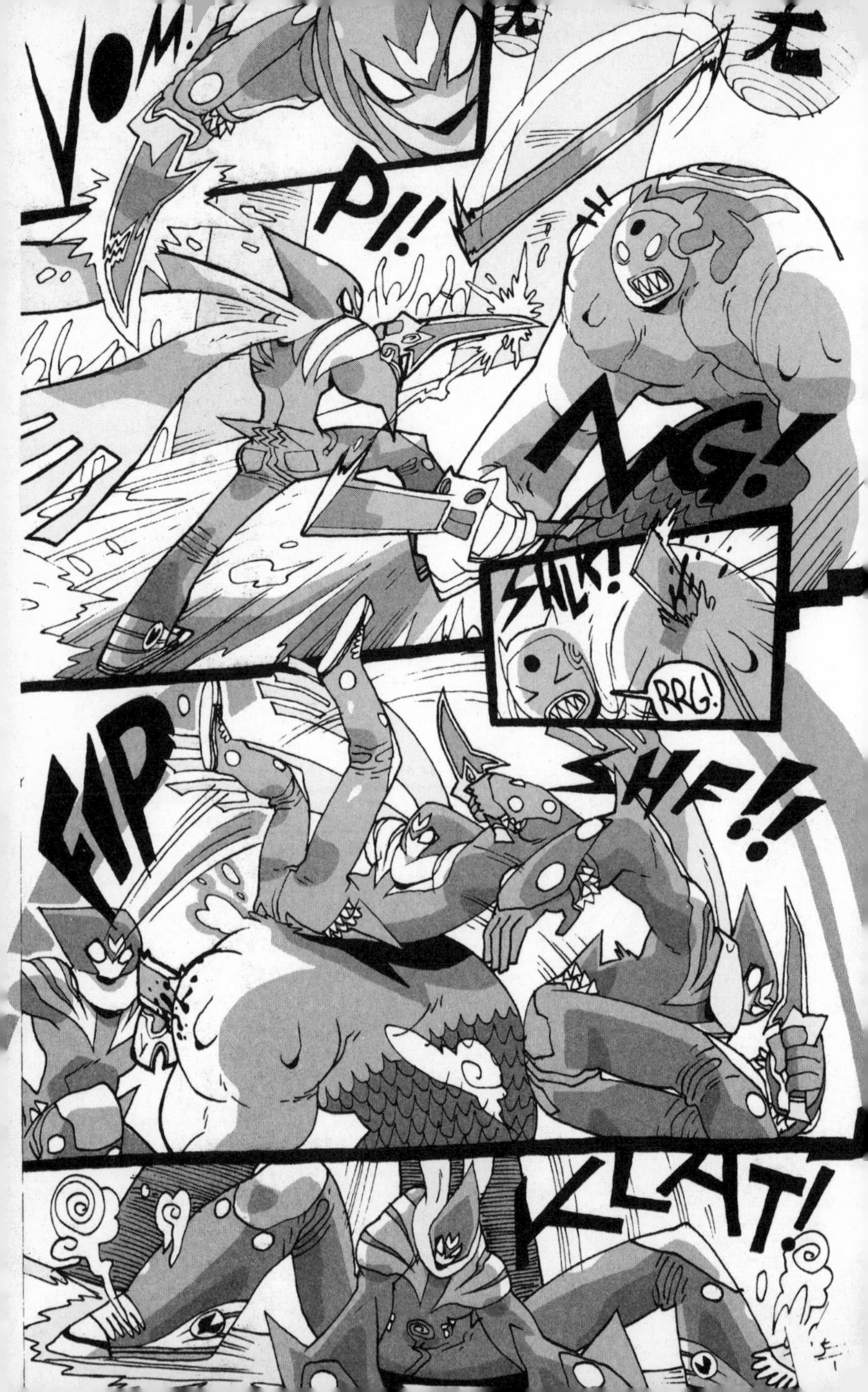
VOM!
PI!!
NG!
SHLK!
RRG!
FIP
SHF!!
KLAT!

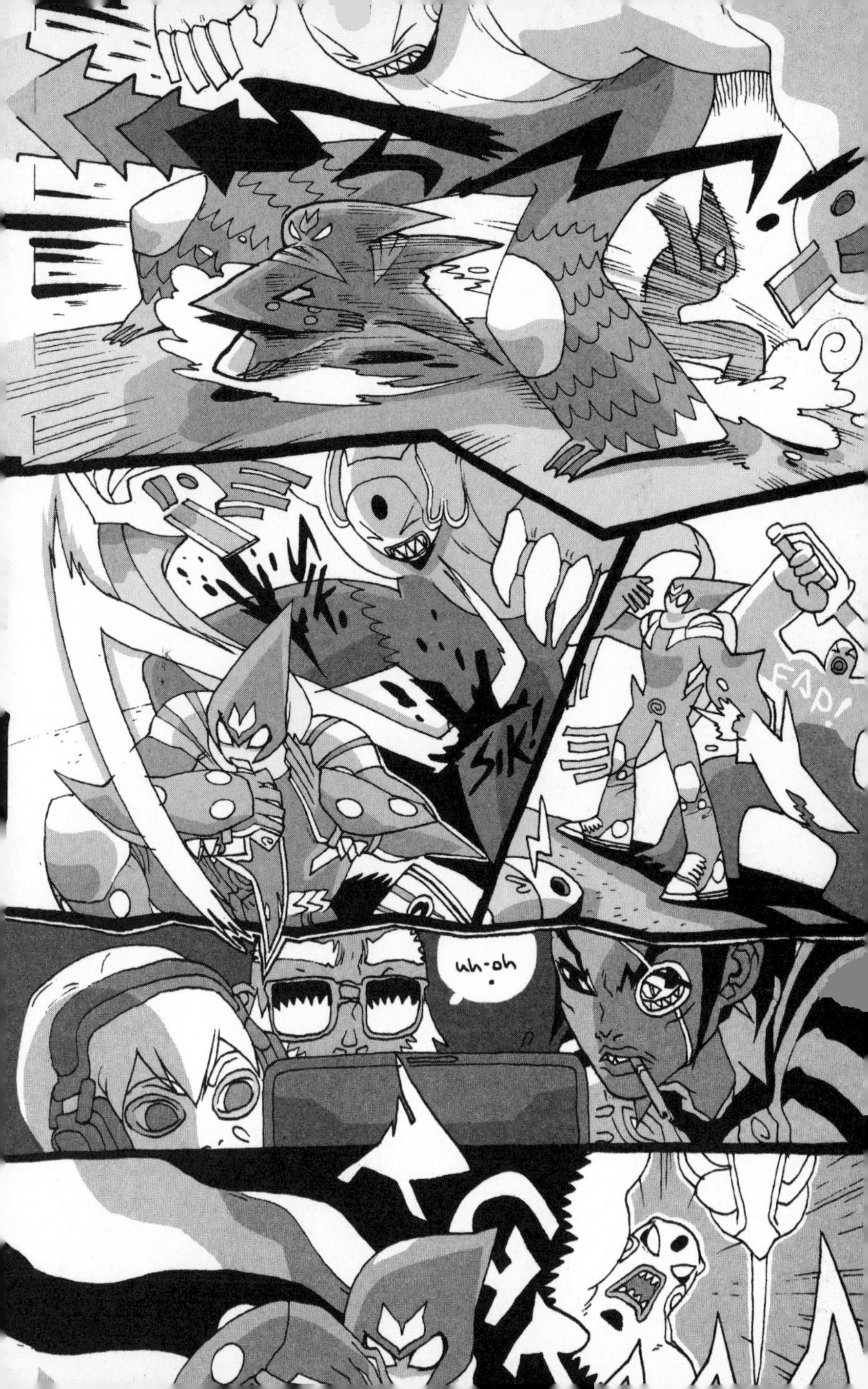
SIK
SIK!
FAP!
uh-oh.

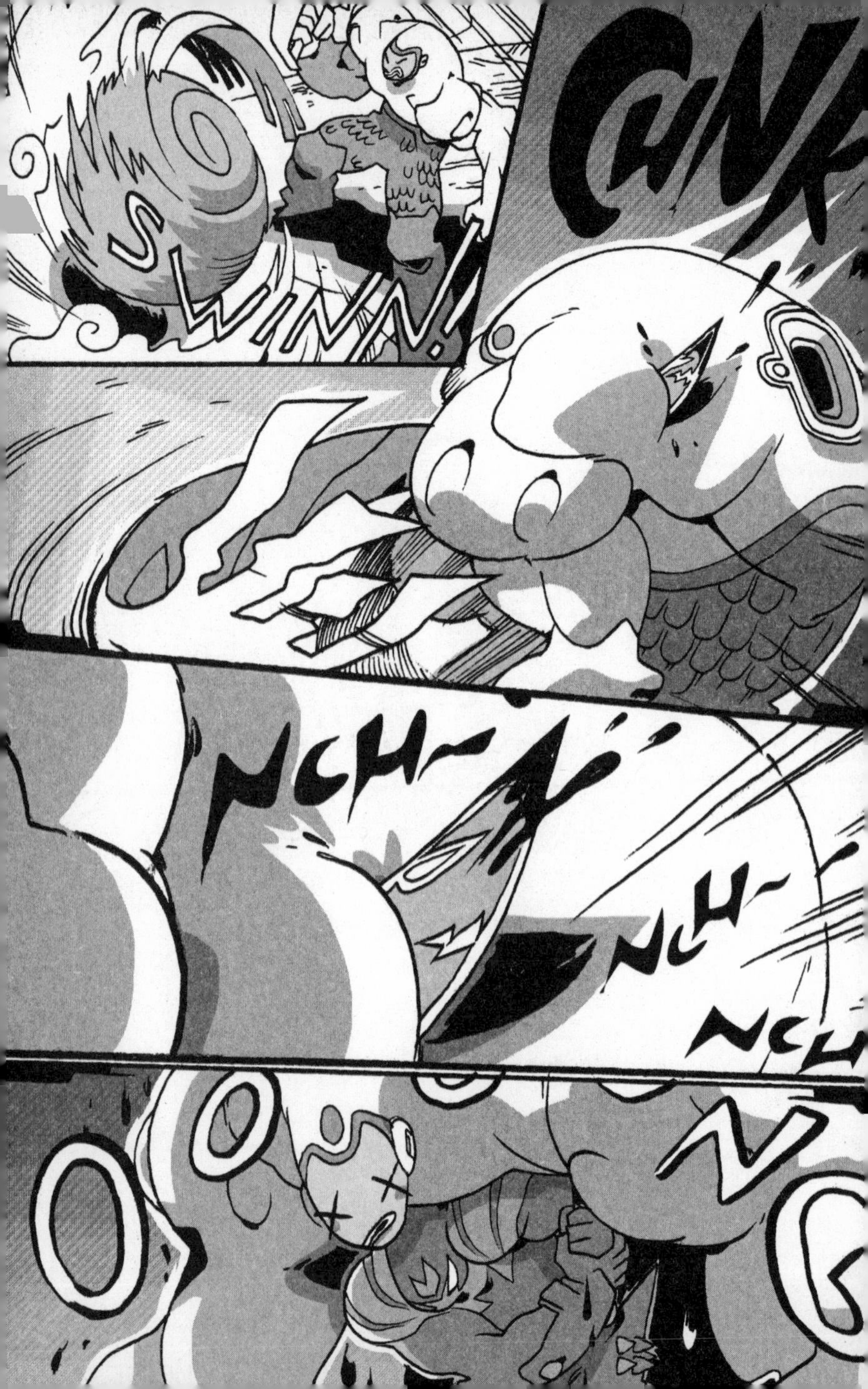
SWINN!
NCH-
NCH-
NCH
OOONG

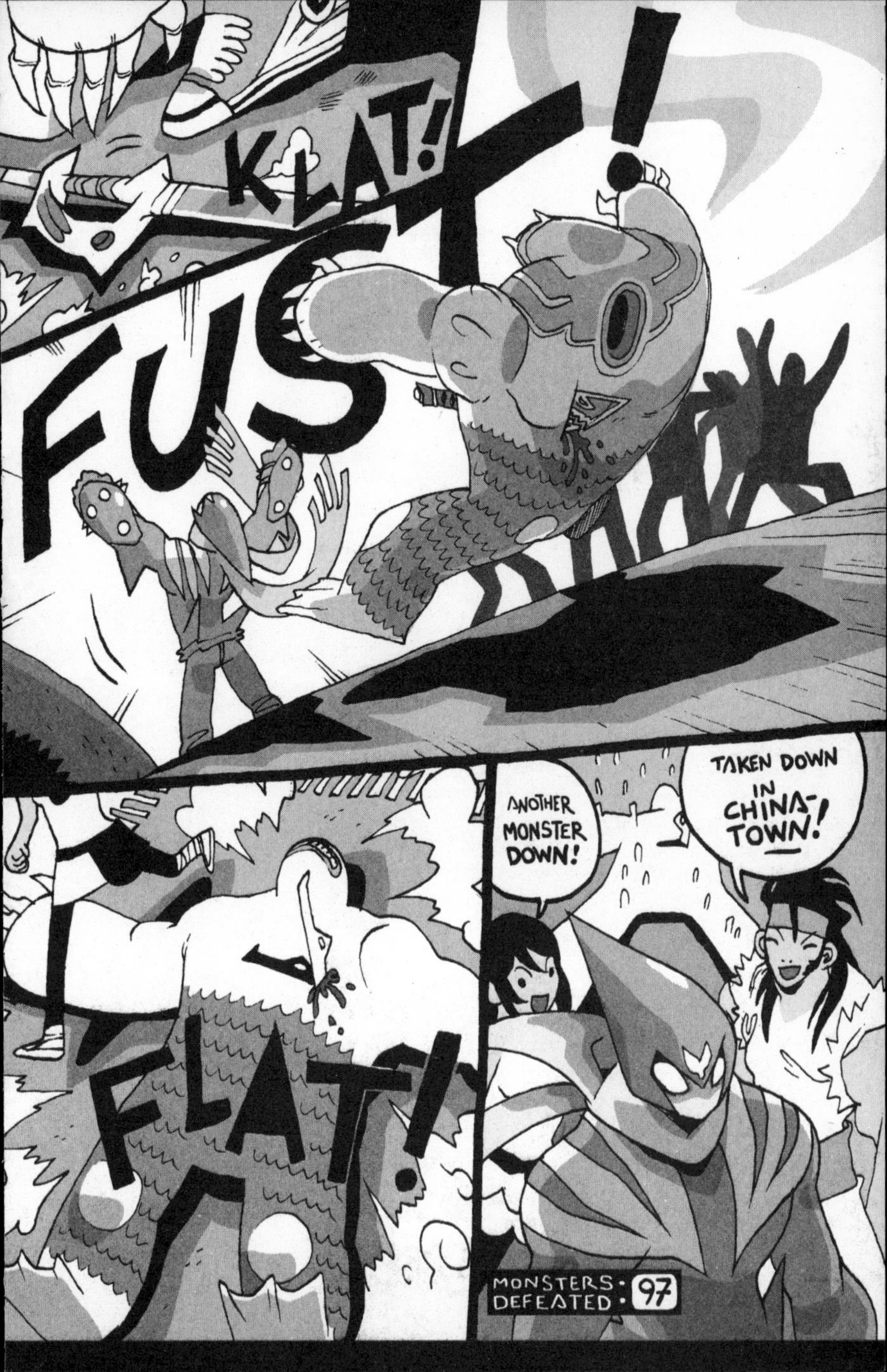
KLAT!
FUST!
FLAT!
ANOTHER MONSTER DOWN!
TAKEN DOWN IN CHINA-TOWN!
MONSTERS DEFEATED • 97

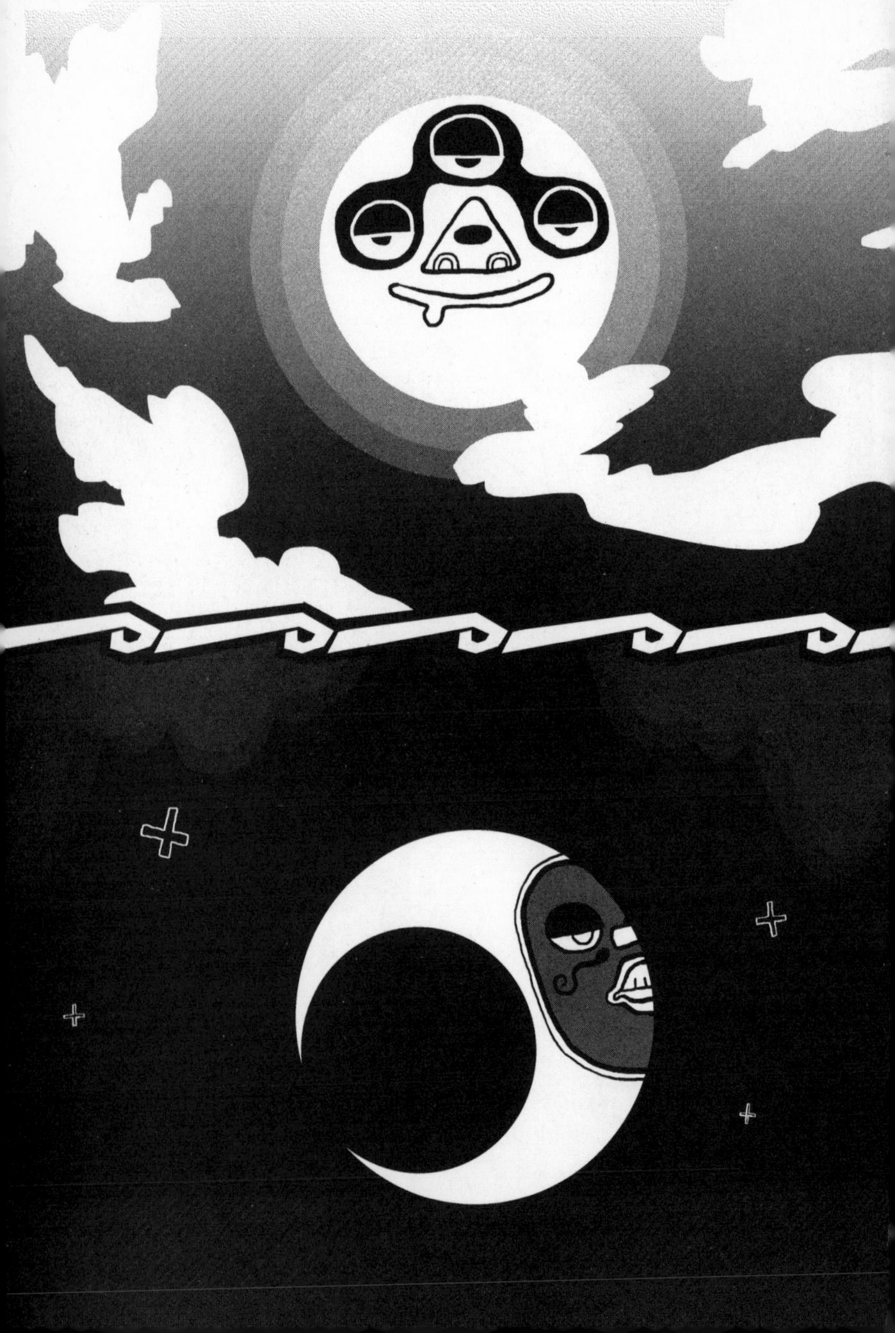

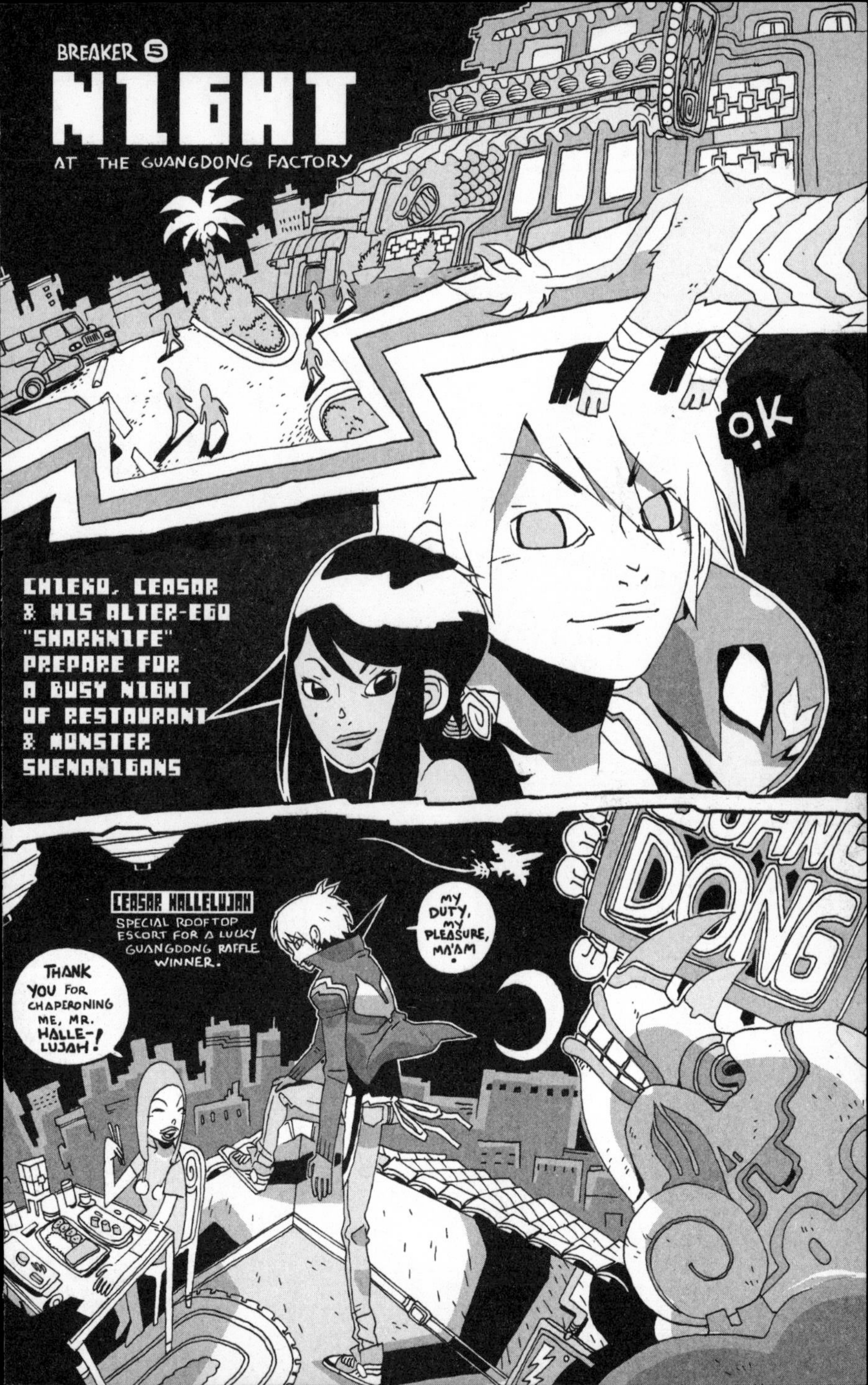

BREAKER 5
NIGHT
AT THE GUANGDONG FACTORY
O.K
CHIEKO, CEASAR & HIS ALTER-EGO "SHARKNIFE" PREPARE FOR A BUSY NIGHT OF RESTAURANT & MONSTER SHENANIGANS
CEASAR HALLELUJAH
SPECIAL ROOFTOP ESCORT FOR A LUCKY GUANGDONG RAFFLE WINNER.
THANK YOU FOR CHAPERONING ME, MR. HALLE-LUJAH!
MY DUTY, MY PLEASURE, MA'AM.
DONG

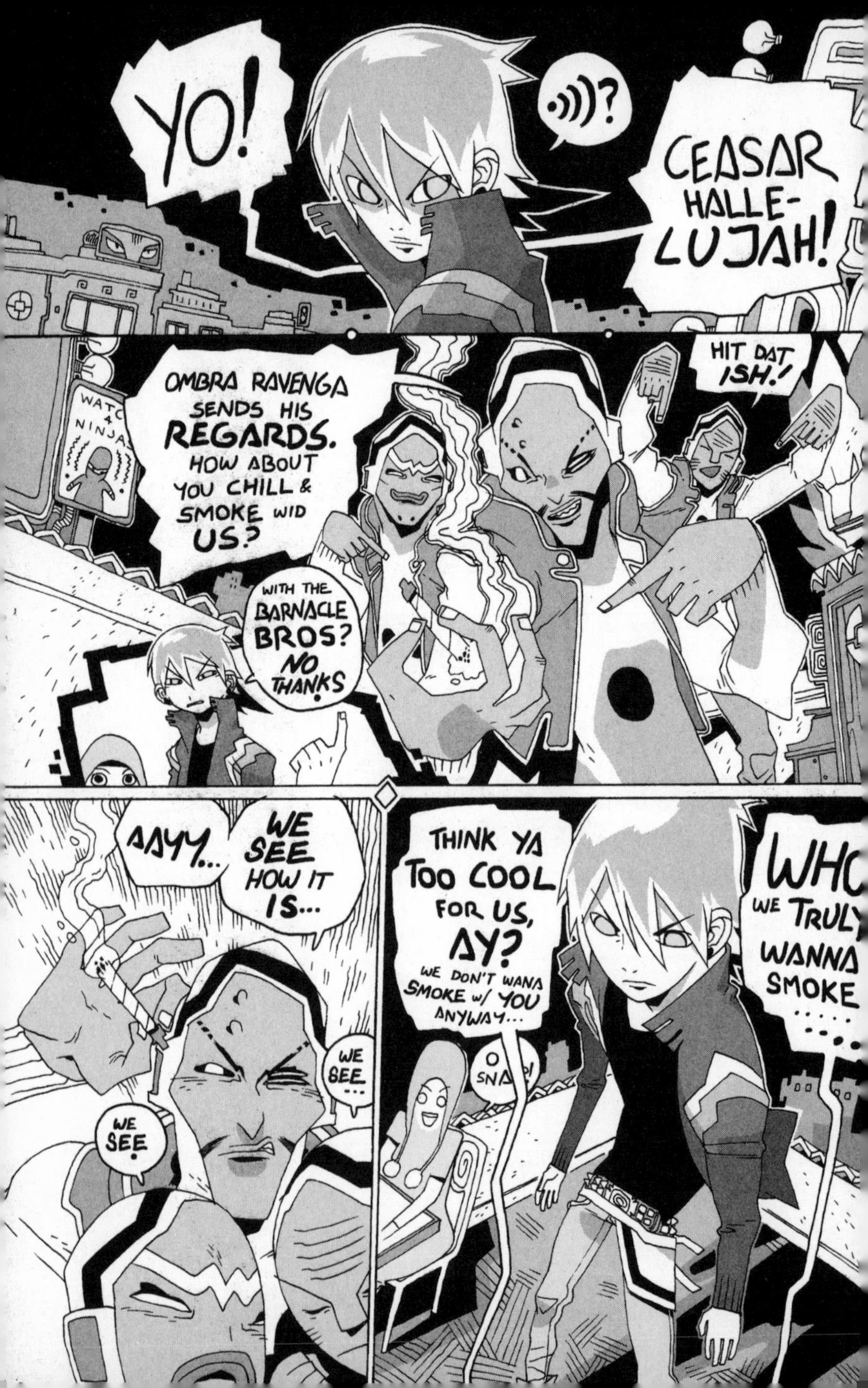
YO!
•)))?
CEASAR HALLE-LUJAH!
OMBRA RAVENGA SENDS HIS REGARDS. HOW ABOUT YOU CHILL & SMOKE WID US?
HIT DAT ISH!
WATC 4 NINJA
WITH THE BARNACLE BROS? NO THANKS.
AAYY...
WE SEE HOW IT IS...
WE SEE...
WE SEE.
THINK YA TOO COOL FOR US, AY? WE DON'T WANA SMOKE w/ YOU ANYWAY...
WE TRULY WANNA SMOKE

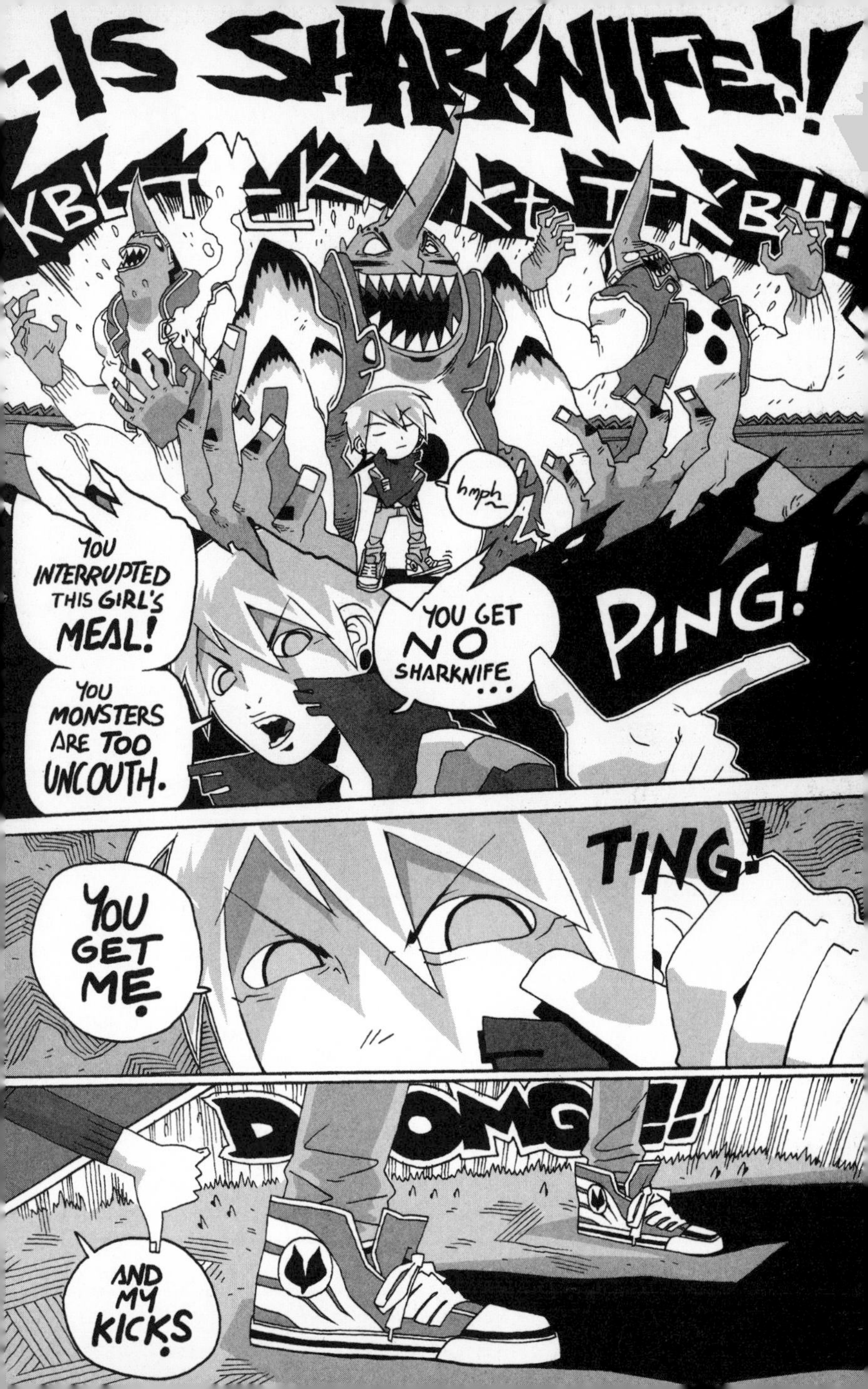

--IS SHARKNIFE!!
hmph~
YOU INTERRUPTED THIS GIRL'S MEAL!
YOU MONSTERS ARE TOO UNCOUTH.
YOU GET NO SHARKNIFE...
PING!
TING!
YOU GET ME.
AND MY KICKS.

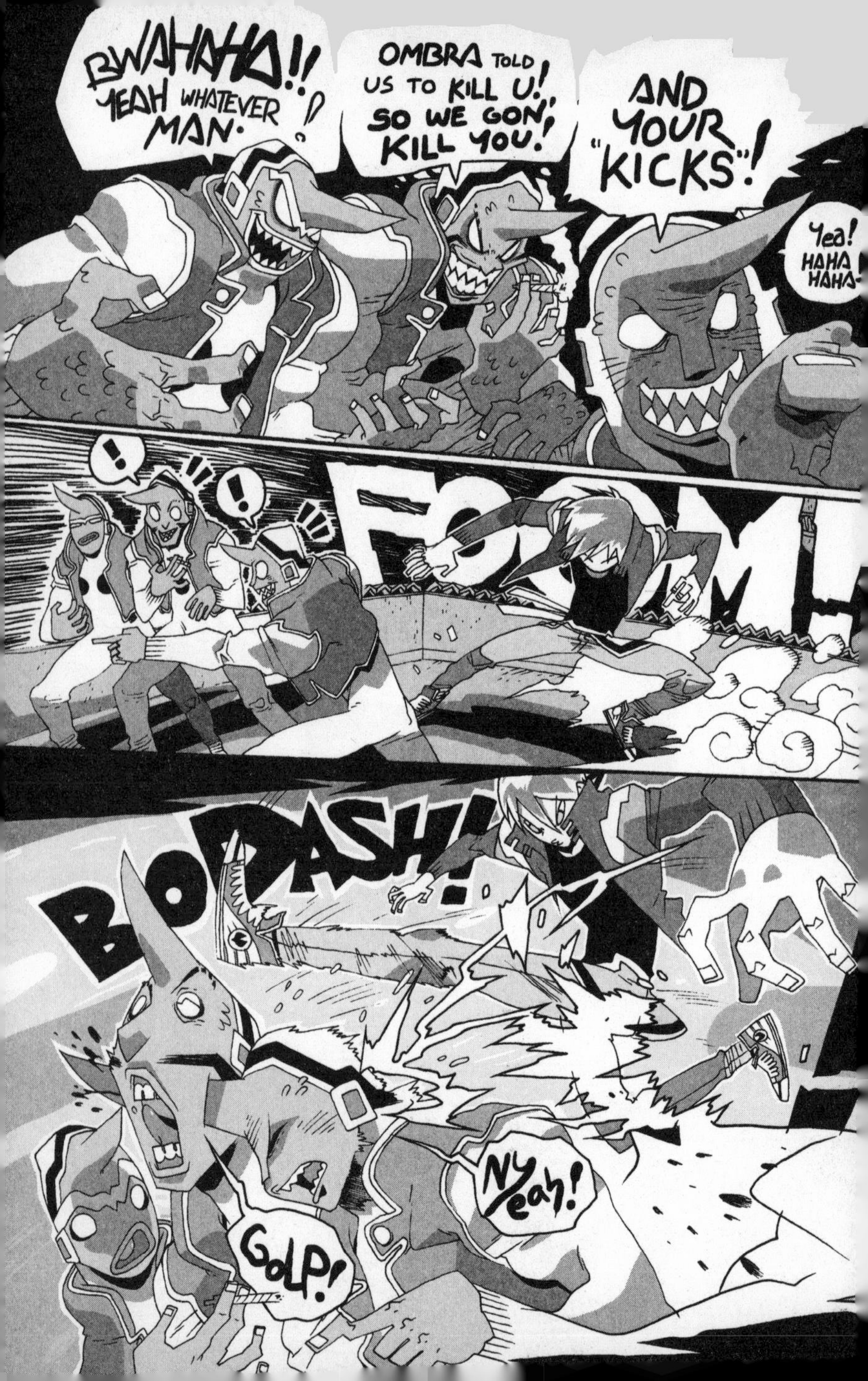

BWAHAHA!! YEAH WHATEVER MAN.
OMBRA TOLD US TO KILL U!, SO WE GON' KILL YOU!
AND YOUR "KICKS"!
Yea! HAHA! HAHA.
!
!
FOOM!
BOOSH!
Nyeah!
GOLP!

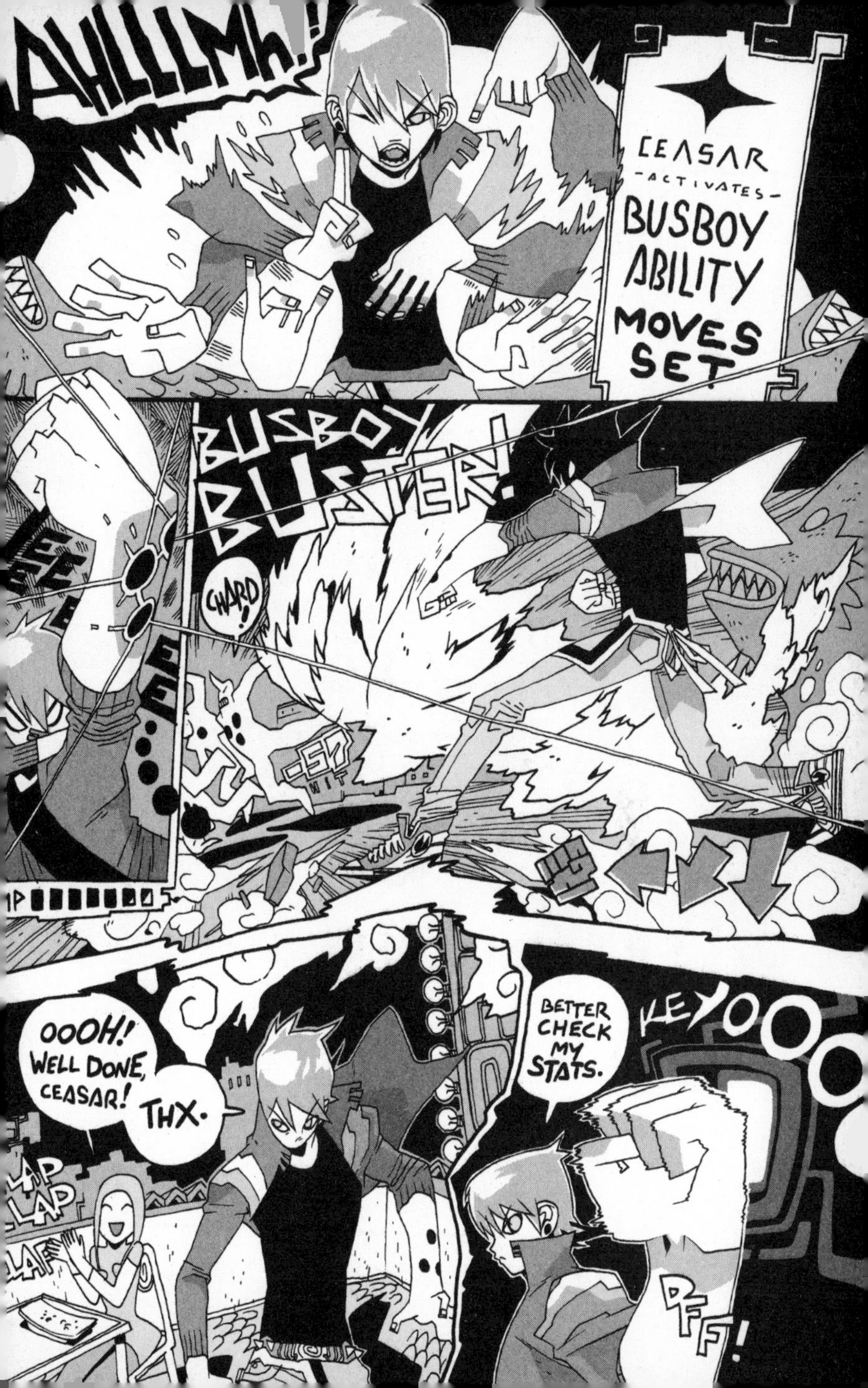
AHLLLMh!
CEASAR
-ACTIVATES-
BUSBOY
ABILITY
MOVES
SET
BUSBOY
BUSTER!
CHARD!
1P
OOOH! WELL DONE, CEASAR!
THX.
BETTER CHECK MY STATS.
KEYOOO
DFF!

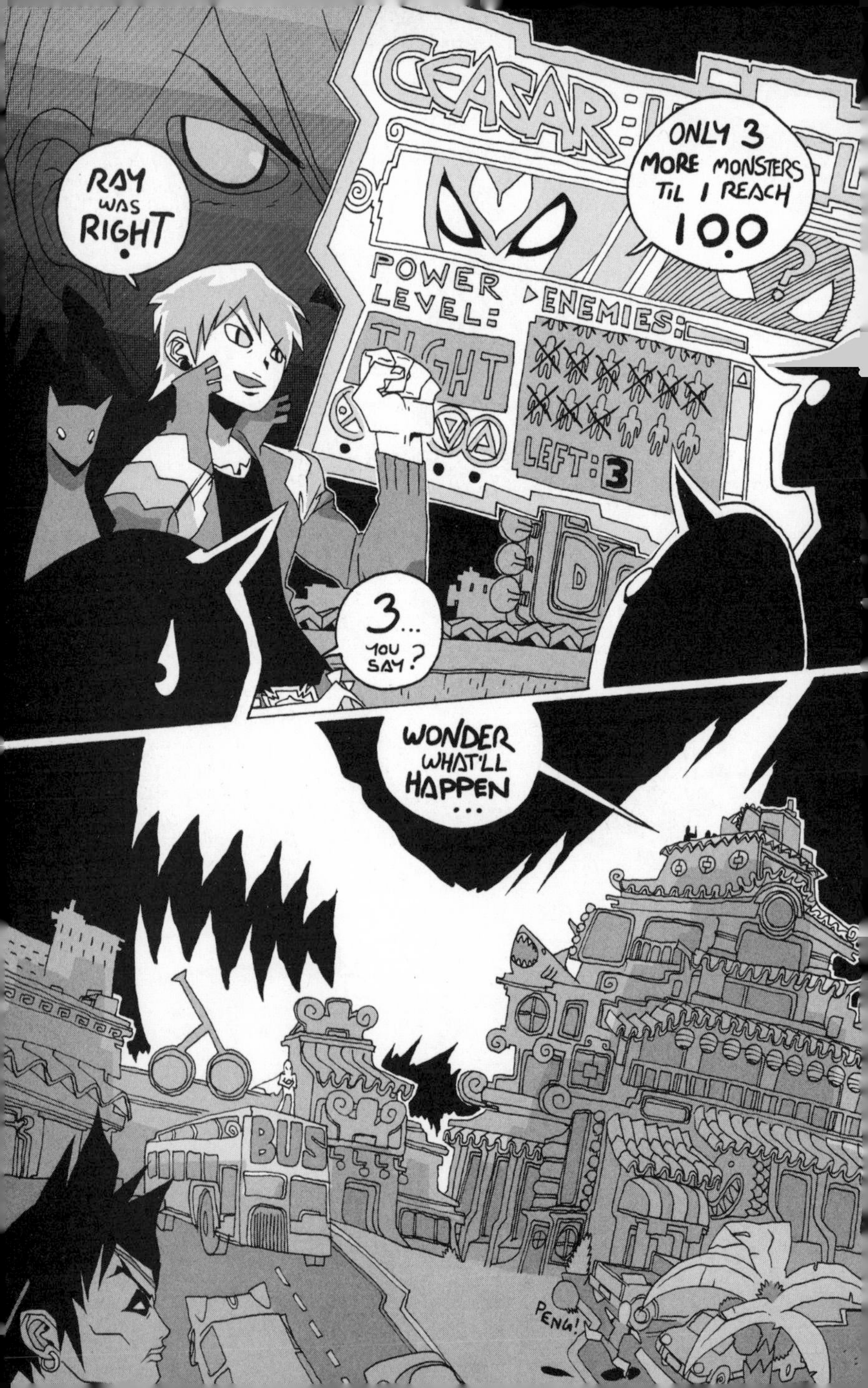
CEASAR
RAY WAS RIGHT.
ONLY 3 MORE MONSTERS TIL I REACH 100.
POWER LEVEL:
TIGHT
ENEMIES:
LEFT: 3
3... YOU SAY?
WONDER WHAT'LL HAPPEN...
BUS
PENG!

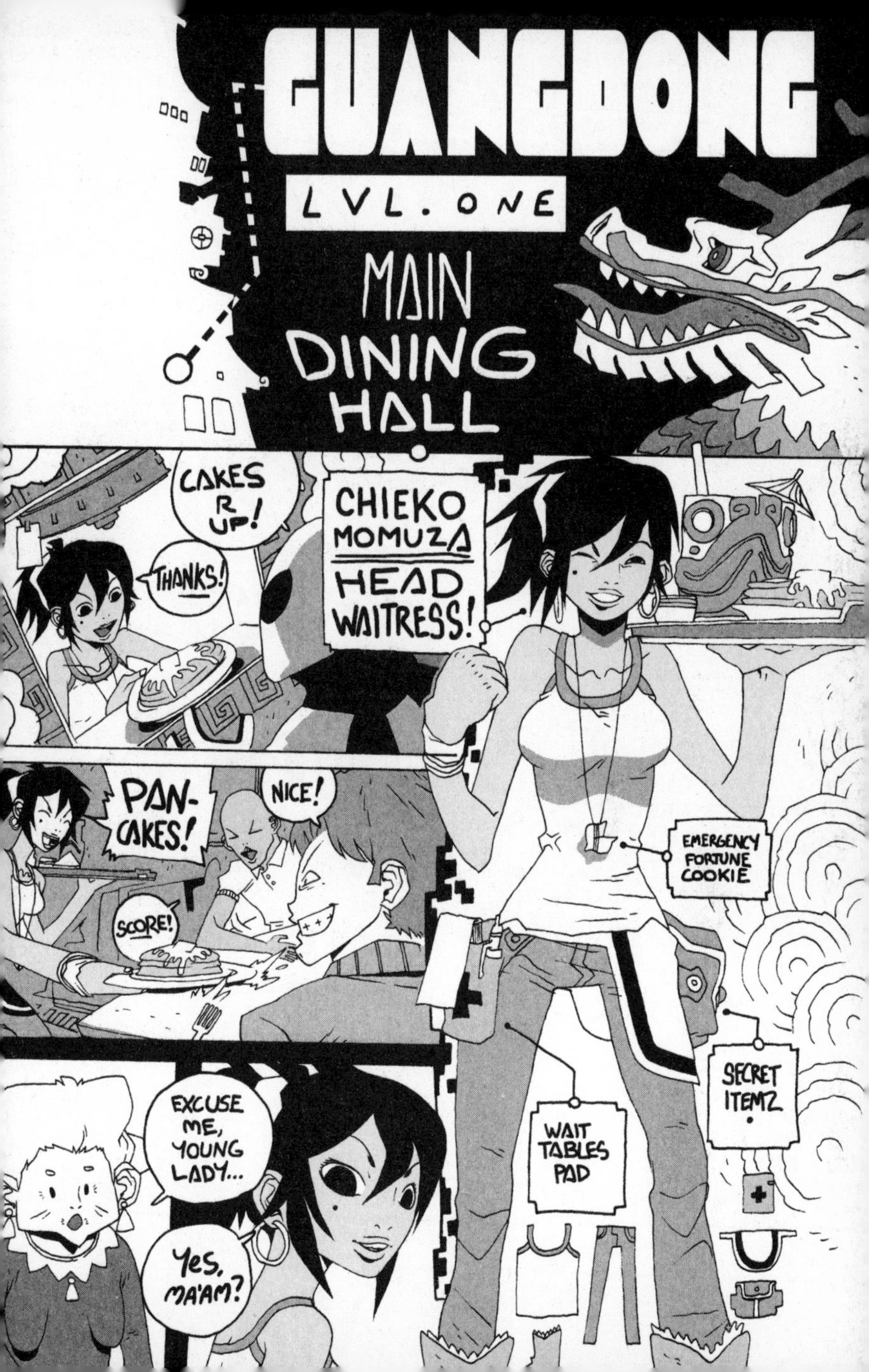
GUANGDONG
LVL. ONE
MAIN DINING HALL
CAKES R UP!
THANKS!
CHIEKO MOMUZA
HEAD WAITRESS!
PAN-CAKES!
NICE!
SCORE!
EMERGENCY FORTUNE COOKIE
SECRET ITEMZ
WAIT TABLES PAD
EXCUSE ME, YOUNG LADY...
Yes, MA'AM?

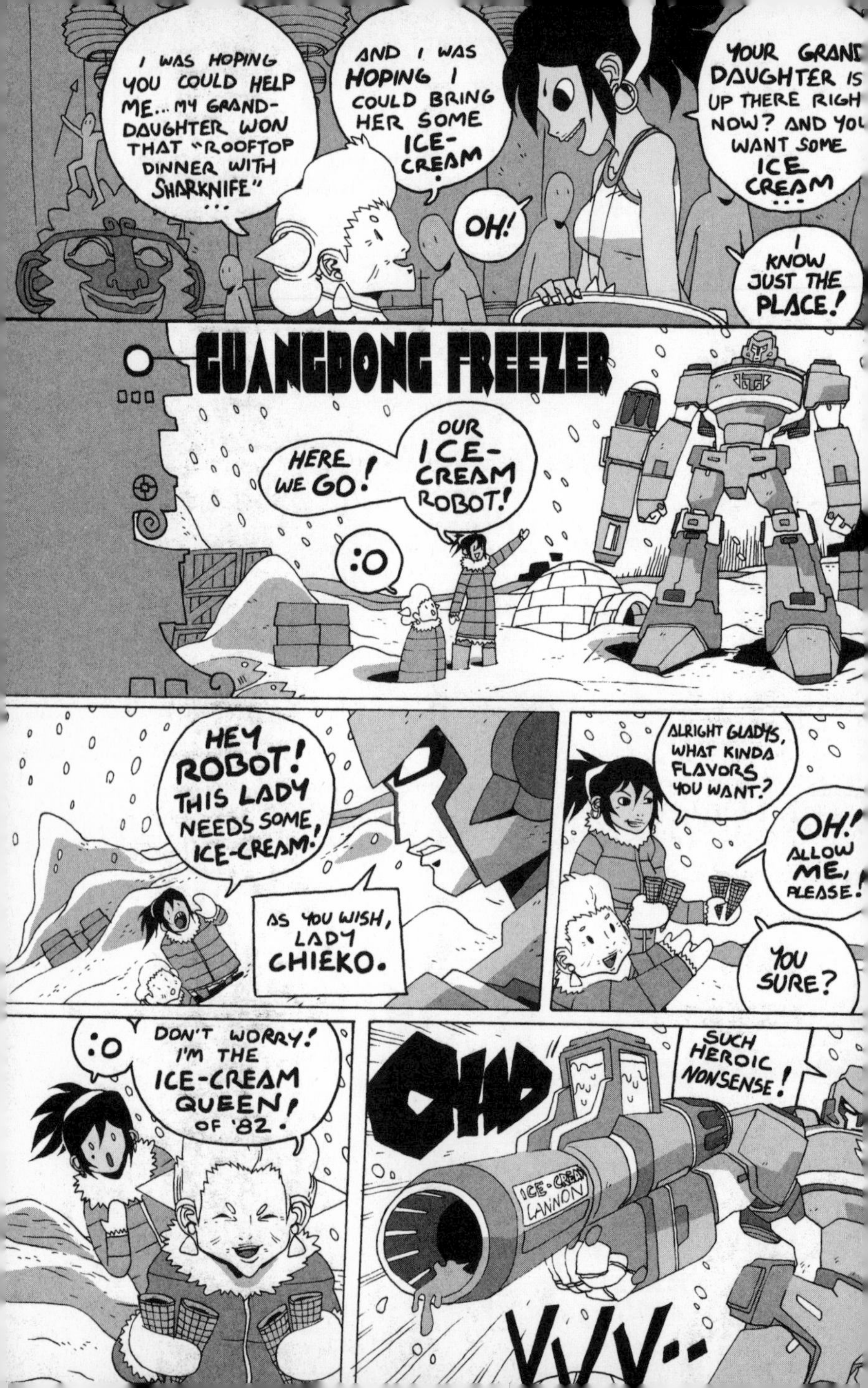

I WAS HOPING YOU COULD HELP ME... MY GRAND-DAUGHTER WON THAT "ROOFTOP DINNER WITH SHARKNIFE"...
AND I WAS HOPING I COULD BRING HER SOME ICE-CREAM.
OH!
YOUR GRAND DAUGHTER IS UP THERE RIGH NOW? AND YOU WANT SOME ICE CREAM...
I KNOW JUST THE PLACE!
GUANGDONG FREEZER
HERE WE GO!
OUR ICE-CREAM ROBOT!
:O
HEY ROBOT! THIS LADY NEEDS SOME ICE-CREAM!
AS YOU WISH, LADY CHIEKO.
ALRIGHT GLADYS, WHAT KINDA FLAVORS YOU WANT?
OH! ALLOW ME, PLEASE!
YOU SURE?
:O
DON'T WORRY! I'M THE ICE-CREAM QUEEN OF '82.
SUCH HEROIC NONSENSE!
ICE-CREAM CANNON
VVV..

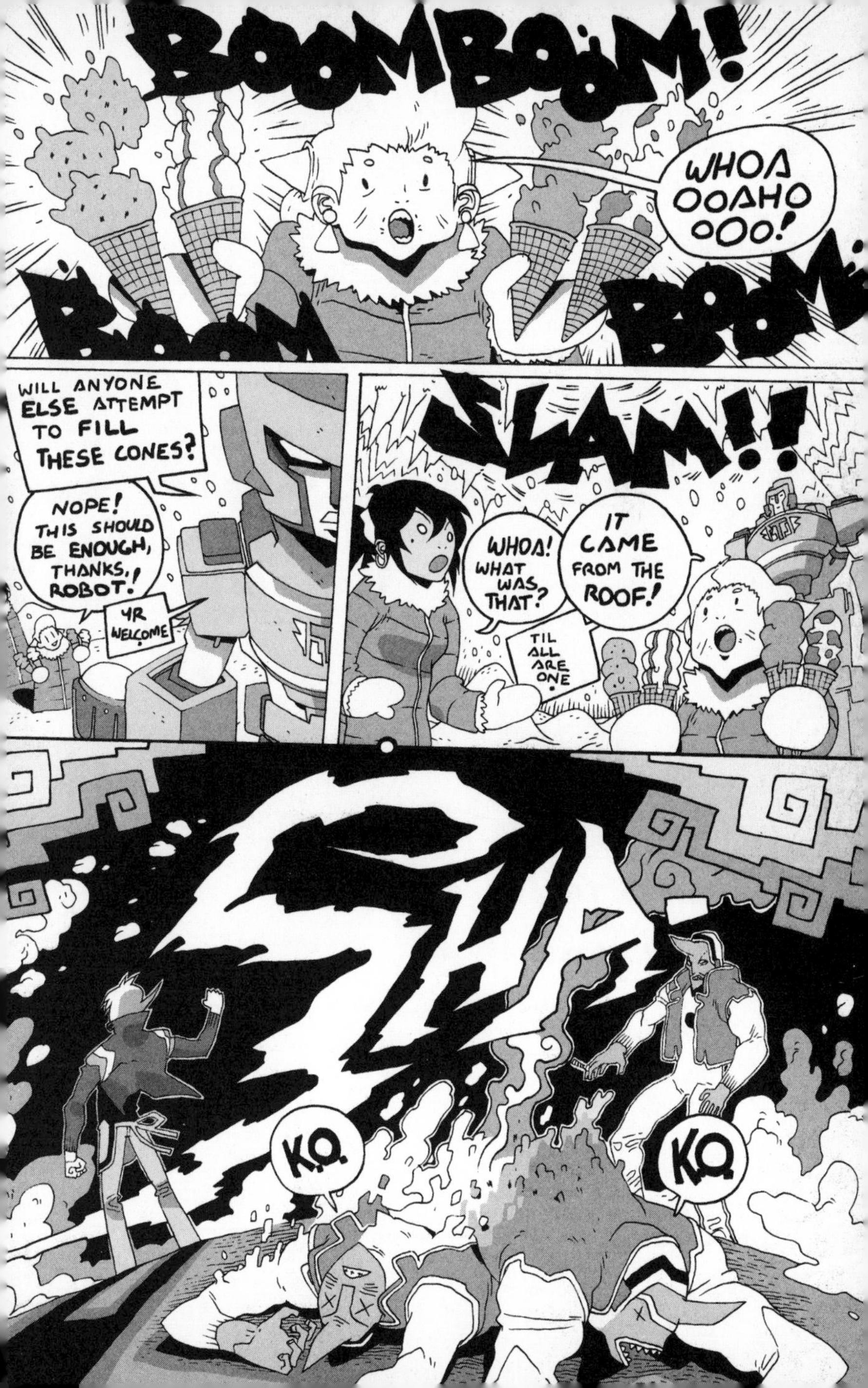
BOOMBOOM!
WHOA OOAHO OOO!
BOOM
BOOM
WILL ANYONE ELSE ATTEMPT TO FILL THESE CONES?
NOPE! THIS SHOULD BE ENOUGH, THANKS, ROBOT!
YR WELCOME
SLAM!!
WHOA! WHAT WAS THAT?
IT CAME FROM THE ROOF!
TIL ALL ARE ONE
K.O.
K.O.

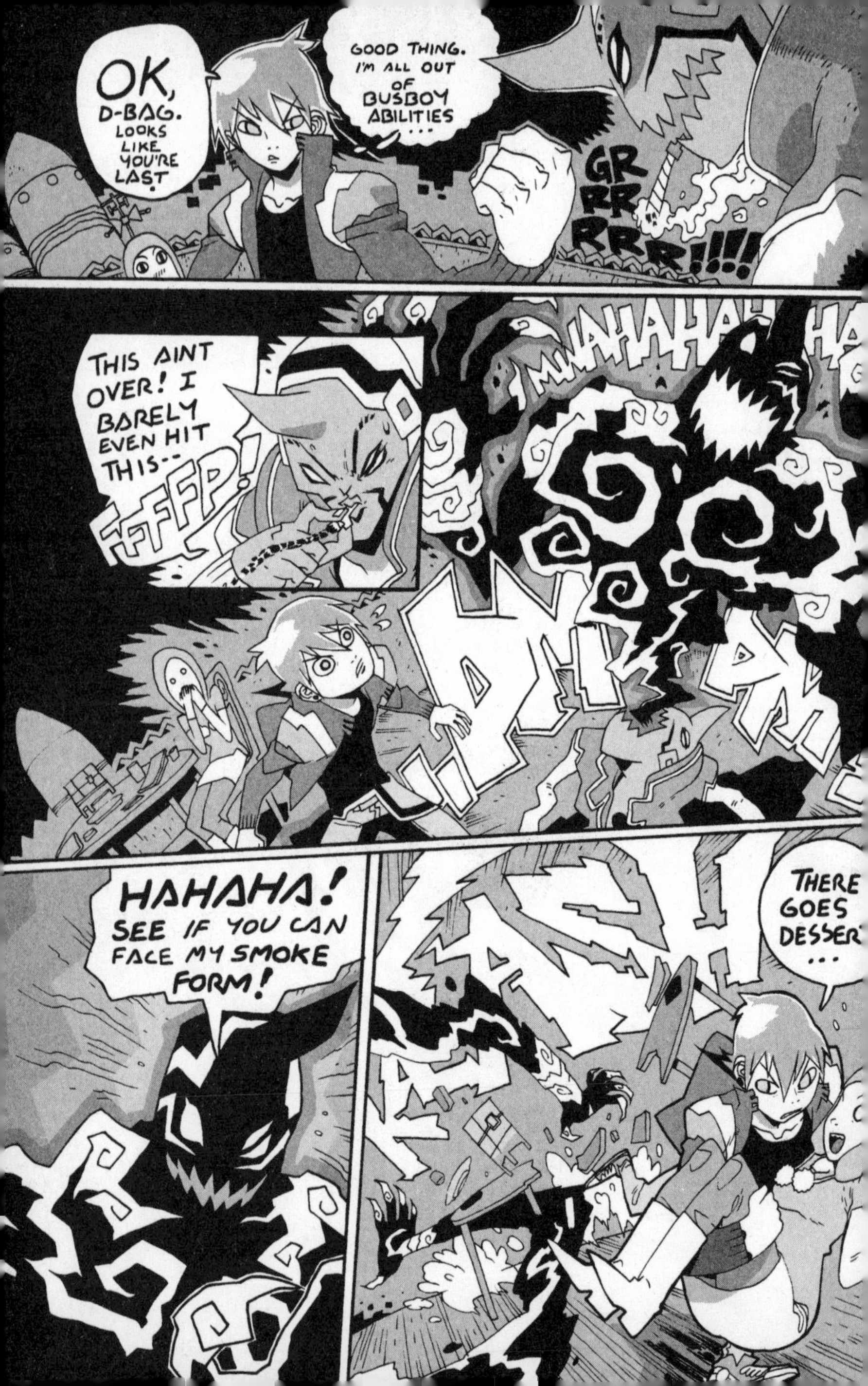
OK, D-BAG. LOOKS LIKE YOU'RE LAST.
GOOD THING. I'M ALL OUT OF BUSBOY ABILITIES...
GRRRRRR!!!!
THIS AINT OVER! I BARELY EVEN HIT THIS--
FFFFP!
MWAHAHAHAHA
HAHAHA! SEE IF YOU CAN FACE MY SMOKE FORM!
THERE GOES DESSERT...

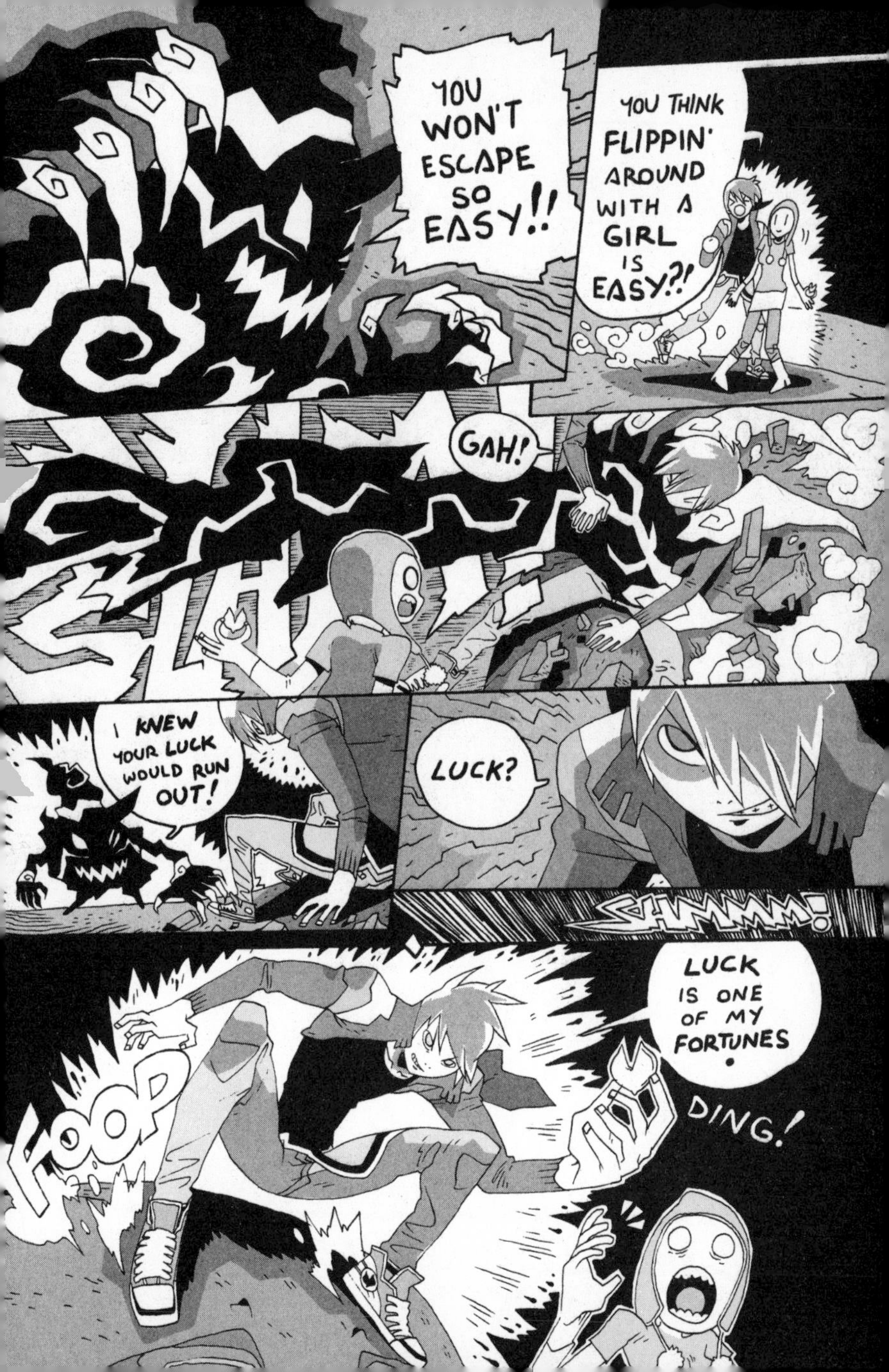
YOU WON'T ESCAPE SO EASY!!
YOU THINK FLIPPIN' AROUND WITH A GIRL IS EASY?!
GAH!
I KNEW YOUR LUCK WOULD RUN OUT!
LUCK?
SHWMM!
LUCK IS ONE OF MY FORTUNES.
FOOP
DING!

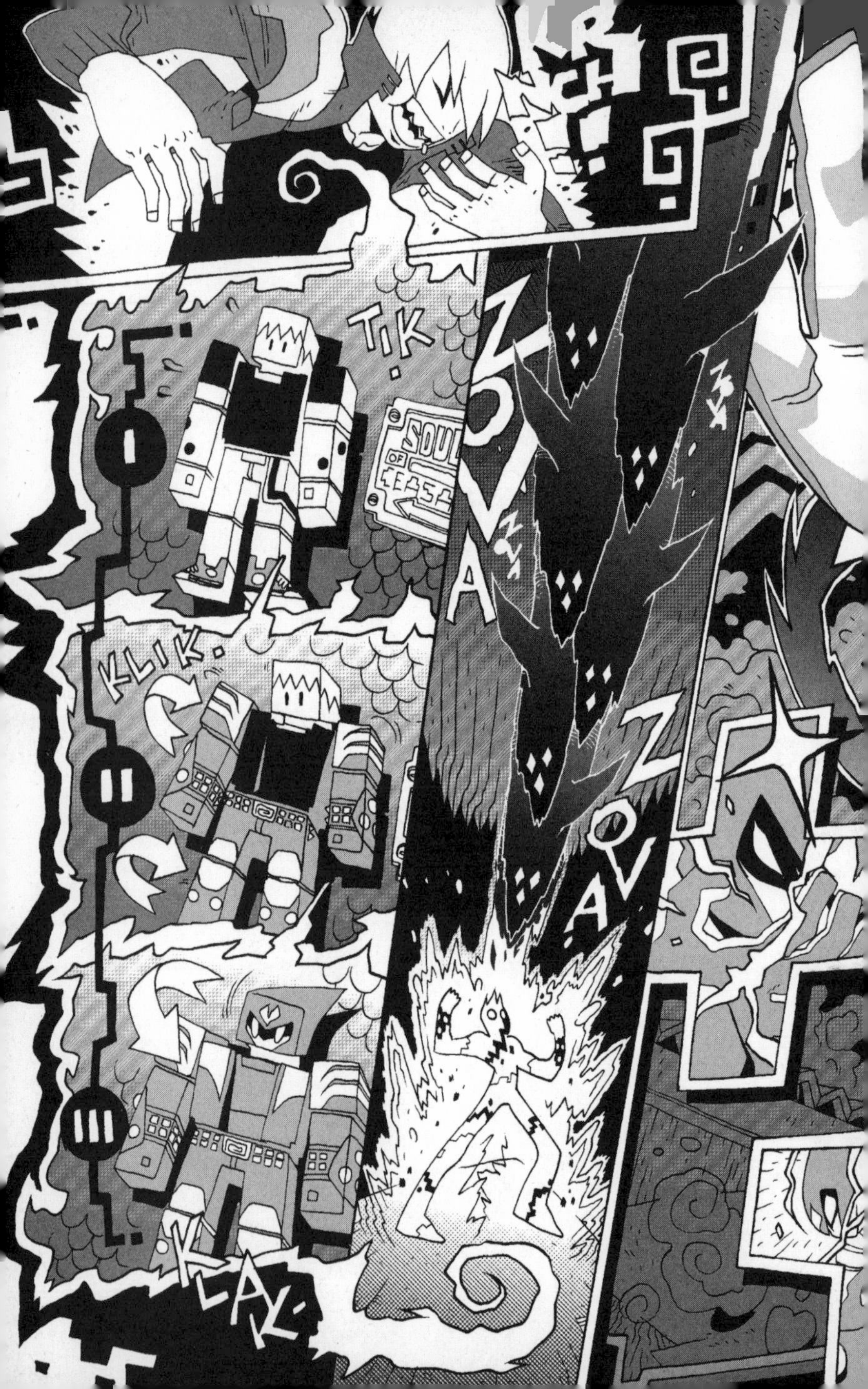

TIK
SOUL
KLIK

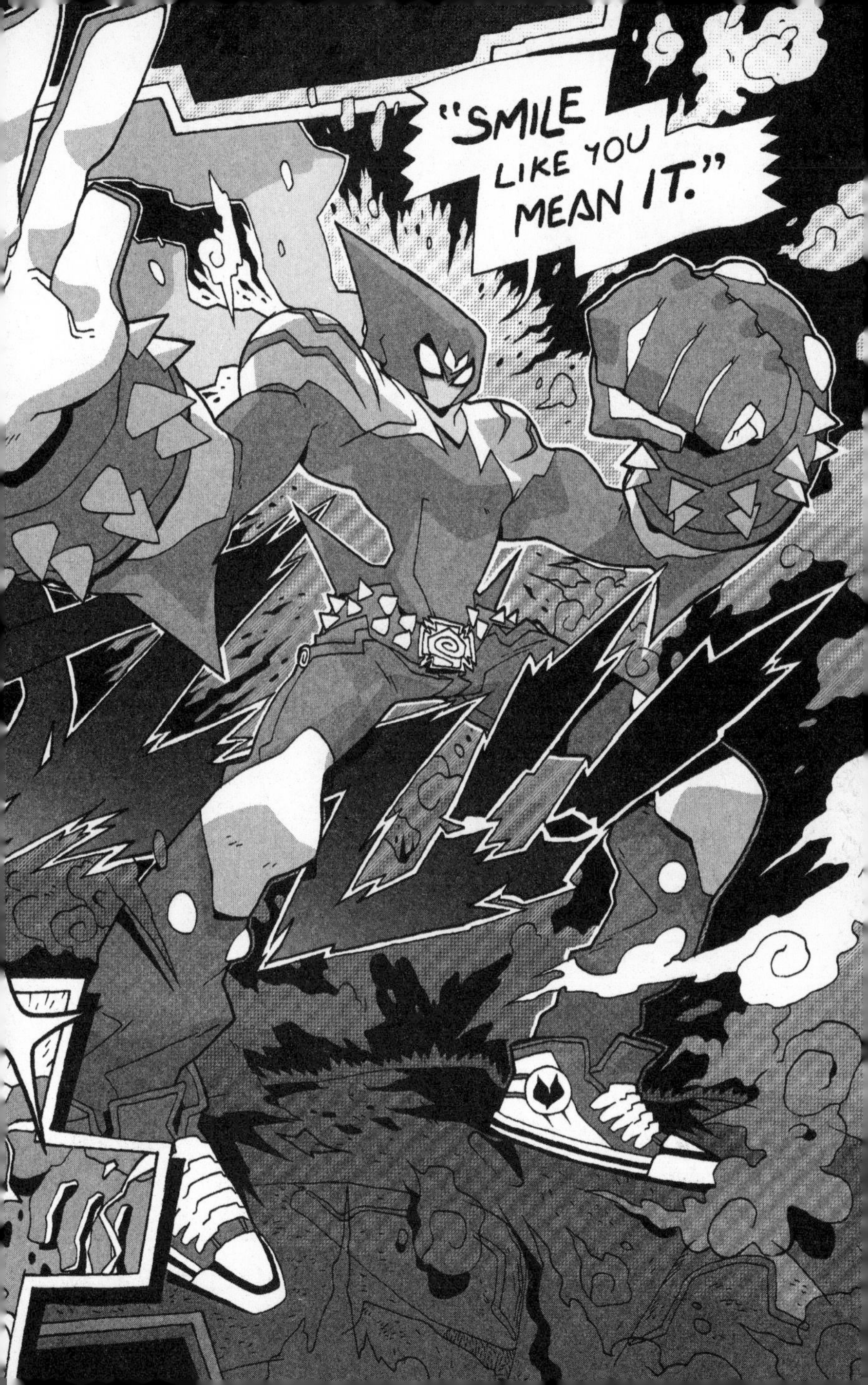
"SMILE LIKE YOU MEAN IT."

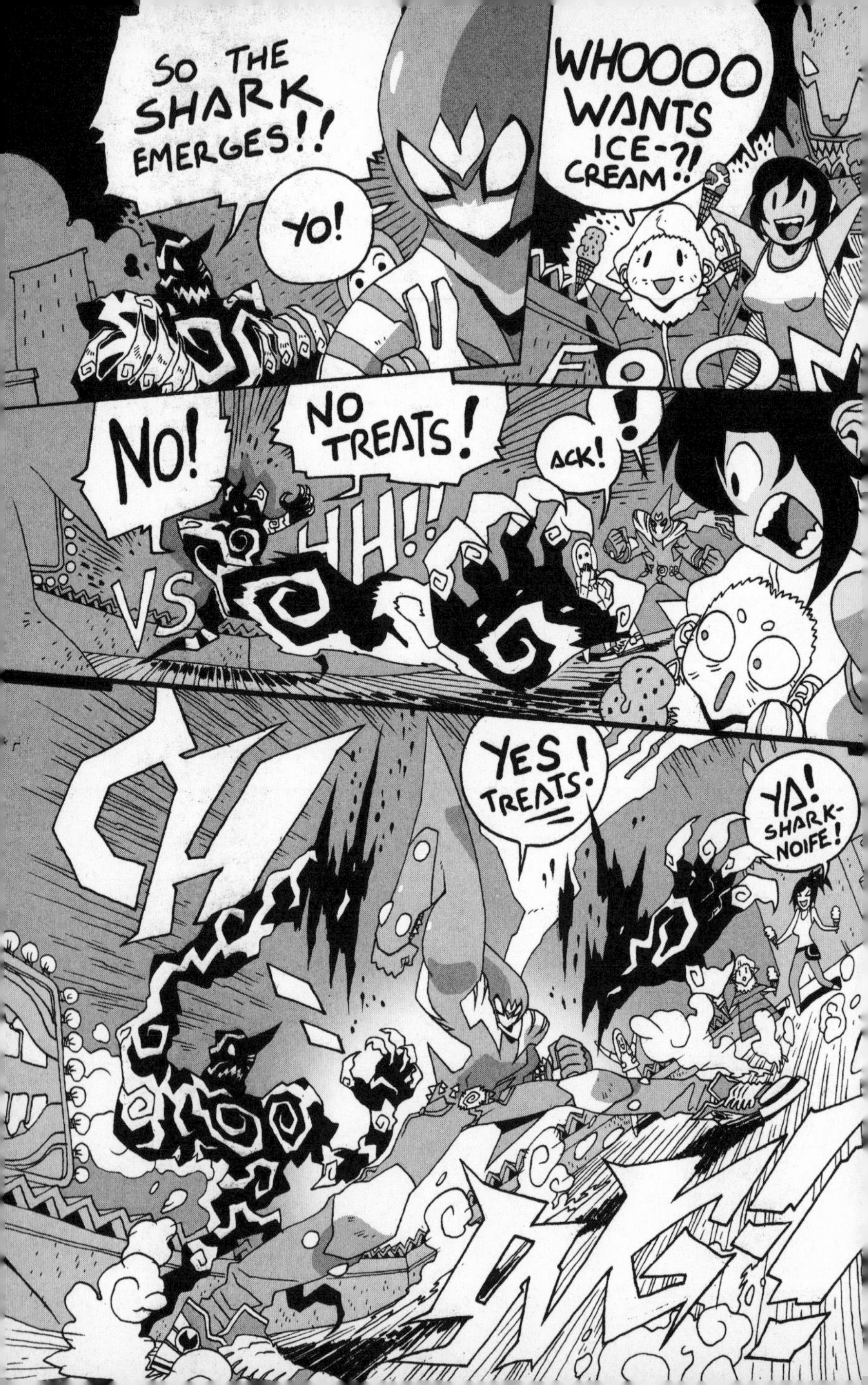
SO THE SHARK EMERGES!!
YO!
WHOOOO WANTS ICE-?! CREAM?!
FOOM
NO!
NO TREATS!
HH!!
VS
ACK!
!
YES TREATS!
YA! SHARK-NOIFE!

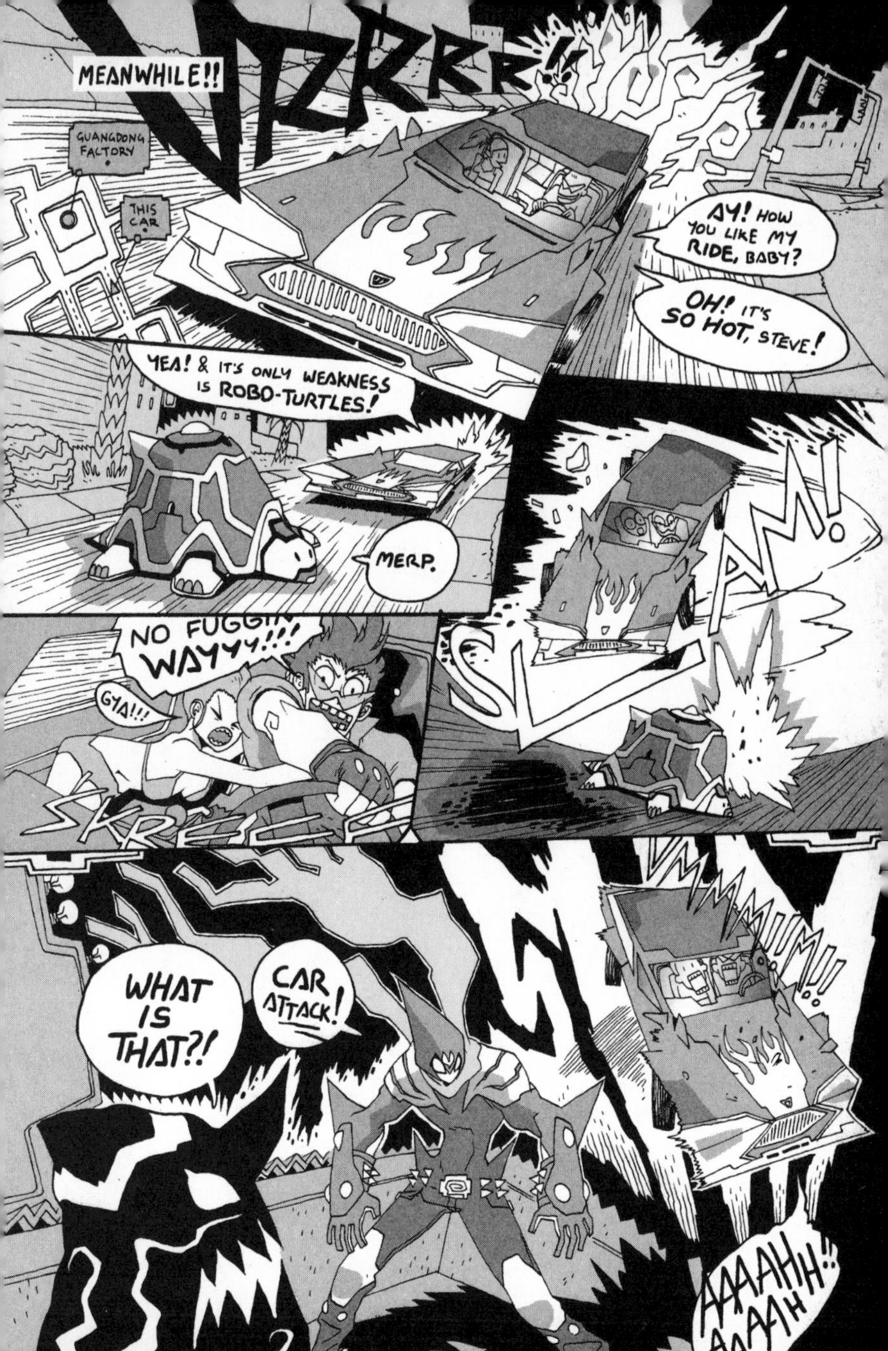
MEANWHILE!!
VRRRR!!
GUANGDONG FACTORY
THIS CAR
AY! HOW YOU LIKE MY RIDE, BABY?
OH! IT'S SO HOT, STEVE!
YEA! & IT'S ONLY WEAKNESS IS ROBO-TURTLES!
MERP.
NO FUGGIN WAYYY!!!
GYA!!!
SLAM!
WHAT IS THAT?!
CAR ATTACK!
AAAAHH!! AAAAH

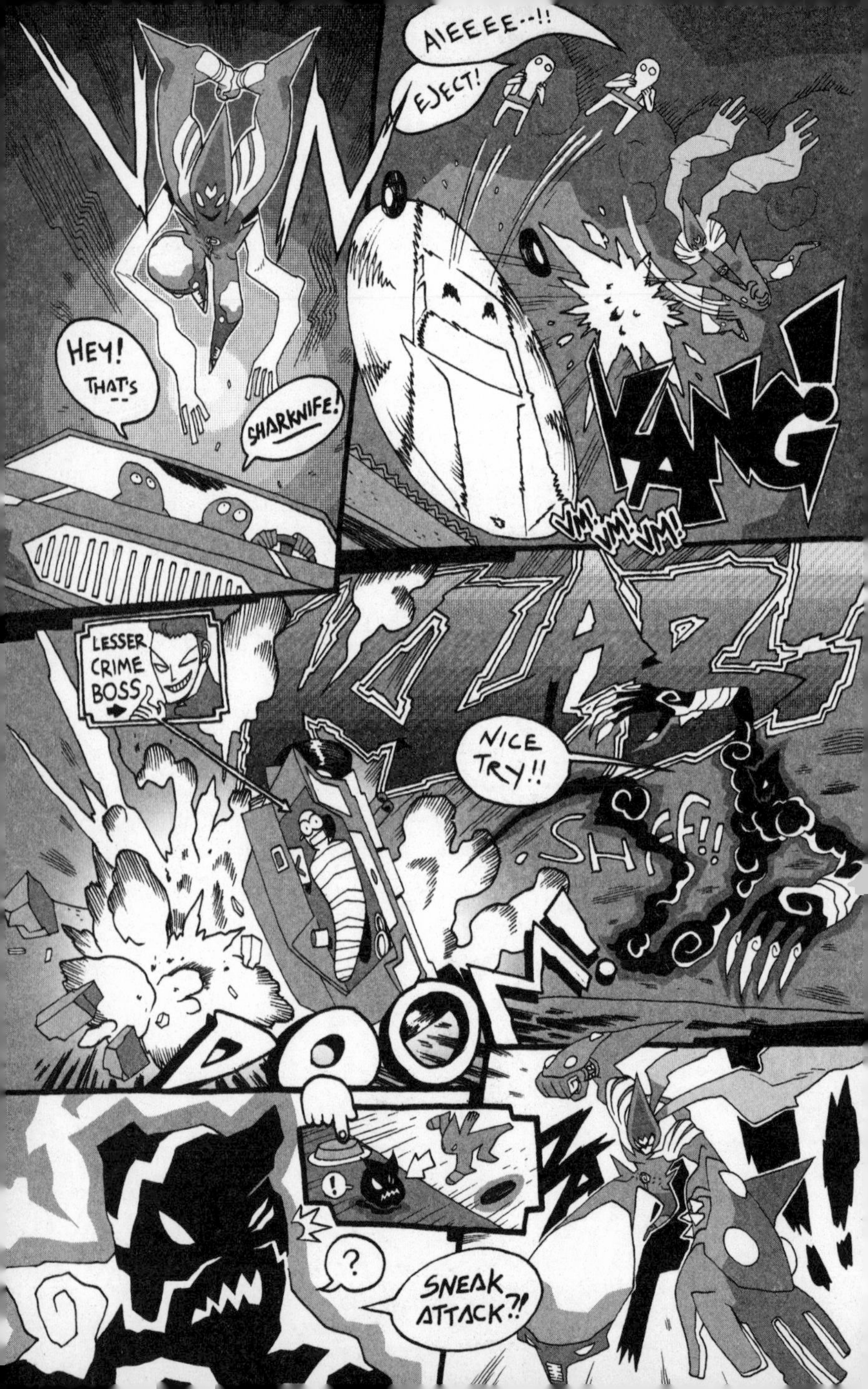

HEY! THAT'S --
SHARKNIFE!
AIEEEE--!!
EJECT!
KANG!
VM! VM! VM!
LESSER CRIME BOSS
NICE TRY!!
SHFF!!
DOOM!
?
SNEAK ATTACK?!

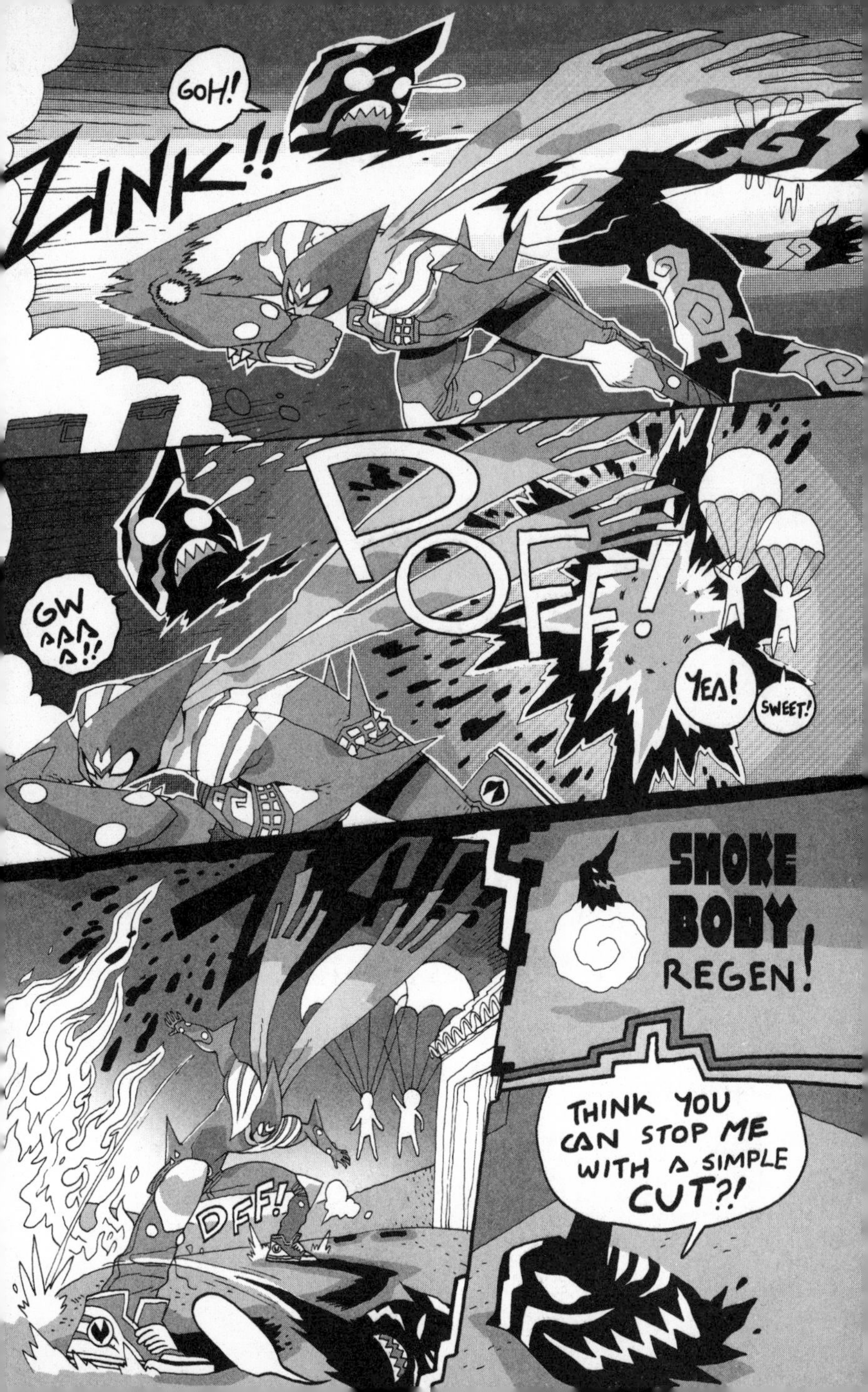

GOH!
ZINK!!
POFF!
GW AAA A!!
YEA!
SWEET!
SMOKE BODY REGEN!
DFF!
THINK YOU CAN STOP ME WITH A SIMPLE CUT?!

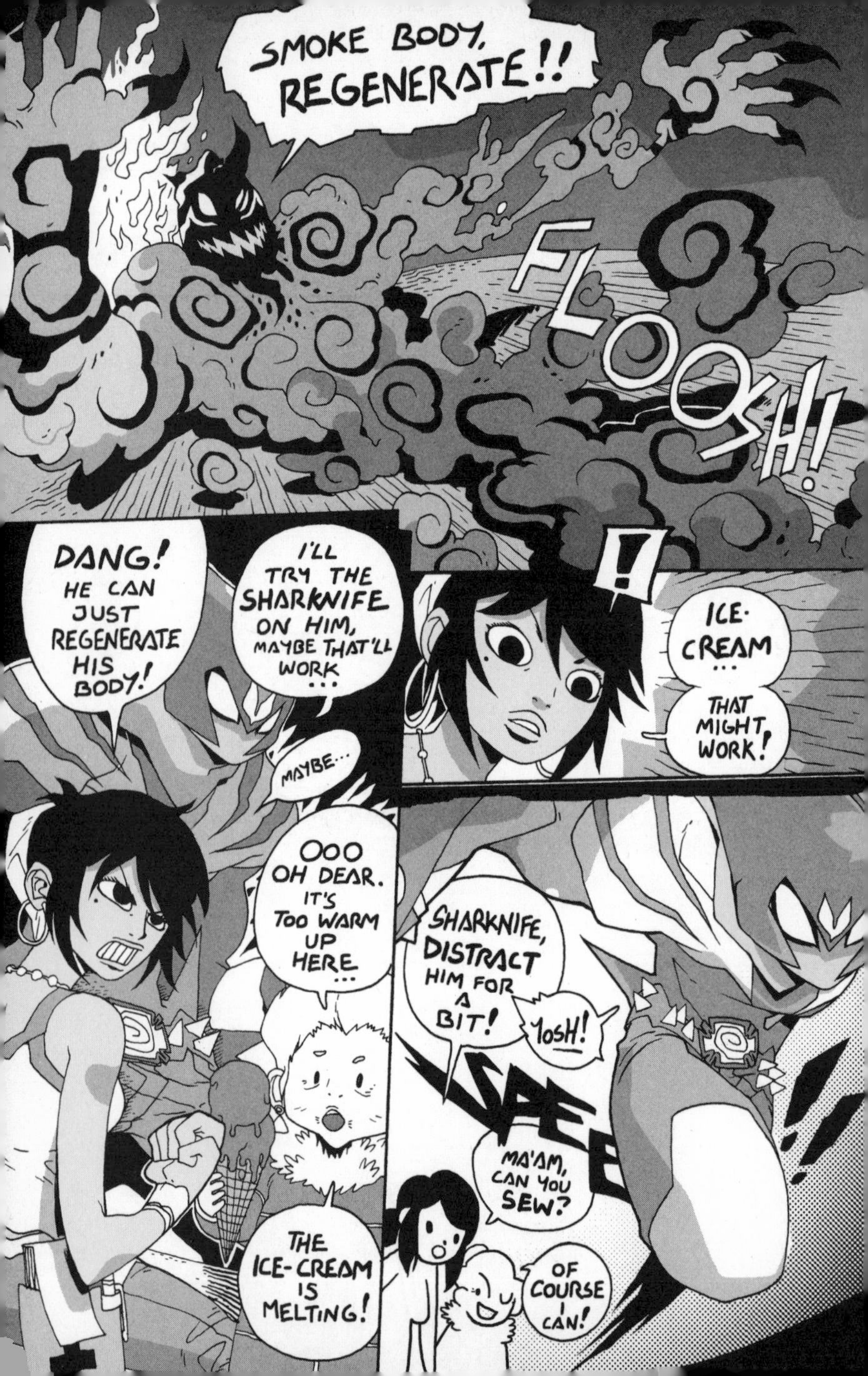
SMOKE BODY, REGENERATE!!
FLOOSH!
DANG! HE CAN JUST REGENERATE HIS BODY!
I'LL TRY THE SHARKNIFE ON HIM, MAYBE THAT'LL WORK ...
MAYBE...
!
ICE-CREAM ...
THAT MIGHT WORK!
OOO OH DEAR. IT'S TOO WARM UP HERE ...
THE ICE-CREAM IS MELTING!
SHARKNIFE, DISTRACT HIM FOR A BIT!
YOSH!
SPEE
MA'AM, CAN YOU SEW?
OF COURSE I CAN!

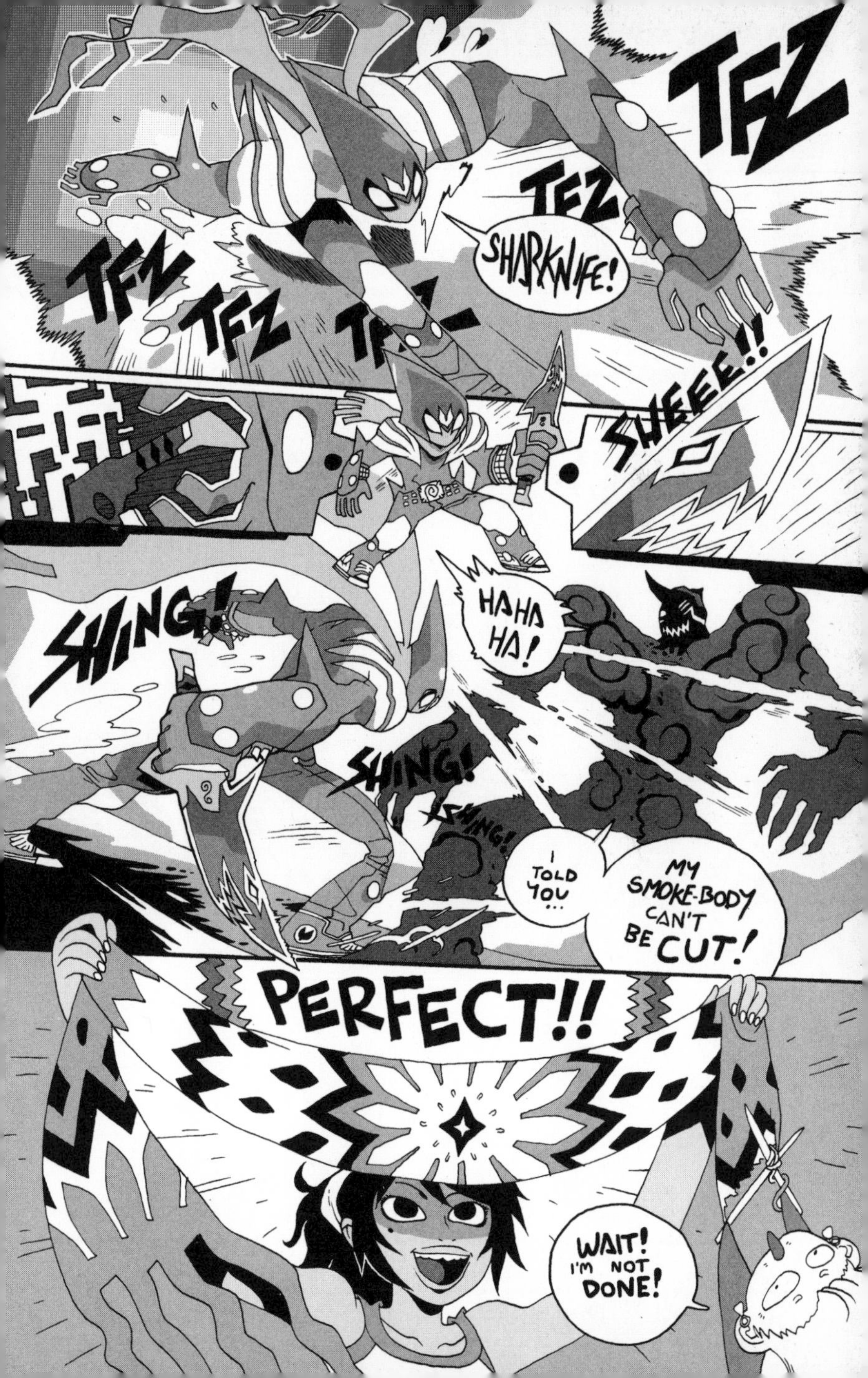

TFZ
TFZ
SHARKNIFE!
TFZ
TFZ
SWEEE!!
SHING!
HAHA HA!
SHING!
SHING!
I TOLD YOU...
MY SMOKE-BODY CAN'T BE CUT!
PERFECT!!
WAIT! I'M NOT DONE!

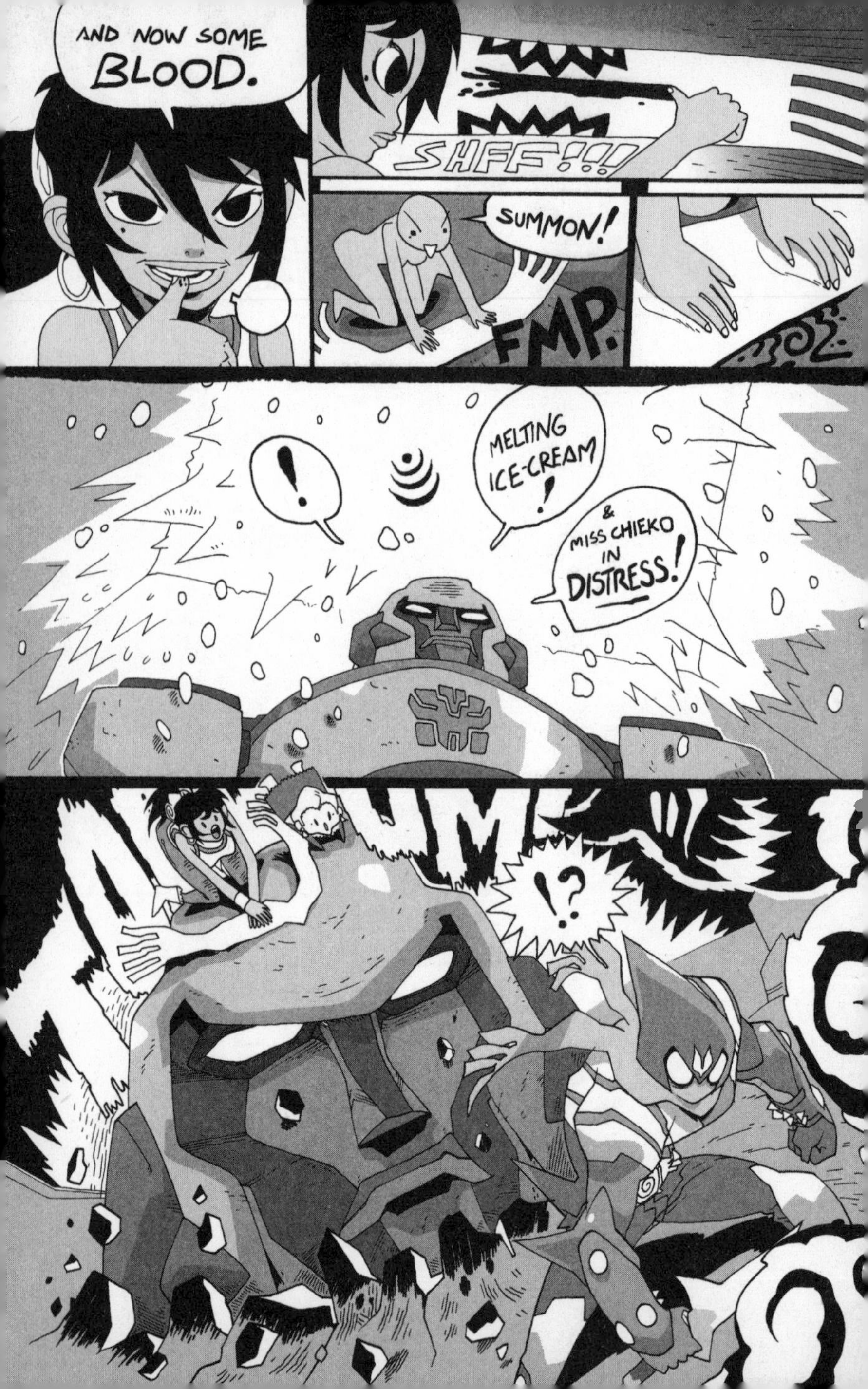
AND NOW SOME BLOOD.
SHFF!!!
SUMMON!
FMP.
!
MELTING ICE-CREAM!
& MISS CHIEKO IN DISTRESS!
!?

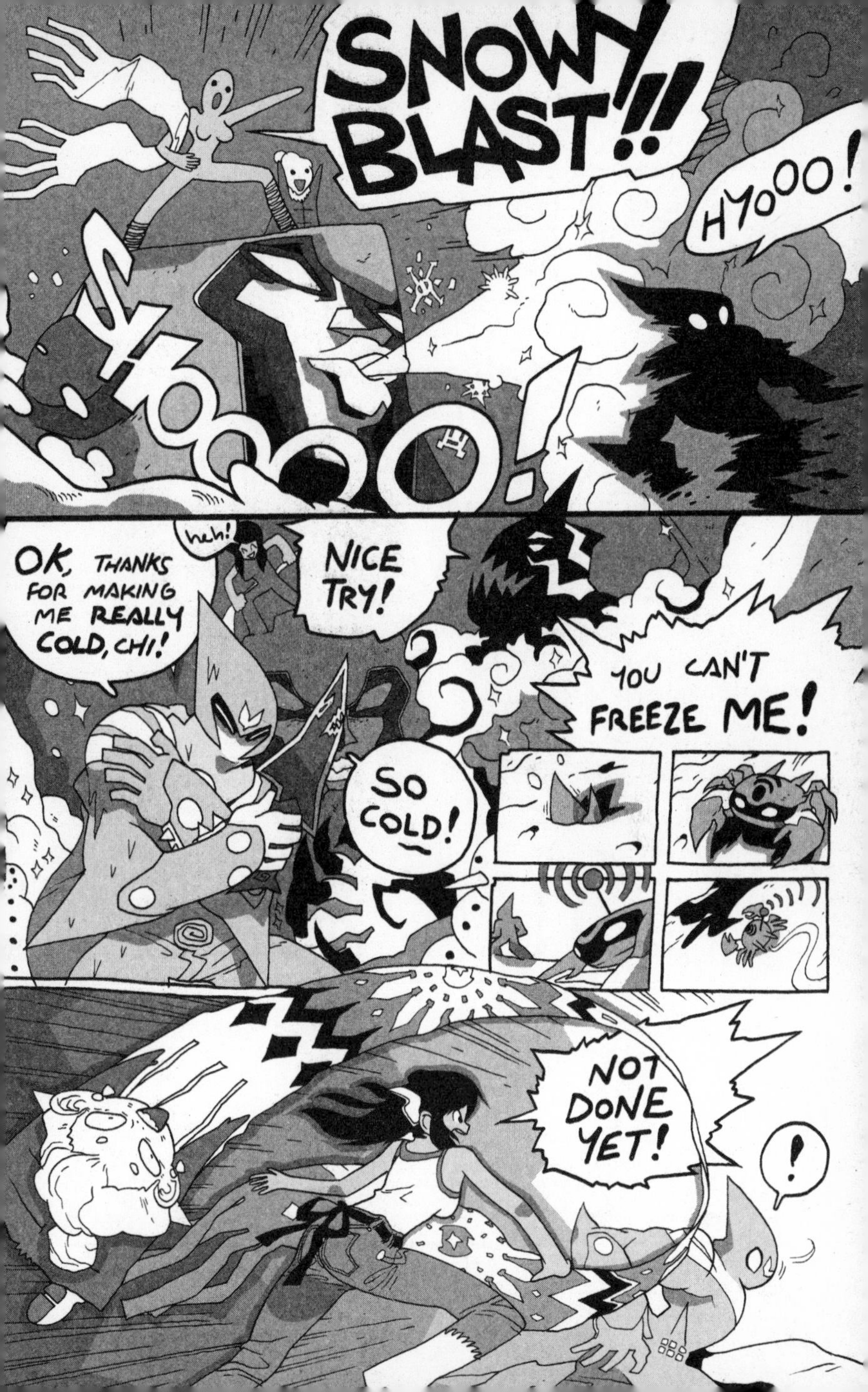
SNOWY BLAST!!
HYOOO!
SHOOOOO!
heh!
OK, THANKS FOR MAKING ME REALLY COLD, CHI!
NICE TRY!
YOU CAN'T FREEZE ME!
SO COLD!
NOT DONE YET!
!

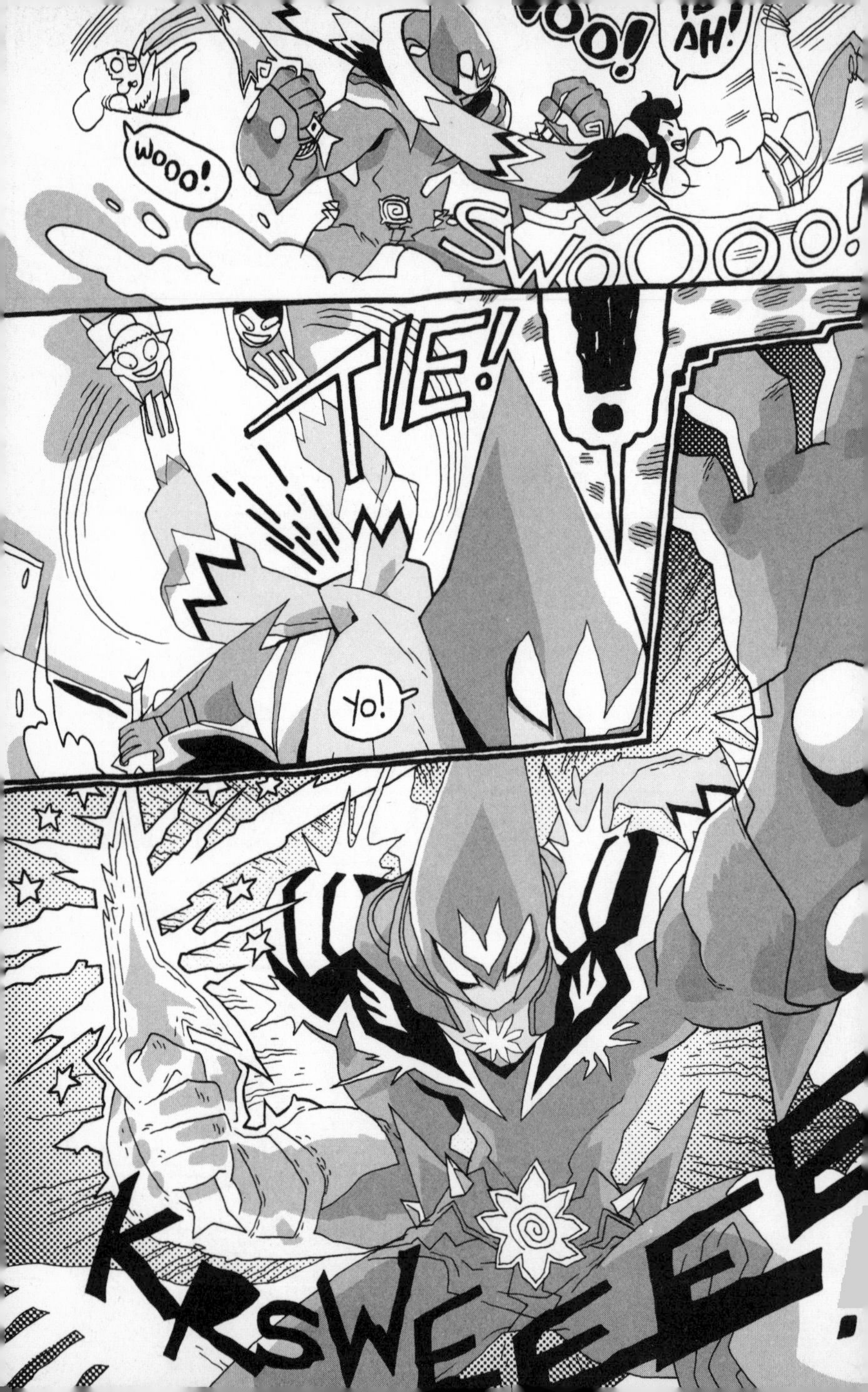
OO!
AH!
WOOO!
SWOOOOO!
TIE!
!
YO!
KRSWEEE

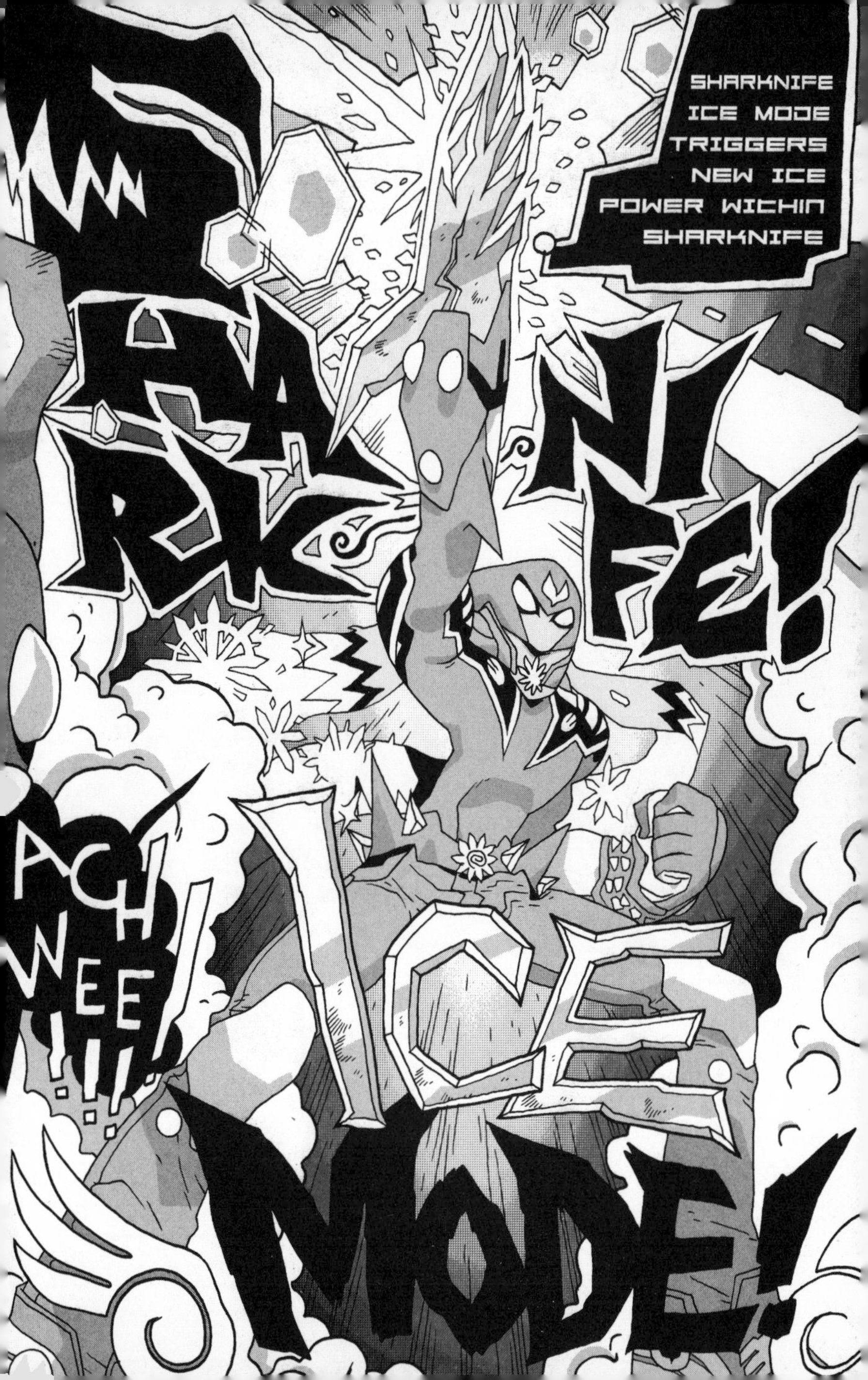
SHARKNIFE ICE MODE TRIGGERS NEW ICE POWER WITHIN SHARKNIFE
ICE MODE!
ACHWEE!!!

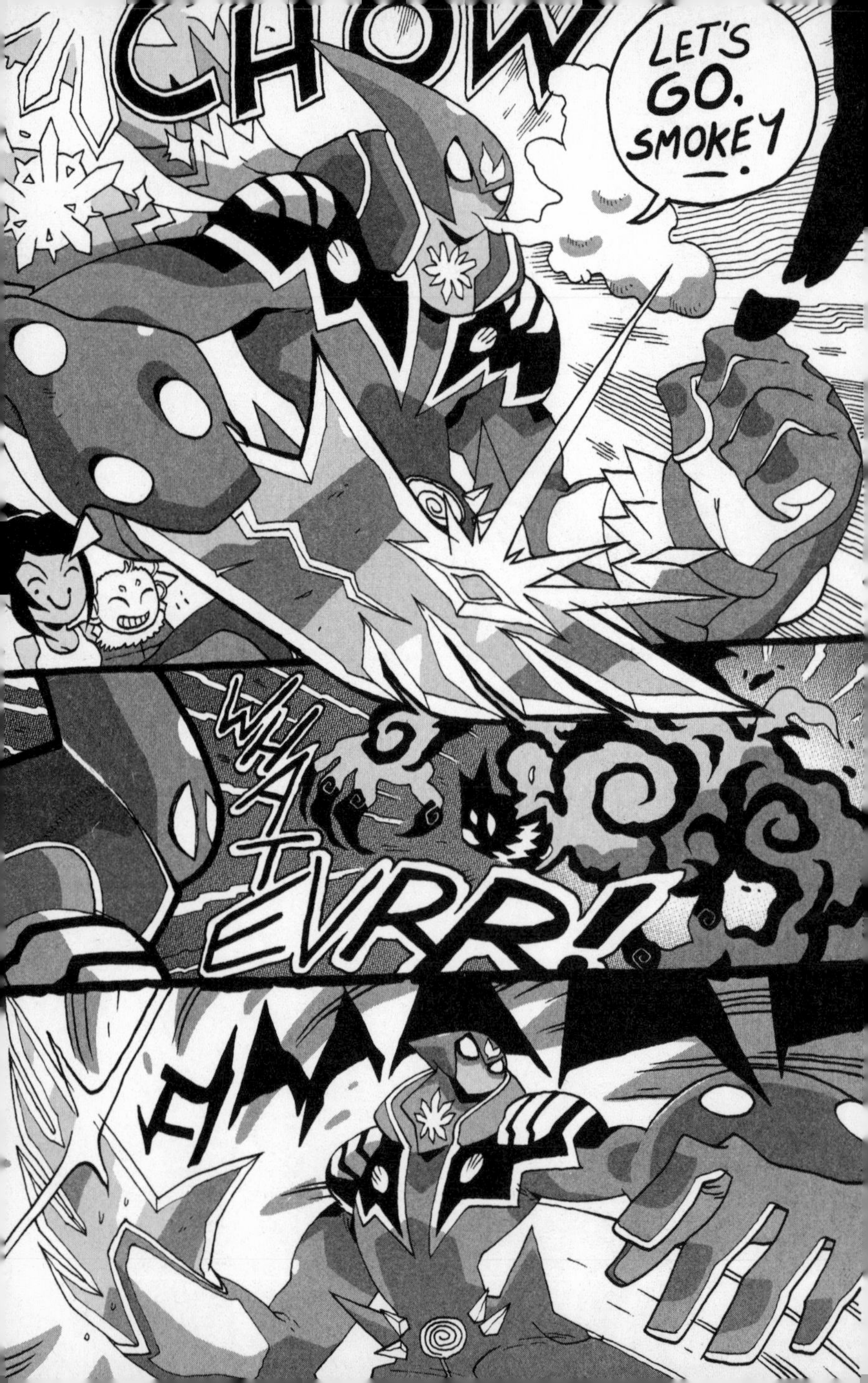
CHOW
LET'S GO, SMOKEY—!
WHAAAT EVRR!

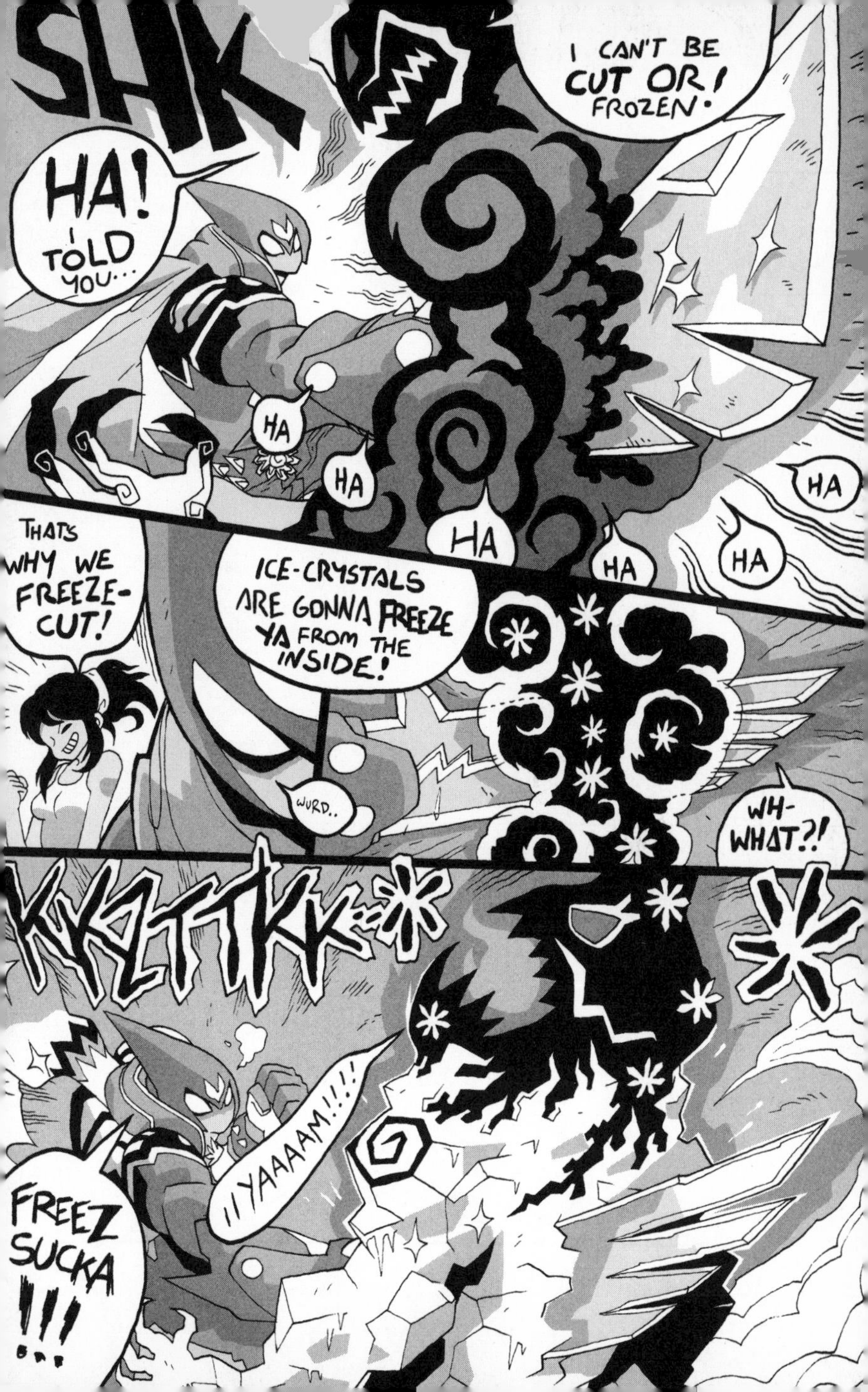
SHIK
I CAN'T BE CUT OR! FROZEN.
HA! I TOLD YOU...
HA
HA
HA
HA
HA
HA
THAT'S WHY WE FREEZE-CUT!
ICE-CRYSTALS ARE GONNA FREEZE YA FROM THE INSIDE!
WURD..
WH-WHAT?!
KKZTTKK
YAAAAM!!!!
FREEZ SUCKA !!!

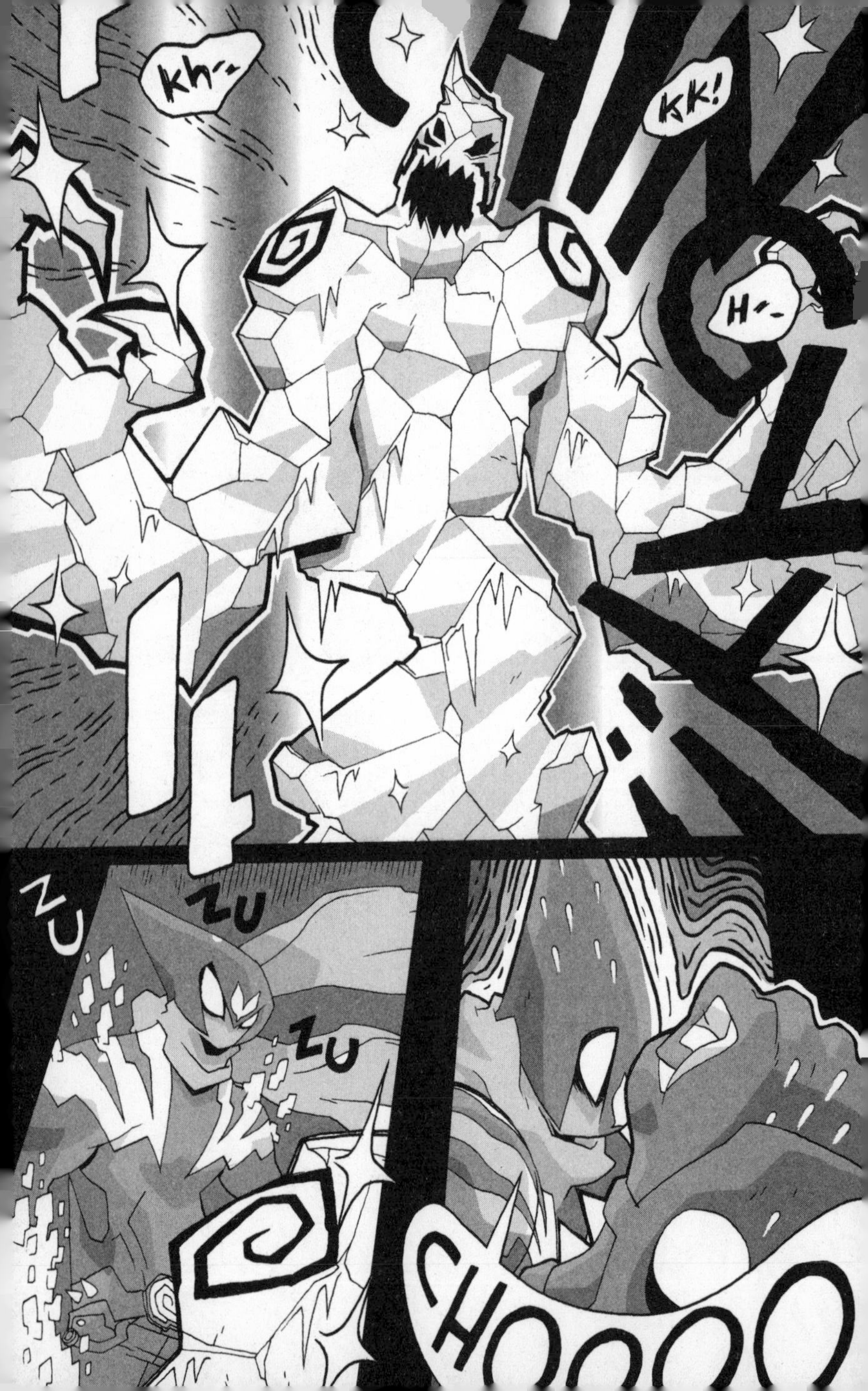

Kh-
KK!
H-
ZU
ZU
ZU
CHOOOO

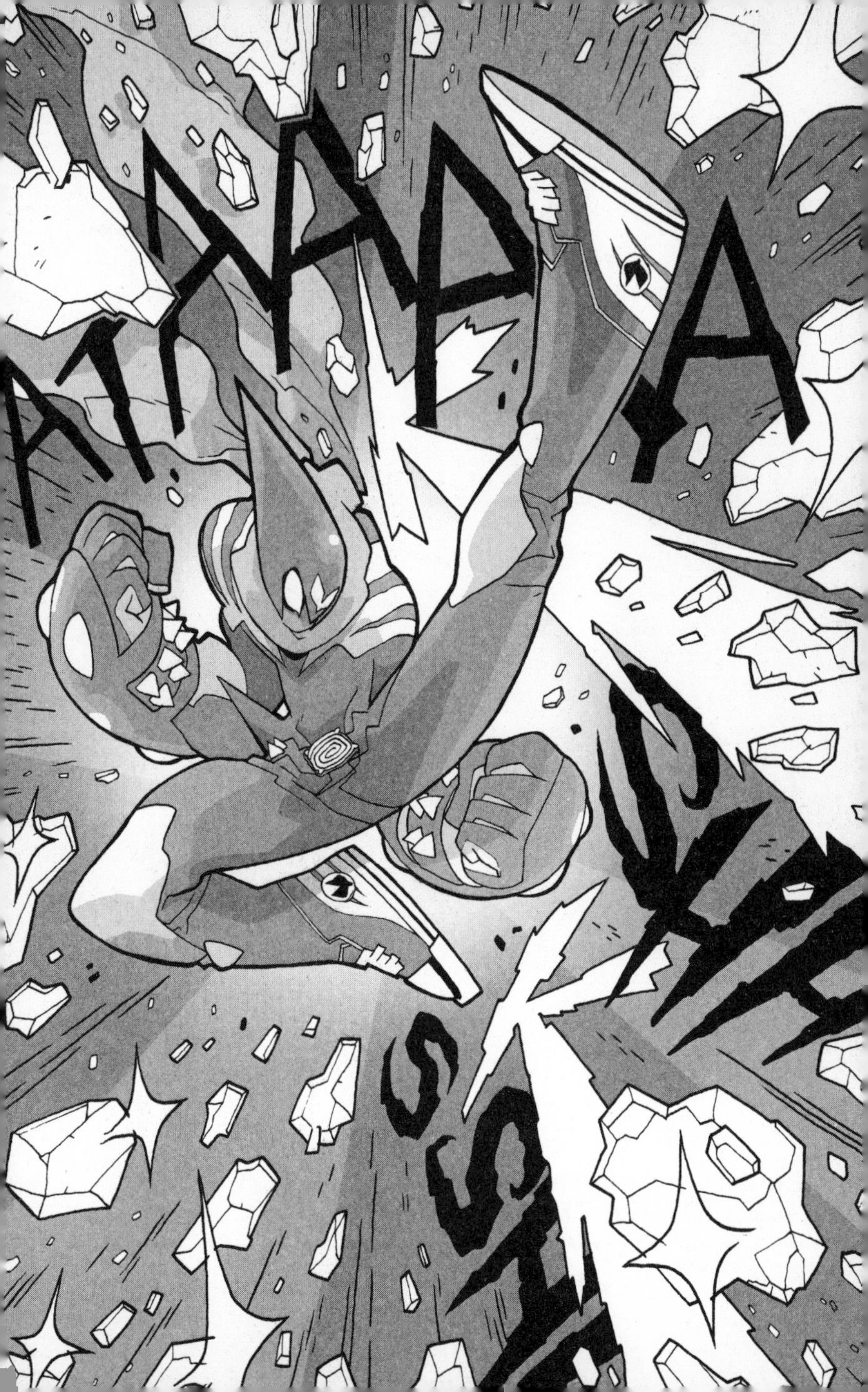

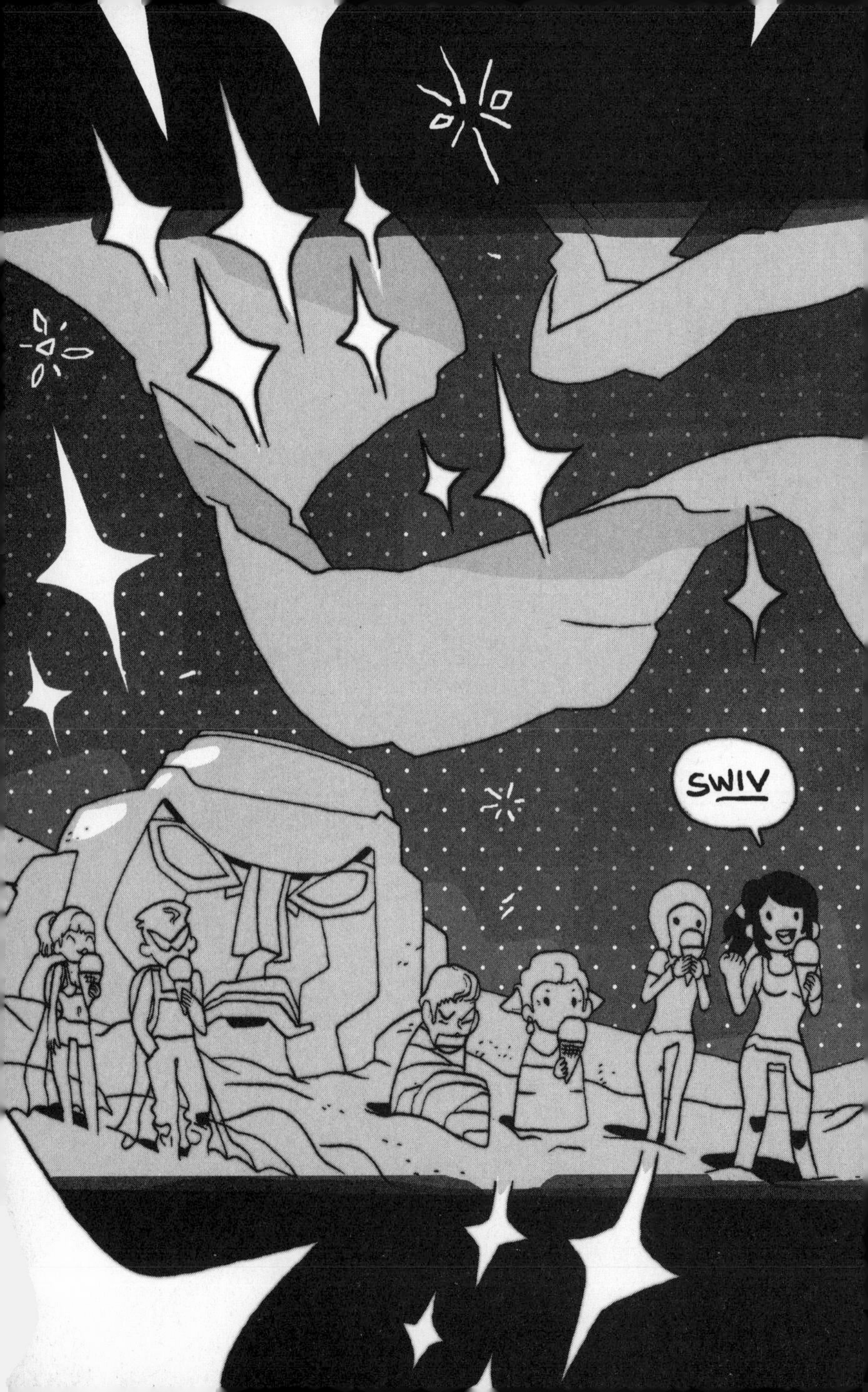
SWIV

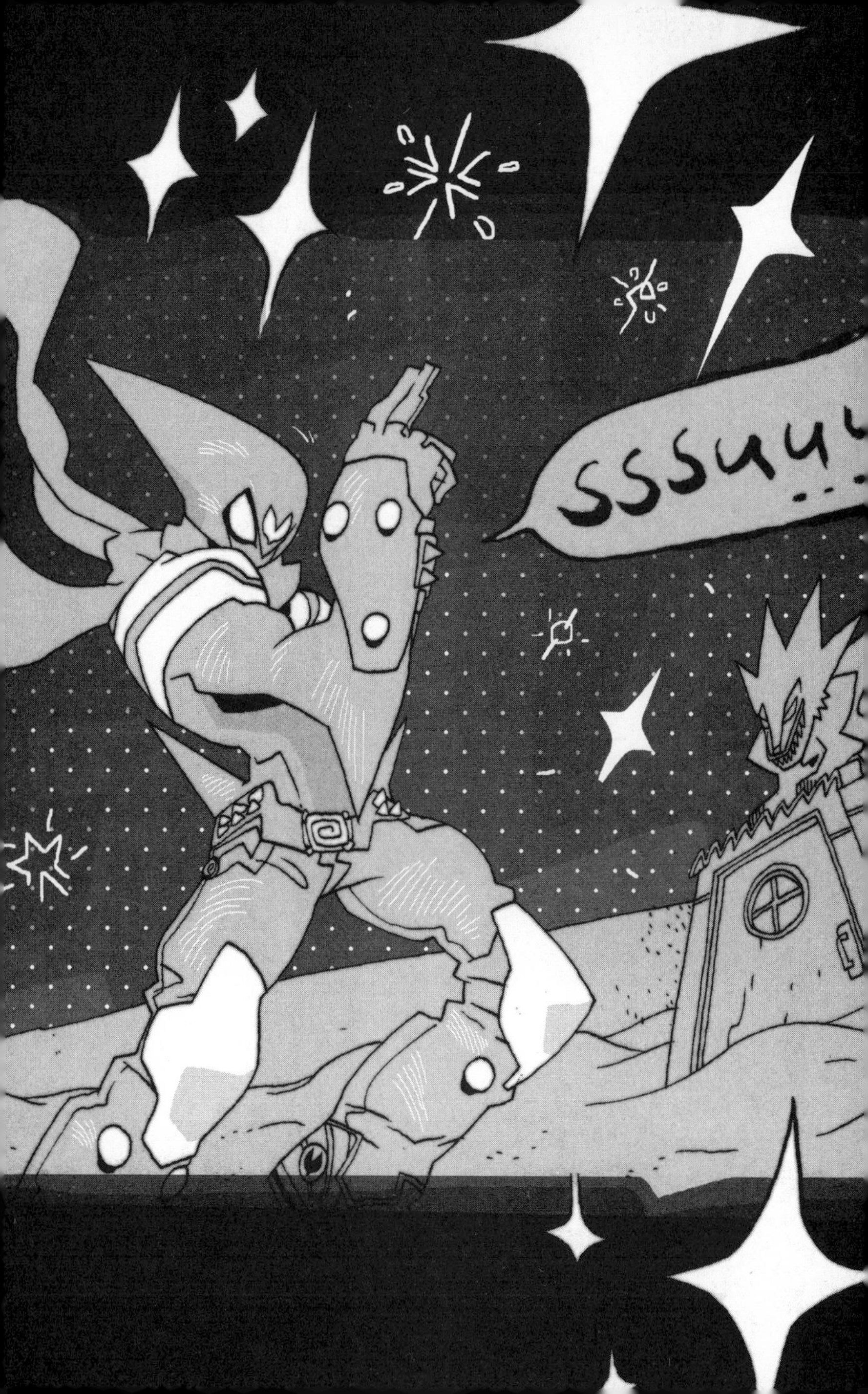
SSSUUU...

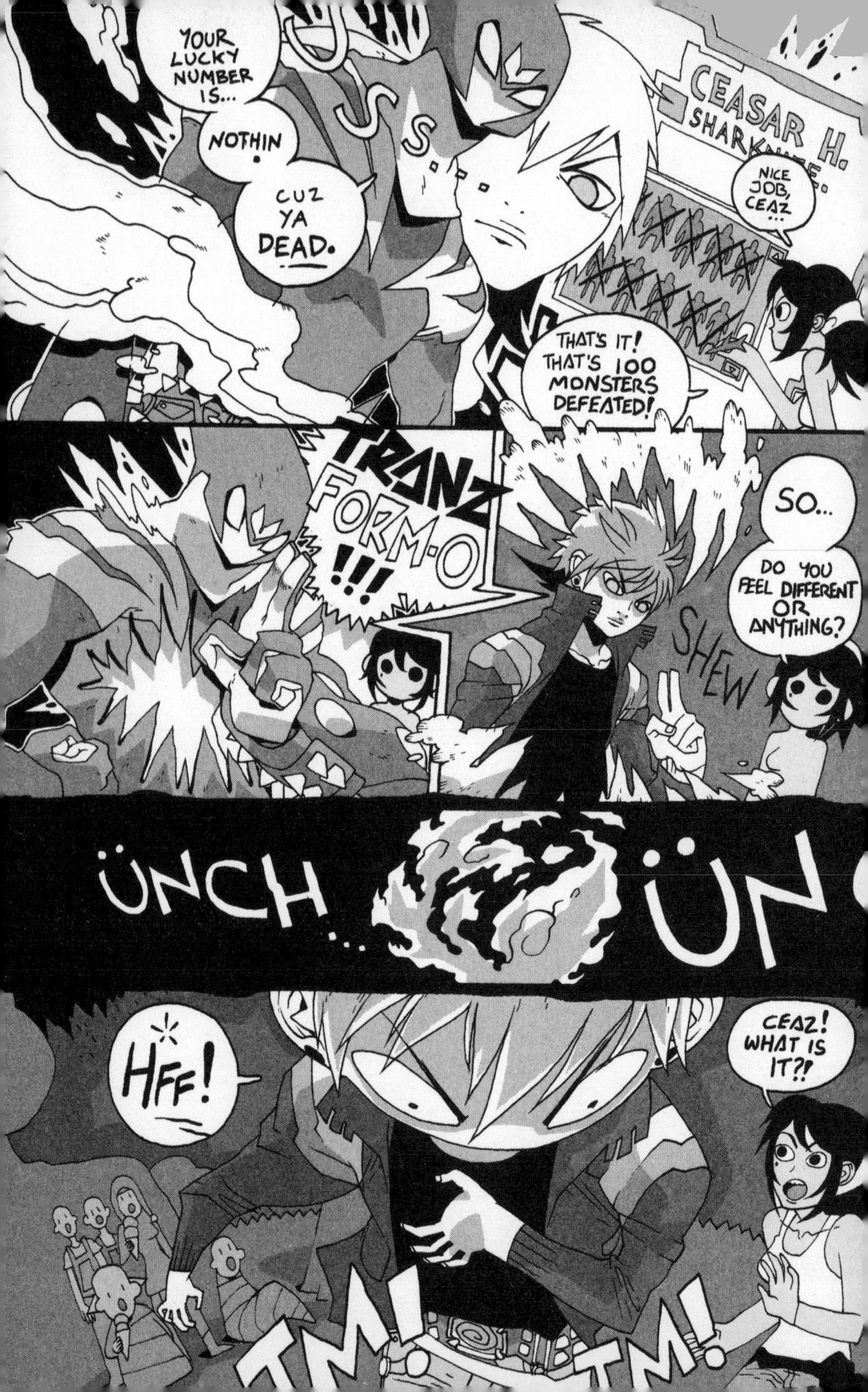

YOUR LUCKY NUMBER IS...
NOTHIN.
CUZ YA DEAD.
CEASAR H. SHARKNIFE.
NICE JOB, CEAZ...
THAT'S IT! THAT'S 100 MONSTERS DEFEATED!
TRANZ FORM-O !!!
SO...
DO YOU FEEL DIFFERENT OR ANYTHING?
SHEW
ÜNCH...
ÜN
HFF!
CEAZ! WHAT IS IT?!
TM! TM!

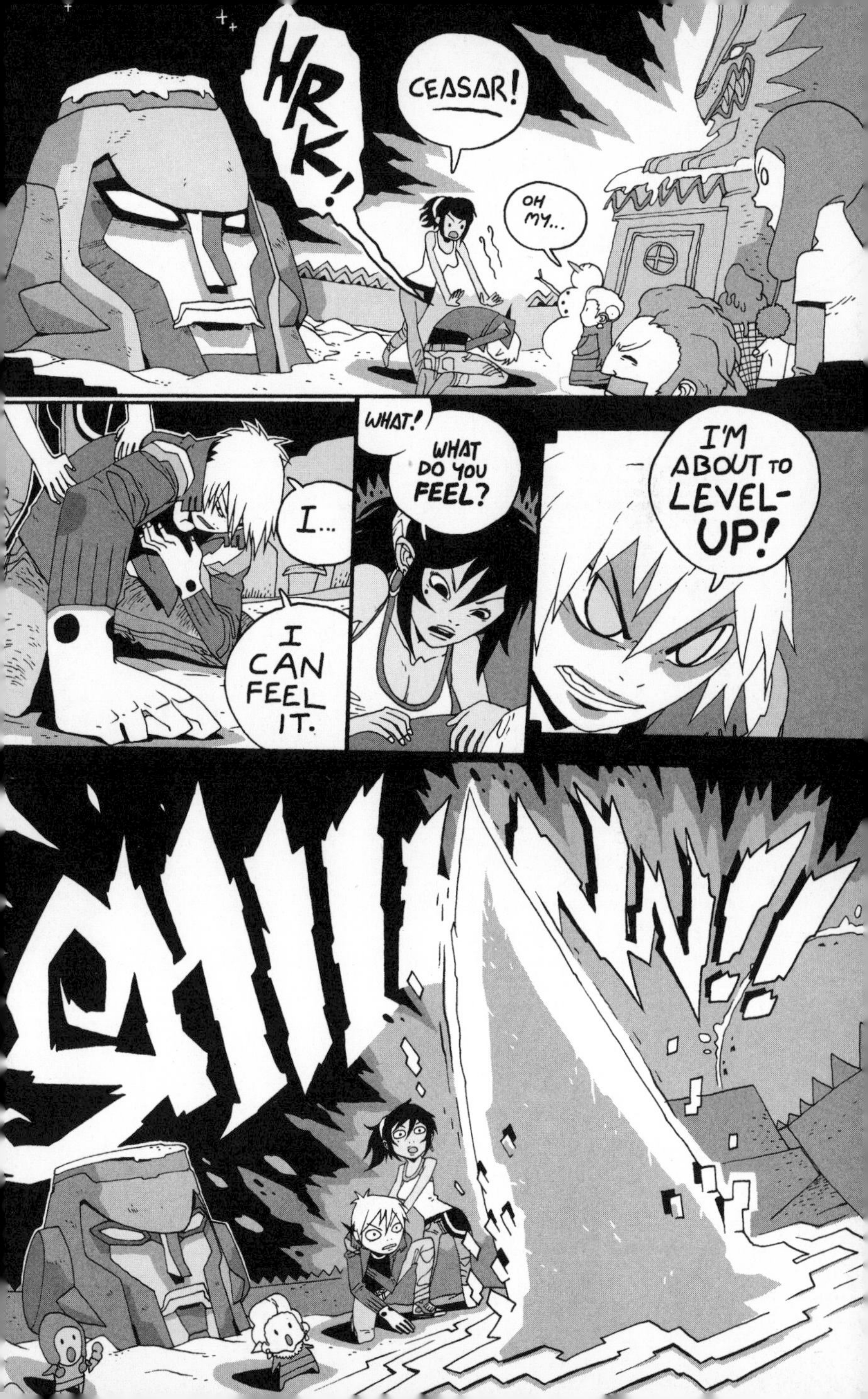
HRK!
CEASAR!
OH MY...
I...
I CAN FEEL IT.
WHAT!
WHAT DO YOU FEEL?
I'M ABOUT TO LEVEL-UP!

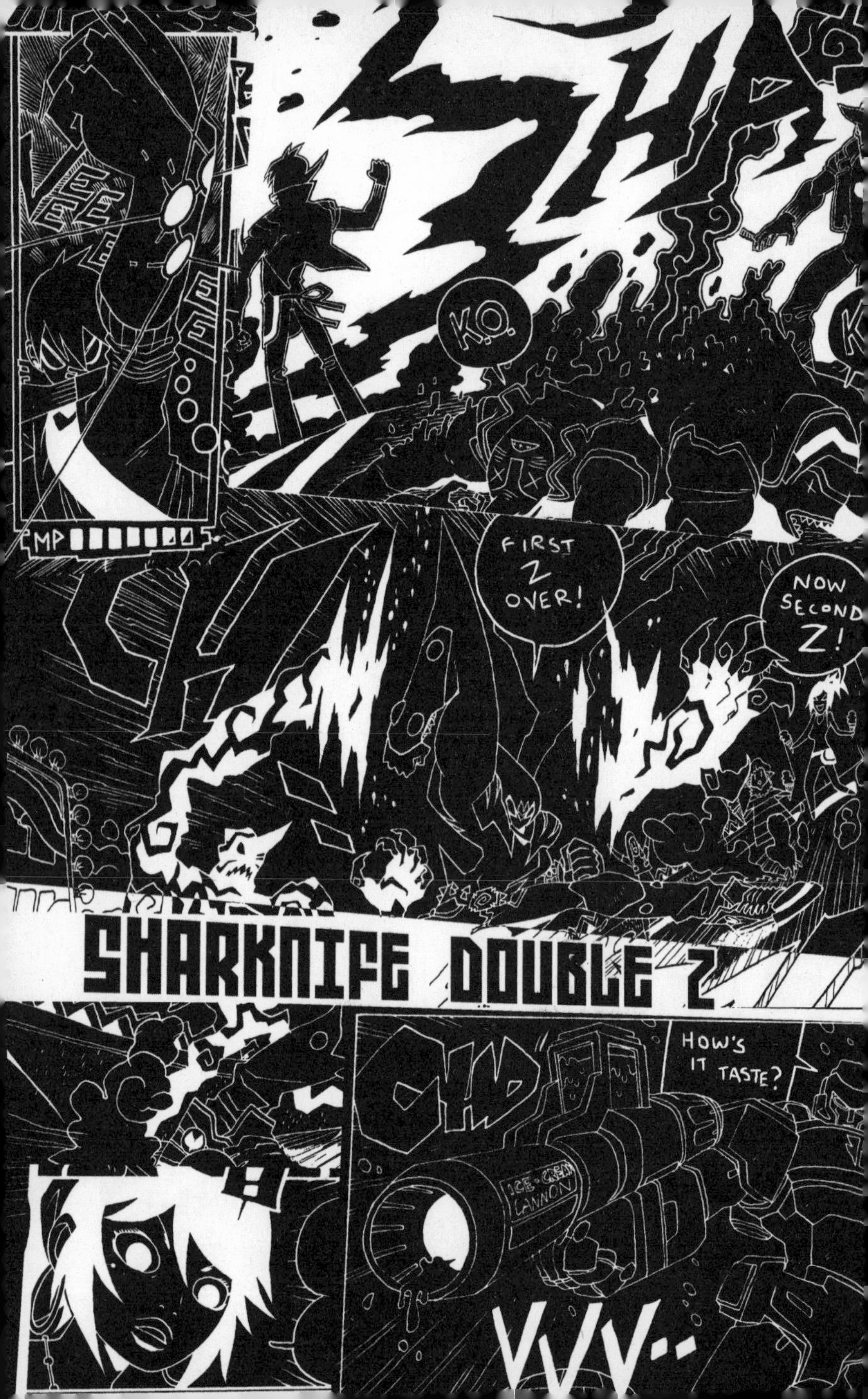

MP
K.O.
FIRST Z OVER!
NOW SECOND Z!
SHARKNIFE DOUBLE Z
HOW'S IT TASTE?
ICE-CREAM CANNON

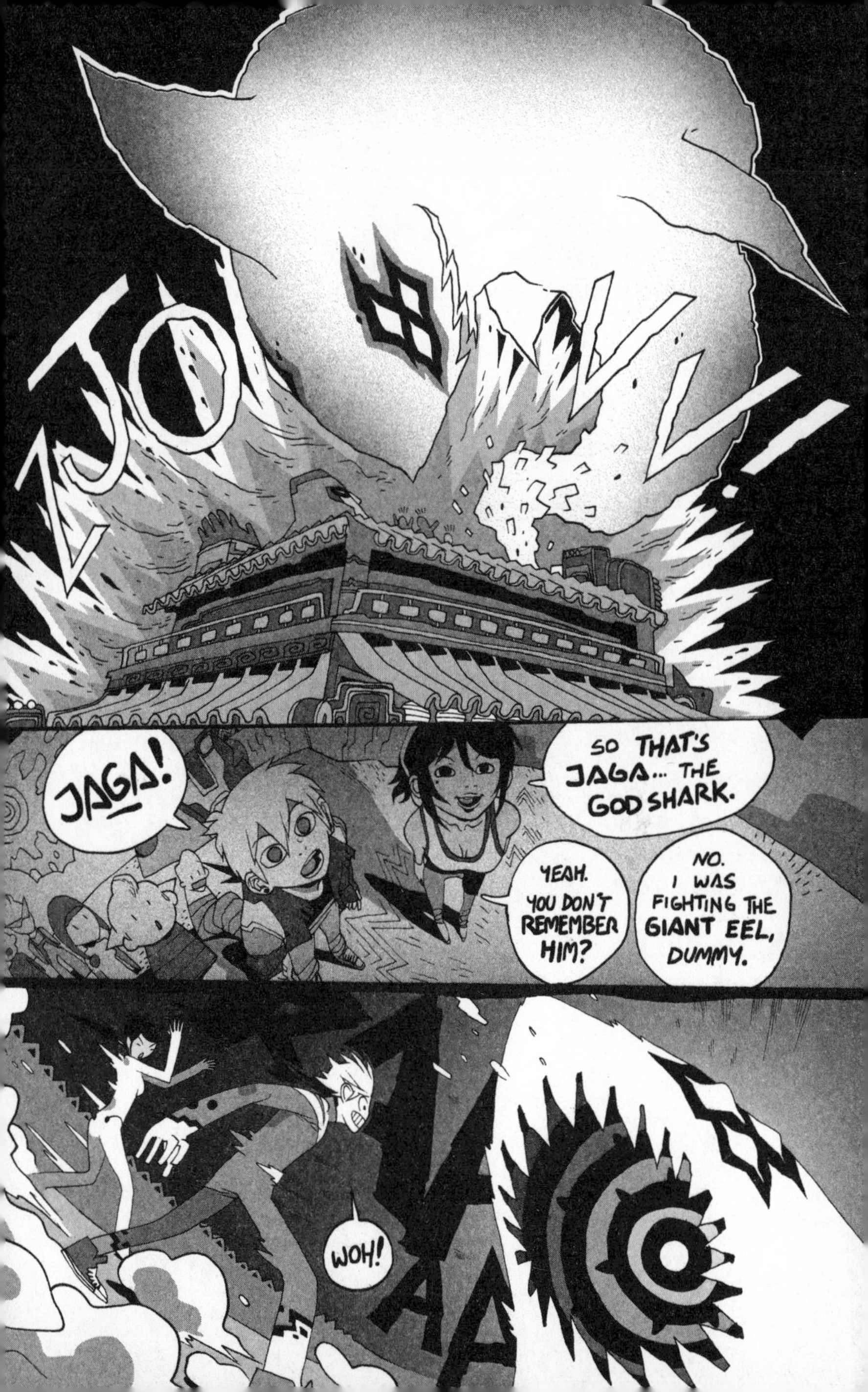
JAGA!
SO THAT'S JAGA... THE GOD SHARK.
YEAH. YOU DON'T REMEMBER HIM?
NO. I WAS FIGHTING THE GIANT EEL, DUMMY.
WOH!

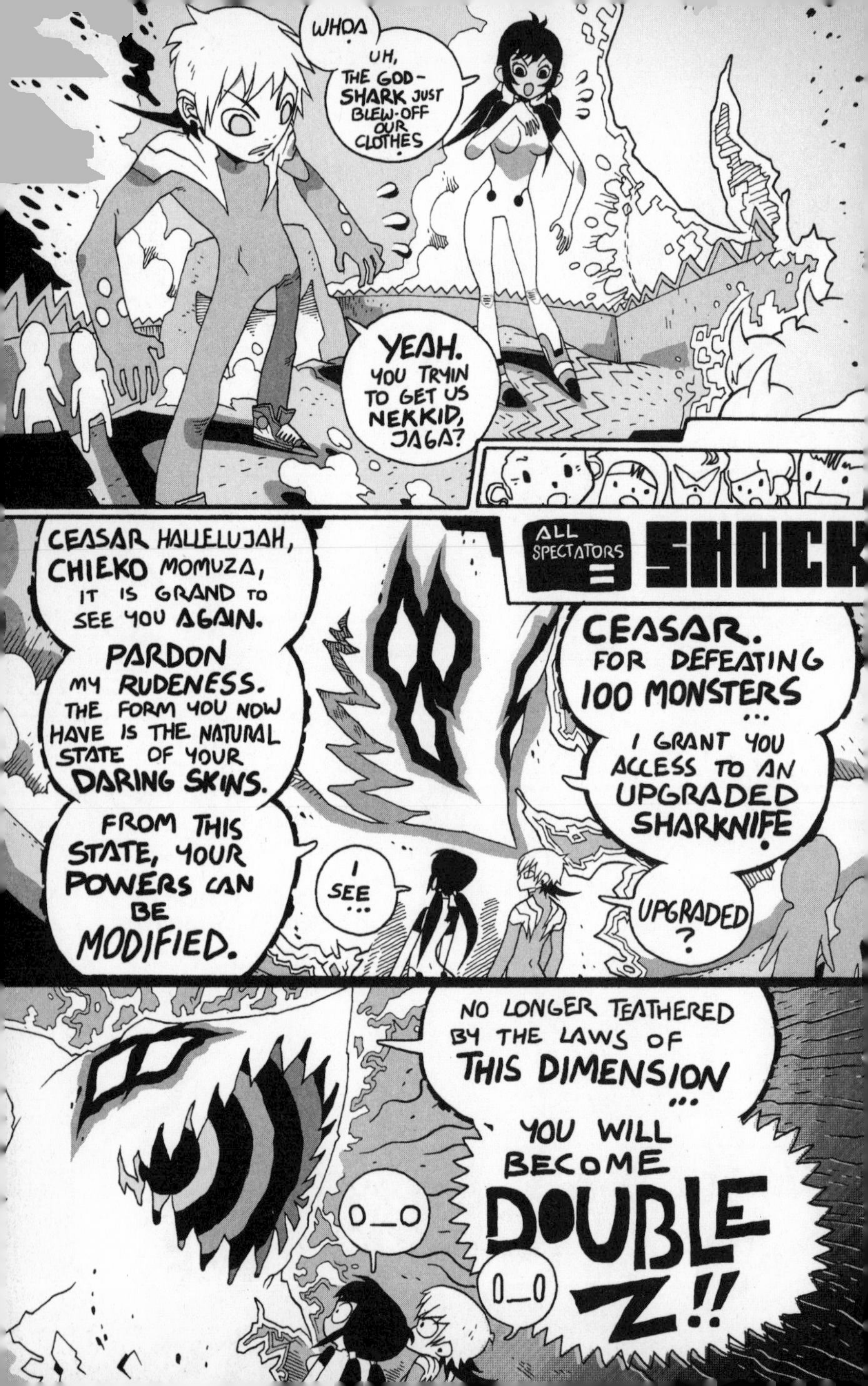
WHOA
UH, THE GOD-SHARK JUST BLEW-OFF OUR CLOTHES
YEAH. YOU TRYIN TO GET US NEKKID, JAGA?
ALL SPECTATORS = SHOCK
CEASAR HALLELUJAH, CHIEKO MOMUZA, IT IS GRAND TO SEE YOU AGAIN.
PARDON MY RUDENESS. THE FORM YOU NOW HAVE IS THE NATURAL STATE OF YOUR DARING SKINS.
FROM THIS STATE, YOUR POWERS CAN BE MODIFIED.
I SEE...
CEASAR. FOR DEFEATING 100 MONSTERS...
I GRANT YOU ACCESS TO AN UPGRADED SHARKNIFE.
UPGRADED?
NO LONGER TEATHERED BY THE LAWS OF THIS DIMENSION...
YOU WILL BECOME DOUBLE Z!!
0_0
0_0

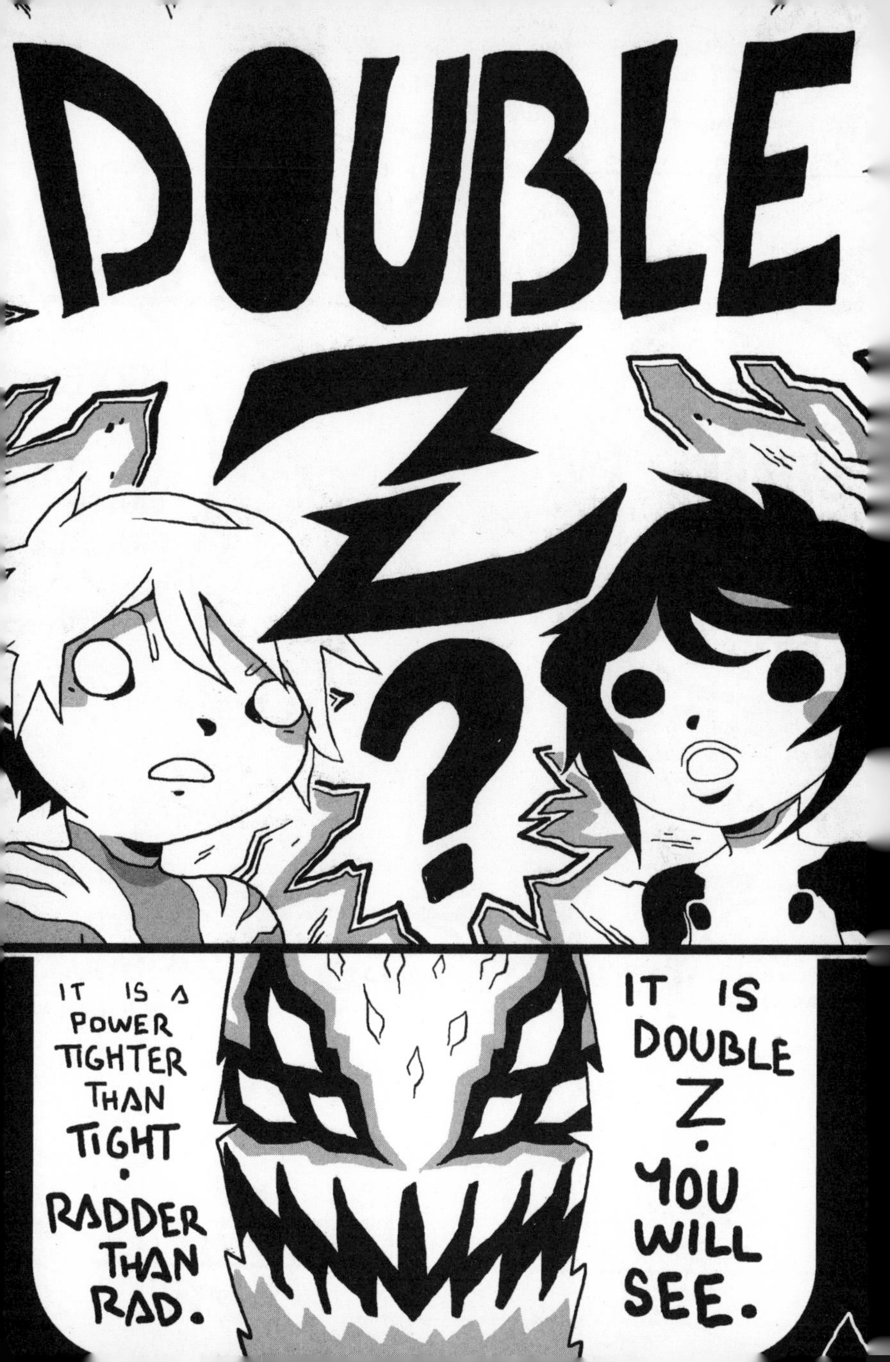
DOUBLE
Z
?
IT IS A POWER TIGHTER THAN TIGHT. RADDER THAN RAD.
IT IS DOUBLE Z. YOU WILL SEE.

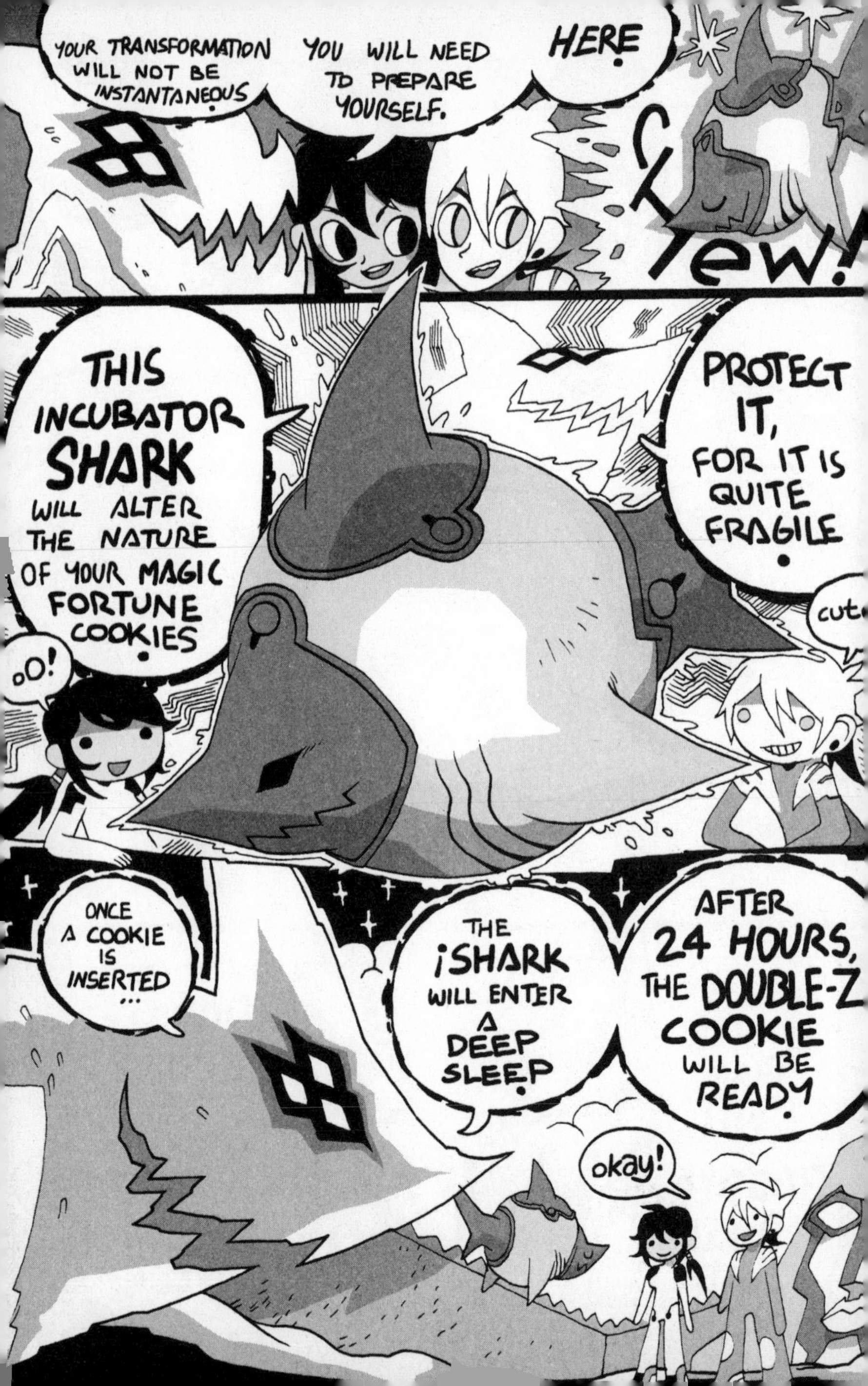
YOUR TRANSFORMATION WILL NOT BE INSTANTANEOUS
YOU WILL NEED TO PREPARE YOURSELF.
HERE!
FTEW!
THIS INCUBATOR SHARK WILL ALTER THE NATURE OF YOUR MAGIC FORTUNE COOKIES.
PROTECT IT, FOR IT IS QUITE FRAGILE.
oO!
cut
ONCE A COOKIE IS INSERTED...
THE iSHARK WILL ENTER A DEEP SLEEP.
AFTER 24 HOURS, THE DOUBLE-Z COOKIE WILL BE READY.
okay!

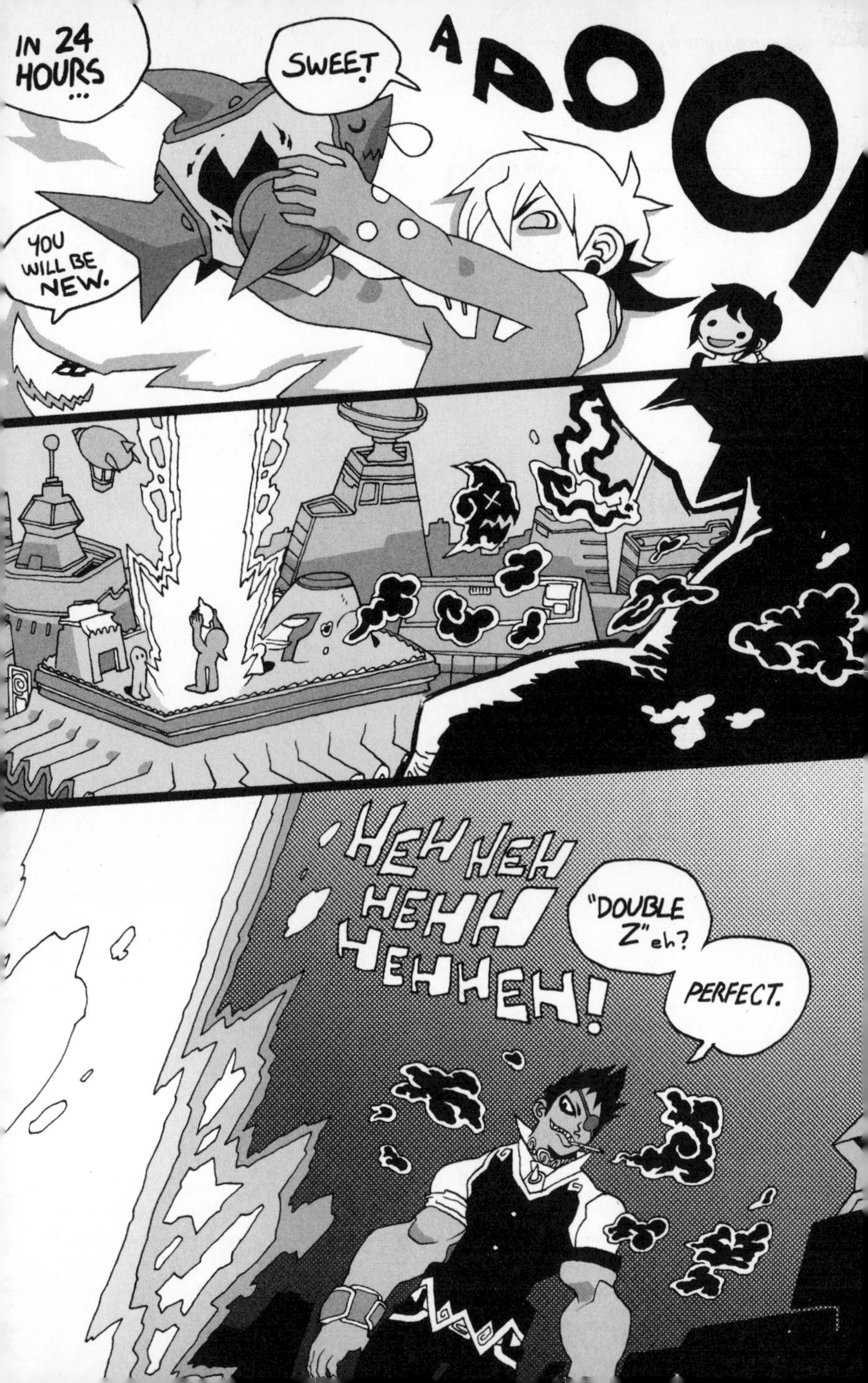
IN 24 HOURS...
SWEET!
YOU WILL BE NEW.
APOO
HEH HEH HEHH HEHHEH!
"DOUBLE Z" eh?
PERFECT.

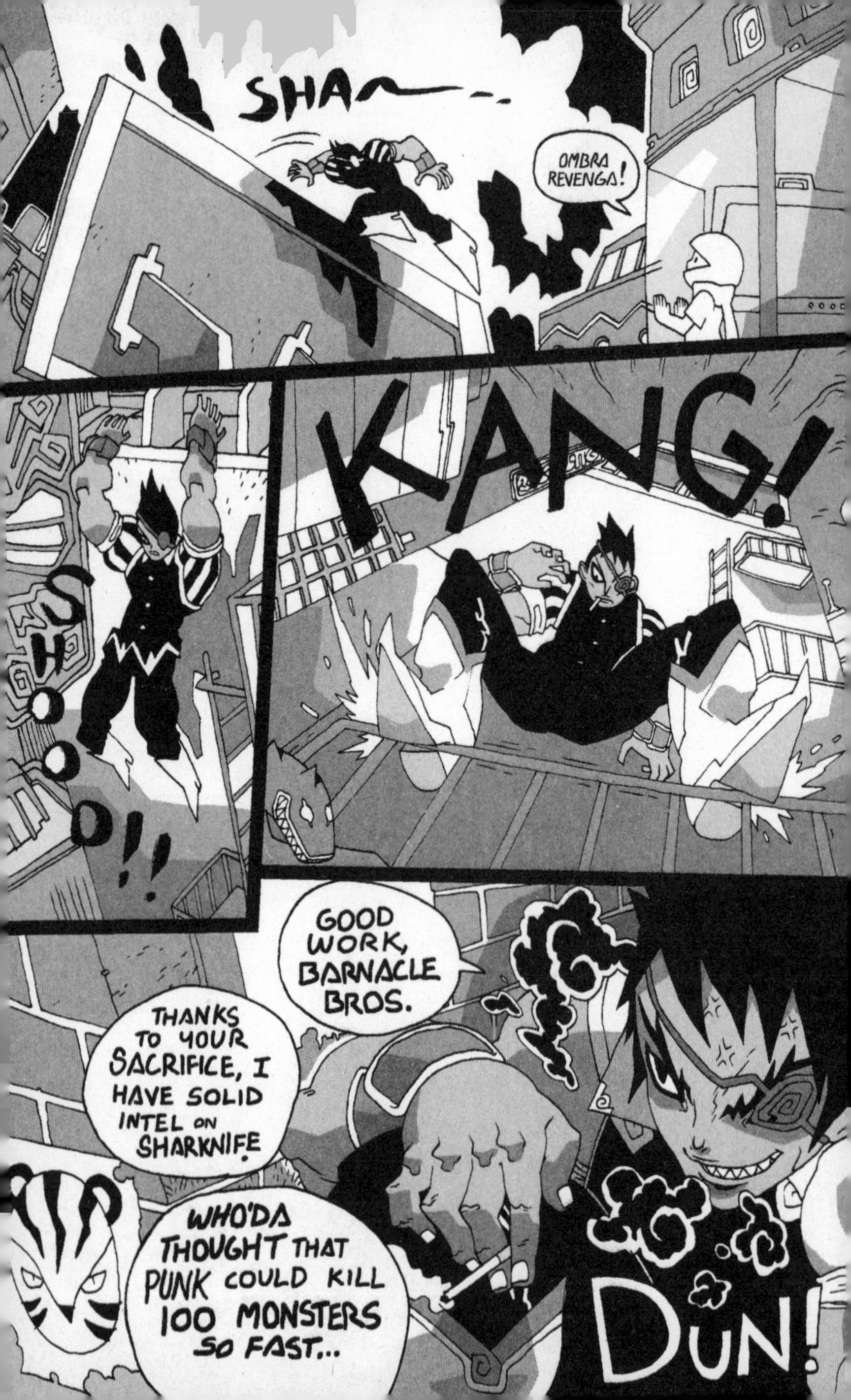
SHA~
OMBRA REVENGA!
KANG!
SHOOOO!!
GOOD WORK, BARNACLE BROS.
THANKS TO YOUR SACRIFICE, I HAVE SOLID INTEL ON SHARKNIFE.
WHO'DA THOUGHT THAT PUNK COULD KILL 100 MONSTERS SO FAST...
DUN!

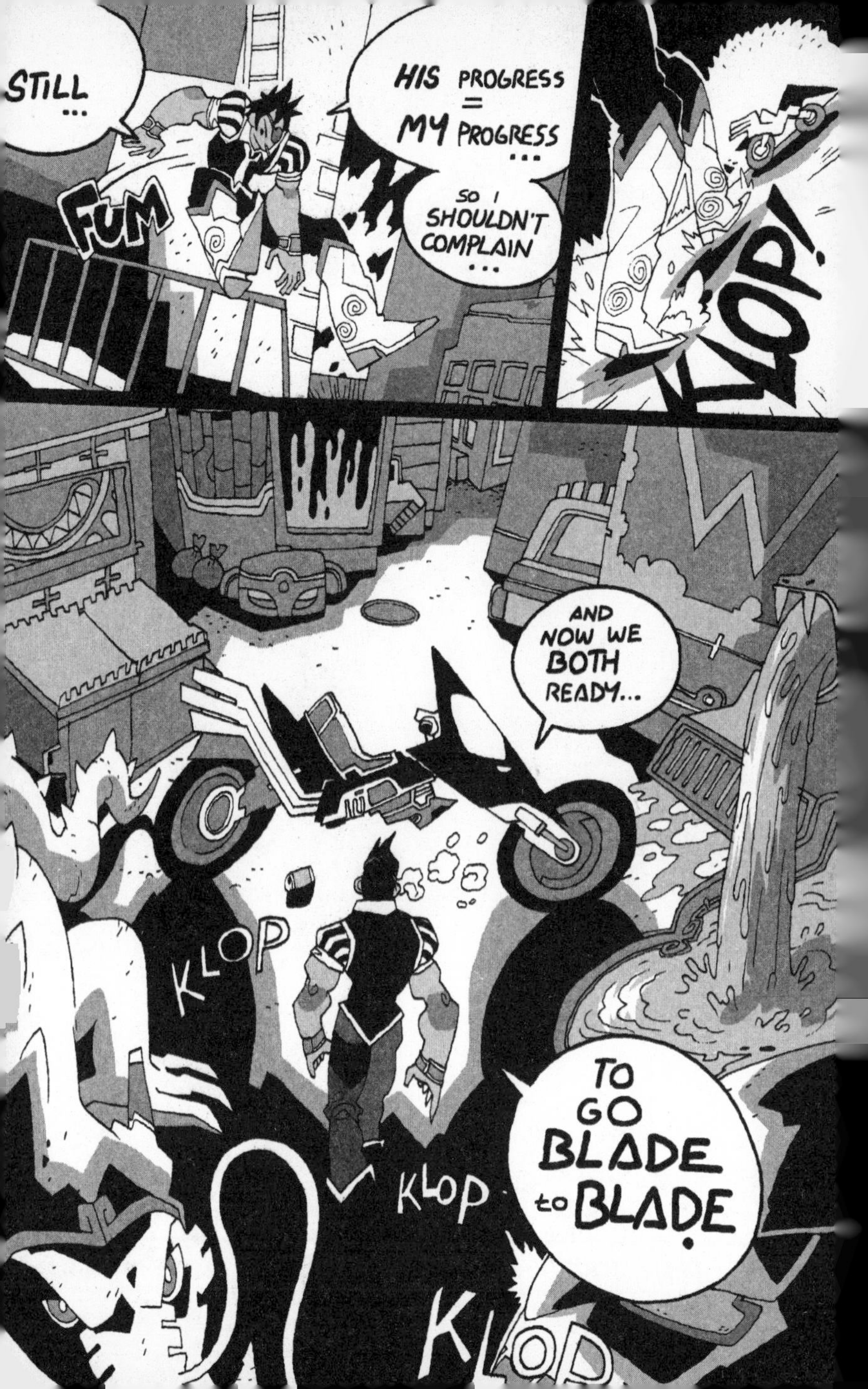
STILL ...
FUM
HIS PROGRESS = MY PROGRESS ...
SO I SHOULDN'T COMPLAIN ...
KLOP!
AND NOW WE BOTH READY...
KLOP
TO GO BLADE to BLADE.
KLOP
KLOP

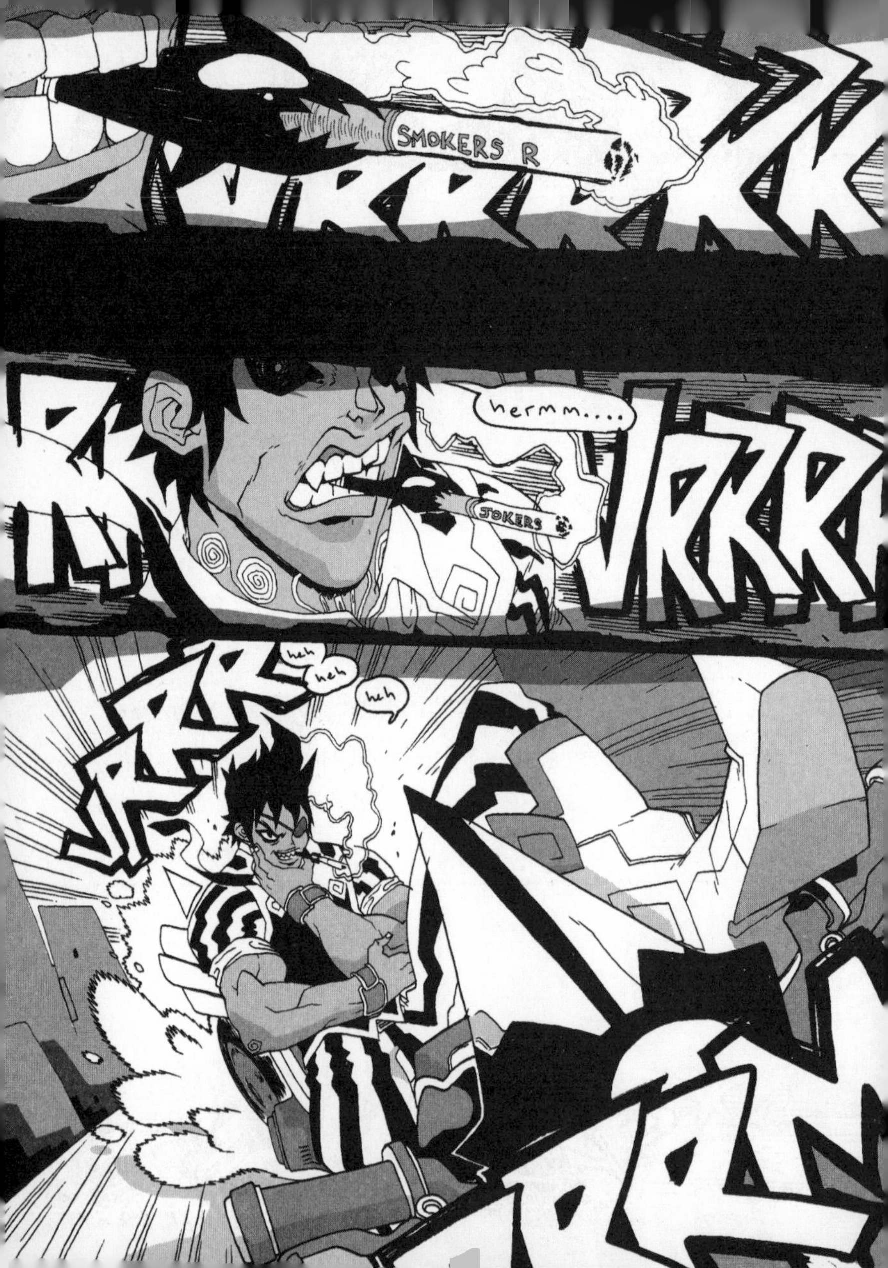
SMOKERS R
hermm.....
JOKERS
heh
heh
heh

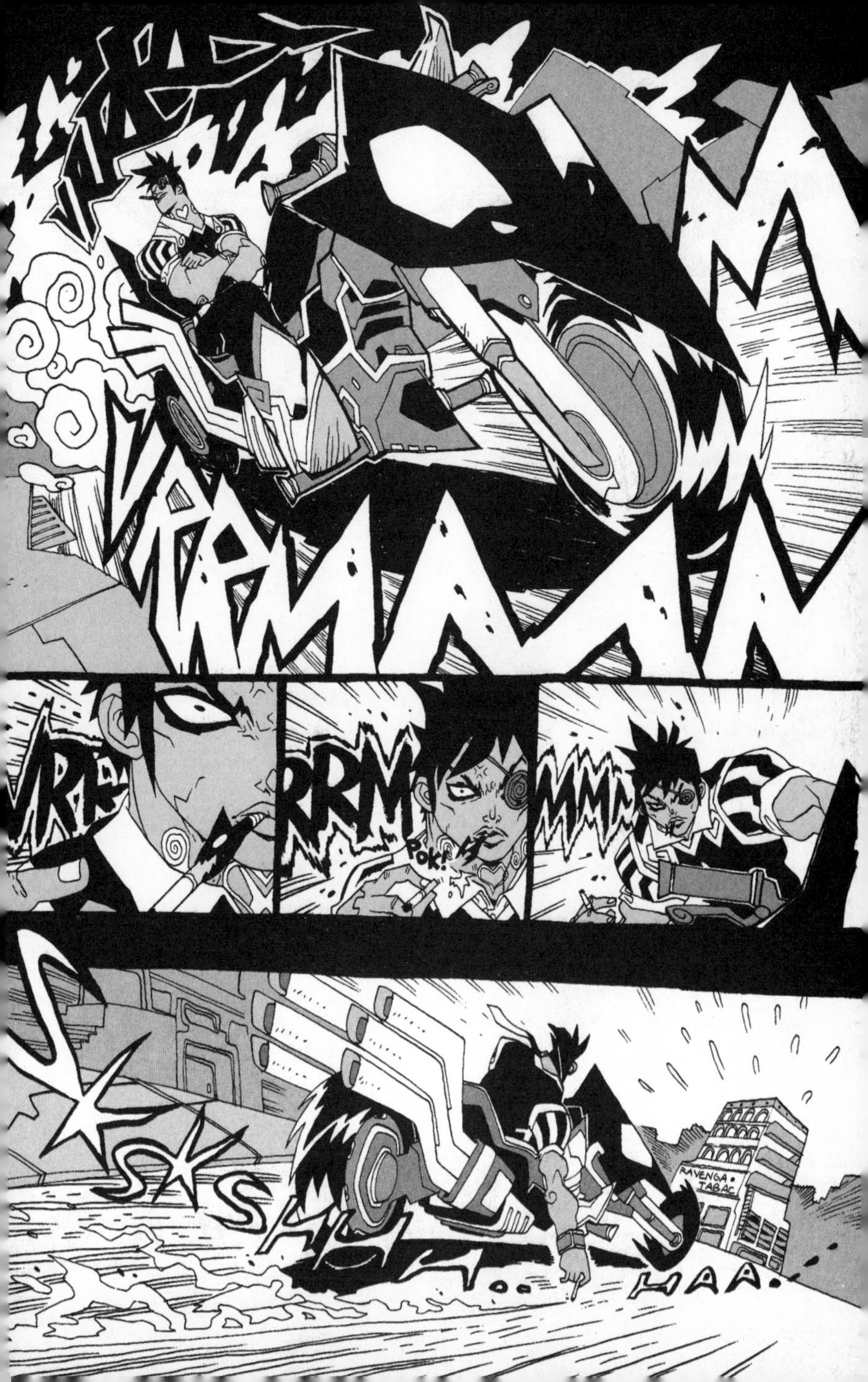
POK!
RAVENGA TABAC
HAA...

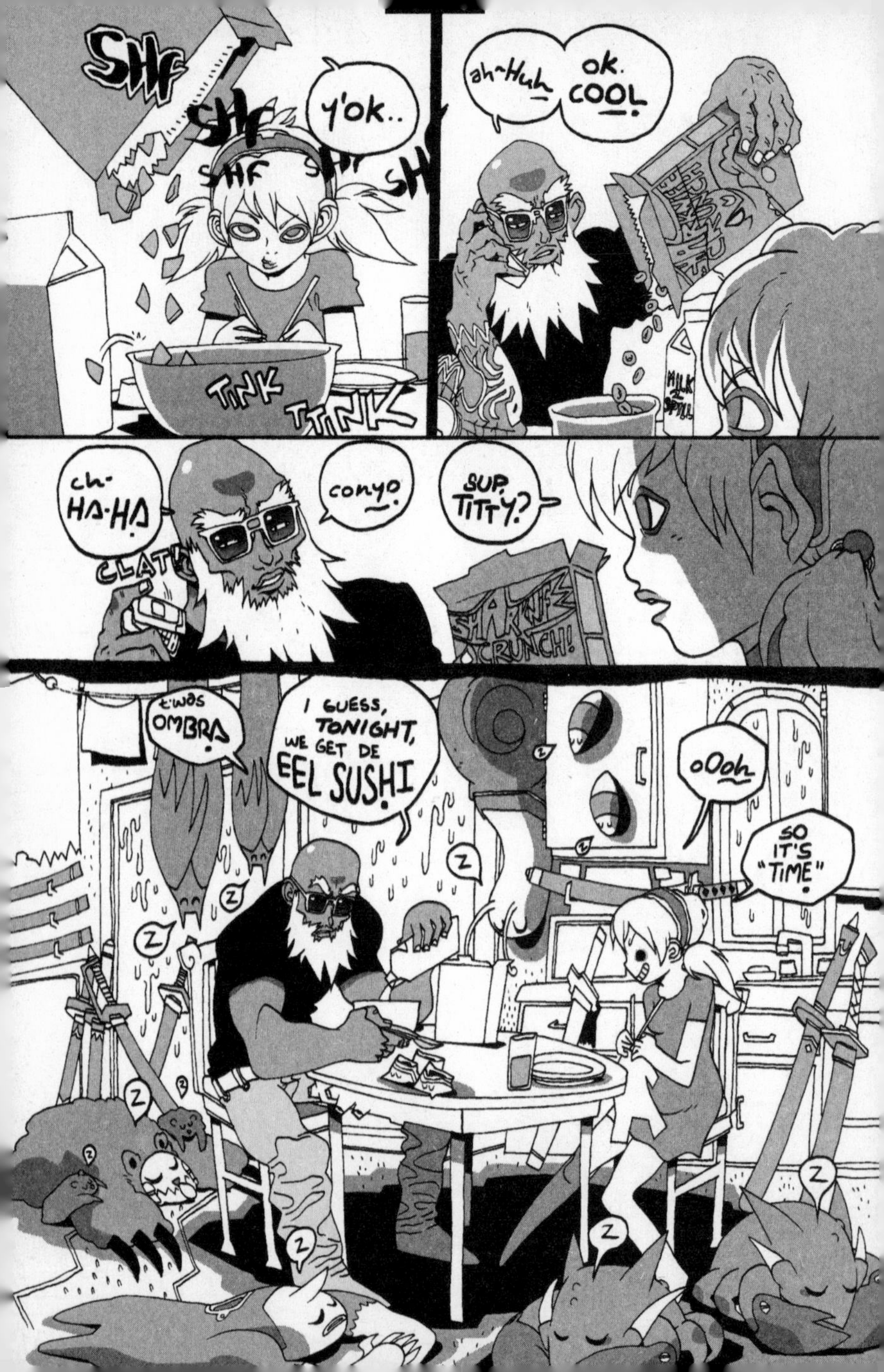
SHF
SHF
SHF
SHF
SH
y'ok..
TINK
TTINK
ah-Huh
ok. COOL
MILK 2 SPILL
ch-HA-HA
CLAT
conyo
SUP, TITTY?
SHARKNIFE CRUNCH!
t'was OMBRA
I GUESS, TONIGHT, WE GET DE EEL SUSHI
oOoh
SO IT'S "TIME"

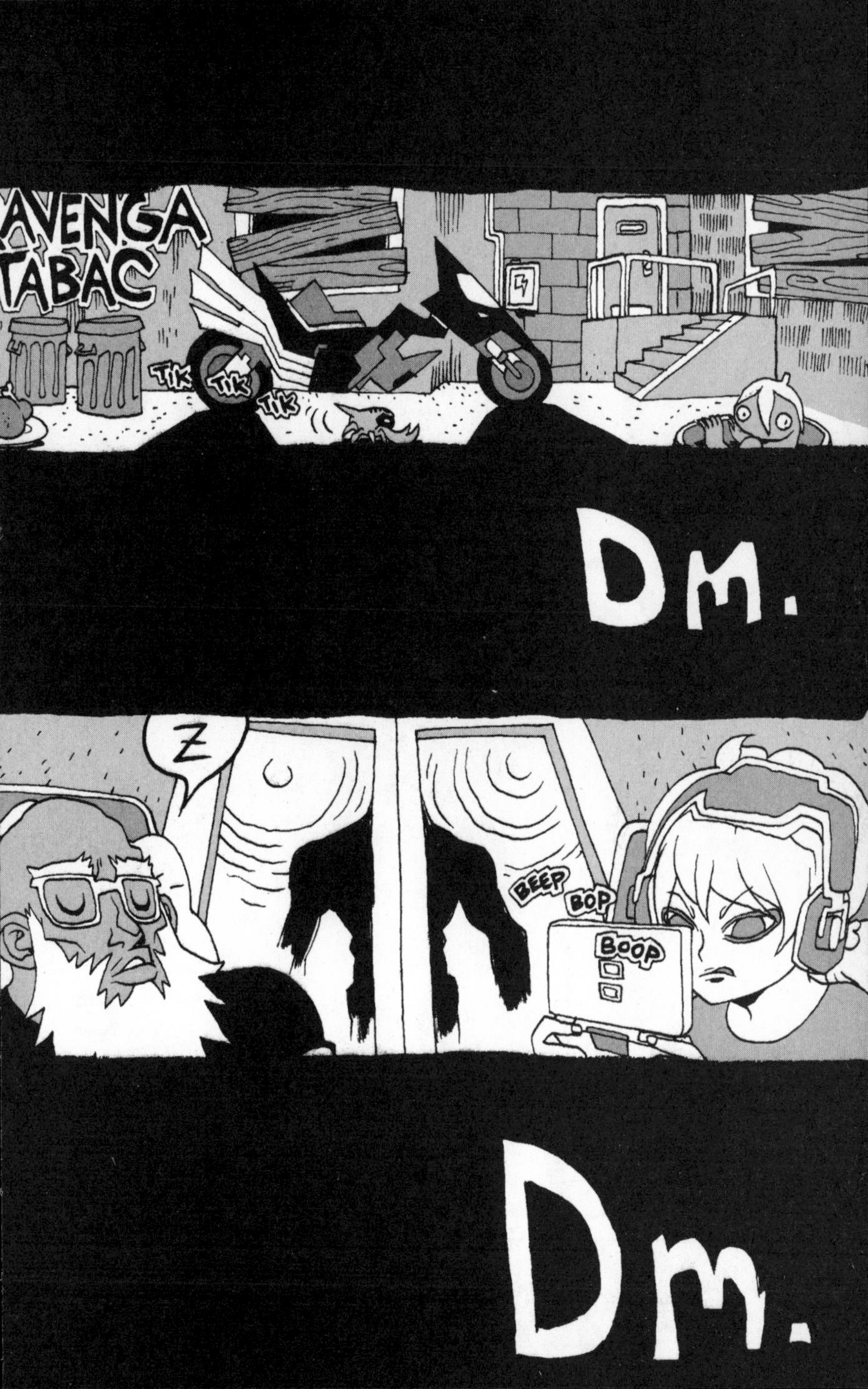
AVENGA
TABAC
TIK
TIK
TIK
Dm.
Z
BEEP
BOP
BOOP
Dm.

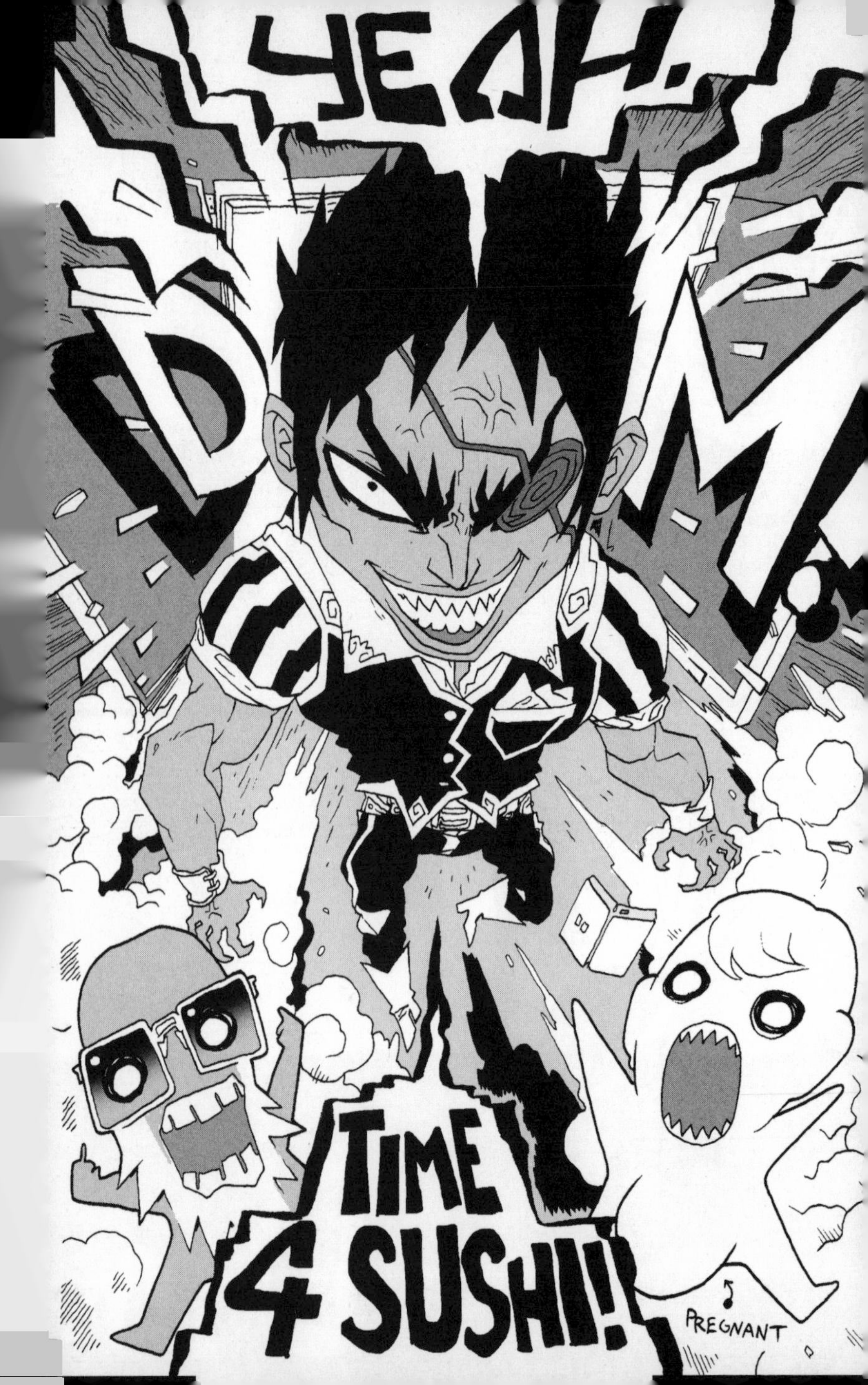
YEAH!
TIME 4 SUSHI!!
PREGNANT

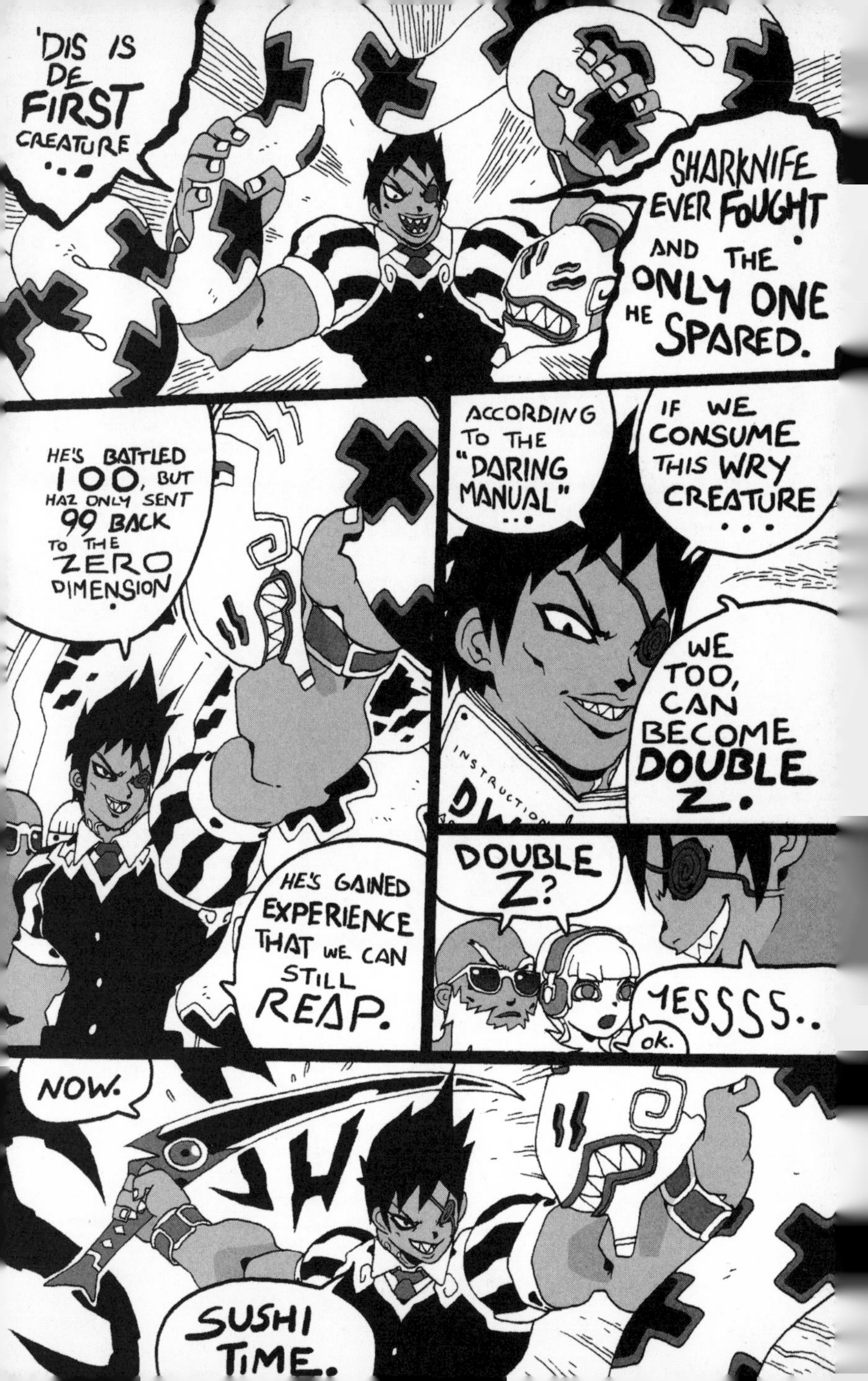
'DIS IS DE FIRST CREATURE ...
SHARKNIFE EVER FOUGHT. AND THE ONLY ONE HE SPARED.
HE'S BATTLED 100, BUT HAZ ONLY SENT 99 BACK TO THE ZERO DIMENSION.
ACCORDING TO THE "DARING MANUAL" ...
IF WE CONSUME THIS WRY CREATURE ...
WE TOO, CAN BECOME DOUBLE Z.
HE'S GAINED EXPERIENCE THAT WE CAN STILL REAP.
DOUBLE Z?
YESSSS..
OK.
NOW.
SUSHI TIME.

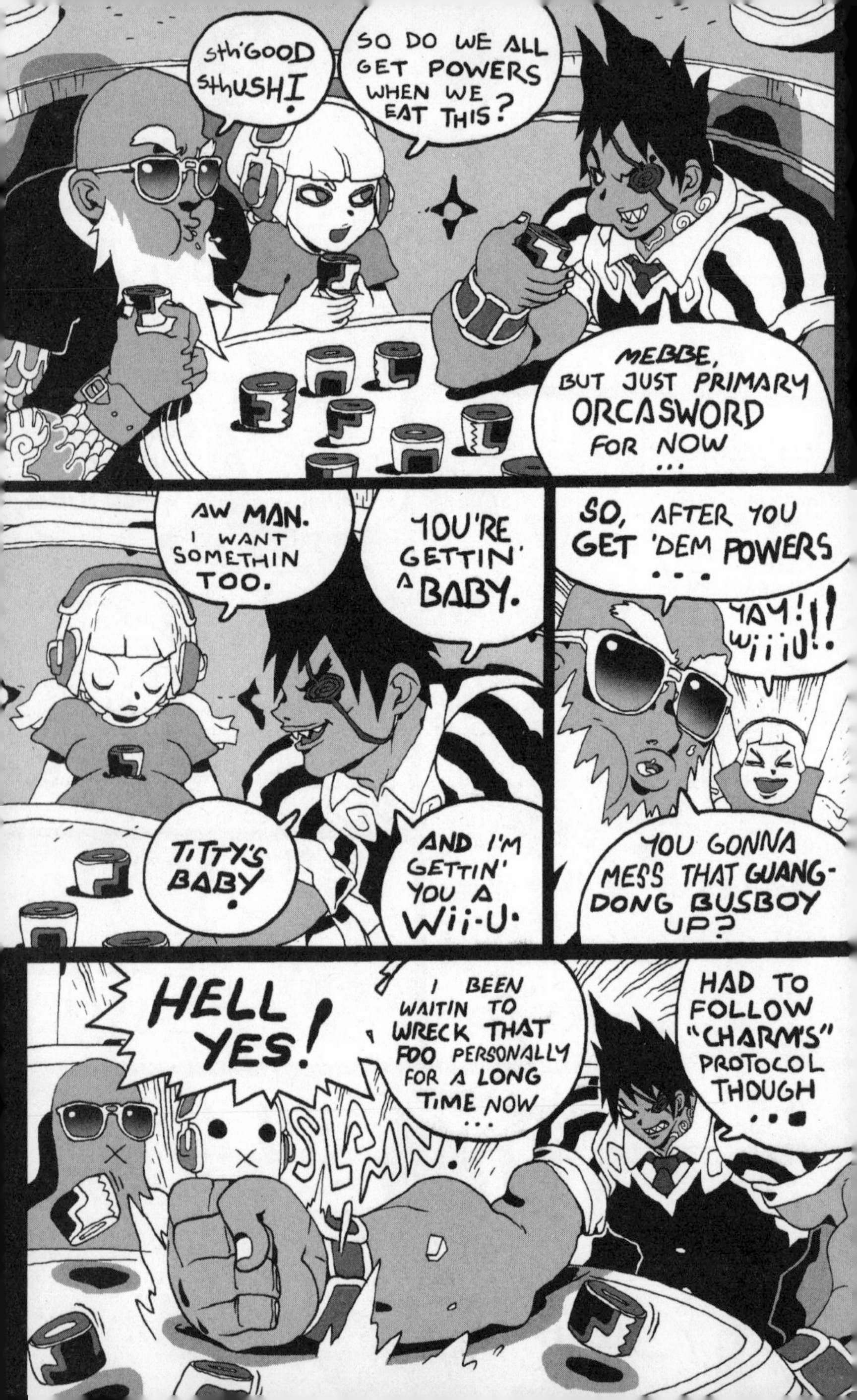
sth'GOOD sthUSHI.
SO DO WE ALL GET POWERS WHEN WE EAT THIS?
MEBBE, BUT JUST PRIMARY ORCASWORD FOR NOW ...
AW MAN. I WANT SOMETHIN TOO.
YOU'RE GETTIN' A BABY.
TITTY'S BABY.
AND I'M GETTIN' YOU A Wii-U.
SO, AFTER YOU GET 'DEM POWERS ...
YAY! WiiiU!!!
YOU GONNA MESS THAT GUANG-DONG BUSBOY UP?
HELL YES!
I BEEN WAITIN TO WRECK THAT FOO PERSONALLY FOR A LONG TIME NOW ...
SLAM!
HAD TO FOLLOW "CHARM'S" PROTOCOL THOUGH ...

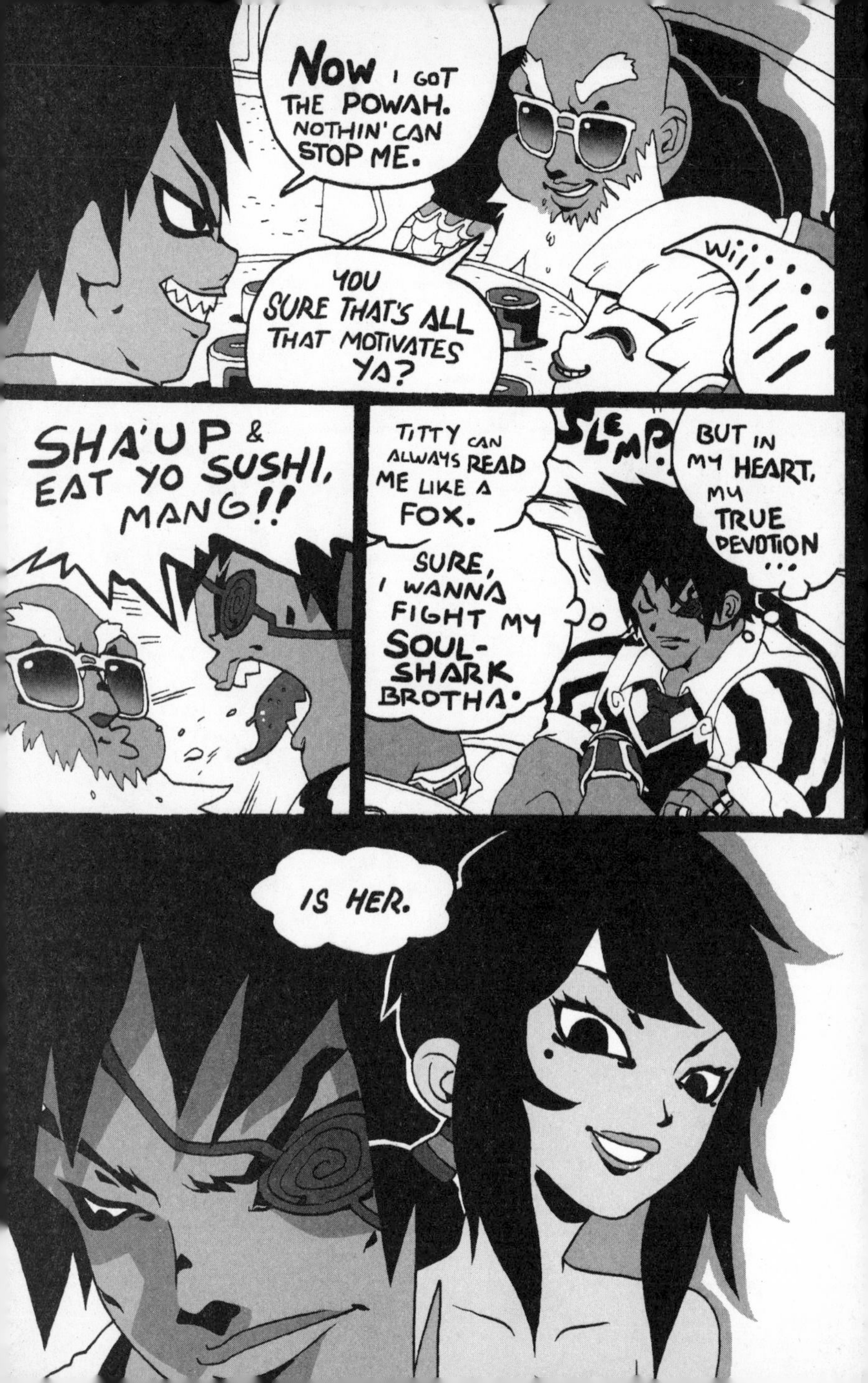
NOW I GOT THE POWAH. NOTHIN' CAN STOP ME.
YOU SURE THAT'S ALL THAT MOTIVATES YA?
Wii
SHA'UP & EAT YO SUSHI, MANG!!
SLEMP.
TITTY CAN ALWAYS READ ME LIKE A FOX.
SURE, I WANNA FIGHT MY SOUL-SHARK BROTHA.
BUT IN MY HEART, MY TRUE DEVOTION ...
IS HER.

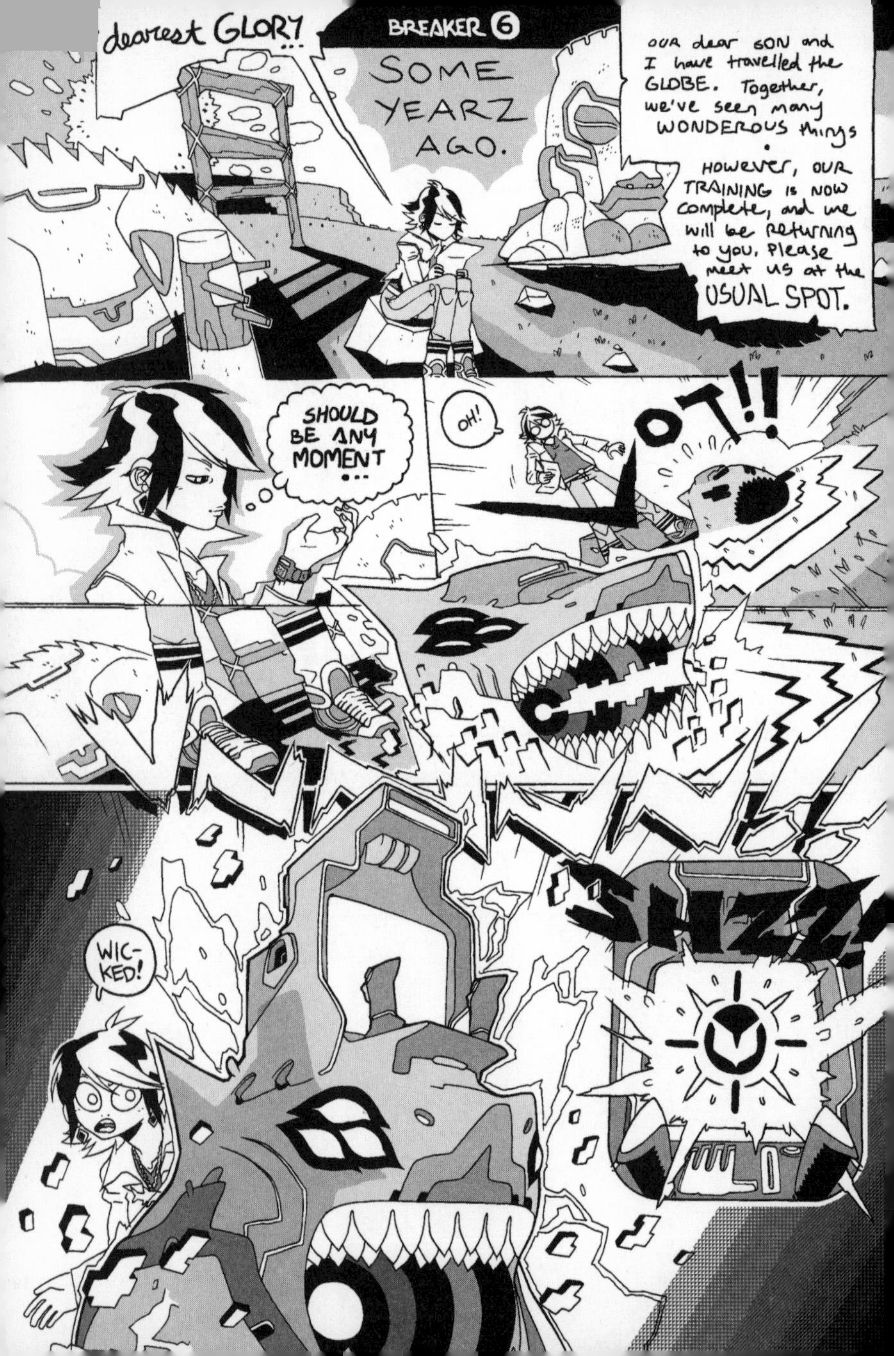
BREAKER 6
dearest GLORY...
SOME YEARZ AGO.
our dear son and I have travelled the GLOBE. Together, we've seen many WONDEROUS things.
HOWEVER, OUR TRAINING is NOW complete, and we will be returning to you. Please meet us at the USUAL SPOT.
SHOULD BE ANY MOMENT...
OH!
WIC-KED!

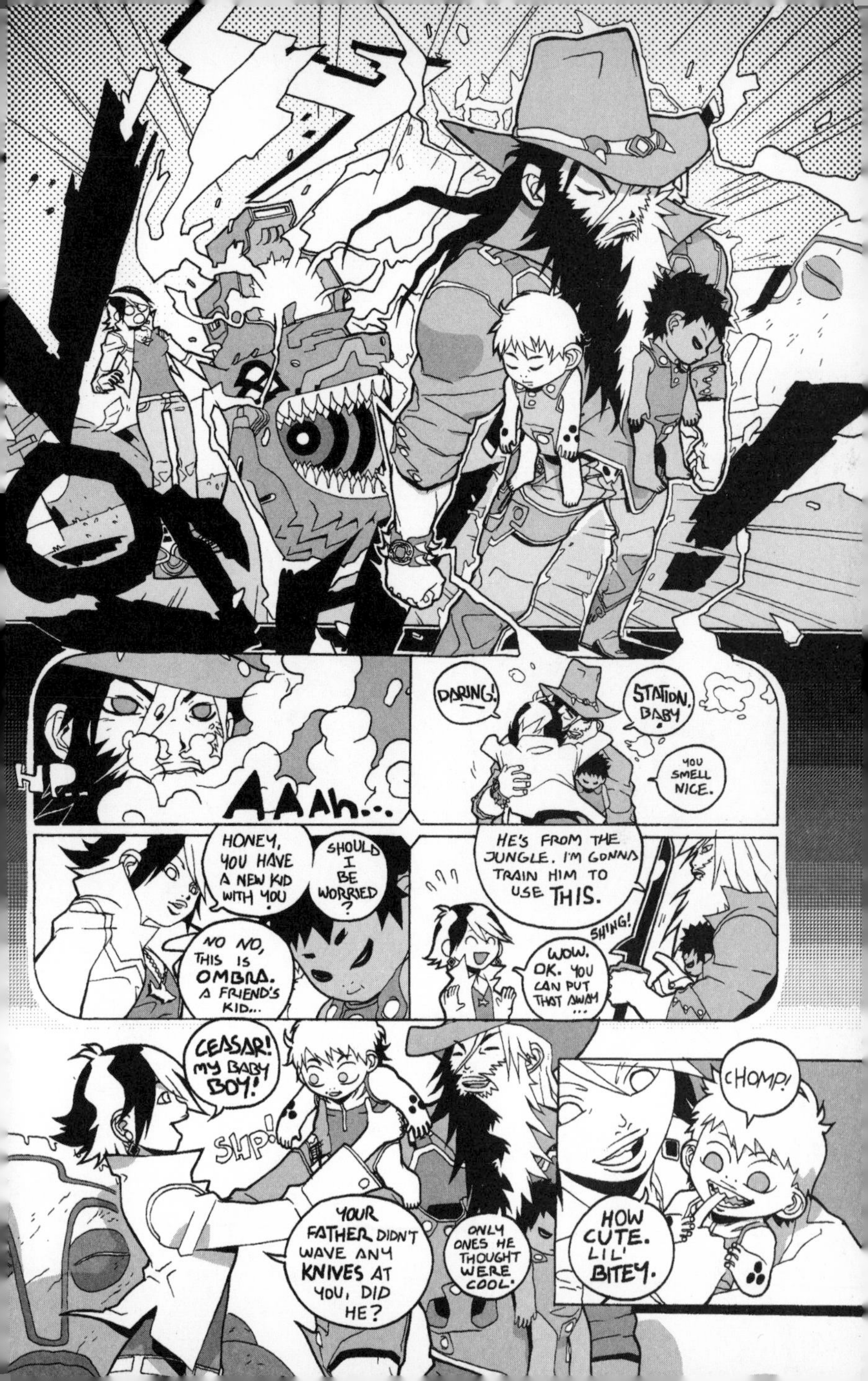
HP...
AAAh...
DARING!
STATION, BABY
YOU SMELL NICE.
HONEY, YOU HAVE A NEW KID WITH YOU
SHOULD I BE WORRIED?
NO NO, THIS IS OMBRA. A FRIEND'S KID...
HE'S FROM THE JUNGLE. I'M GONNA TRAIN HIM TO USE THIS.
SHING!
WOW. OK. YOU CAN PUT THAT AWAY...
CEASAR! MY BABY BOY!
SHP!
YOUR FATHER DIDN'T WAVE ANY KNIVES AT YOU, DID HE?
ONLY ONES HE THOUGHT WERE COOL.
CHOMP!
HOW CUTE. LIL' BITEY.

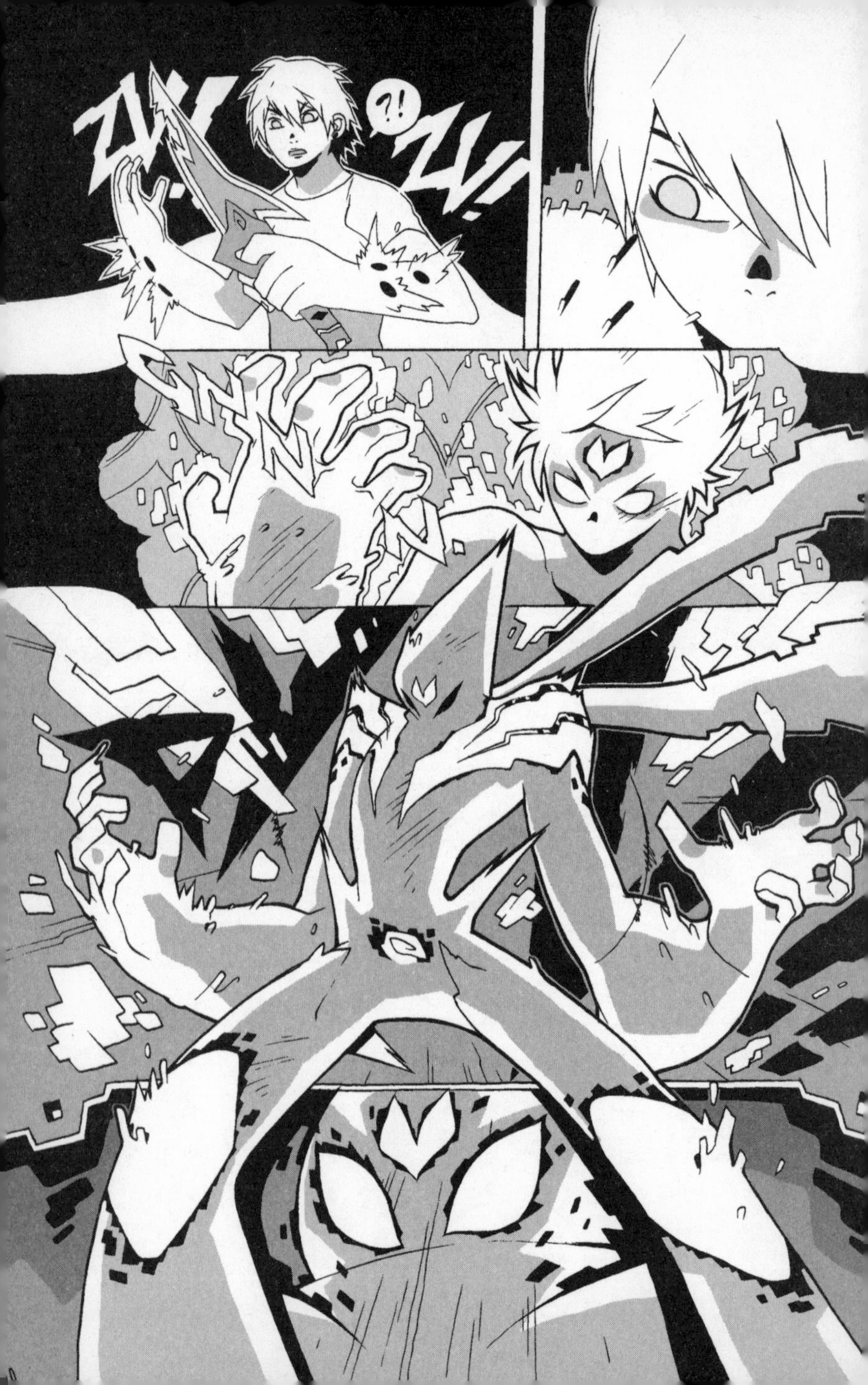

ZZT
?!
ZZT

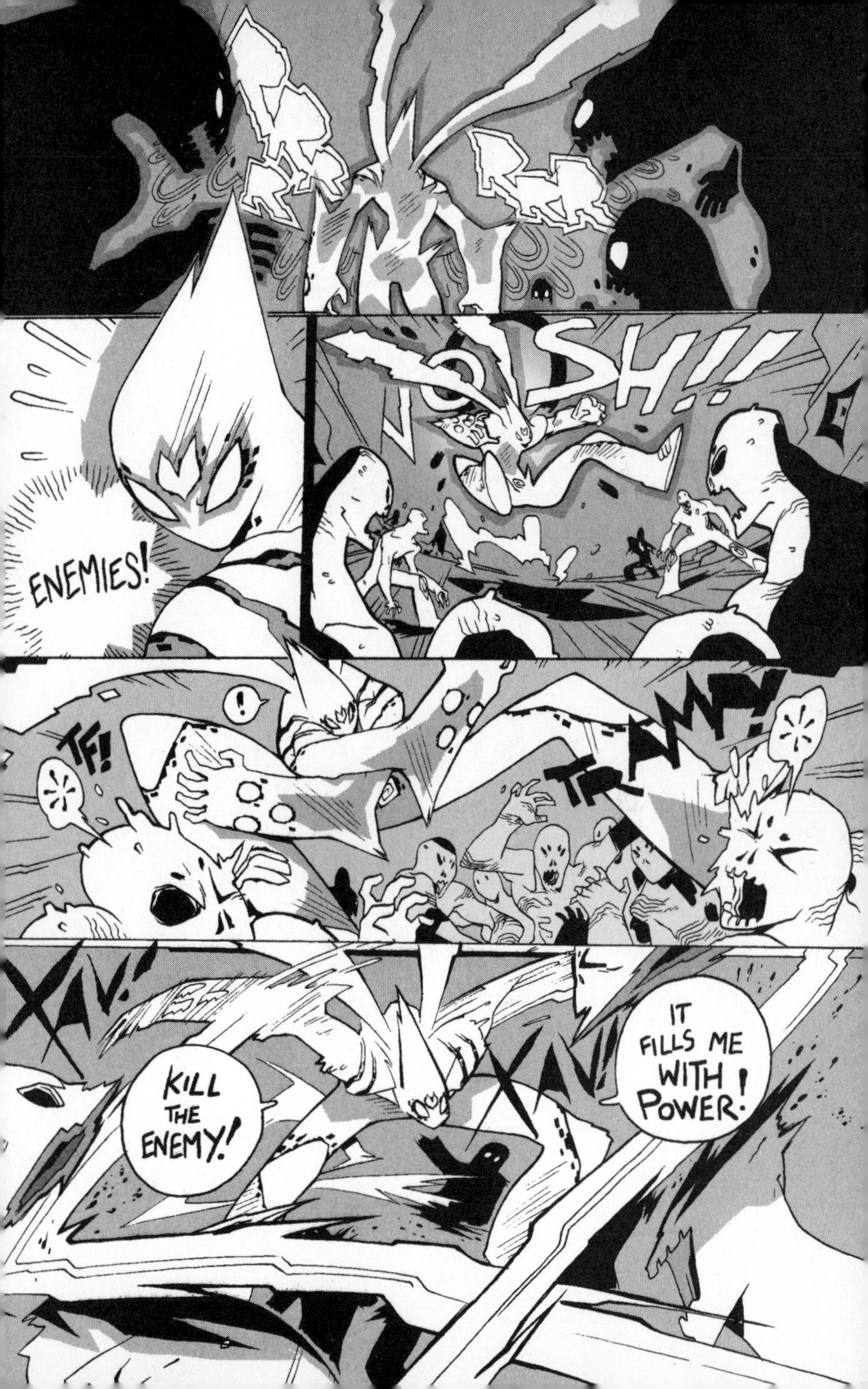

ENEMIES!
KILL THE ENEMY!
IT FILLS ME WITH POWER!

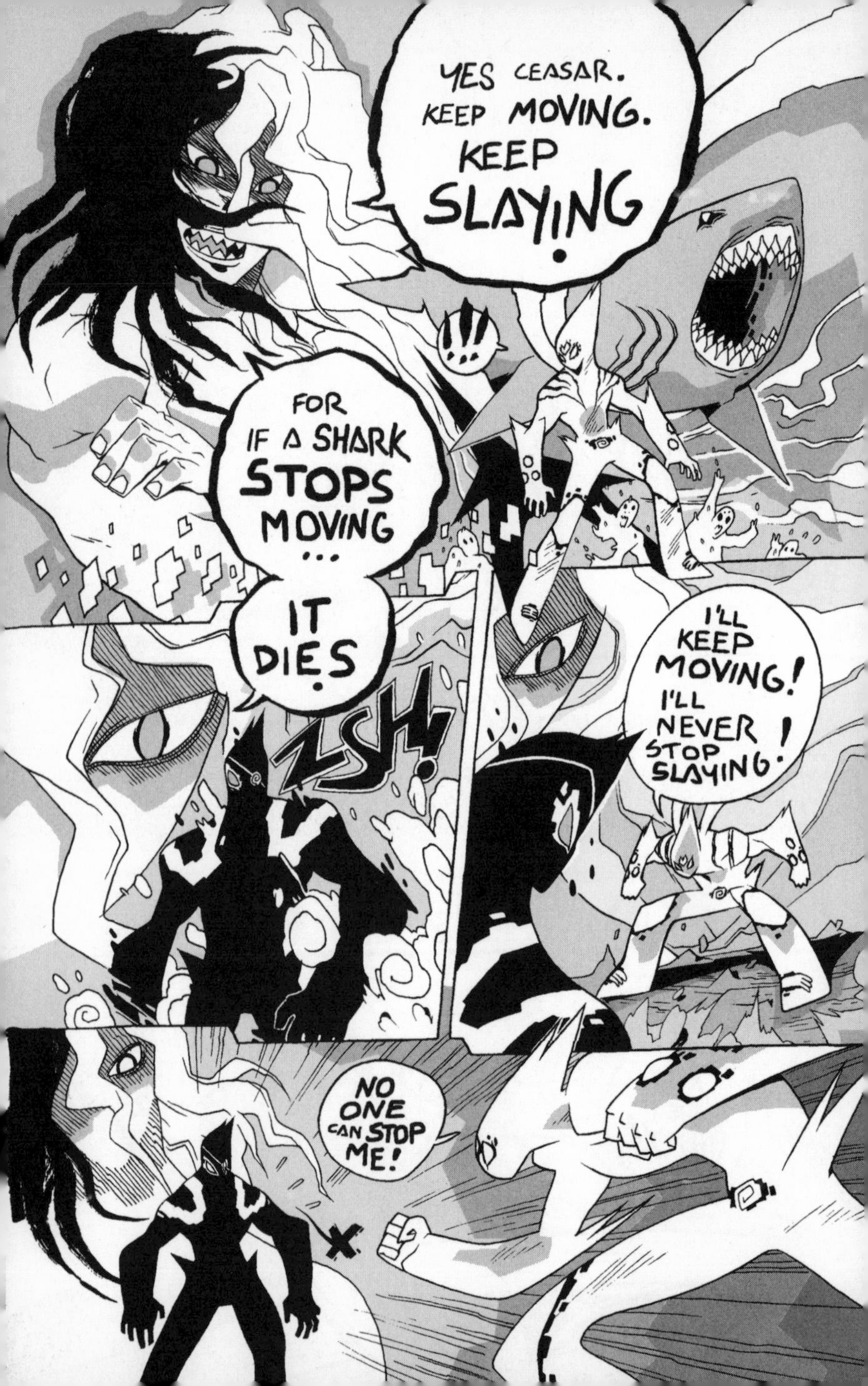
YES CEASAR. KEEP MOVING. KEEP SLAYING!
!!
FOR IF A SHARK STOPS MOVING...
IT DIES.
ZSH!
I'LL KEEP MOVING! I'LL NEVER STOP SLAYING!
NO ONE CAN STOP ME!

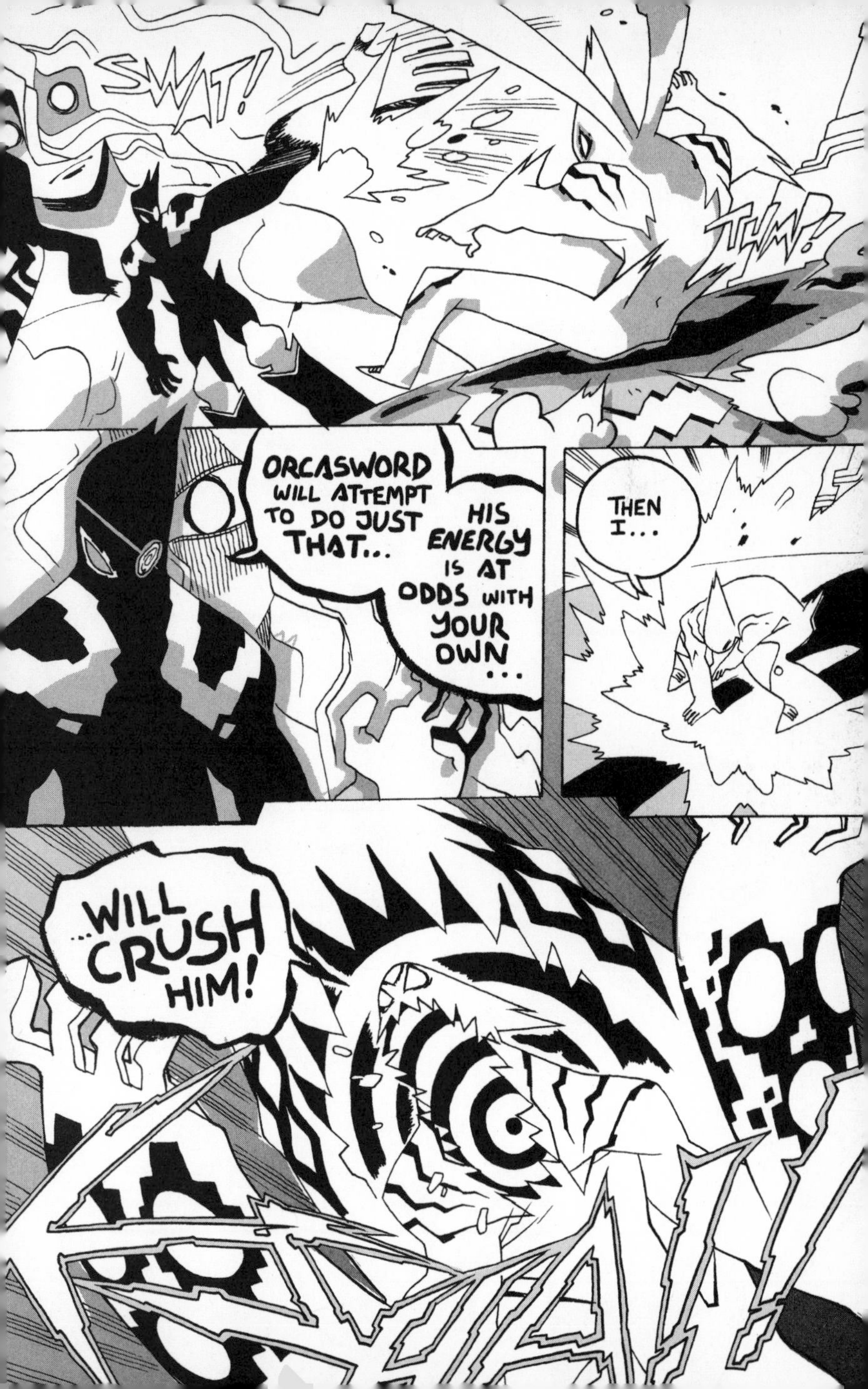
SWAT!
THMP!
ORCASWORD WILL ATTEMPT TO DO JUST THAT...
HIS ENERGY IS AT ODDS WITH YOUR OWN...
THEN I...
...WILL CRUSH HIM!

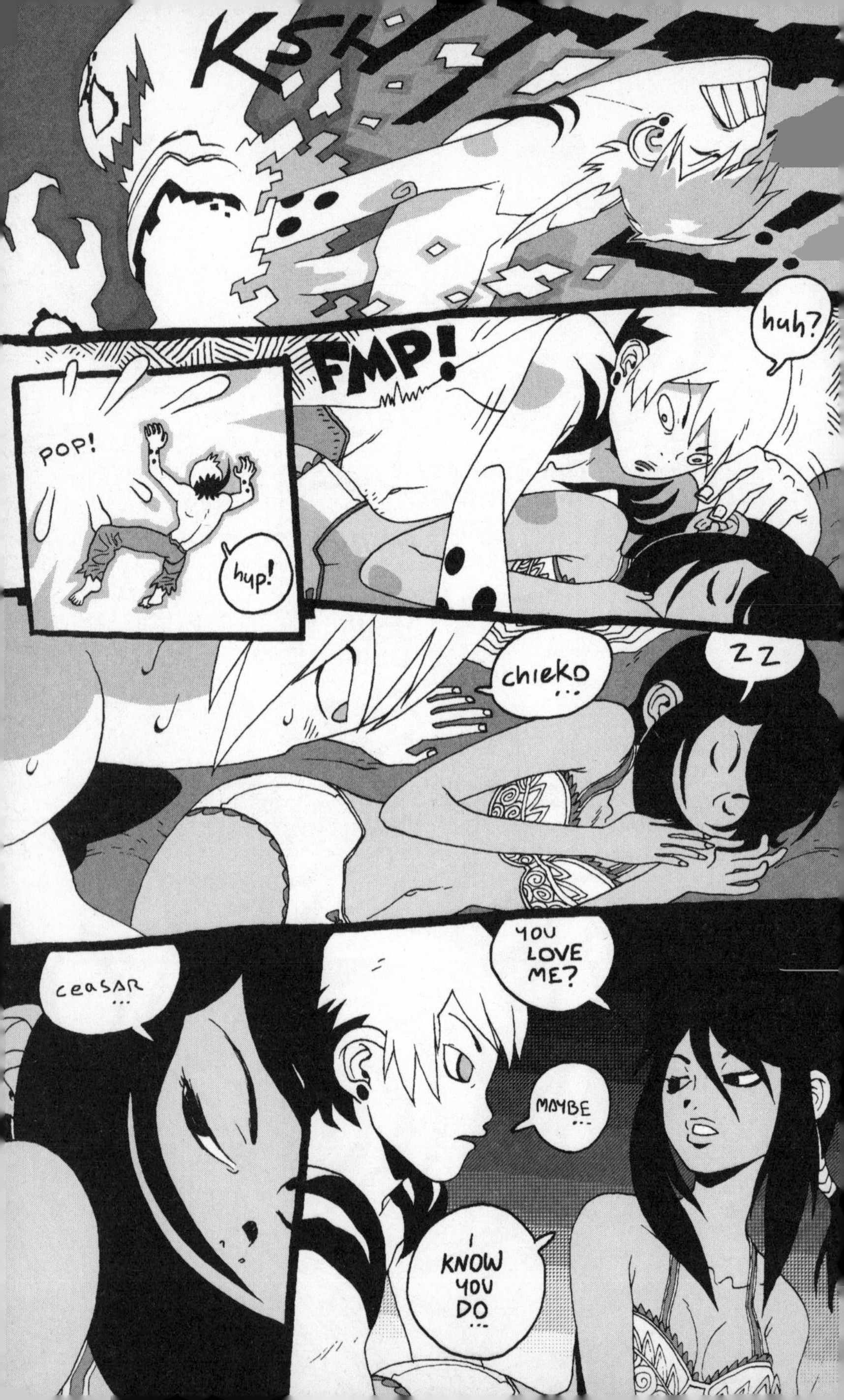
KSHT!
FMP!
huh?
POP!
hup!
chieko ...
ZZ
ceasar ...
YOU LOVE ME?
MAYBE ...
I KNOW YOU DO ...

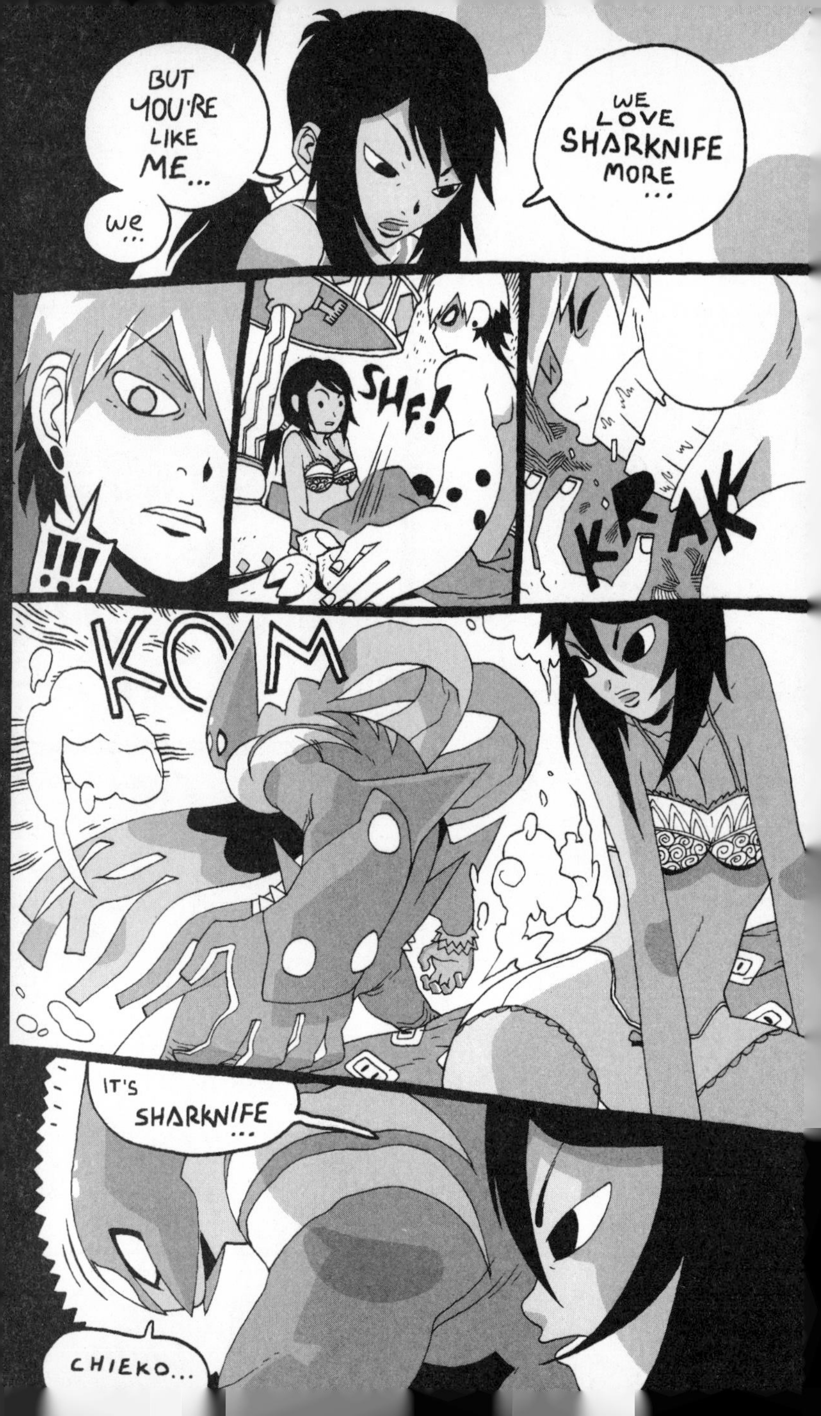
BUT YOU'RE LIKE ME...
WE...
WE LOVE SHARKNIFE MORE...
!!!
SHF!
KRAK
KOM
IT'S SHARKNIFE...
CHIEKO...

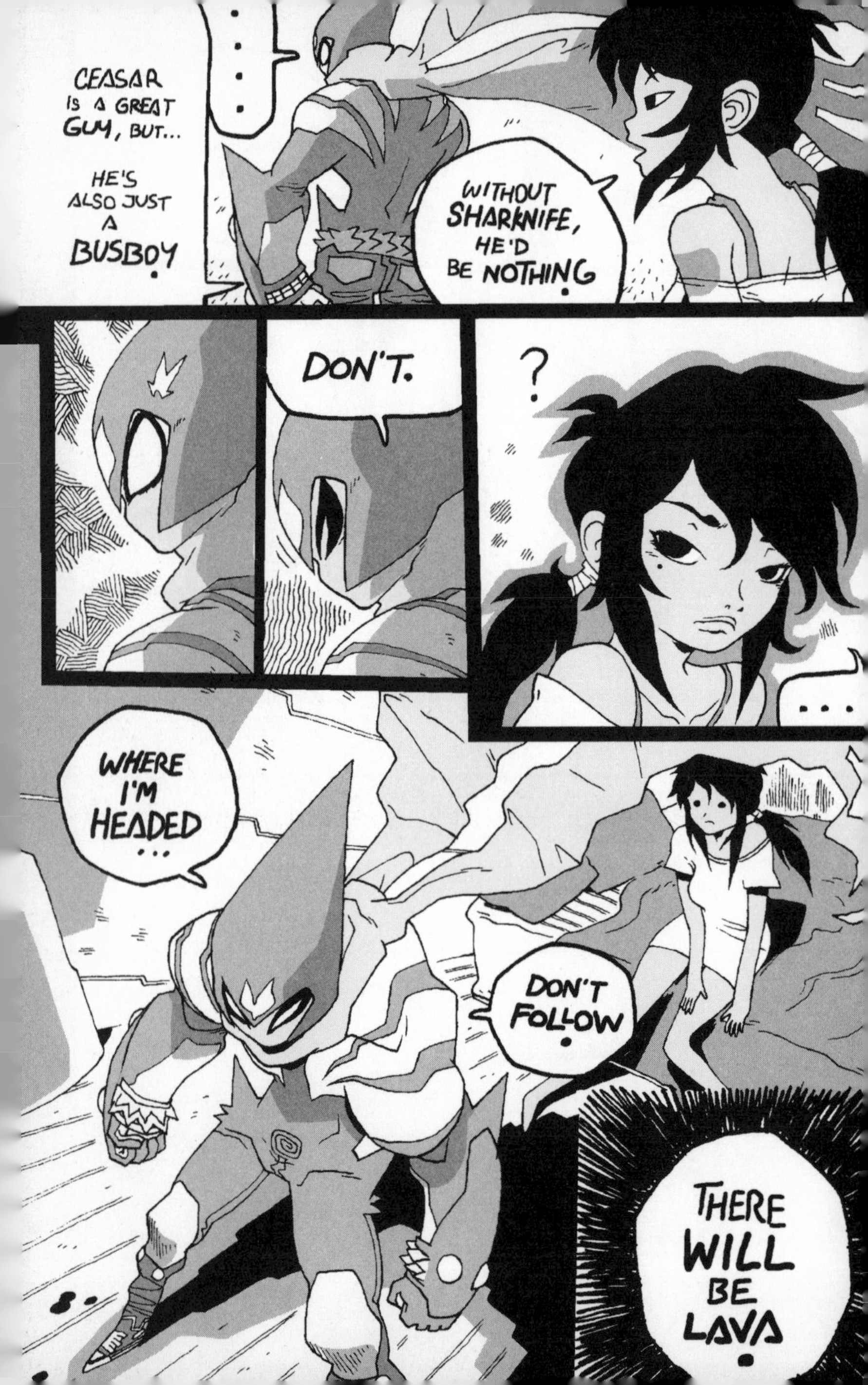
...
CEASAR IS A GREAT GUY, BUT...
HE'S ALSO JUST A BUSBOY.
WITHOUT SHARKNIFE, HE'D BE NOTHING.
DON'T.
?
...
WHERE I'M HEADED...
DON'T FOLLOW.
THERE WILL BE LAVA.

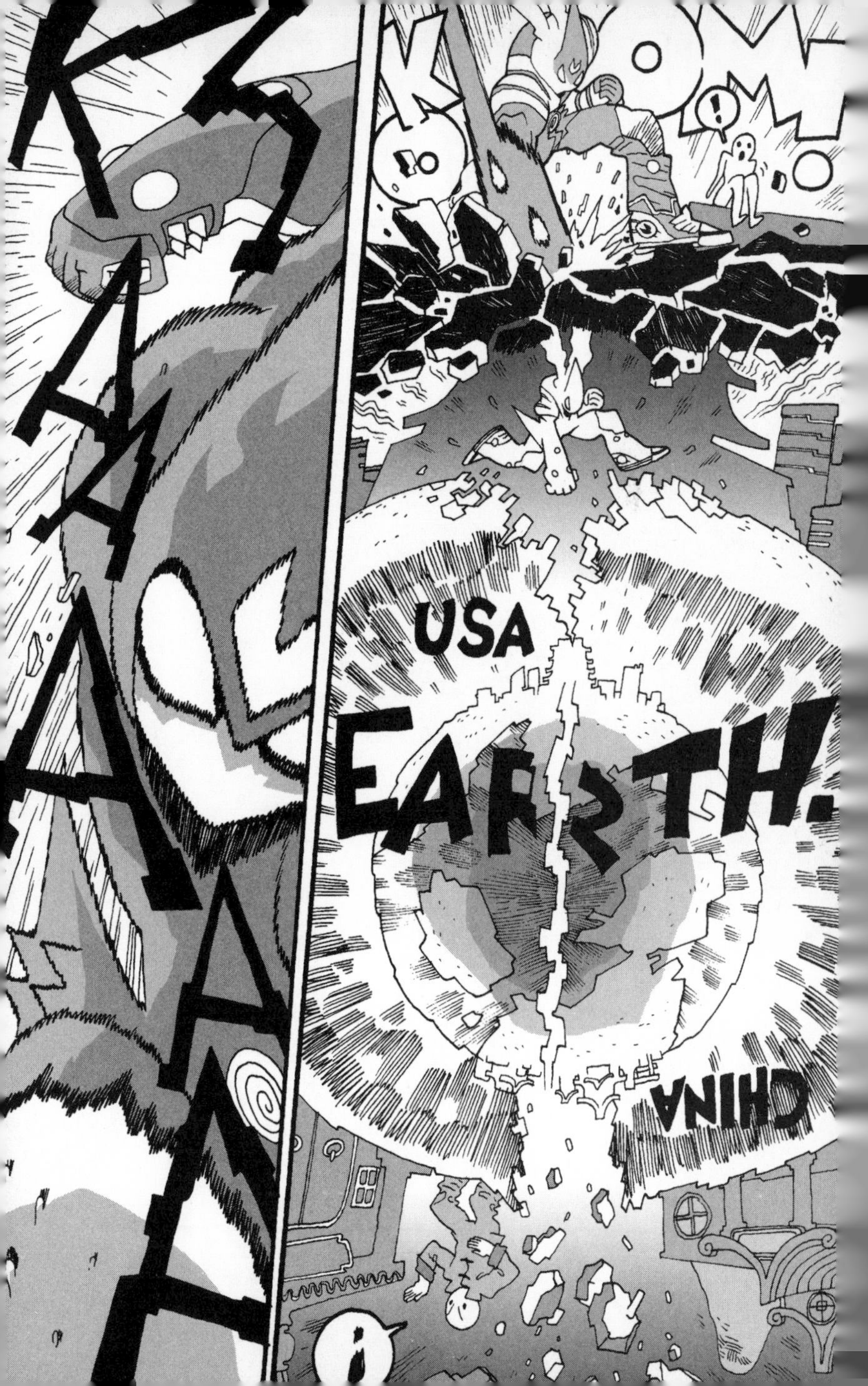
!
USA
EARTH!
CHINA

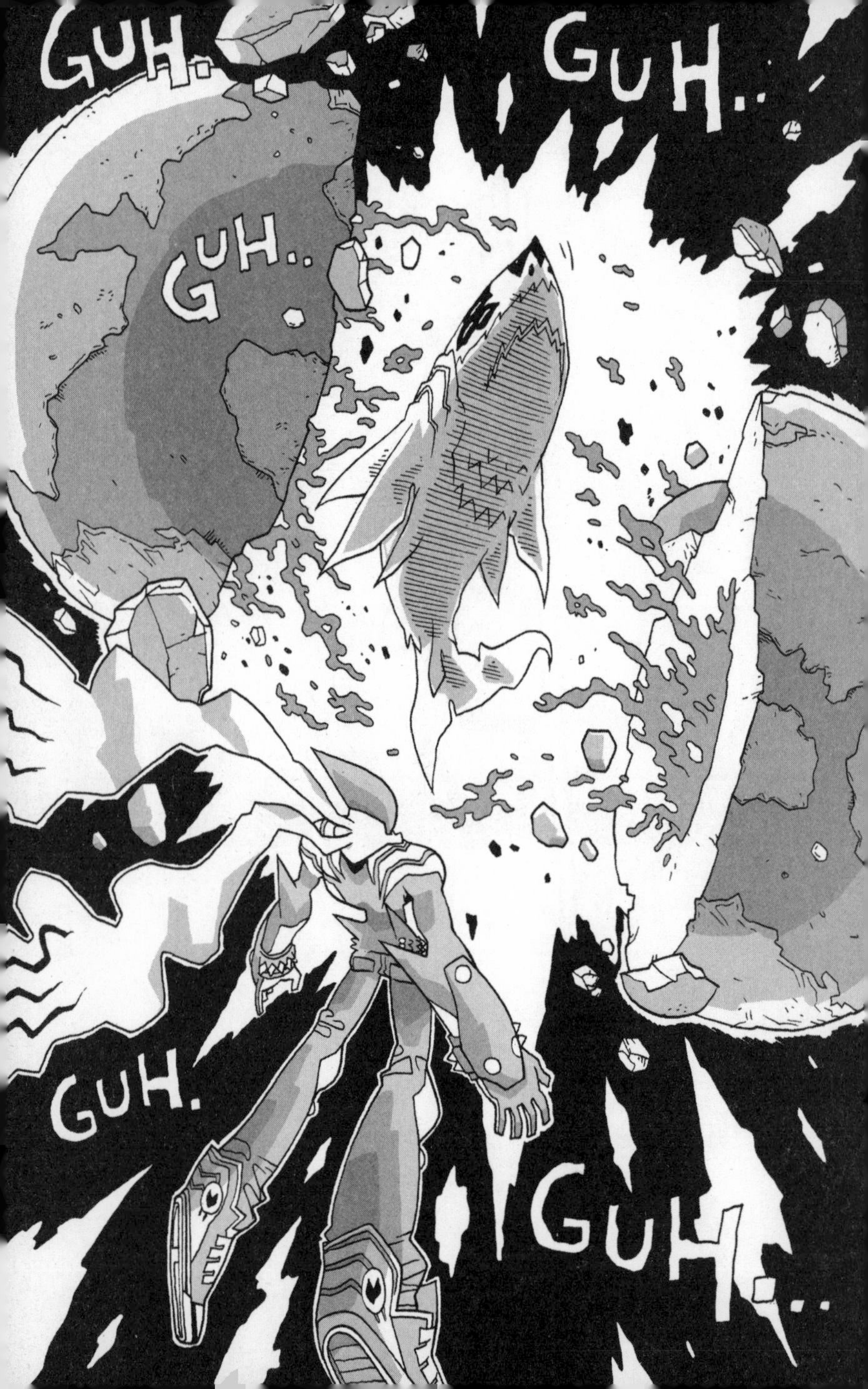
GUH.
GUH..
GUH..
GUH.
GUH...

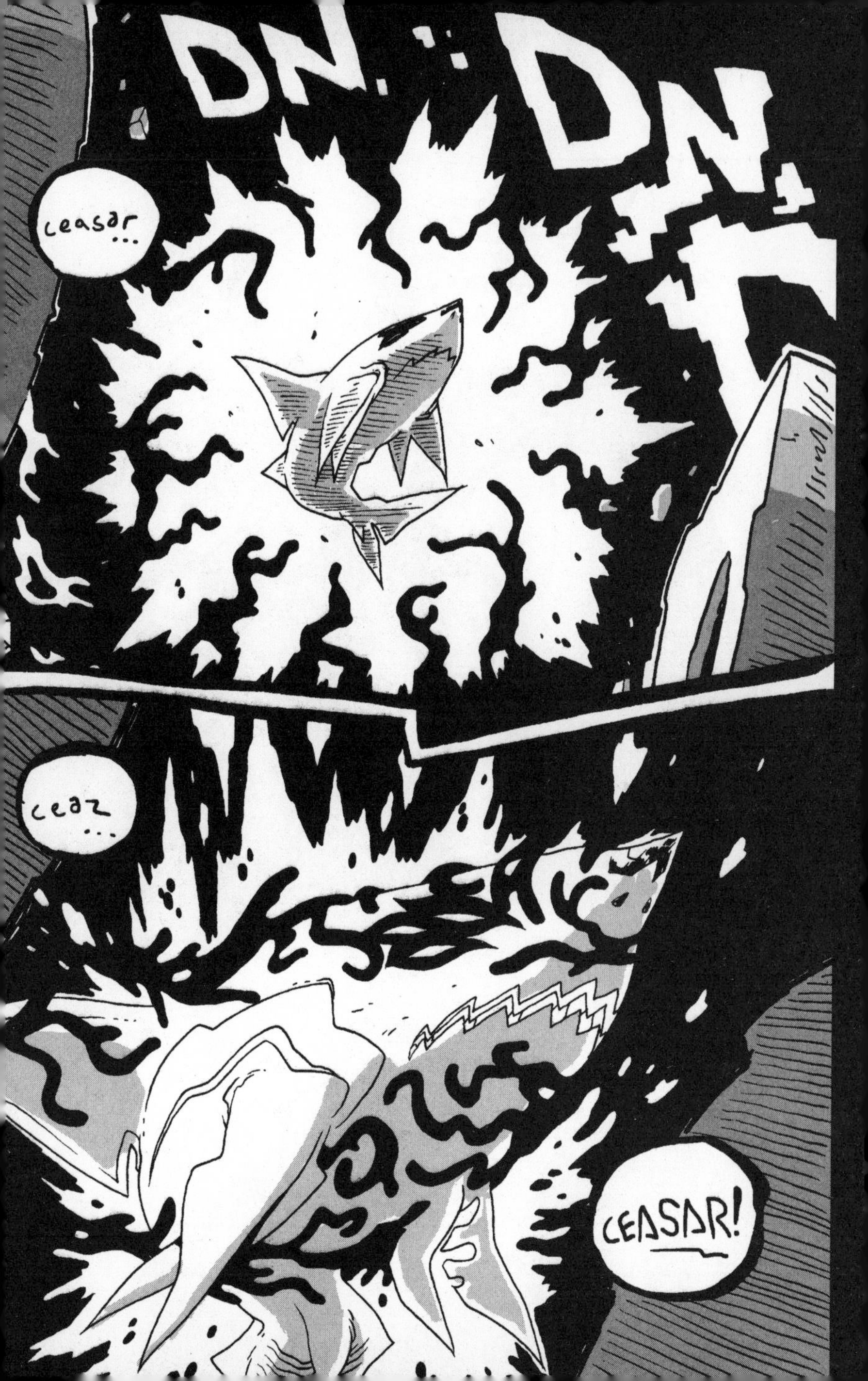
DN. DN.
ceasar...
ceaz...
CEASAR!

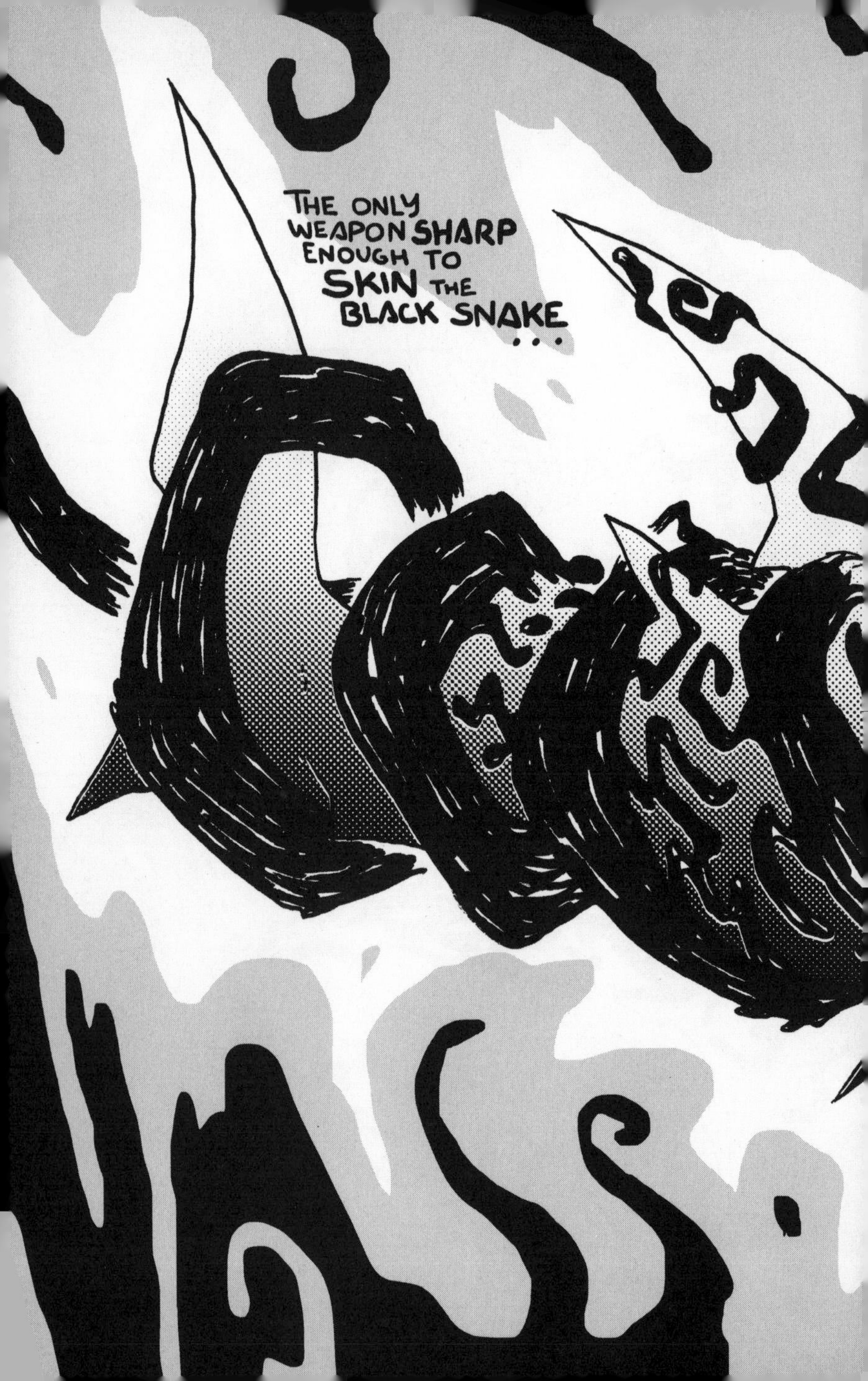
THE ONLY WEAPON SHARP ENOUGH TO SKIN THE BLACK SNAKE . . .

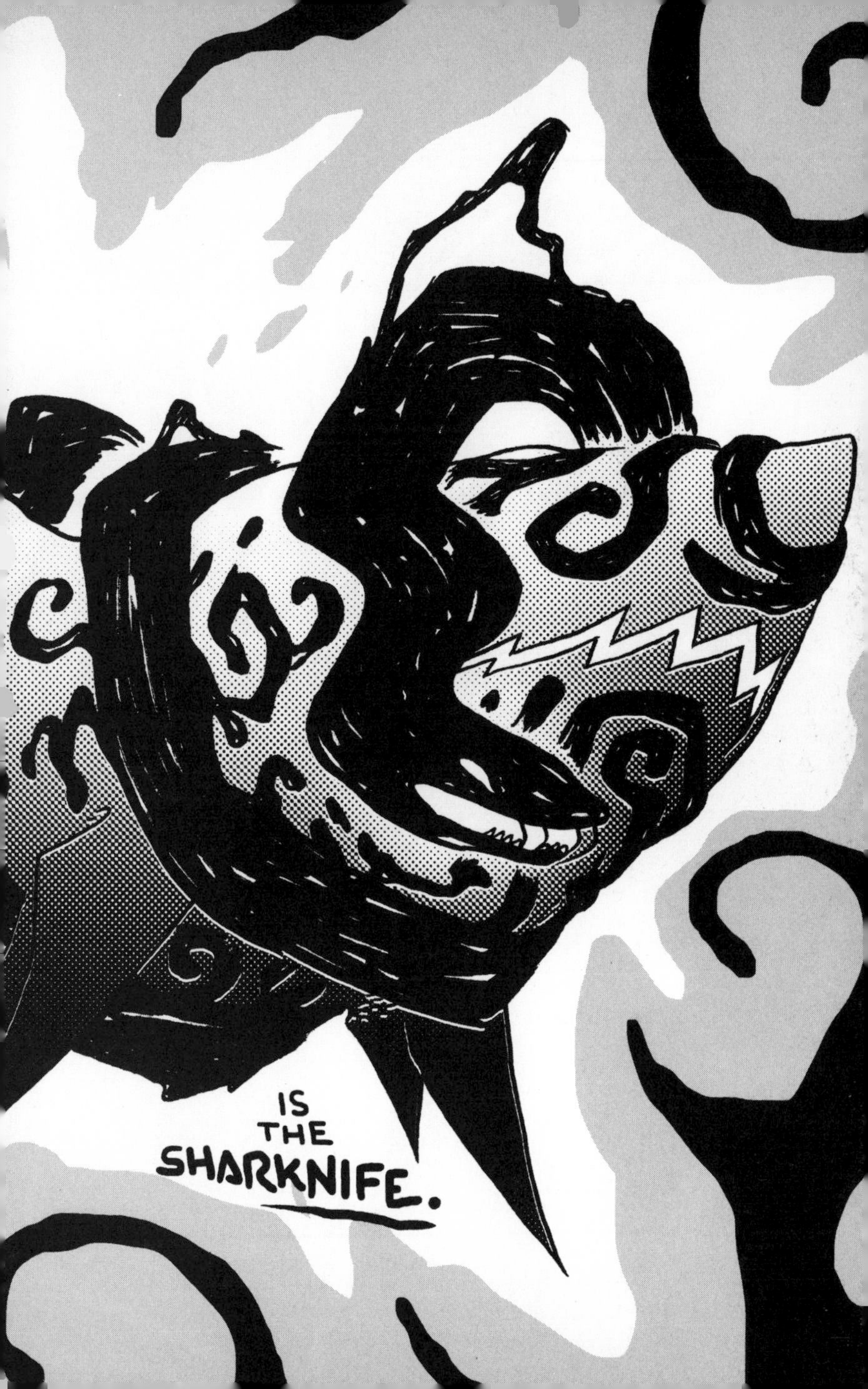
IS
THE
SHARKNIFE.

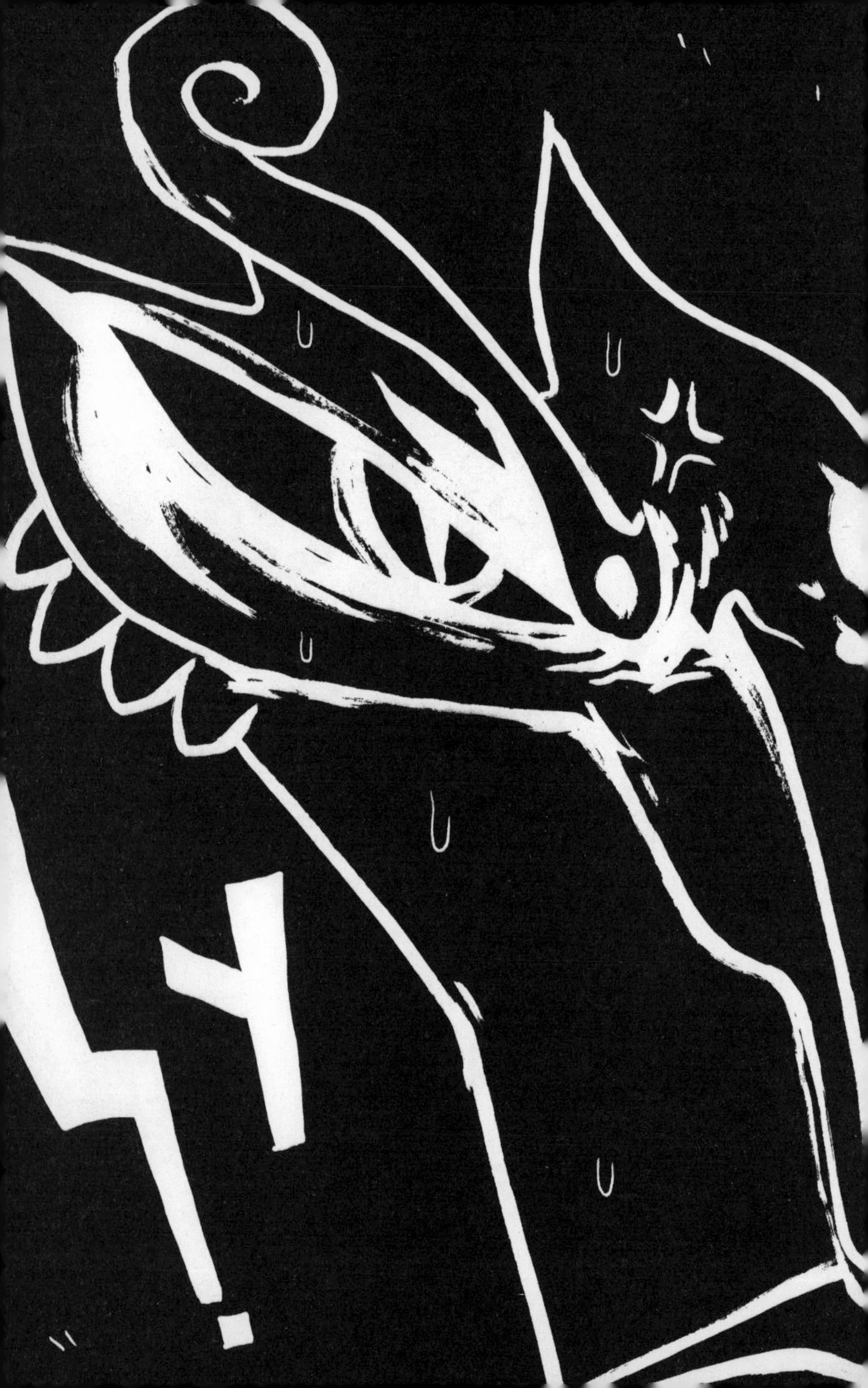

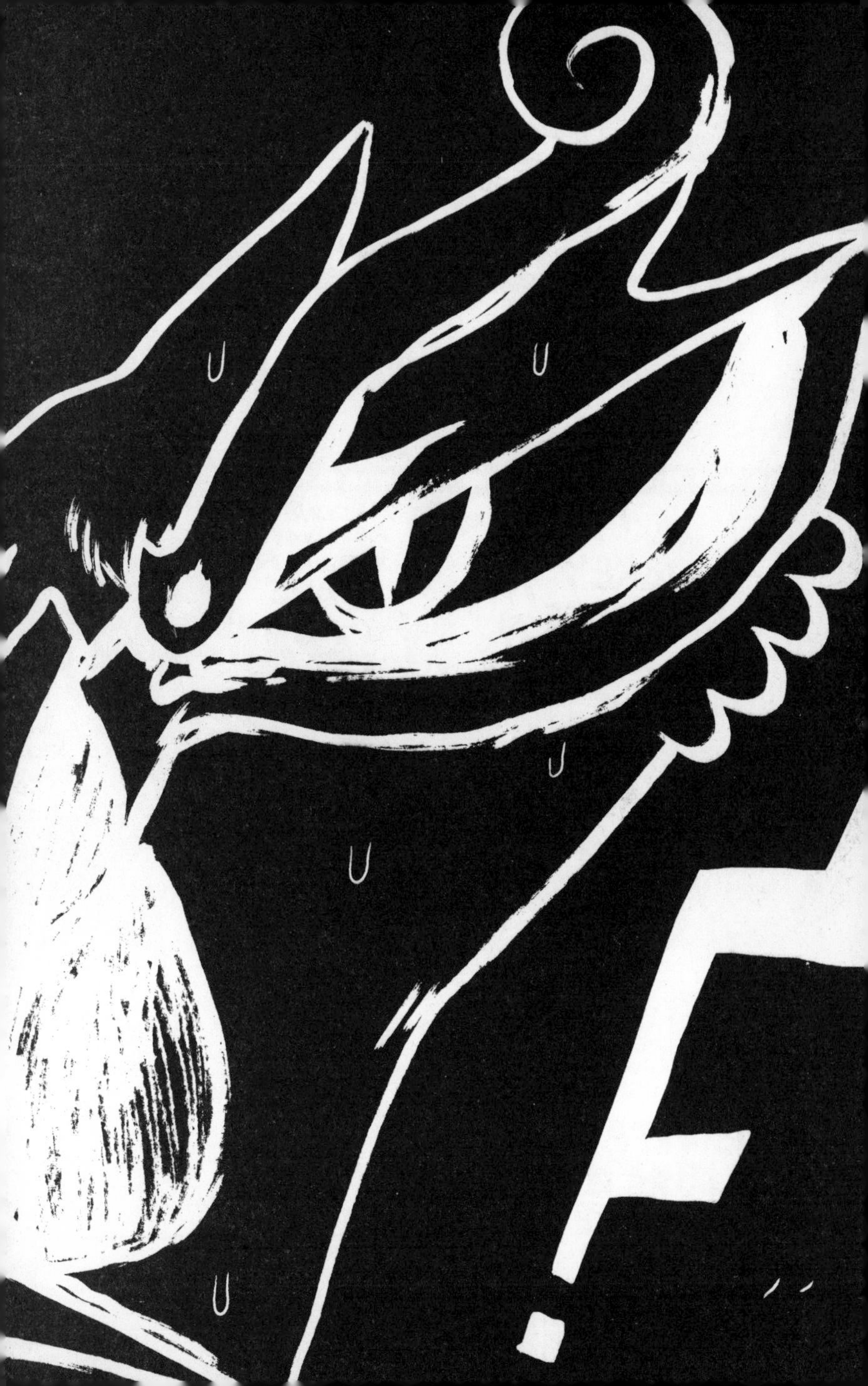

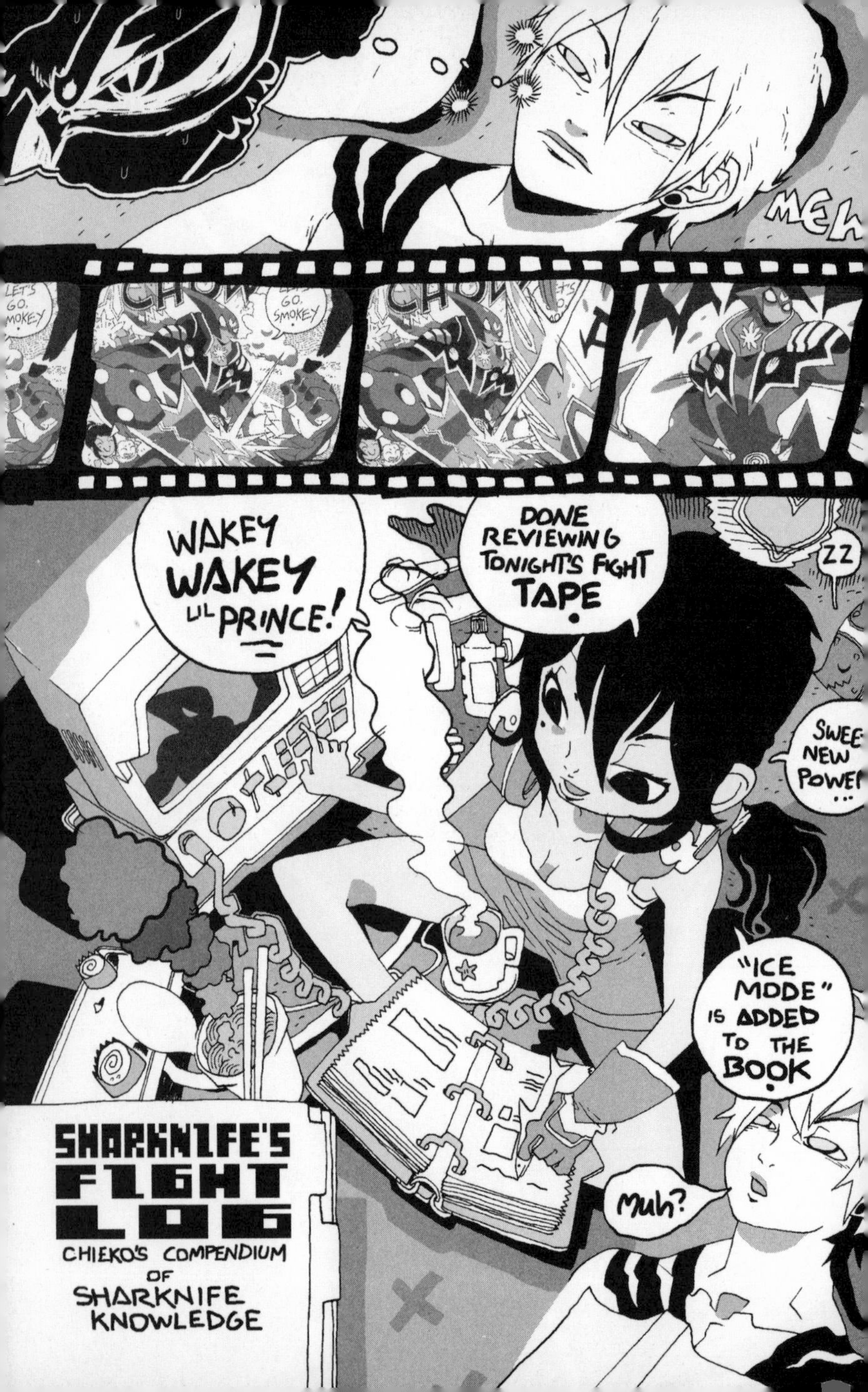
MEH
LET'S GO, SMOKEY
LET'S GO, SMOKEY
WAKEY WAKEY LIL PRINCE!
DONE REVIEWING TONIGHT'S FIGHT TAPE
ZZ
SWEE NEW POWE ...
"ICE MODE" IS ADDED TO THE BOOK
Muh?

SHARKNIFE'S FIGHT LOG

CHIEKO'S COMPENDIUM OF SHARKNIFE KNOWLEDGE

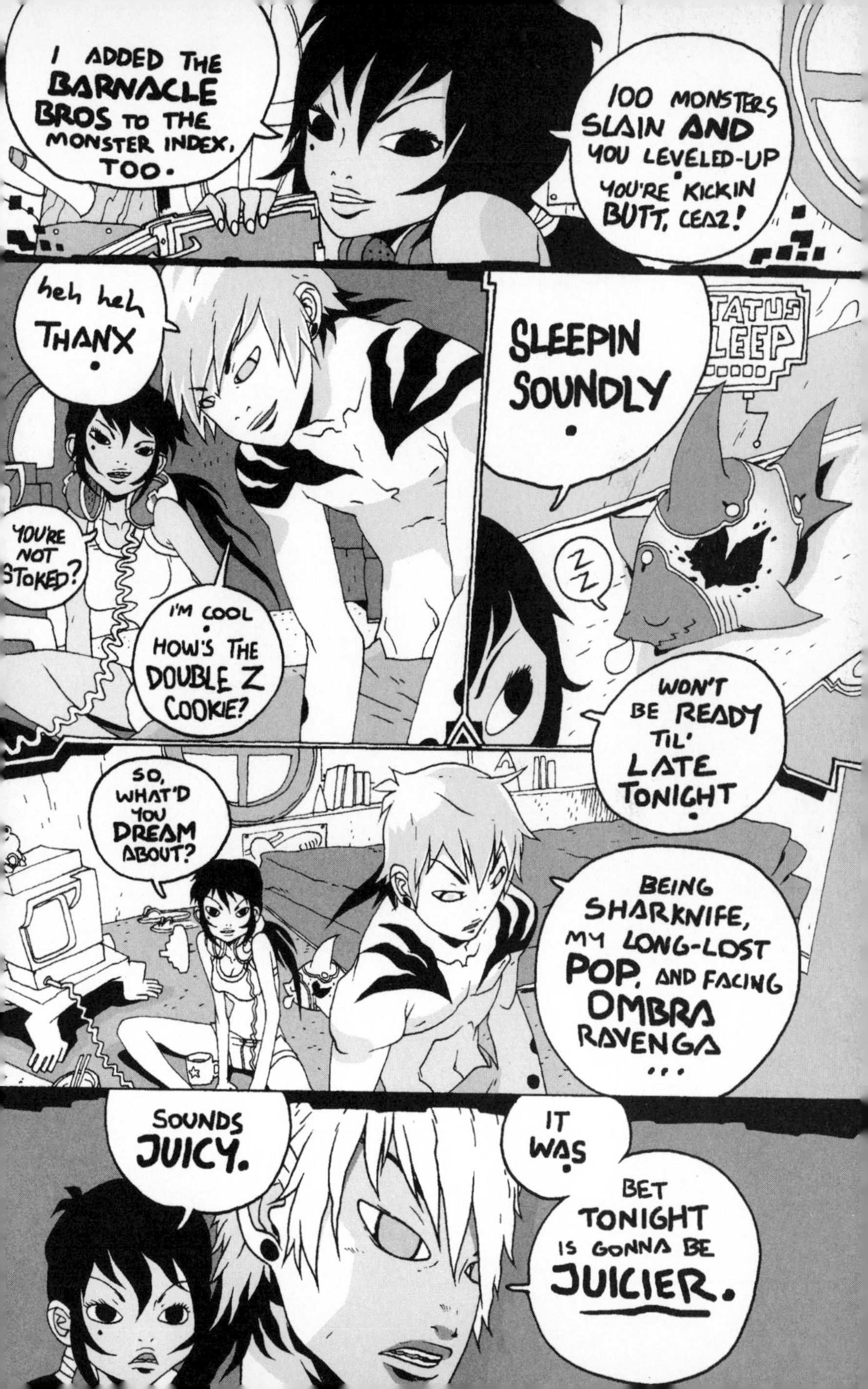
I ADDED THE BARNACLE BROS TO THE MONSTER INDEX, TOO.
100 MONSTERS SLAIN AND YOU LEVELED-UP. YOU'RE KICKIN BUTT, CEAZ!
heh heh THANX.
YOU'RE NOT STOKED?
I'M COOL. HOW'S THE DOUBLE Z COOKIE?
SLEEPIN SOUNDLY.
ZZ
WON'T BE READY TIL' LATE TONIGHT.
SO, WHAT'D YOU DREAM ABOUT?
BEING SHARKNIFE, MY LONG-LOST POP, AND FACING OMBRA RAVENGA...
SOUNDS JUICY.
IT WAS.
BET TONIGHT IS GONNA BE JUICIER.

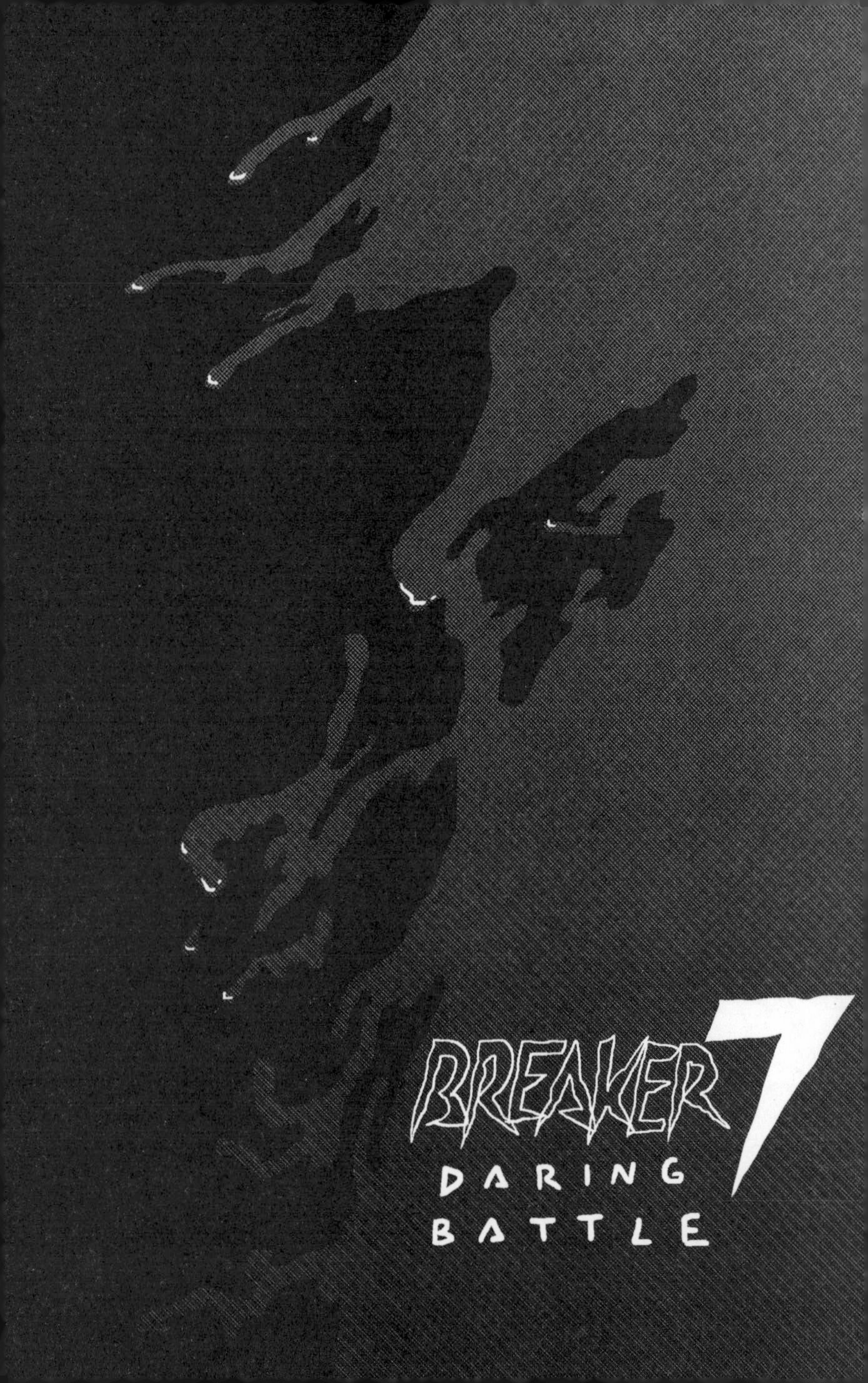
BREAKER 7
DARING BATTLE

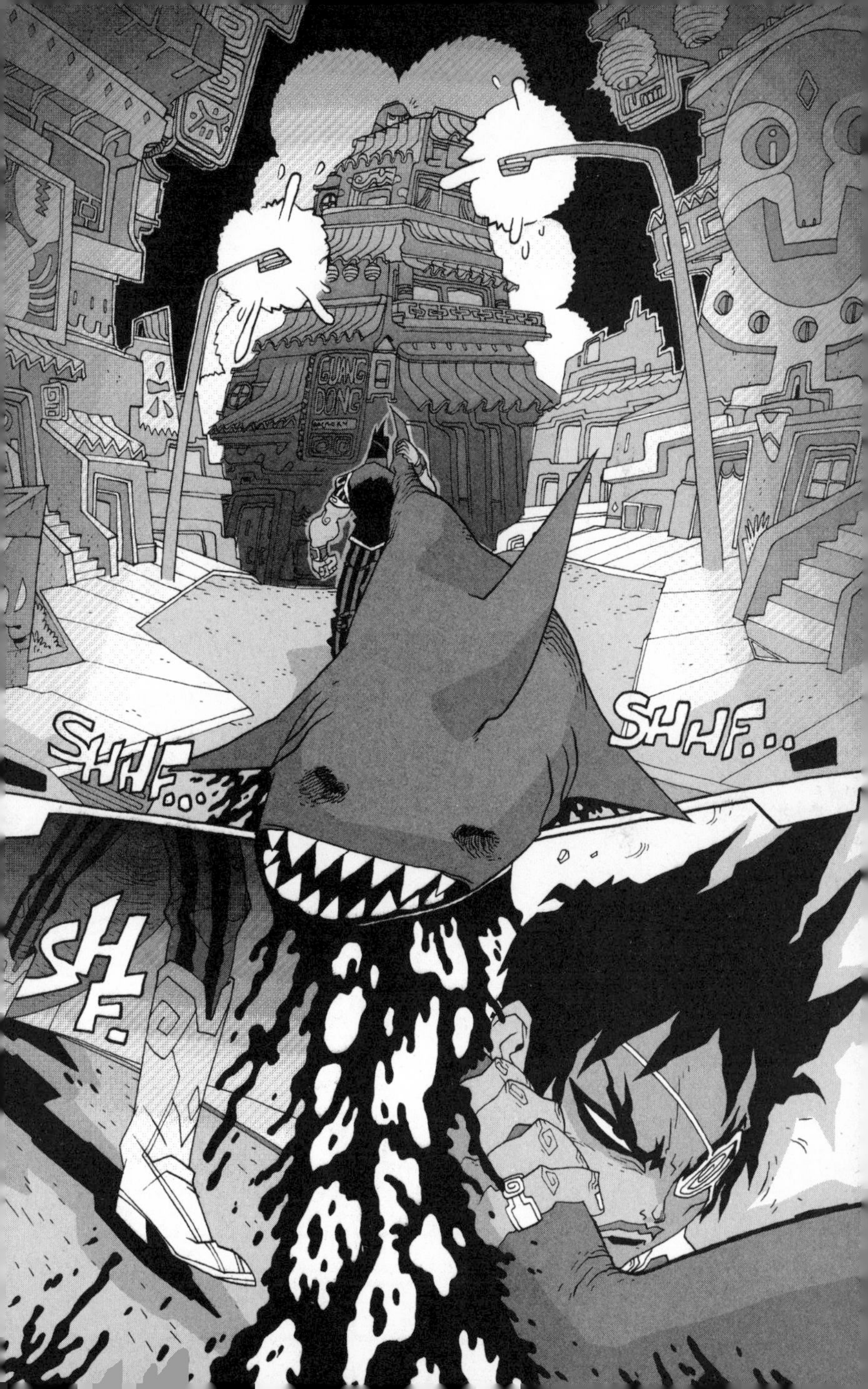
GUANG DONG
SHHF...
SHHF...
SHF.

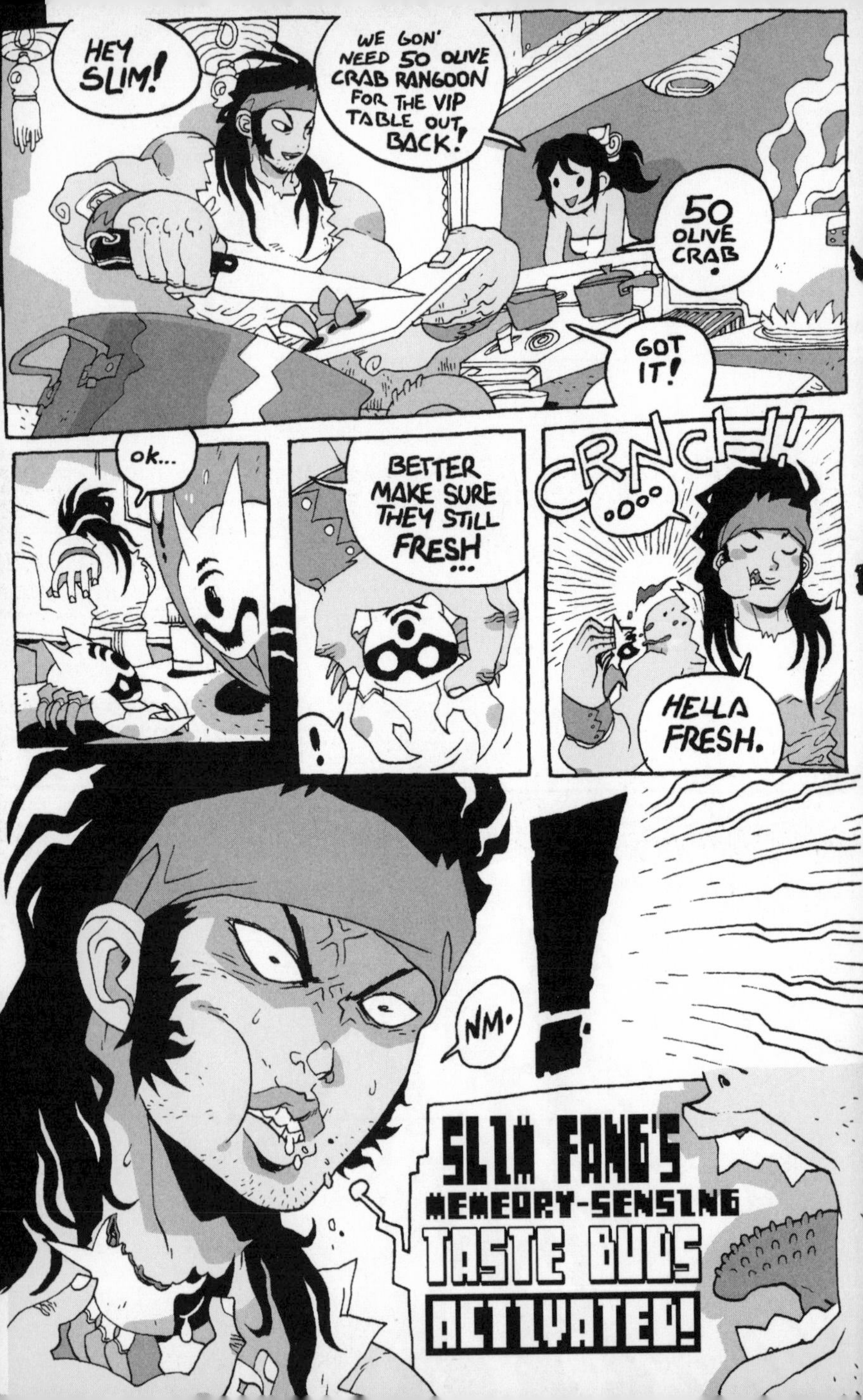
HEY SLIM!
WE GON' NEED 50 OLIVE CRAB RANGOON FOR THE VIP TABLE OUT BACK!
50 OLIVE CRAB.
GOT IT!
ok...
BETTER MAKE SURE THEY STILL FRESH...
!
CRNCH!
.o0o
HELLA FRESH.
NM.
!
SLIM FANG'S MEMORY-SENSING TASTE BUDS ACTIVATED!

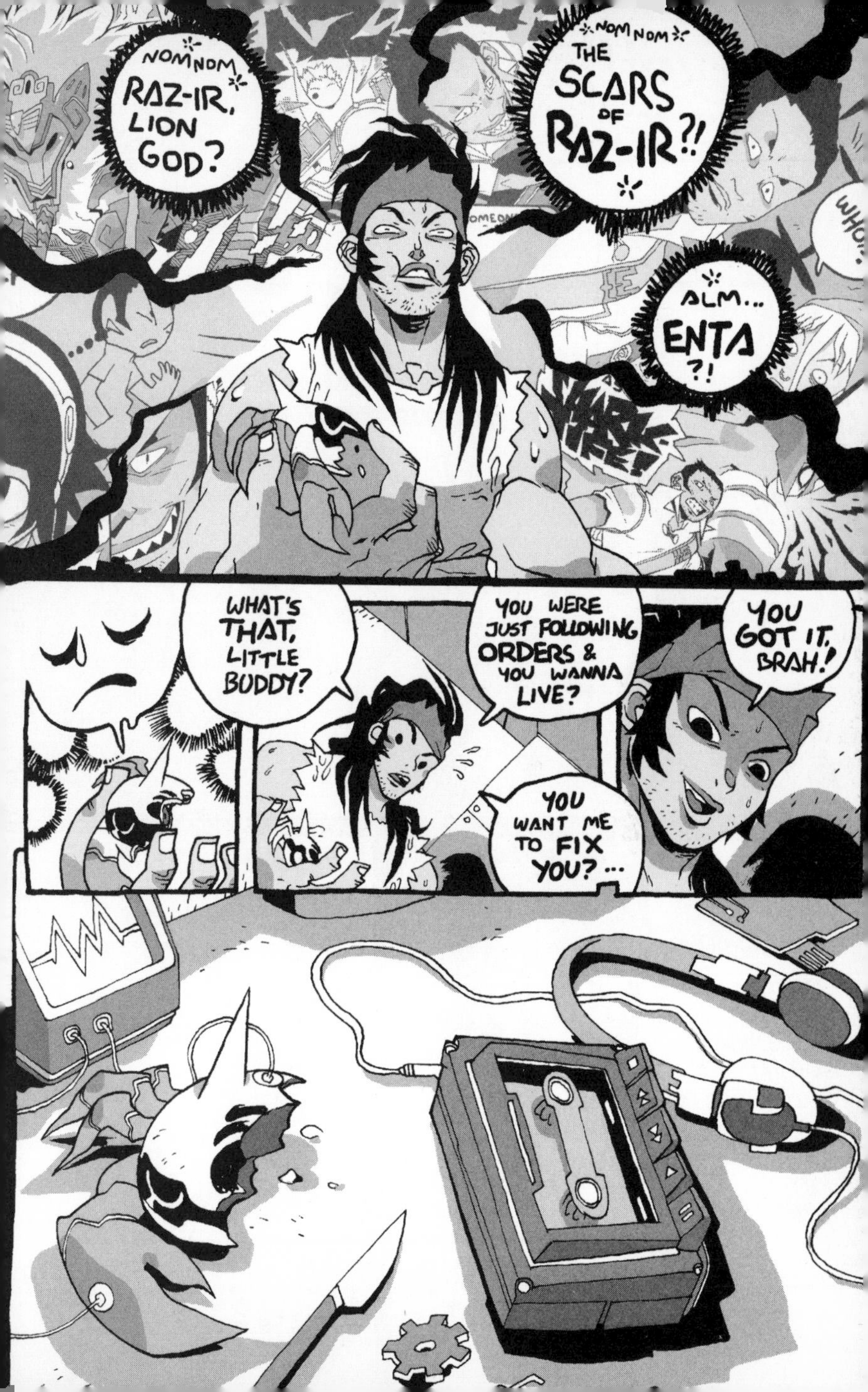
NOM NOM
RAZ-IR, LION GOD?
NOM NOM
THE SCARS OF RAZ-IR?!
WHO...
ALM... ENTA?!
WHAT'S THAT, LITTLE BUDDY?
YOU WERE JUST FOLLOWING ORDERS & YOU WANNA LIVE?
YOU WANT ME TO FIX YOU?...
YOU GOT IT, BRAH!

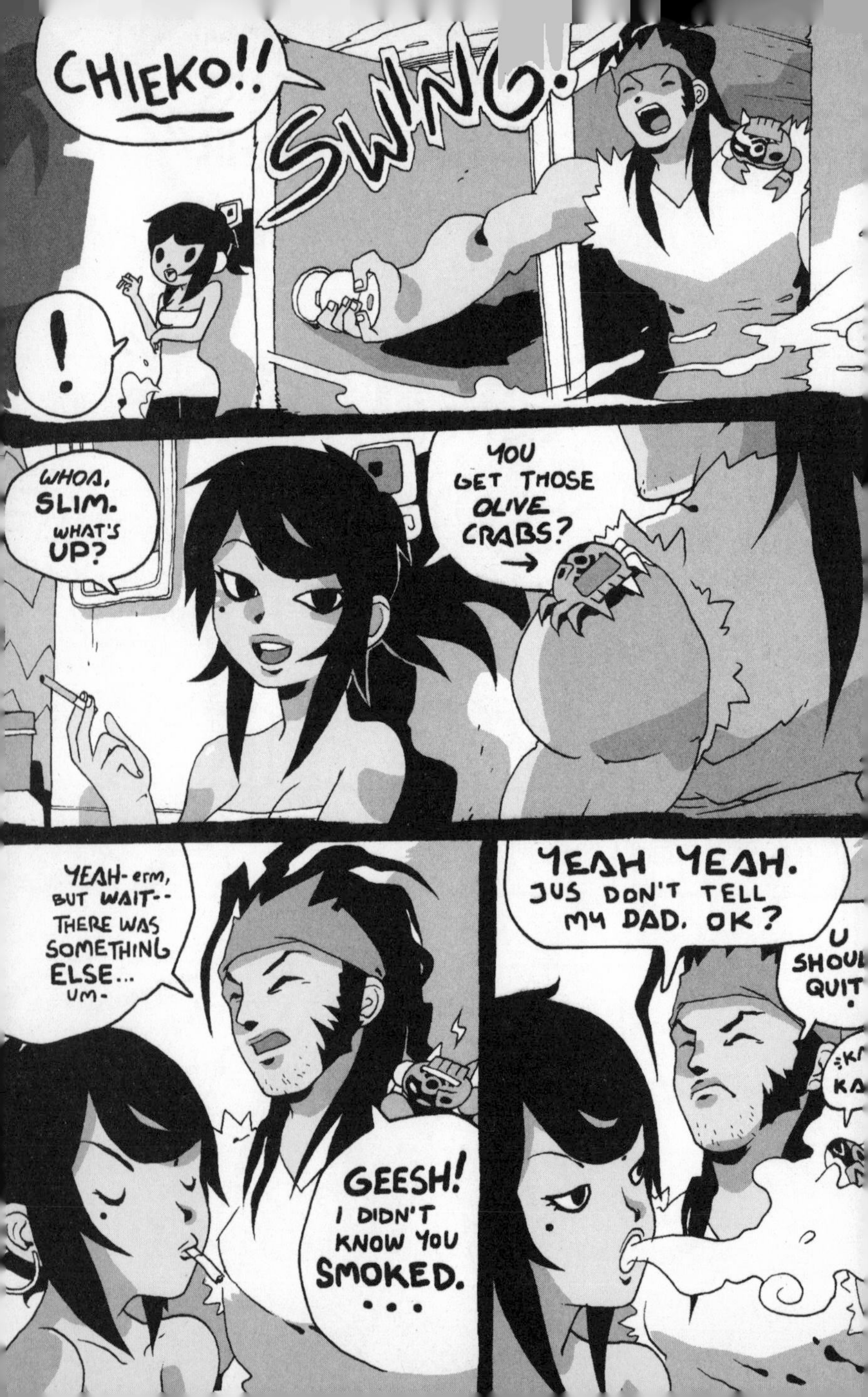

CHIEKO!!
SWING!
!
WHOA, SLIM. WHAT'S UP?
YOU GET THOSE OLIVE CRABS? →
YEAH- erm, BUT WAIT-- THERE WAS SOMETHING ELSE... UM-
GEESH! I DIDN'T KNOW YOU SMOKED. ...
YEAH YEAH. JUS DON'T TELL MY DAD. OK?

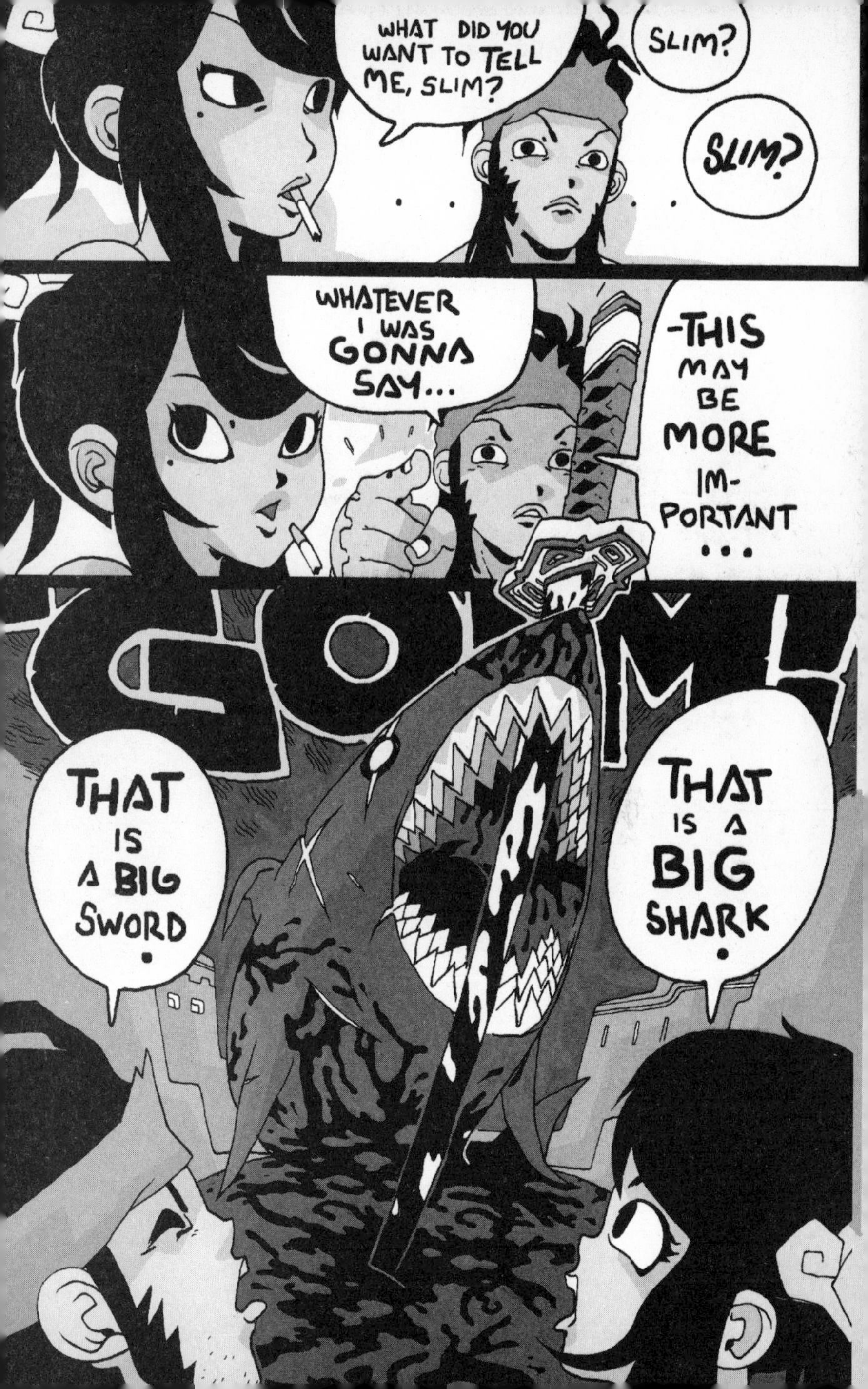
WHAT DID YOU WANT TO TELL ME, SLIM?
SLIM?
SLIM?
WHATEVER I WAS GONNA SAY...
-THIS MAY BE MORE IM-PORTANT ...
THAT IS A BIG SWORD.
THAT IS A BIG SHARK.

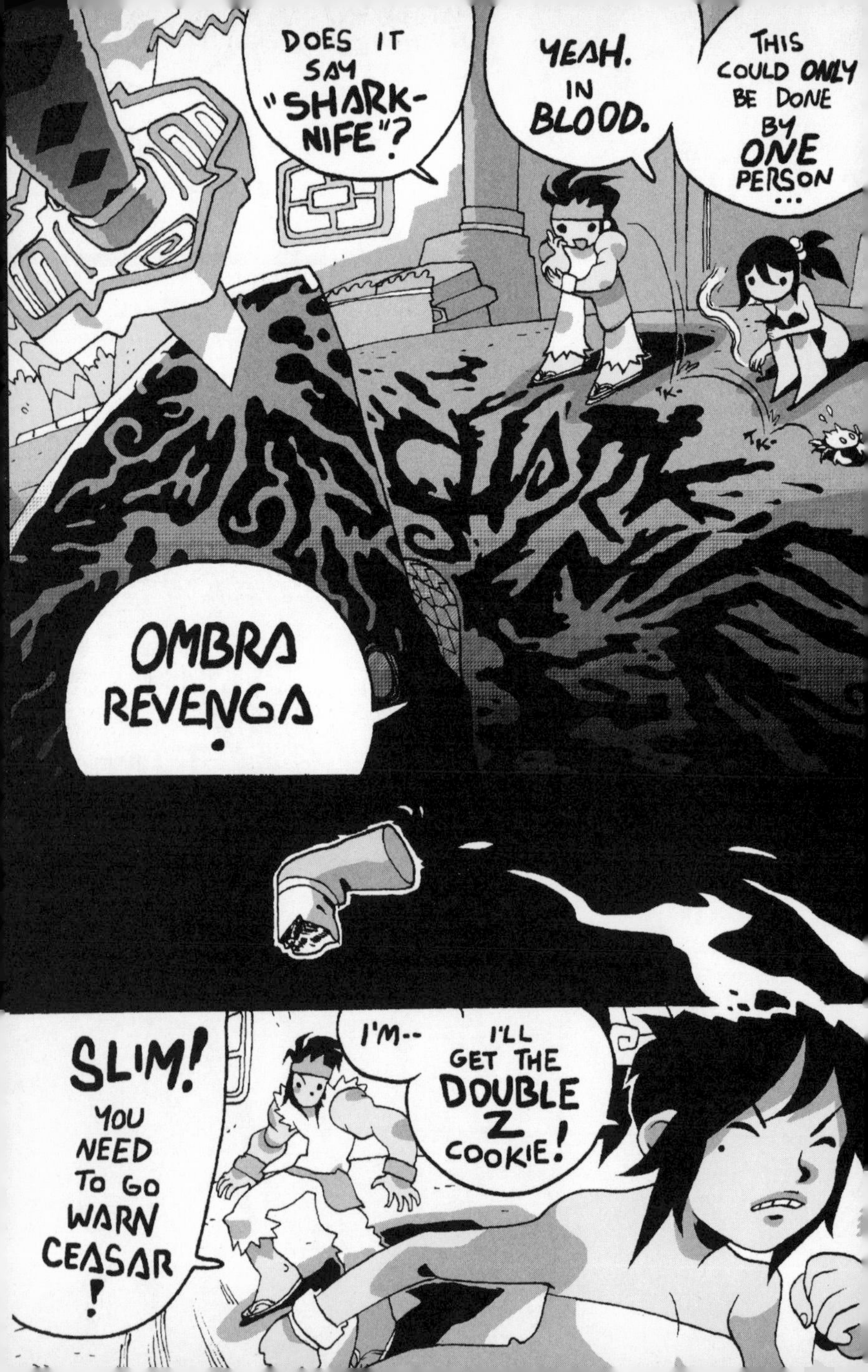
DOES IT SAY "SHARK-NIFE"?
YEAH. IN BLOOD.
THIS COULD ONLY BE DONE BY ONE PERSON...
TK-
TK-
OMBRA REVENGA.
SLIM! YOU NEED TO GO WARN CEASAR!
I'M--
I'LL GET THE DOUBLE Z COOKIE!

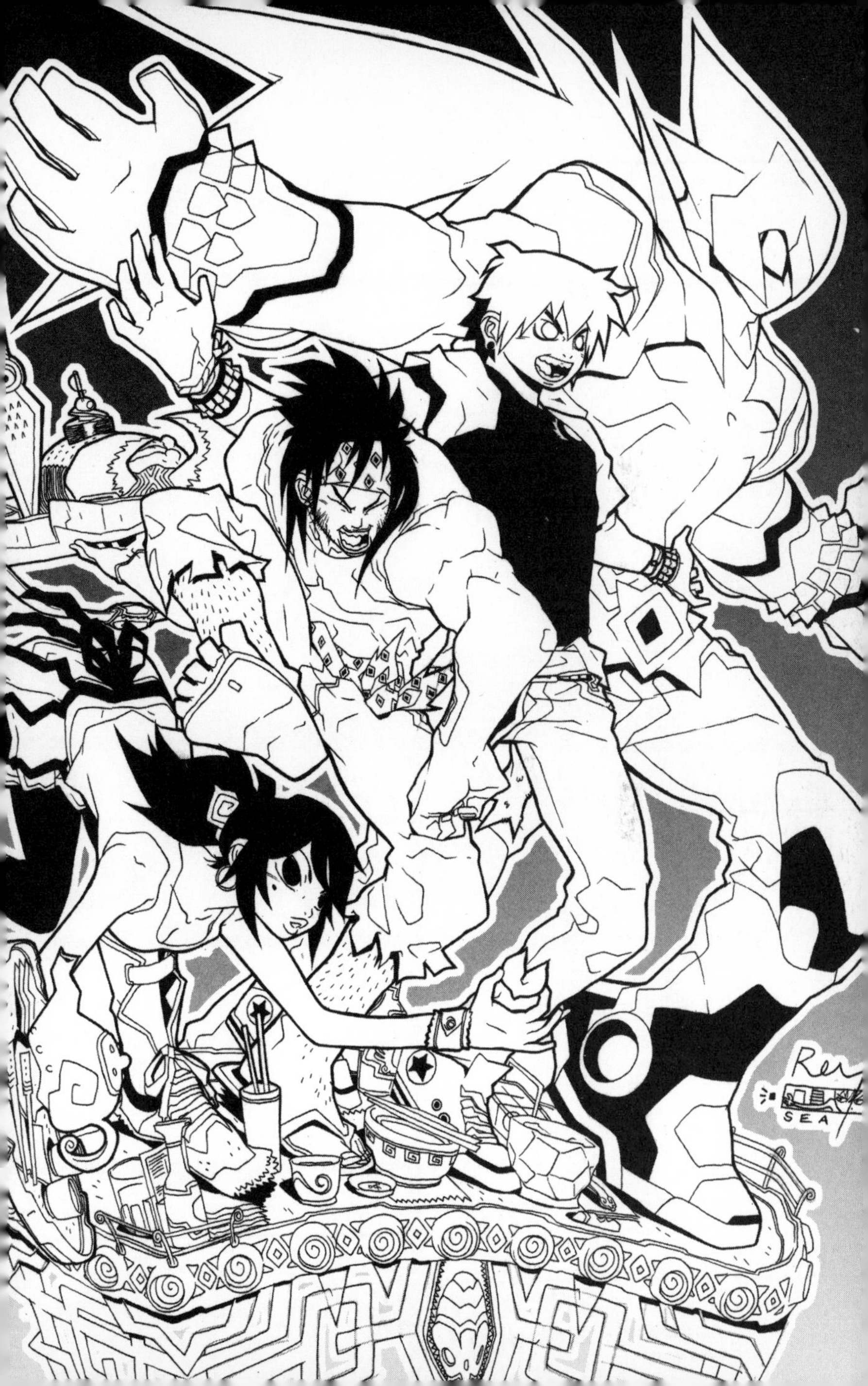
SEA

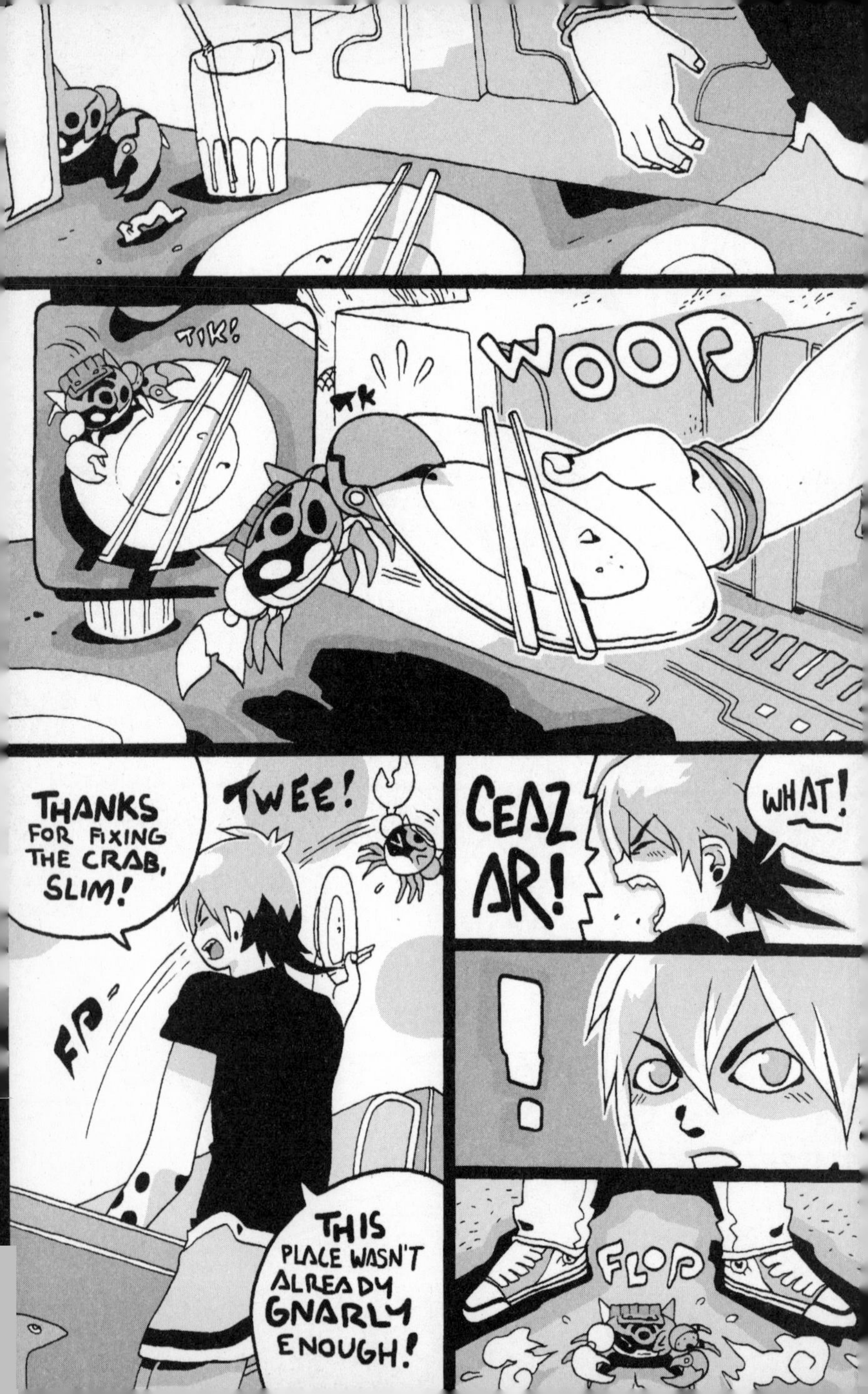
TIK!
TK
WOOP
THANKS FOR FIXING THE CRAB, SLIM!
TWEE!
FP-
THIS PLACE WASN'T ALREADY GNARLY ENOUGH!
CEAZAR!
WHAT!
!
FLOP

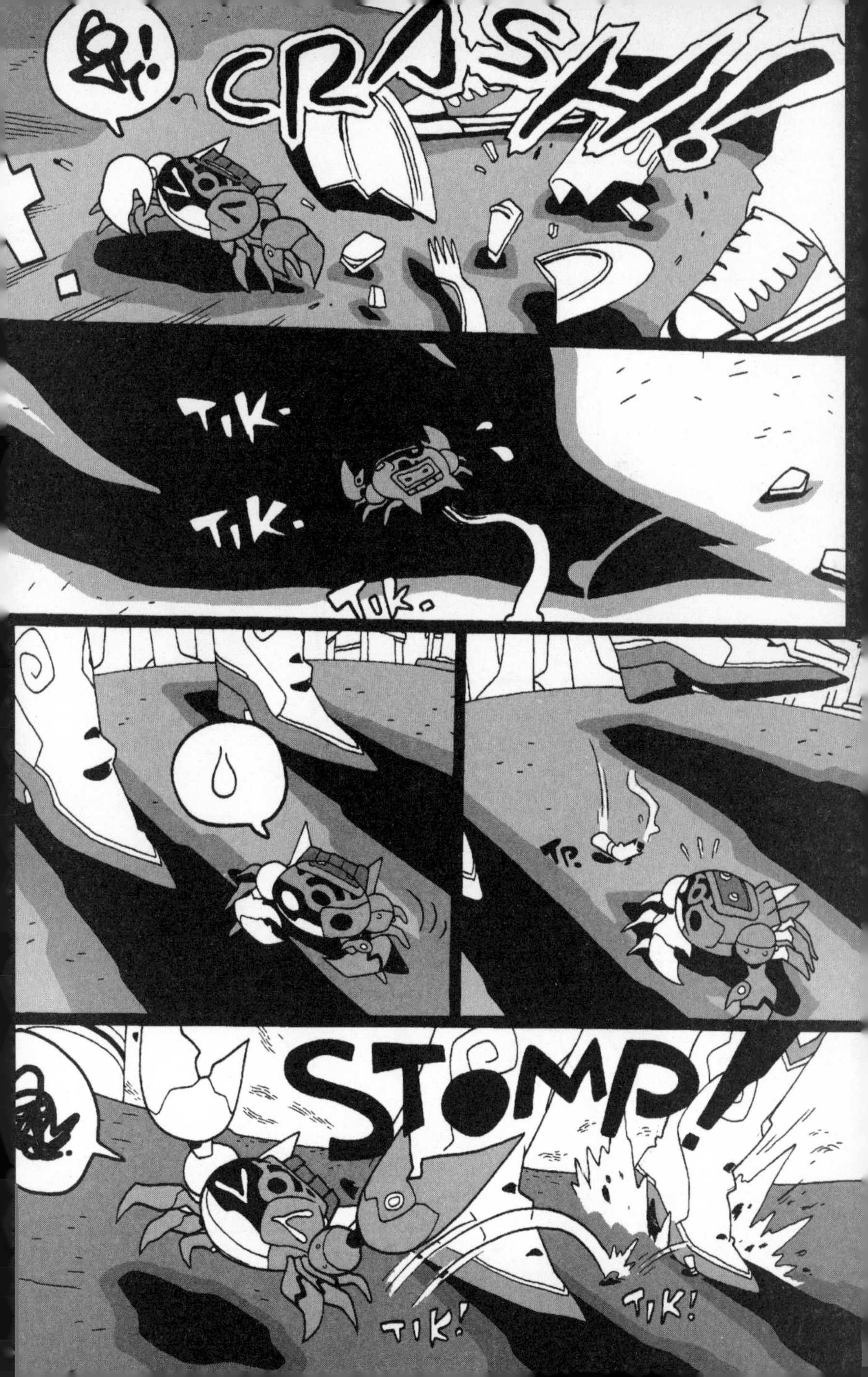
CRASH!
TIK-
TIK-
TOK.
TP.
STOMP!
TIK!
TIK!

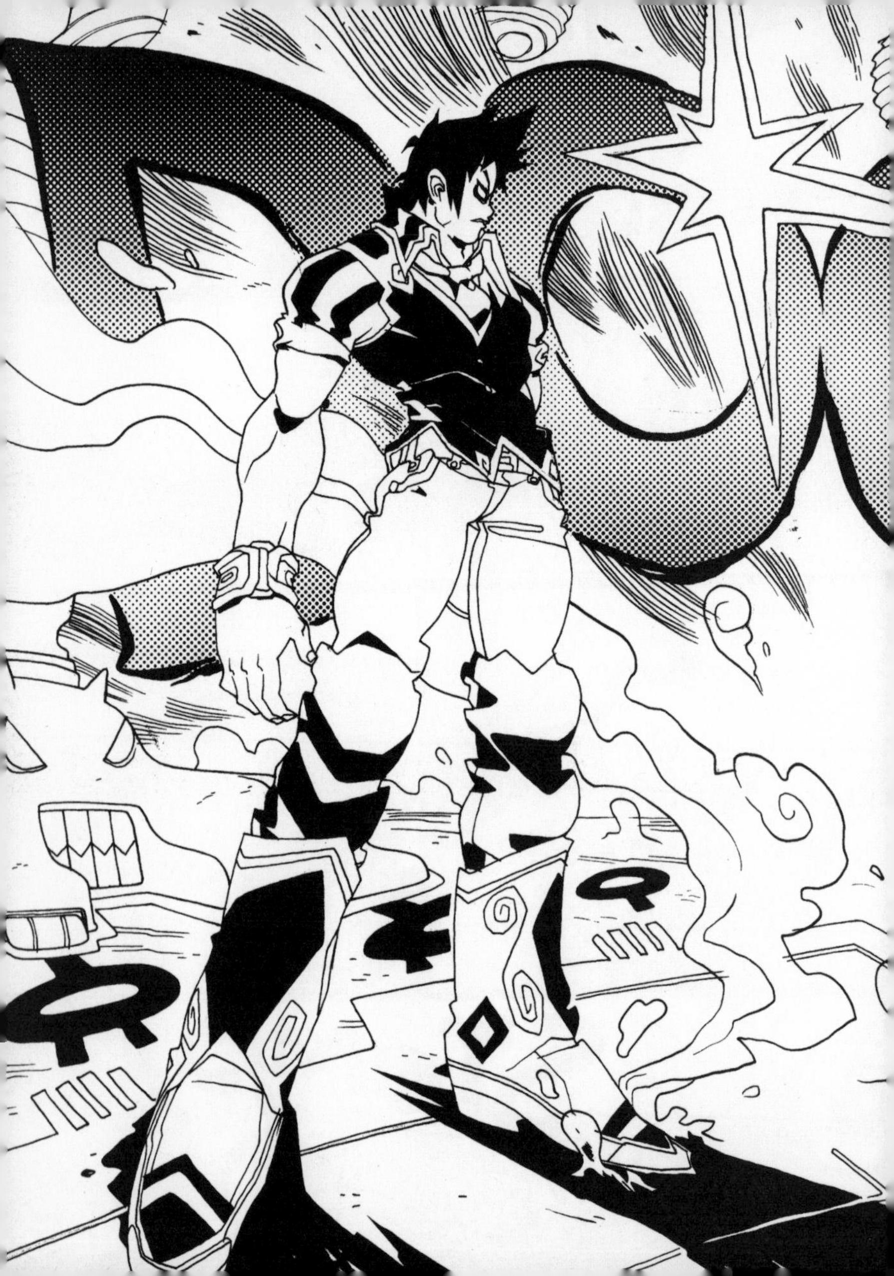

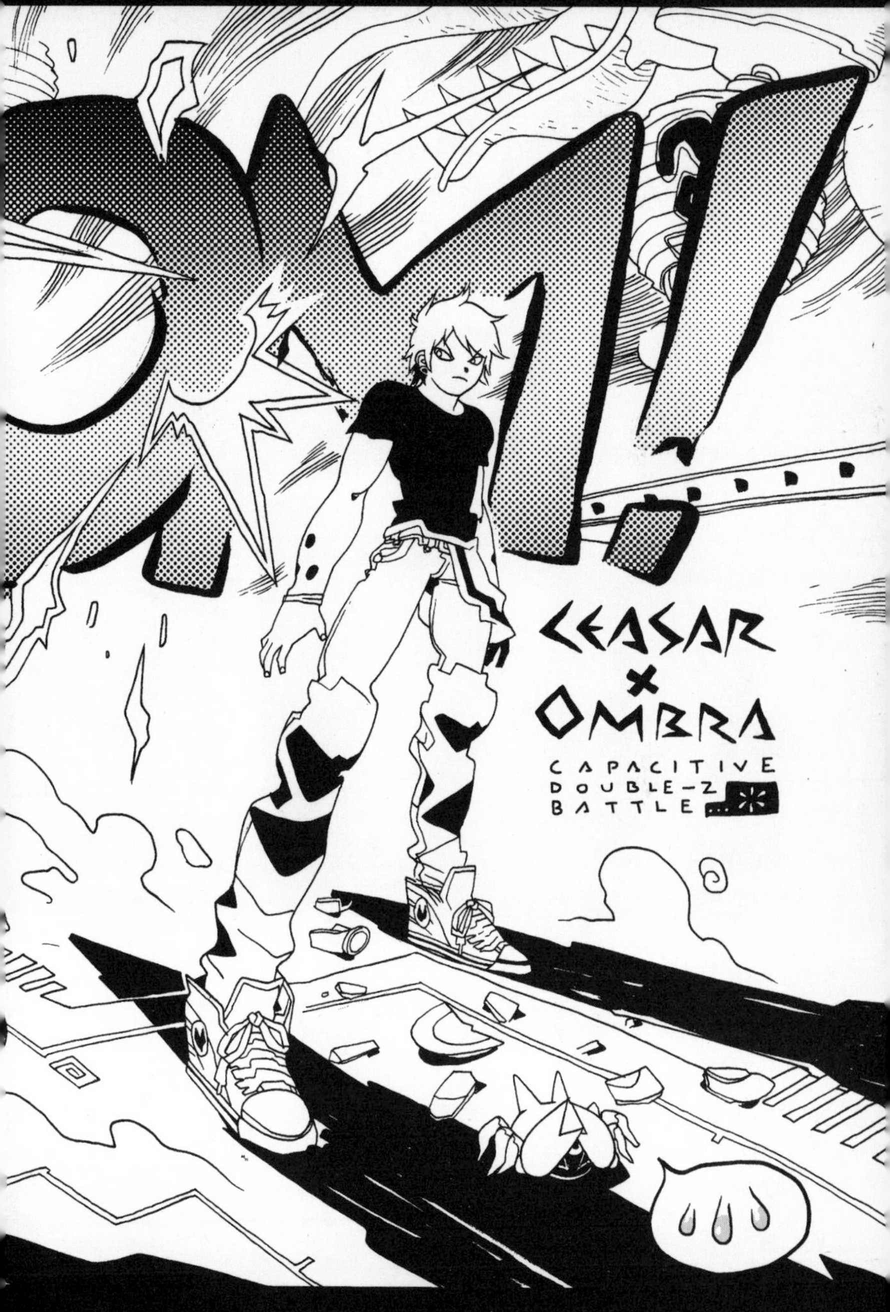
CEASAR
×
OMBRA
CAPACITIVE
DOUBLE-Z
BATTLE

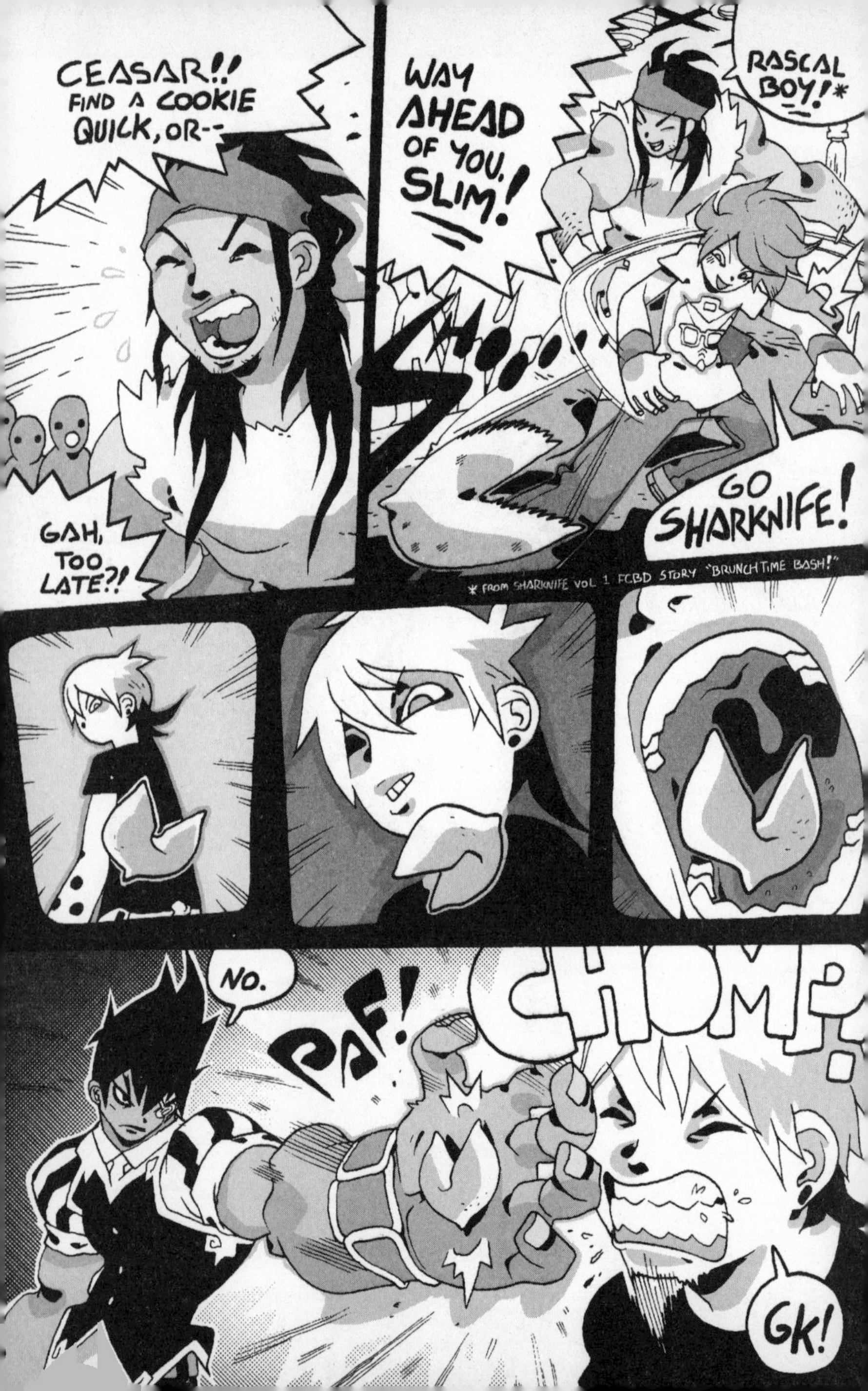
CEASAR!! FIND A COOKIE QUICK, OR--
GAH, TOO LATE?!
WAY AHEAD OF YOU, SLIM!
RASCAL BOY!*
SHOOOO...
GO SHARKNIFE!
* FROM SHARKNIFE VOL 1 FCBD STORY "BRUNCHTIME BASH!"
NO.
PAF!
CHOMP!
GK!

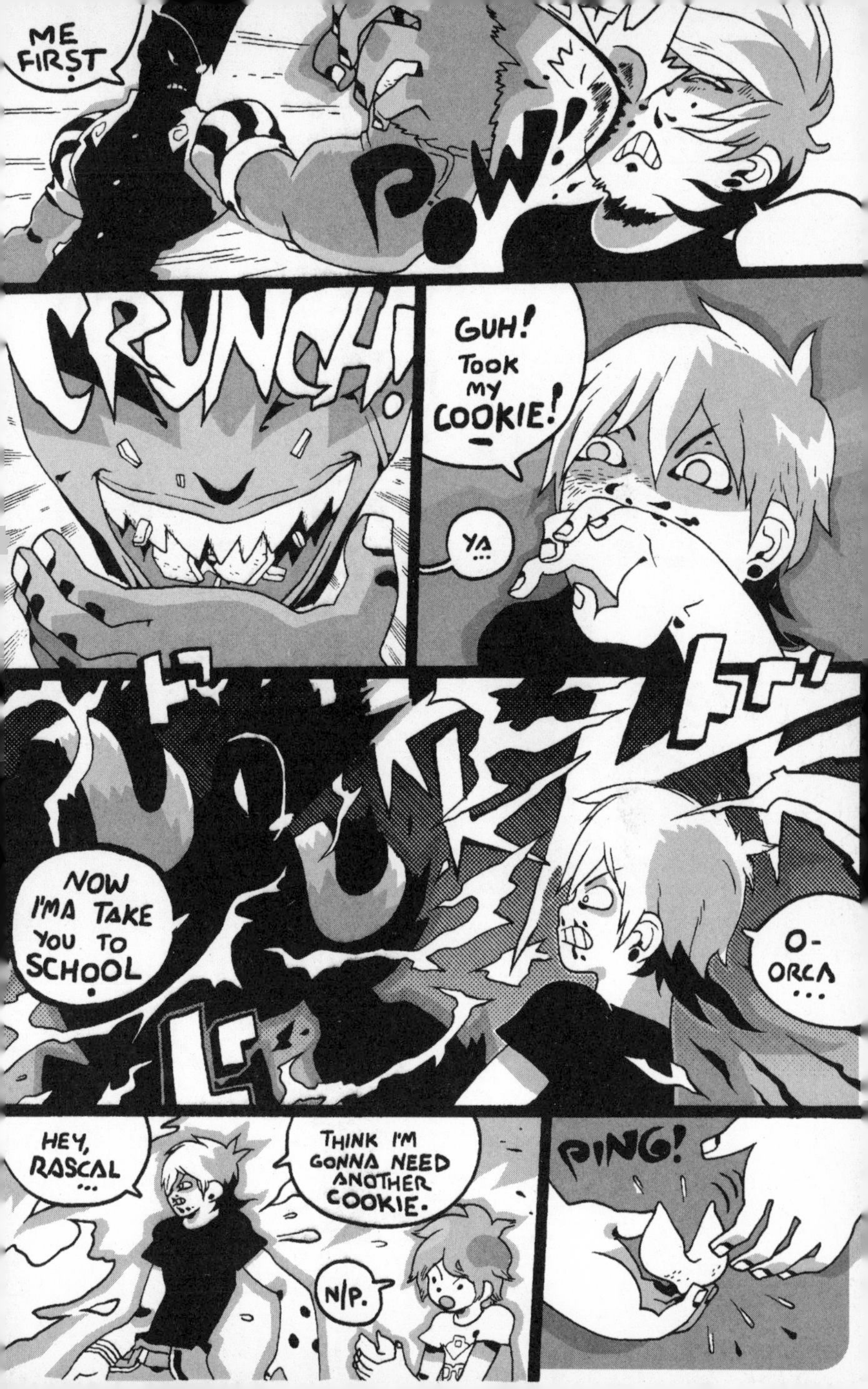
ME FIRST
POW!
CRUNCH!
GUH! TOOK MY COOKIE!
YA...
NOW I'MA TAKE YOU TO SCHOOL
O-ORCA...
HEY, RASCAL...
THINK I'M GONNA NEED ANOTHER COOKIE.
N/P.
PING!

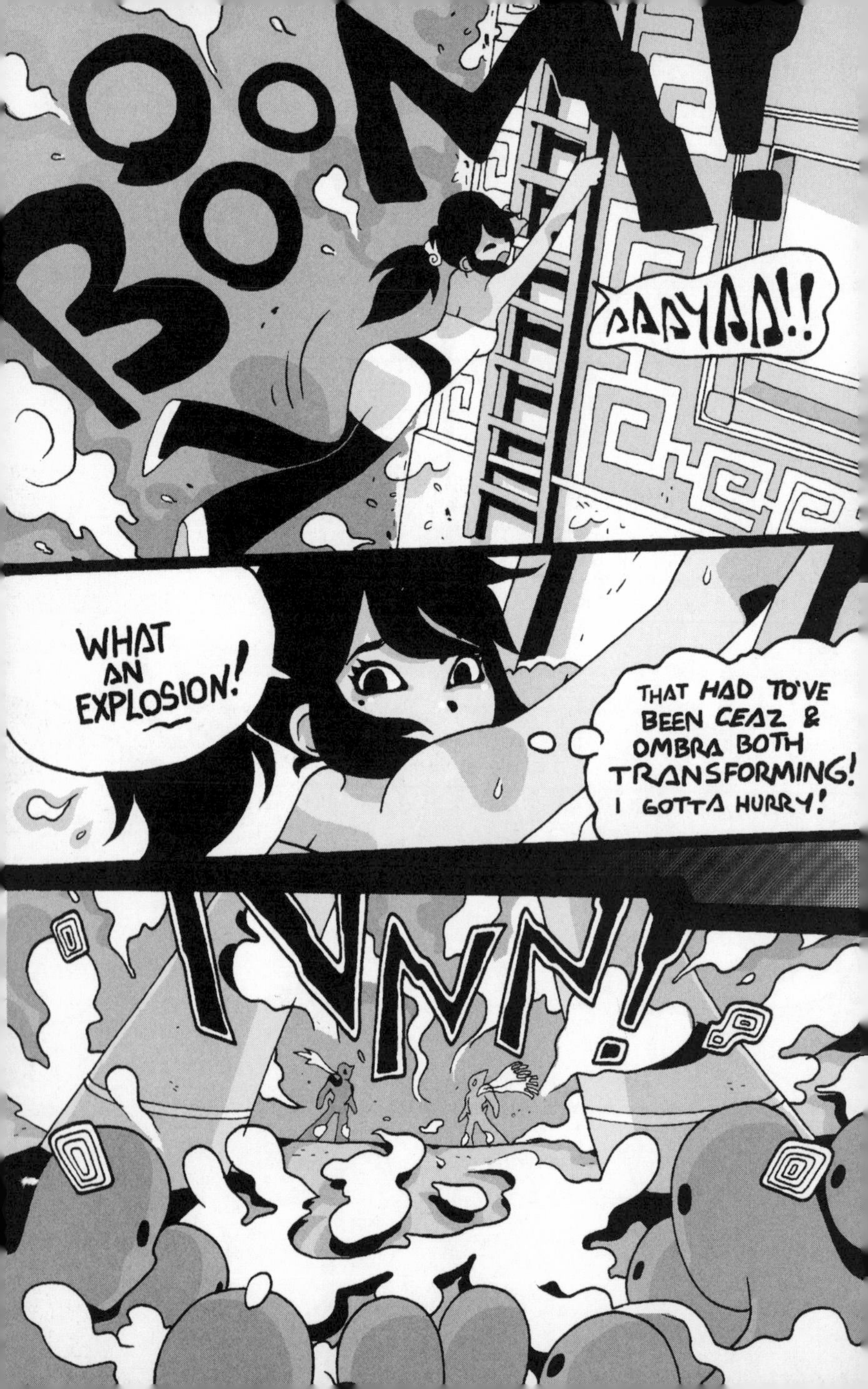
BOOM!
AAAYAA!!
WHAT AN EXPLOSION!
THAT HAD TO'VE BEEN CEAZ & OMBRA BOTH TRANSFORMING! I GOTTA HURRY!
VNNN!

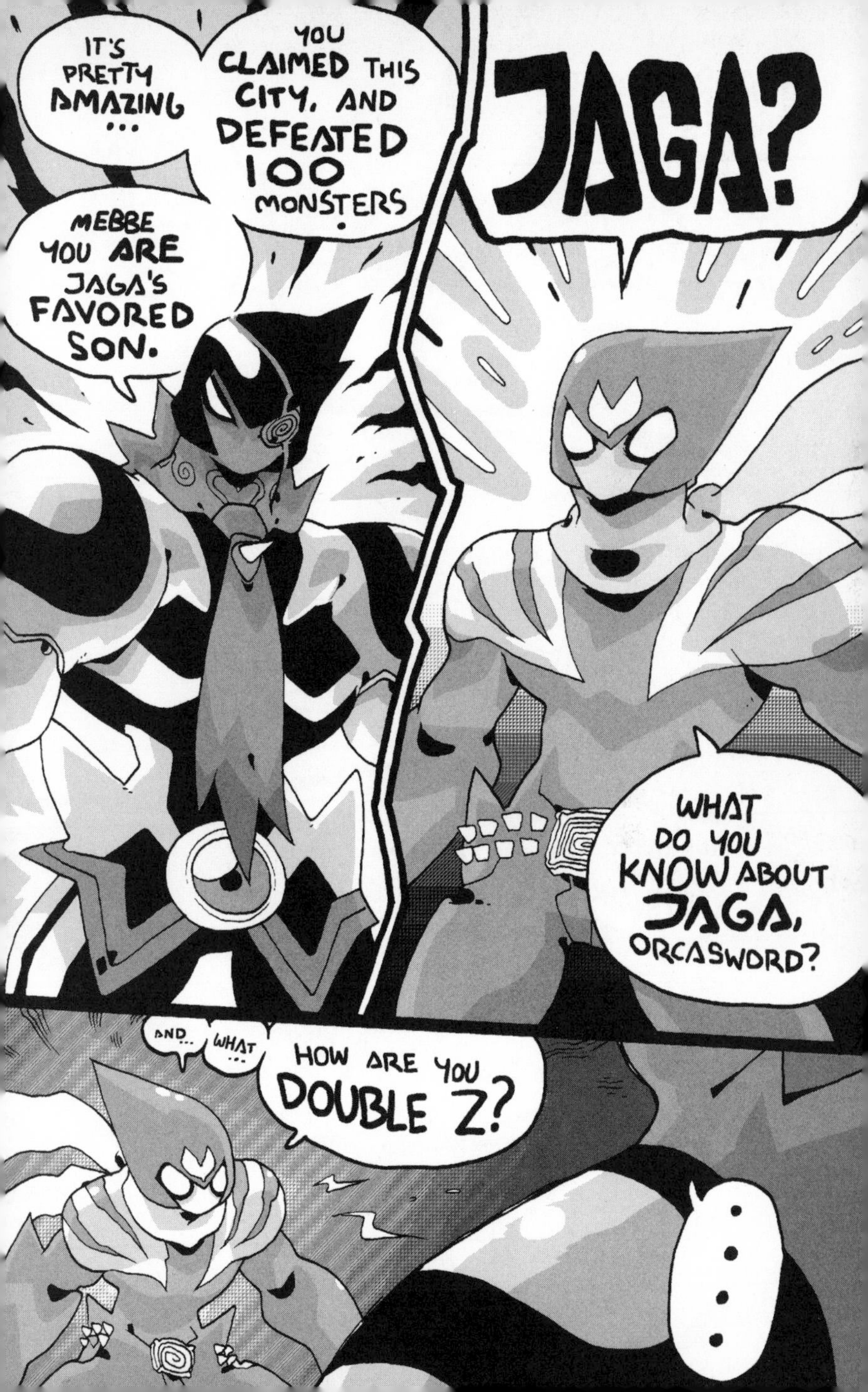
IT'S PRETTY AMAZING...
YOU CLAIMED THIS CITY, AND DEFEATED 100 MONSTERS.
MEBBE YOU ARE JAGA'S FAVORED SON.
JAGA?
WHAT DO YOU KNOW ABOUT JAGA, ORCASWORD?
AND...
WHAT...
HOW ARE YOU DOUBLE Z?
...

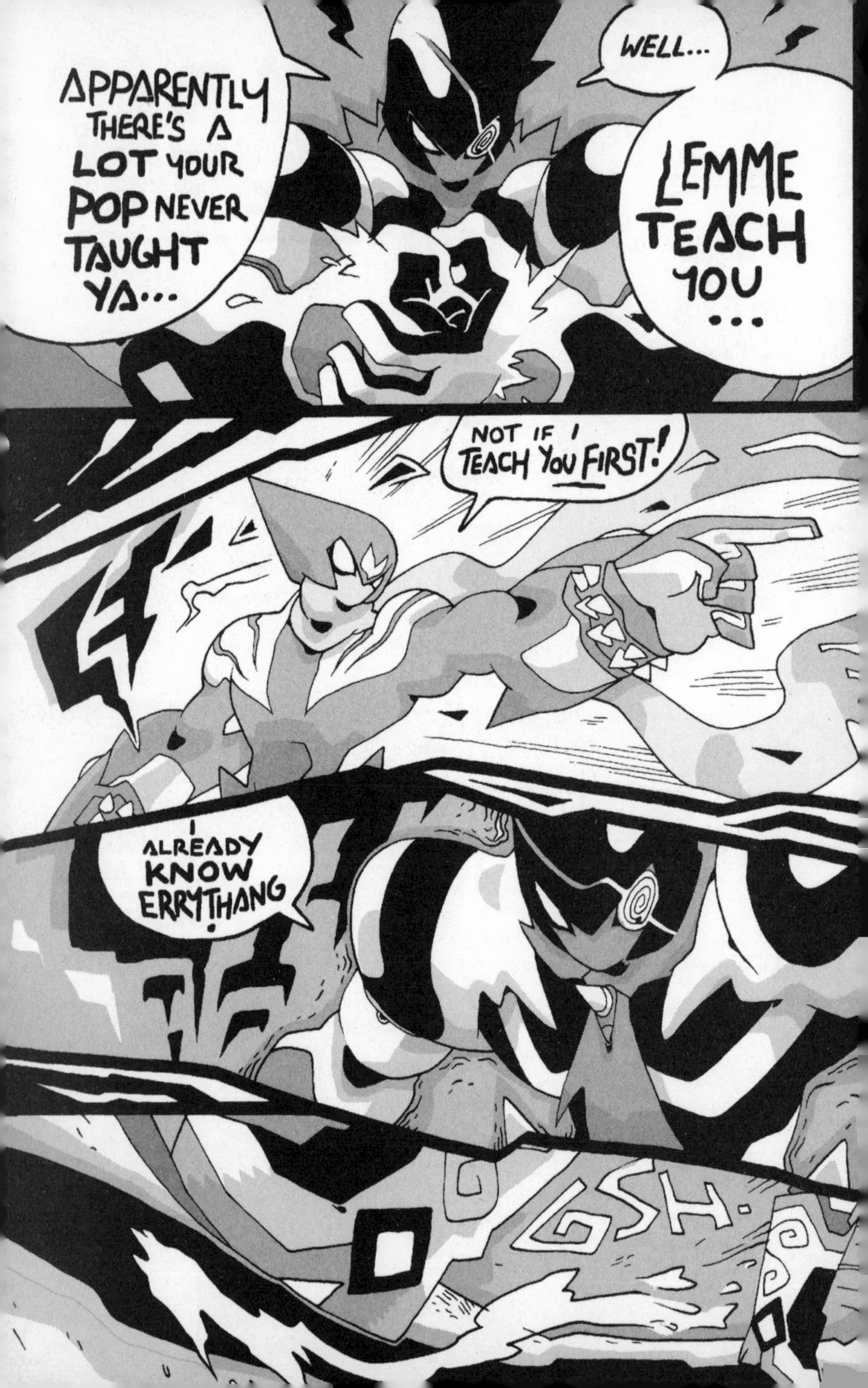
APPARENTLY THERE'S A LOT YOUR POP NEVER TAUGHT YA...
WELL...
LEMME TEACH YOU...
NOT IF I TEACH YOU FIRST!
I ALREADY KNOW ERRYTHANG!
GSH

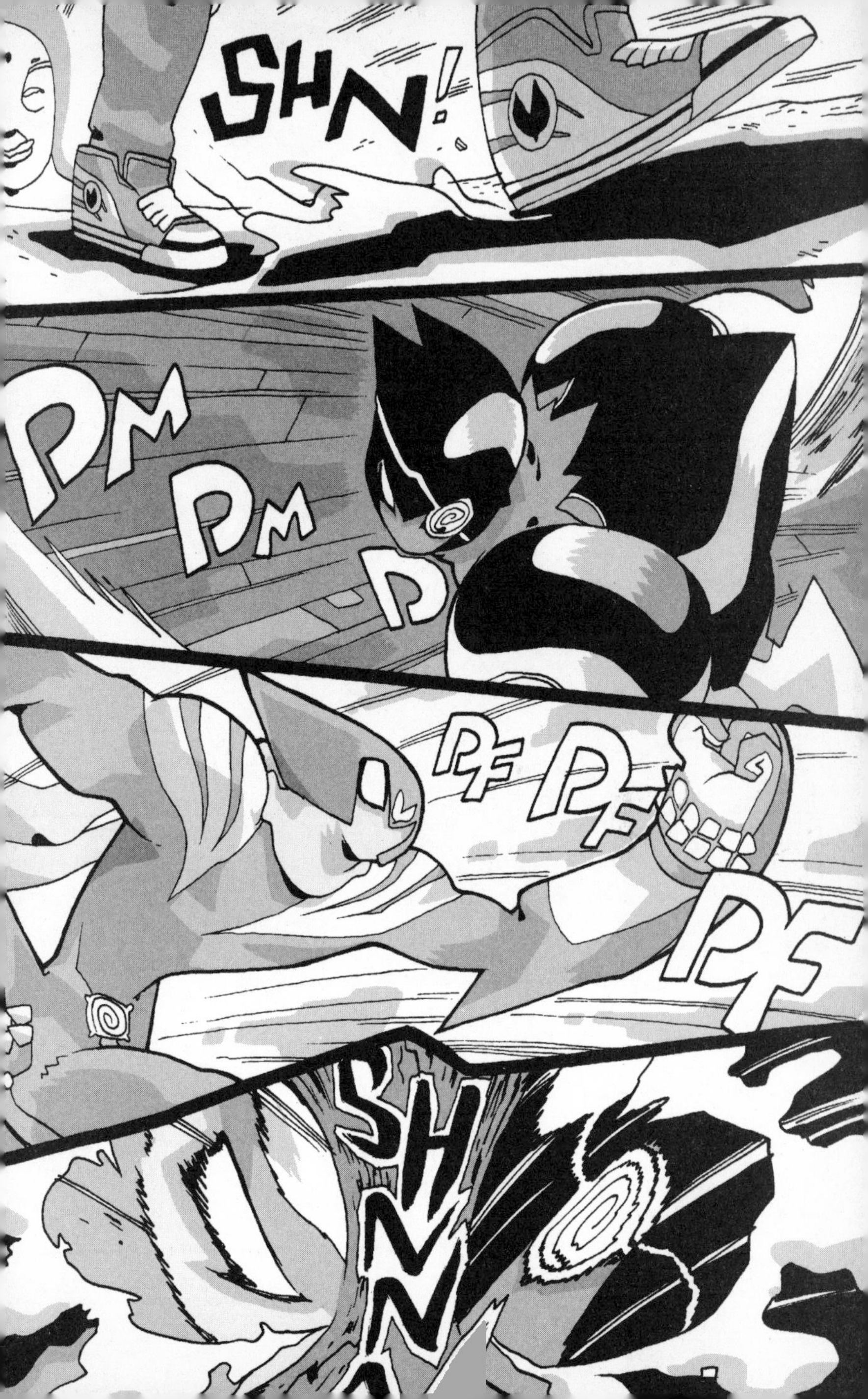
SHN!
DM DM D
DF DF DF
SHNN

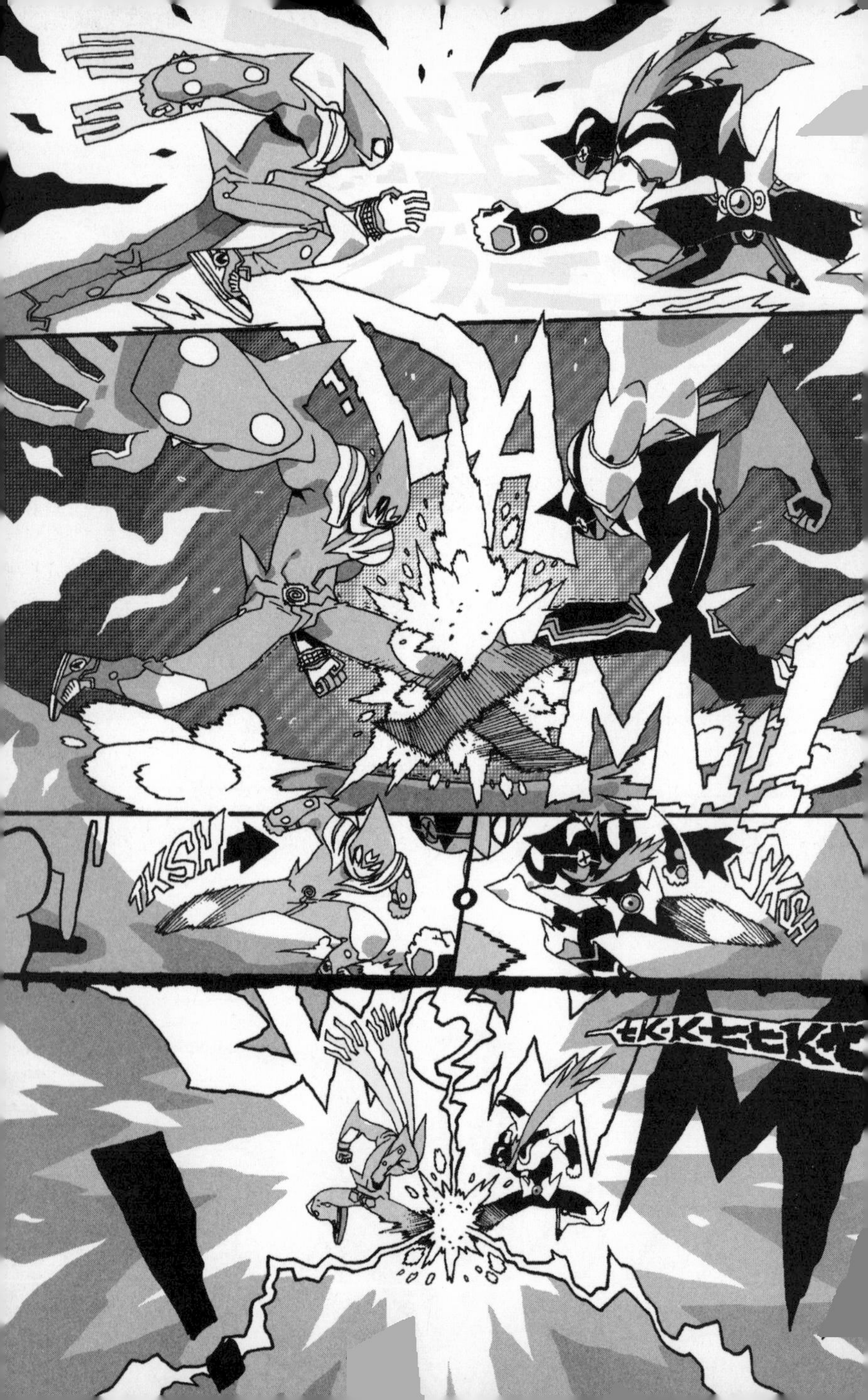
TKSH
SKSH

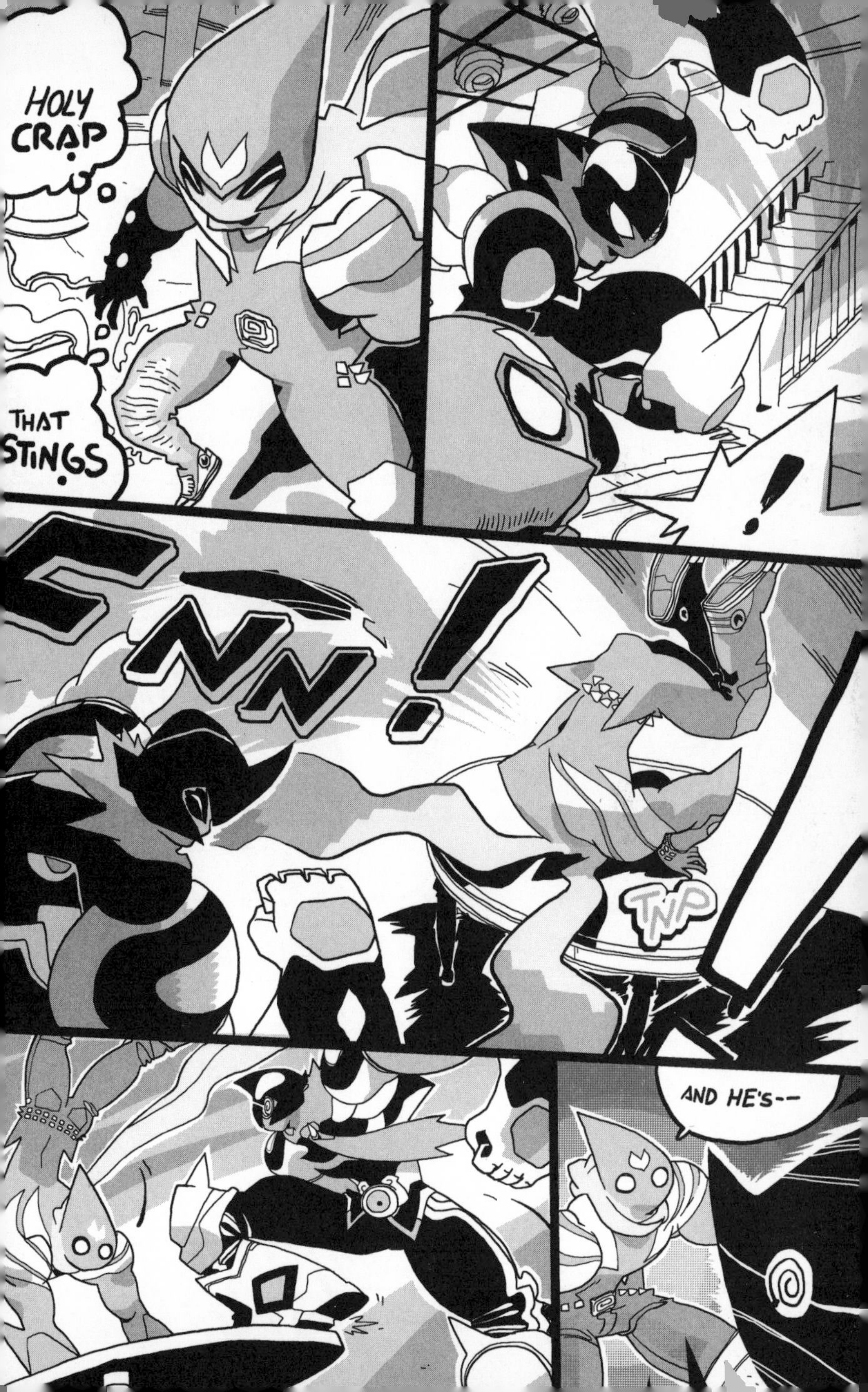
HOLY CRAP
THAT STINGS
!
SNN!
TNP
AND HE'S--

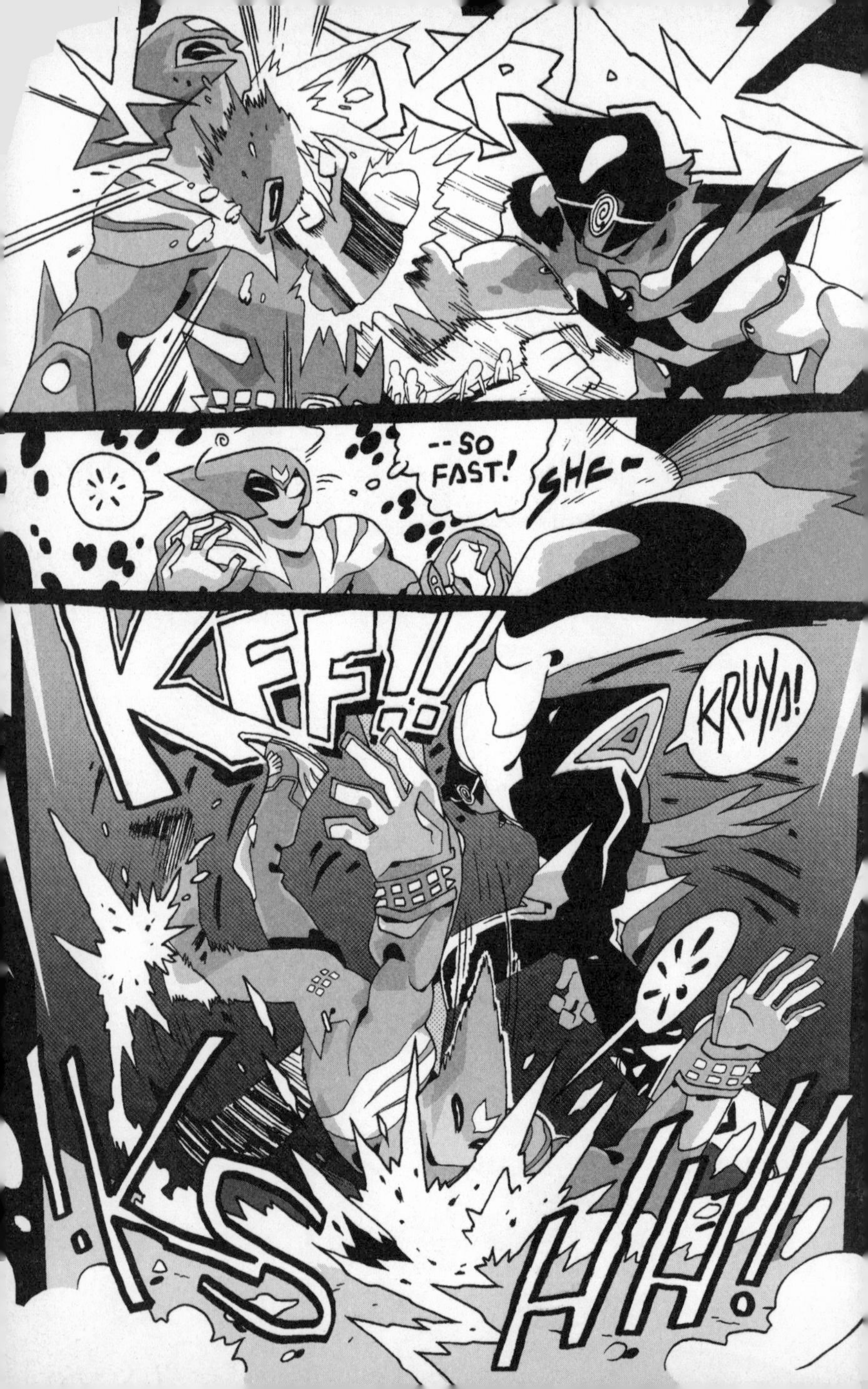
KRAK
--SO FAST!
SHF
KFF!!
KRUYA!
KSHH!

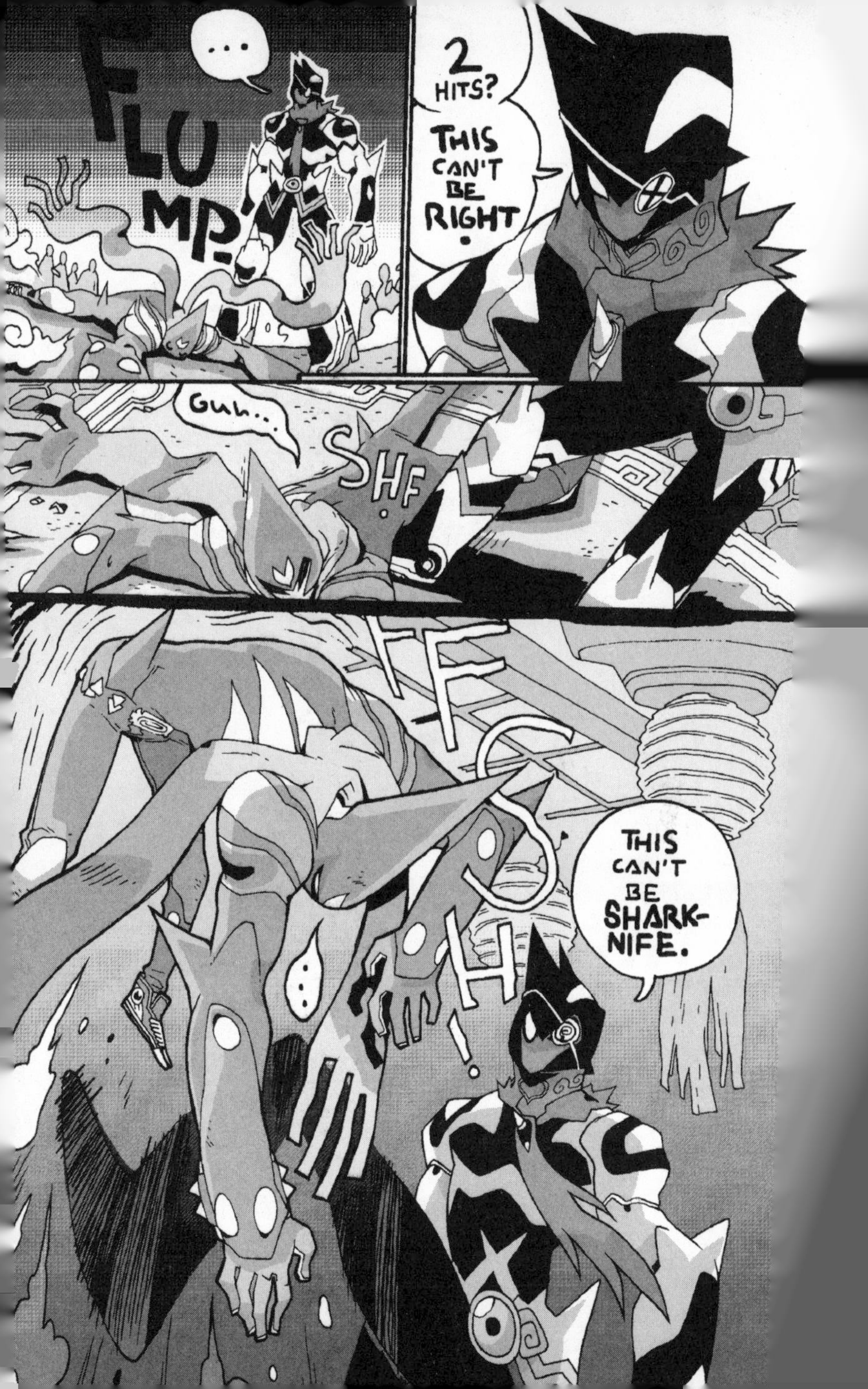

...
FLUMP
2 HITS?
THIS CAN'T BE RIGHT.
Guh...
SHF
FFSH
THIS CAN'T BE SHARK-NIFE.

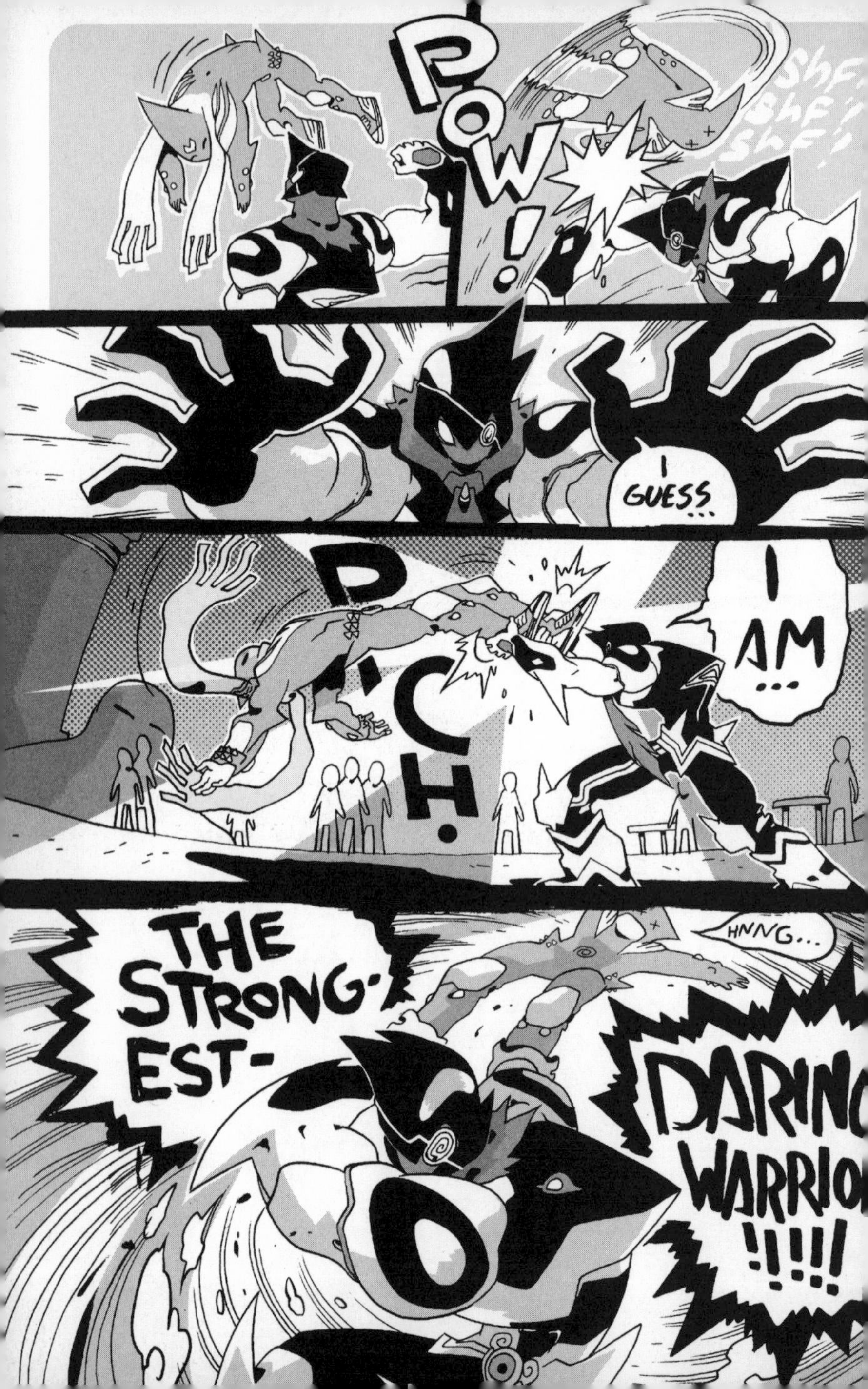

POW!
SHF SHF SHF
I GUESS...
I AM...
PACH!
THE STRONG-EST-
HNNG...
DARING WARRIO!!!!!

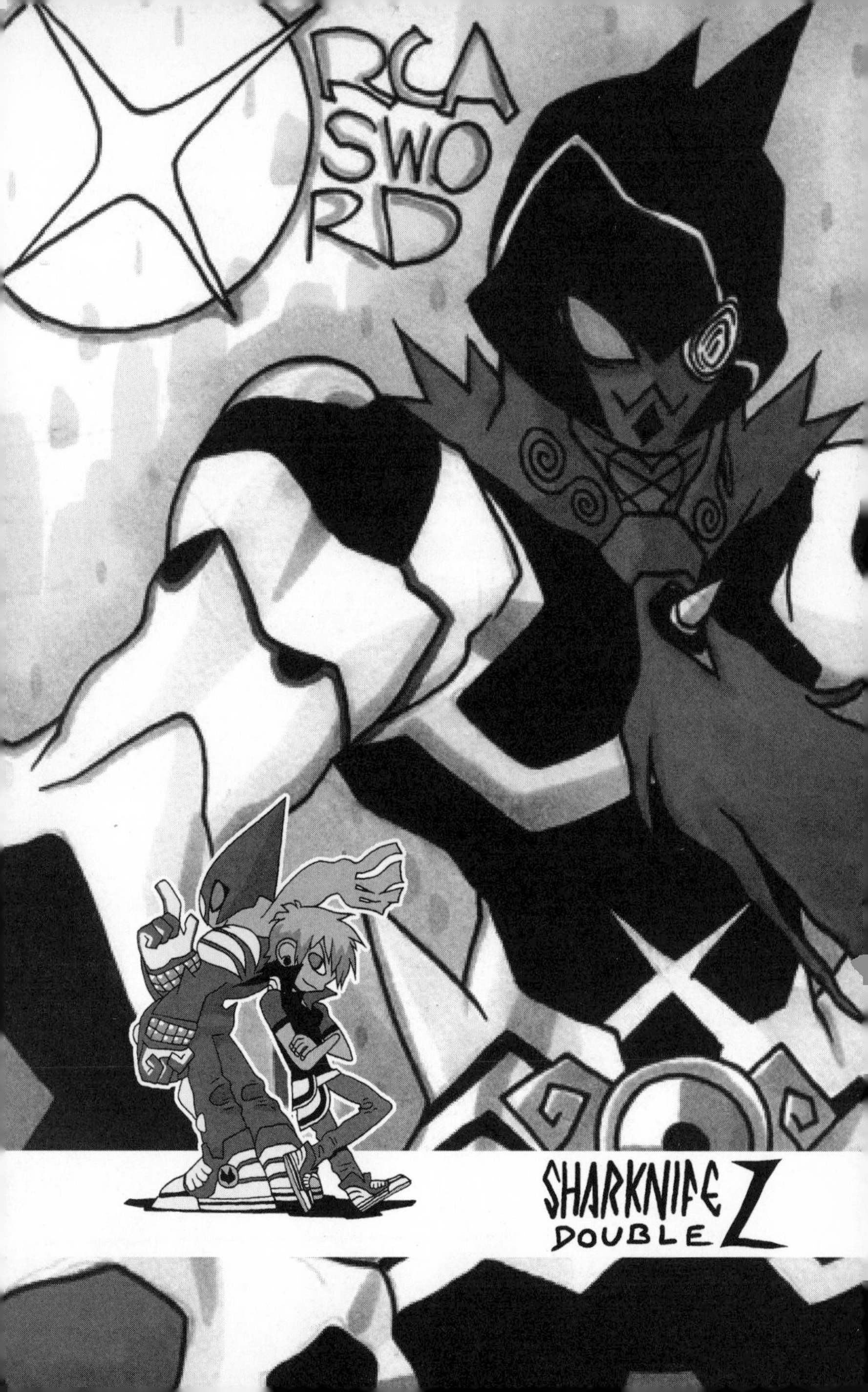
ORCA SWORD
SHARKNIFE DOUBLE Z

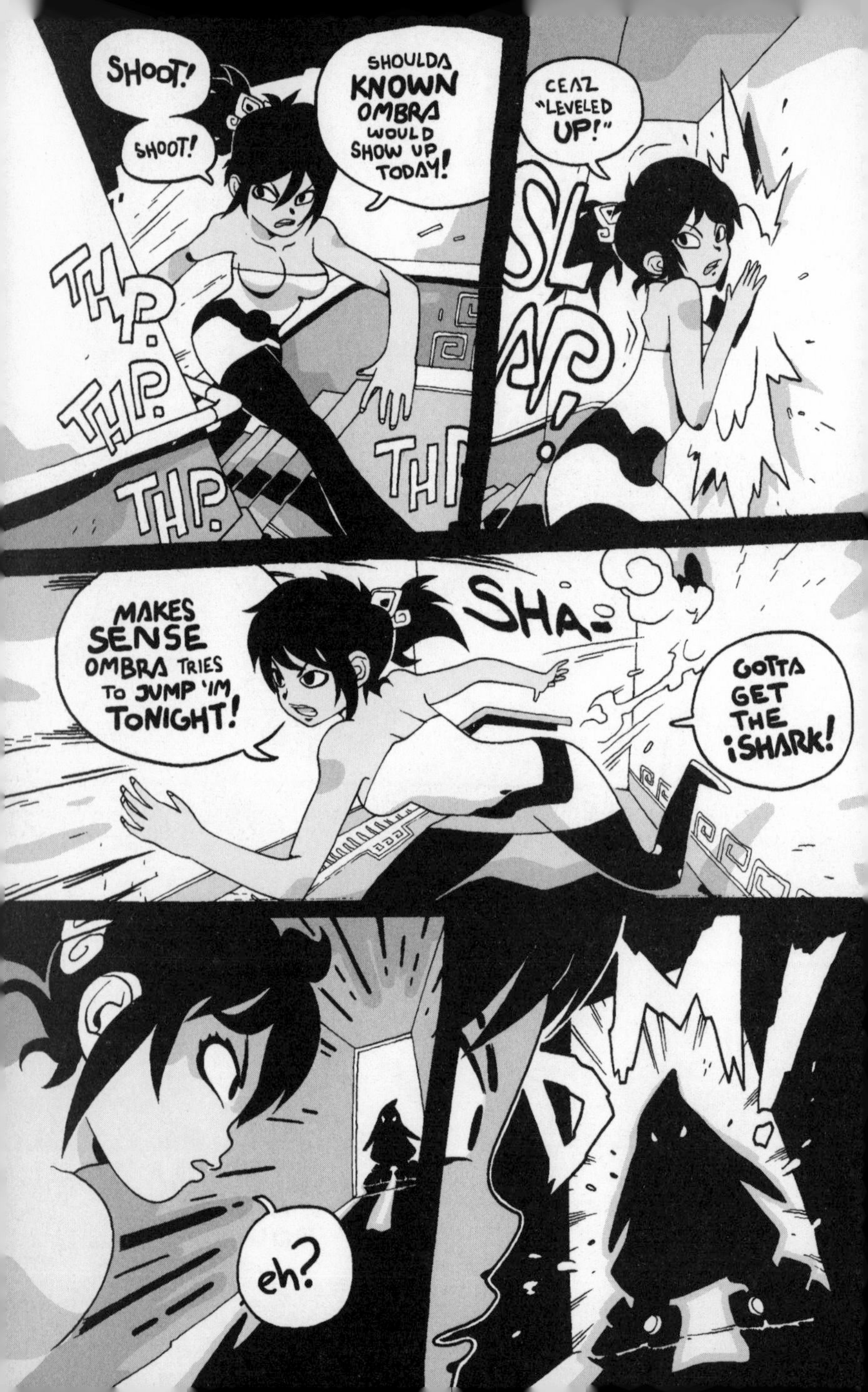
SHOOT!
SHOOT!
SHOULDA KNOWN OMBRA WOULD SHOW UP TODAY!
THP.
THP.
THP.
CEAZ "LEVELED UP!"
SLAP!
MAKES SENSE OMBRA TRIES TO JUMP 'IM TONIGHT!
SHA-
GOTTA GET THE ¡SHARK!
eh?

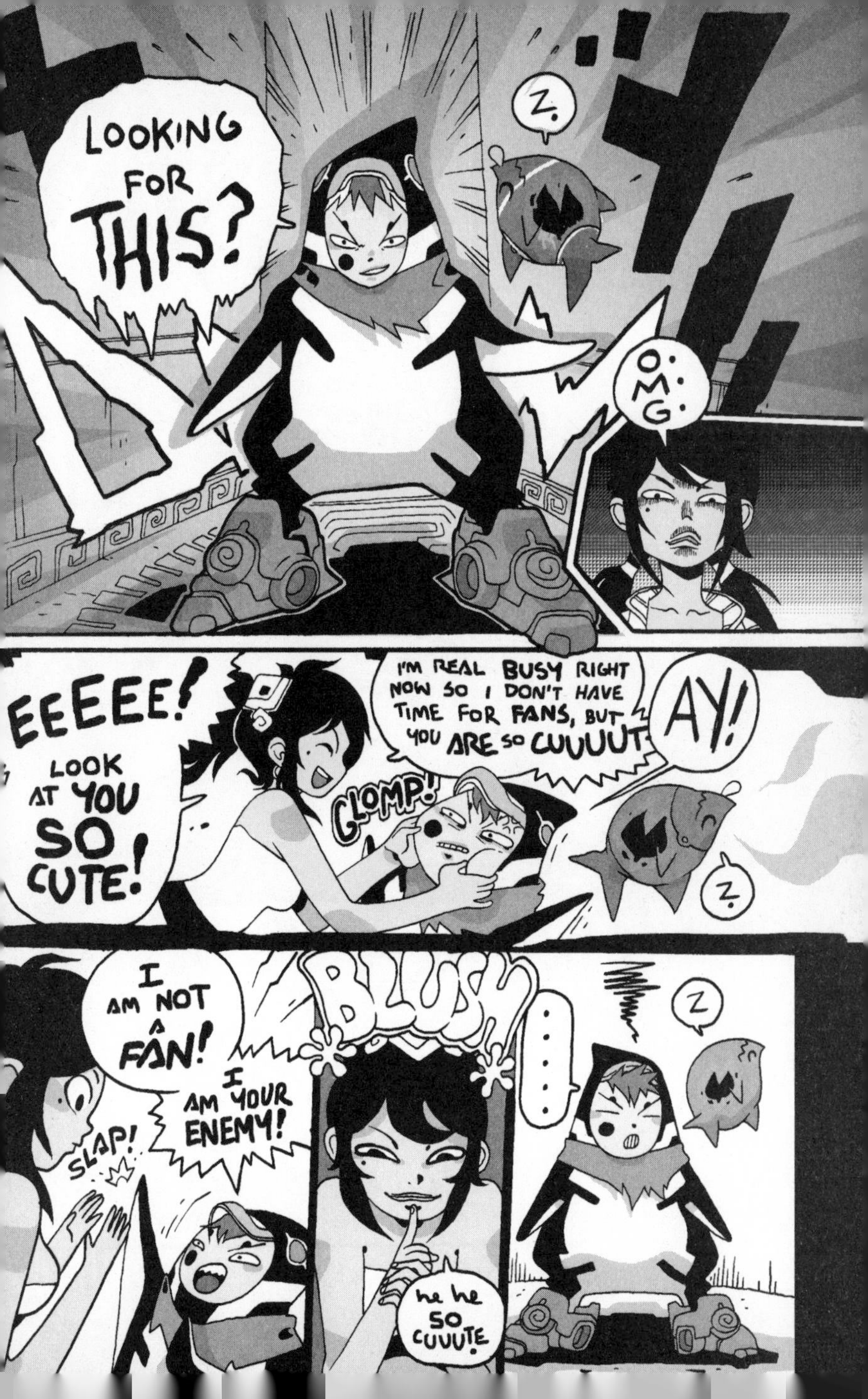
LOOKING FOR THIS?
Z.
OMG
EEEEEE!
LOOK AT YOU SO CUTE!
I'M REAL BUSY RIGHT NOW SO I DON'T HAVE TIME FOR FANS, BUT YOU ARE SO CUUUUT-
AY!
GLOMP!
Z.
I AM NOT A FAN!
I AM YOUR ENEMY!
SLAP!
BLUSH
he he SO CUUUTE
....
Z

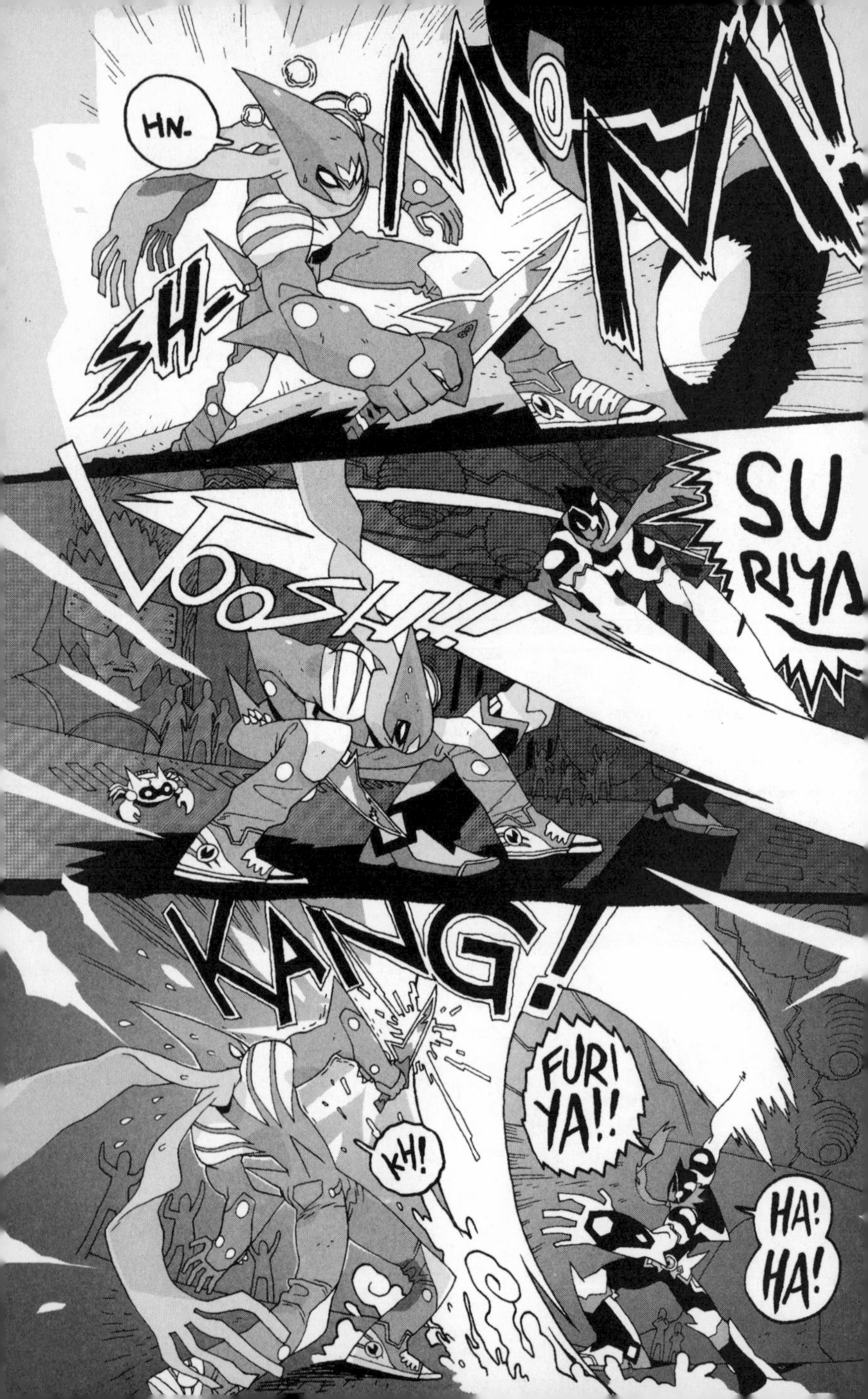

HN.
SH-
MYOM!
VOOSH!!
SU RIYA
KANG!
KH!
FURI YA!!
HA! HA!

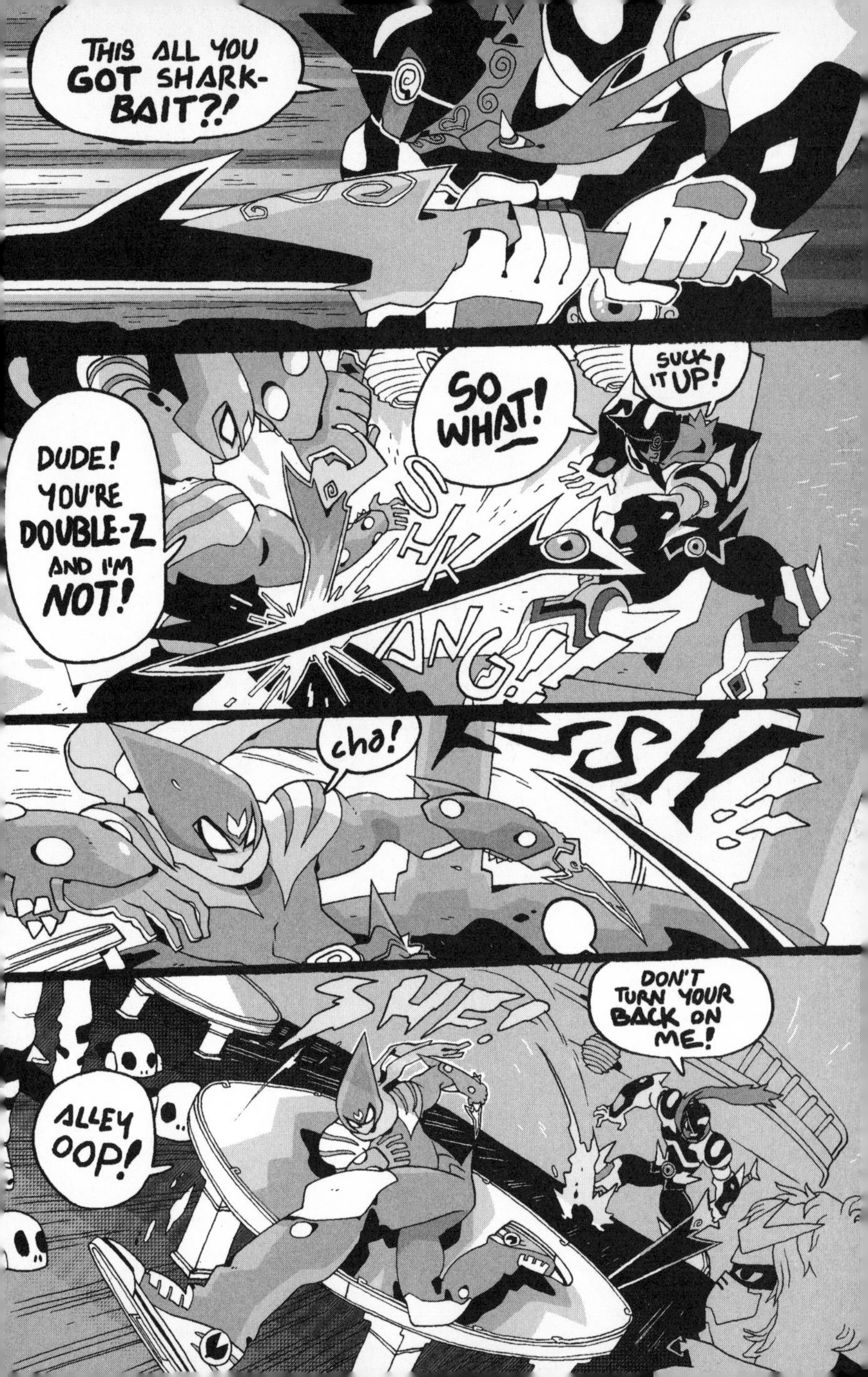
THIS ALL YOU GOT SHARK-BAIT?!
DUDE! YOU'RE DOUBLE-Z AND I'M NOT!
SO WHAT!
SUCK IT UP!
SHK
ANG!!
cha!
SH
DON'T TURN YOUR BACK ON ME!
ALLEY OOP!

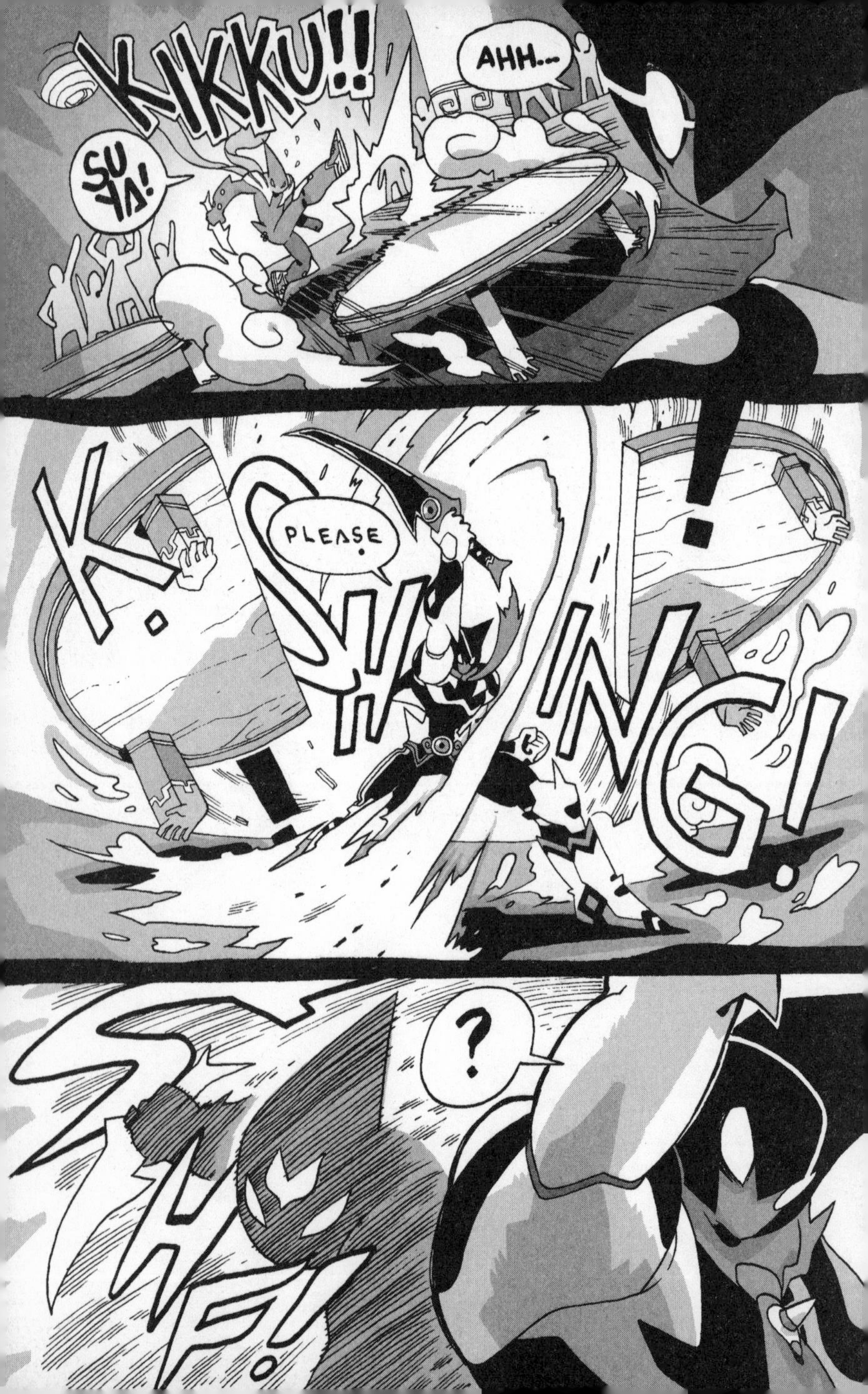

KIKKU!!
SU YA!
AHH...
KA-SWING!
PLEASE.
?
SHF!

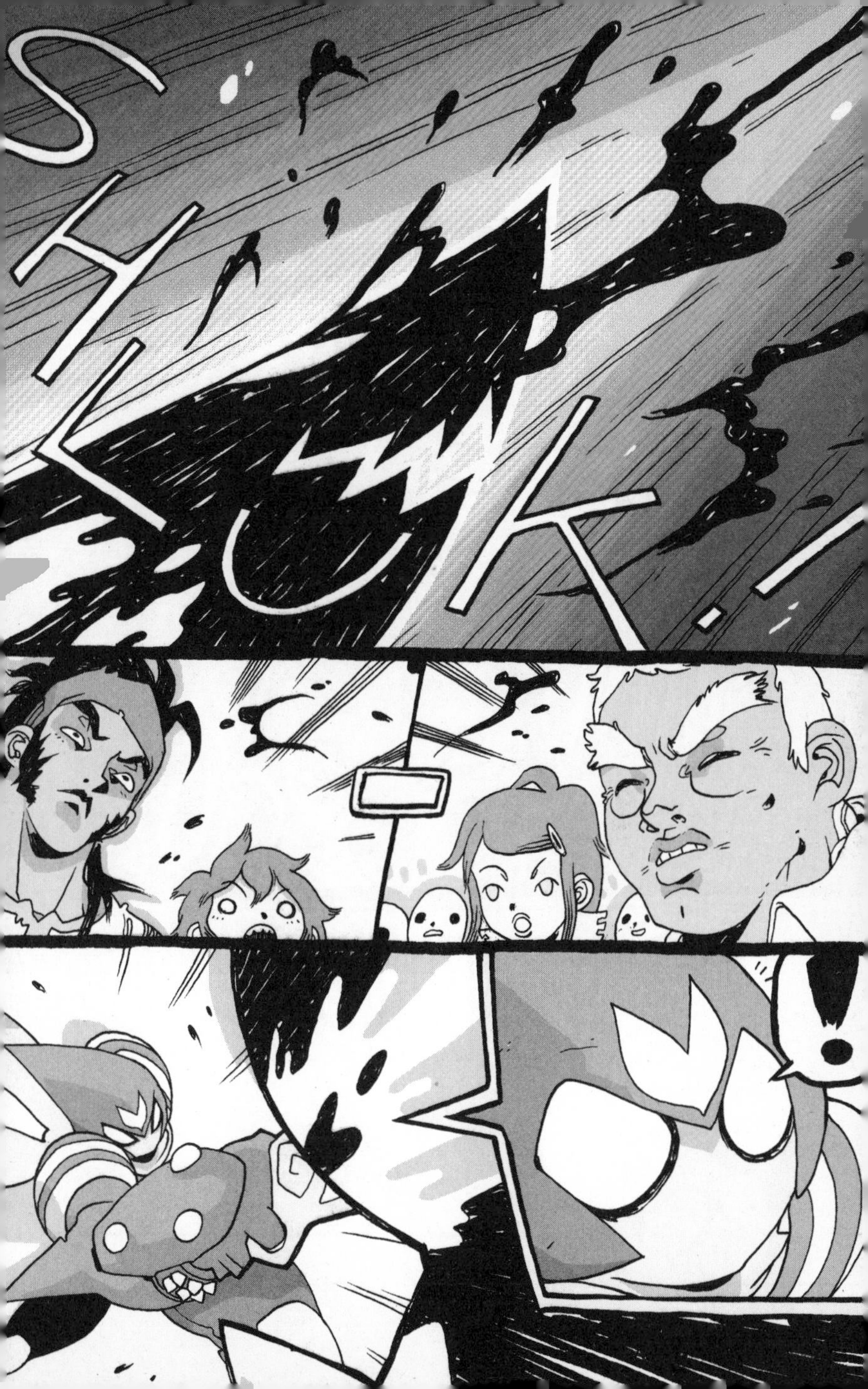
SHLUK!!
!

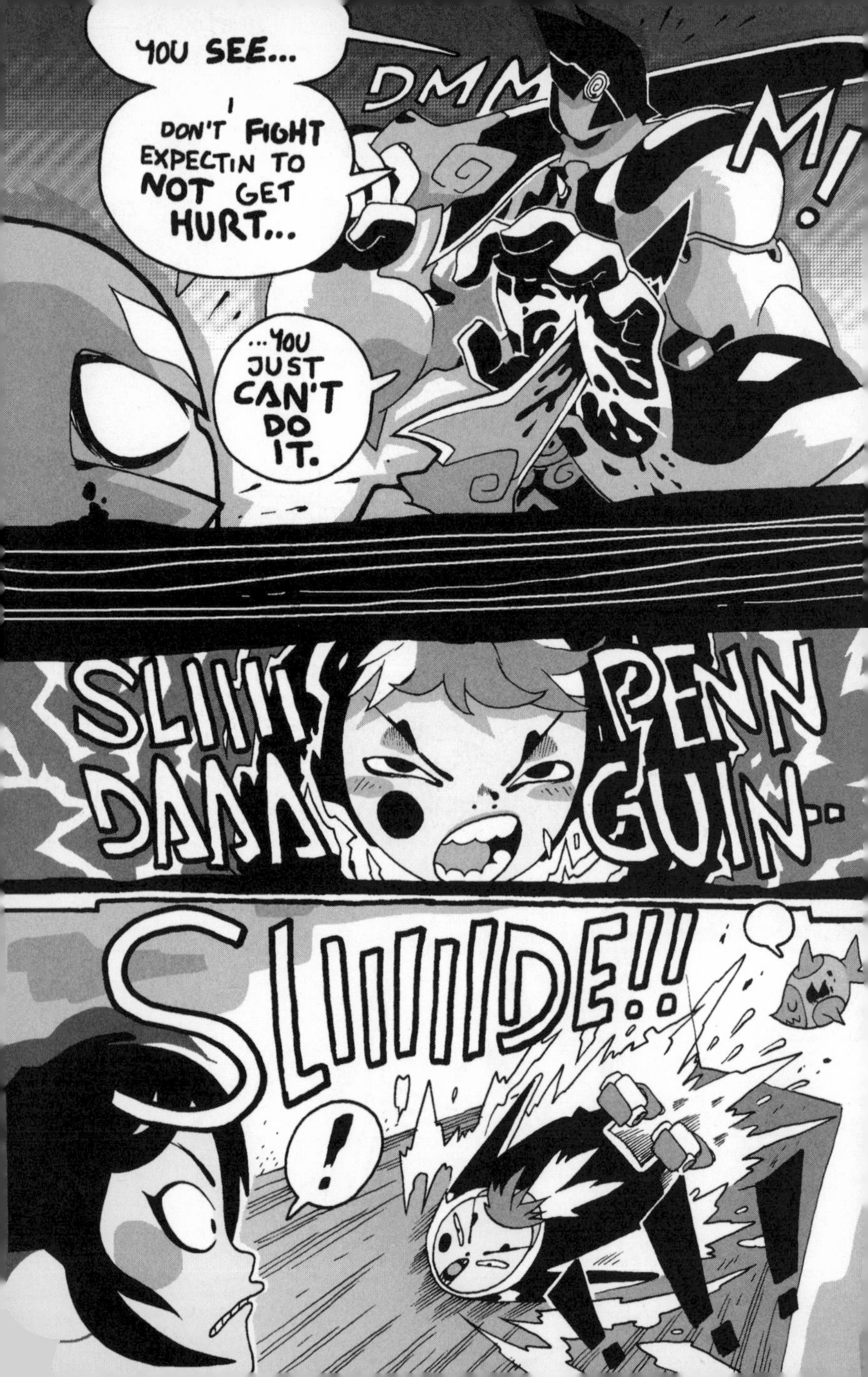
YOU SEE...
I DON'T FIGHT EXPECTIN TO NOT GET HURT...
DMMMM!
...YOU JUST CAN'T DO IT.
SLIIIIS PENN
DAAAA GUIN..
SLIIIIDE!!
!

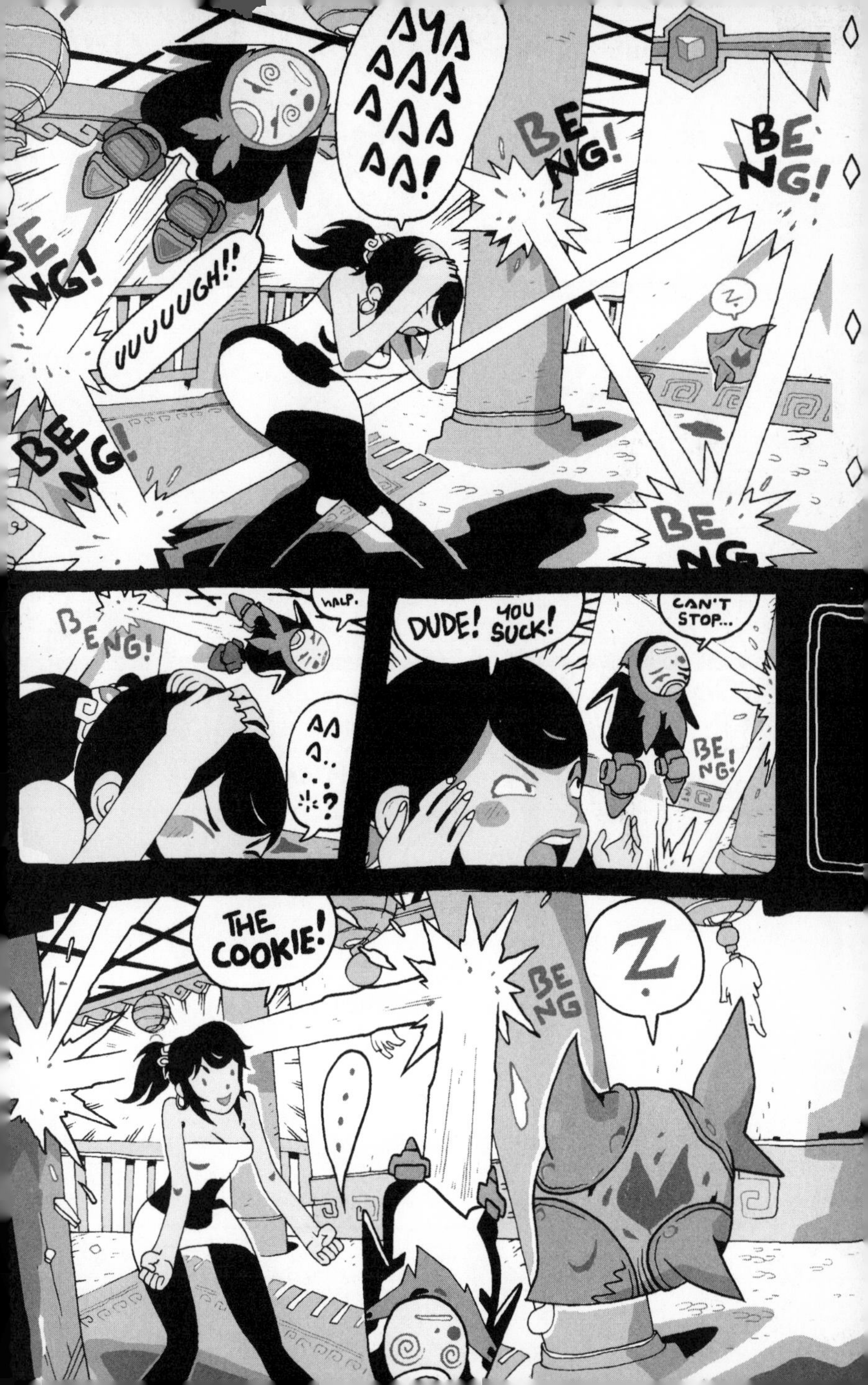

AYAAAAAAAAAAAA!
BENG!
BENG!
UUUUUGH!!
BENG!
BENG!
BENG!
BENG!
halp.
AAA...
...?
DUDE! YOU SUCK!
CAN'T STOP...
BENG!
THE COOKIE!
BENG
Z

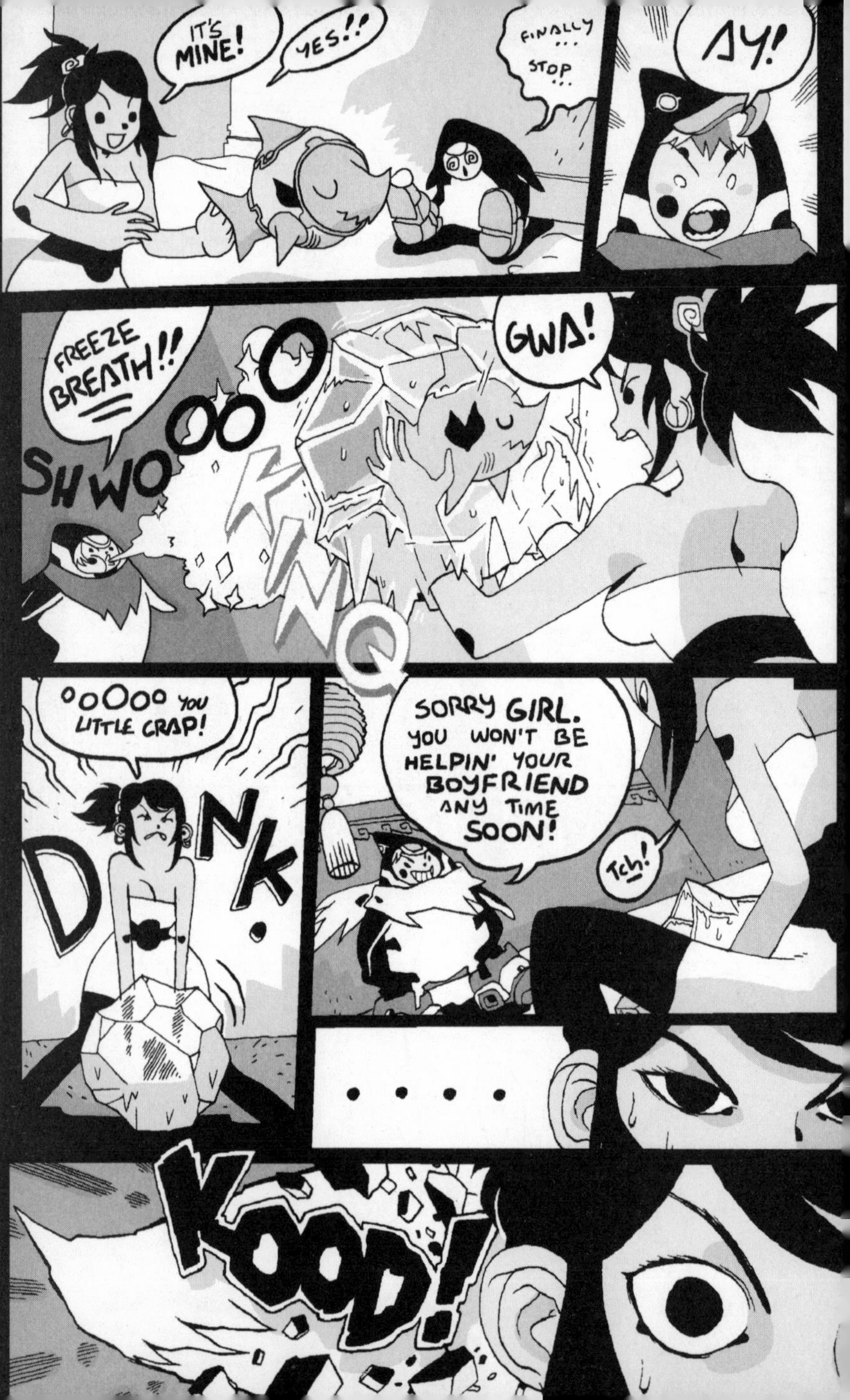
IT'S MINE!
YES!!
FINALLY ... STOP ...
AY!
FREEZE BREATH!!
SHWOOOO
GWA!
KINQ
OOOOO YOU LITTLE CRAP!
DONK
SORRY GIRL. YOU WON'T BE HELPIN' YOUR BOYFRIEND ANY TIME SOON!
Tch!
....
KOOD!

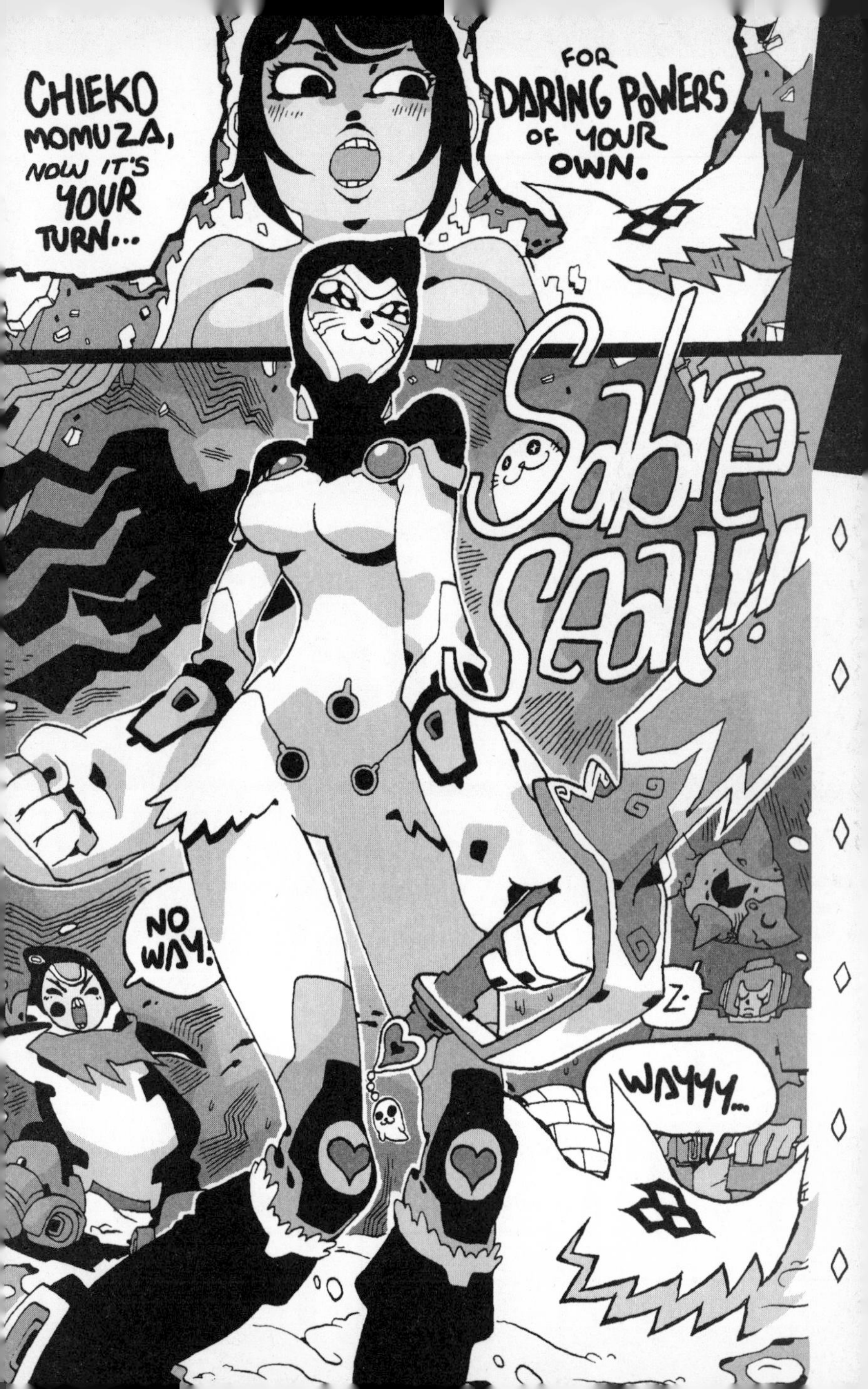
CHIEKO MOMUZA, NOW IT'S YOUR TURN...
FOR DARING POWERS OF YOUR OWN.
Sabre Seal!!
NO WAY!
Z
WAYYY...

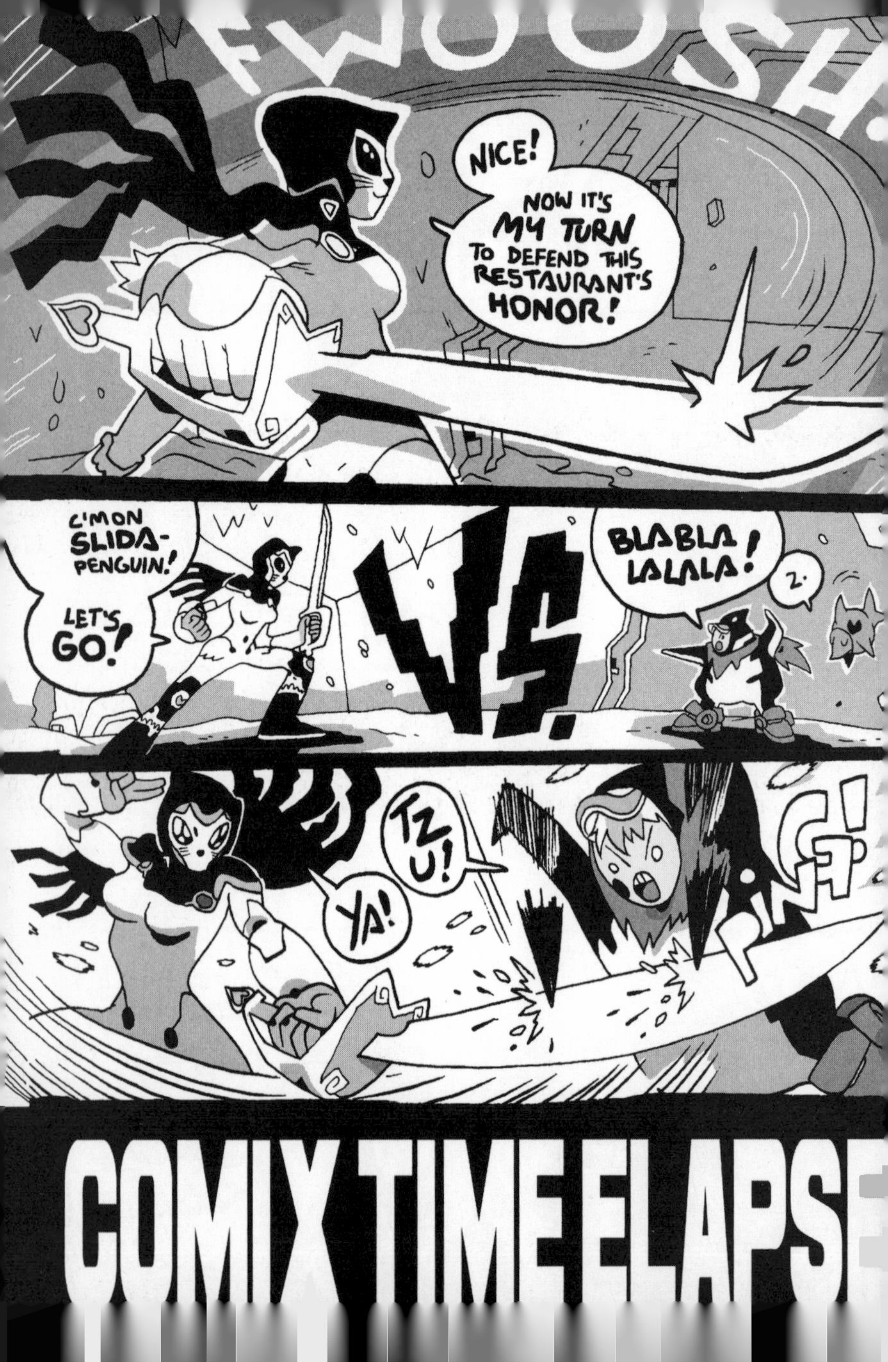
FWOOSH!
NICE!
NOW IT'S MY TURN TO DEFEND THIS RESTAURANT'S HONOR!
C'MON SLIDA-PENGUIN!
LET'S GO!
VS.
BLABLA! LALALA!
YA!
TZU!
PING!
COMIX TIME ELAPSE

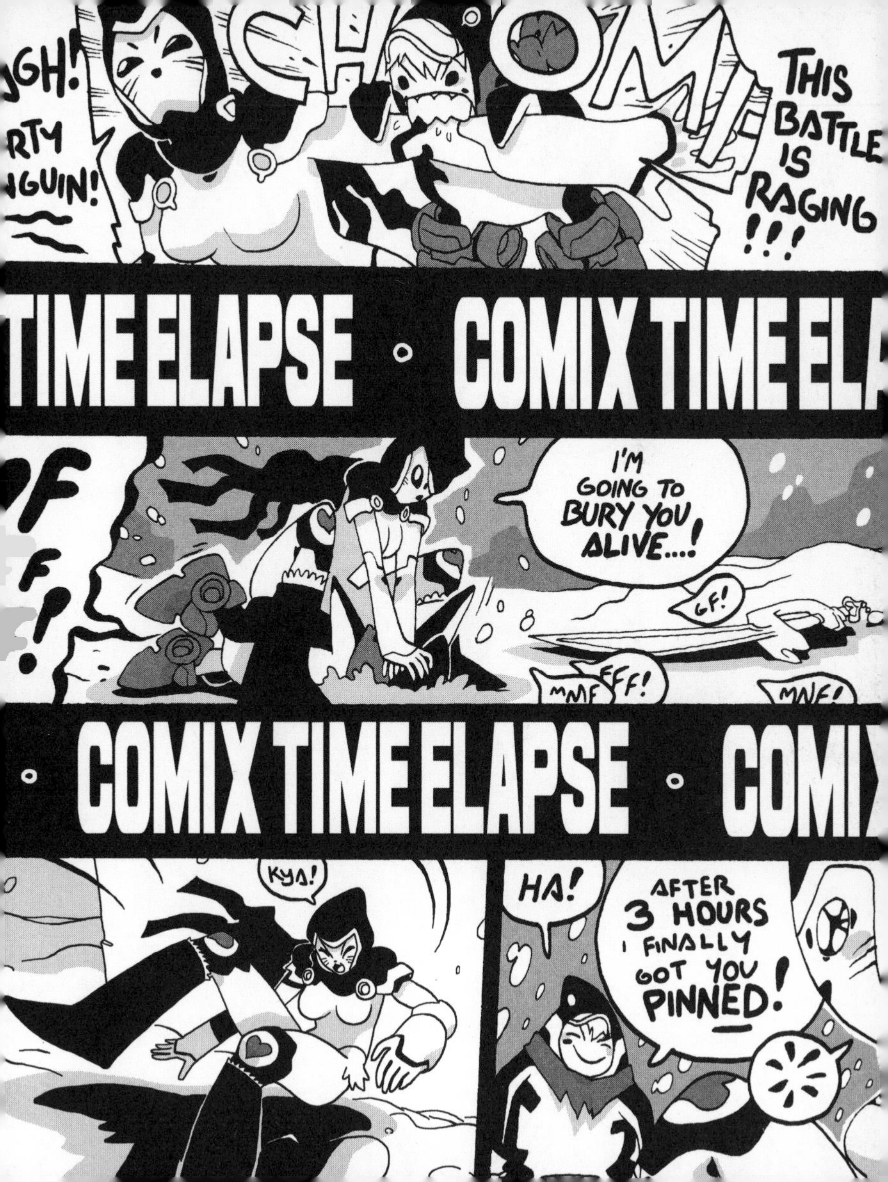
GH!
RTY
NGUIN!
THIS BATTLE IS RAGING!!!
TIME ELAPSE • COMIX TIME ELA
I'M GOING TO BURY YOU ALIVE...!
GF!
MNF
FFF!
MNF!
• COMIX TIME ELAPSE • COMI
KYA!
HA!
AFTER 3 HOURS I FINALLY GOT YOU PINNED!

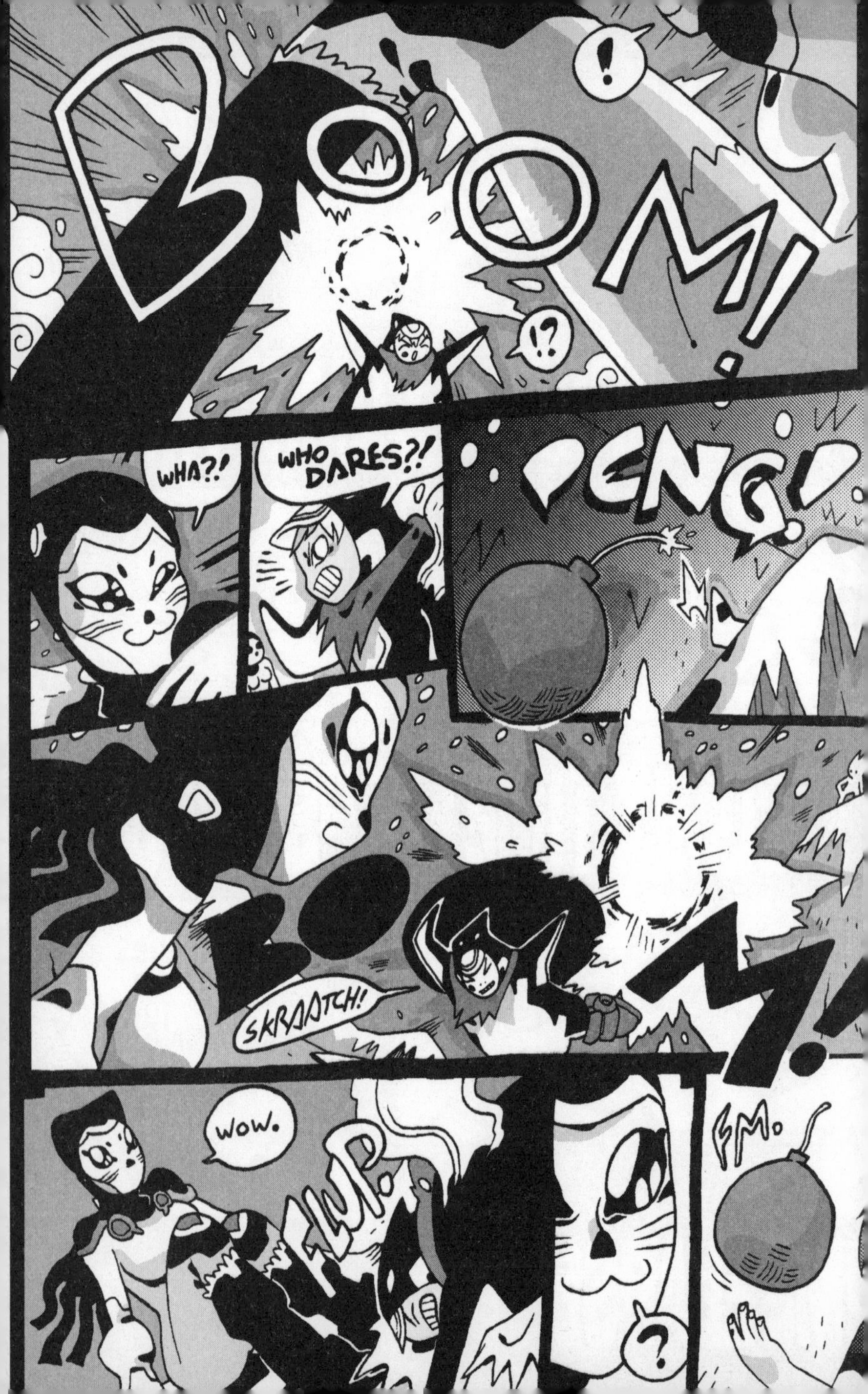
BOOM!
!
!?
WHA?!
WHO DARES?!
PENG!
BOOM!
SKRAATCH!
WOW.
FM.
?

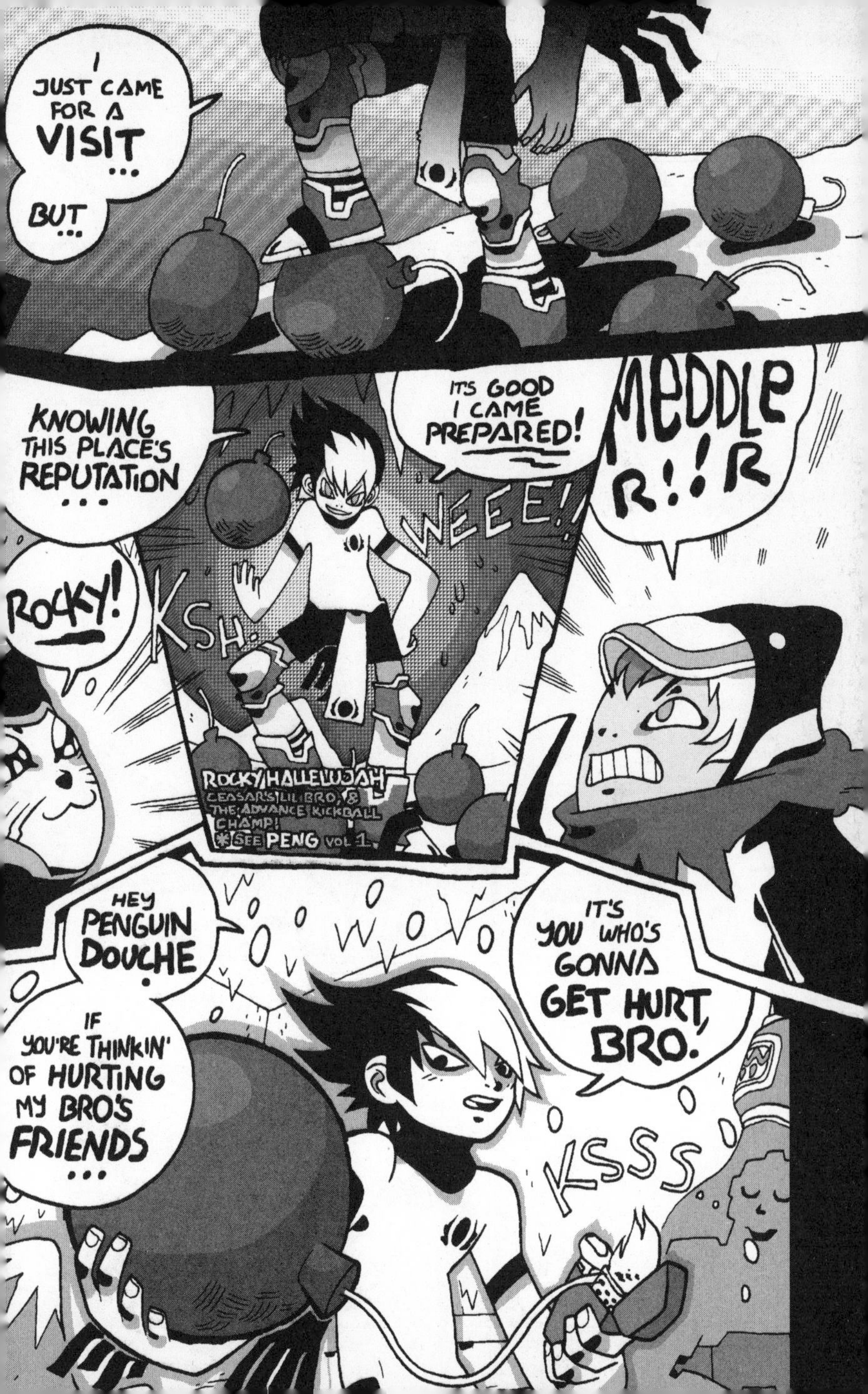
I JUST CAME FOR A VISIT ...
BUT ...
KNOWING THIS PLACE'S REPUTATION ...
IT'S GOOD I CAME PREPARED!
MEDDLE R!!R
WEEE!!
ROCKY!
KSH.
ROCKY HALLELUJAH
CEASAR'S LIL BRO, & THE ADVANCE KICKBALL CHAMP!
* SEE PENG VOL 1.
HEY PENGUIN DOUCHE.
IF YOU'RE THINKIN' OF HURTING MY BRO'S FRIENDS ...
IT'S YOU WHO'S GONNA GET HURT, BRO.
KSSS

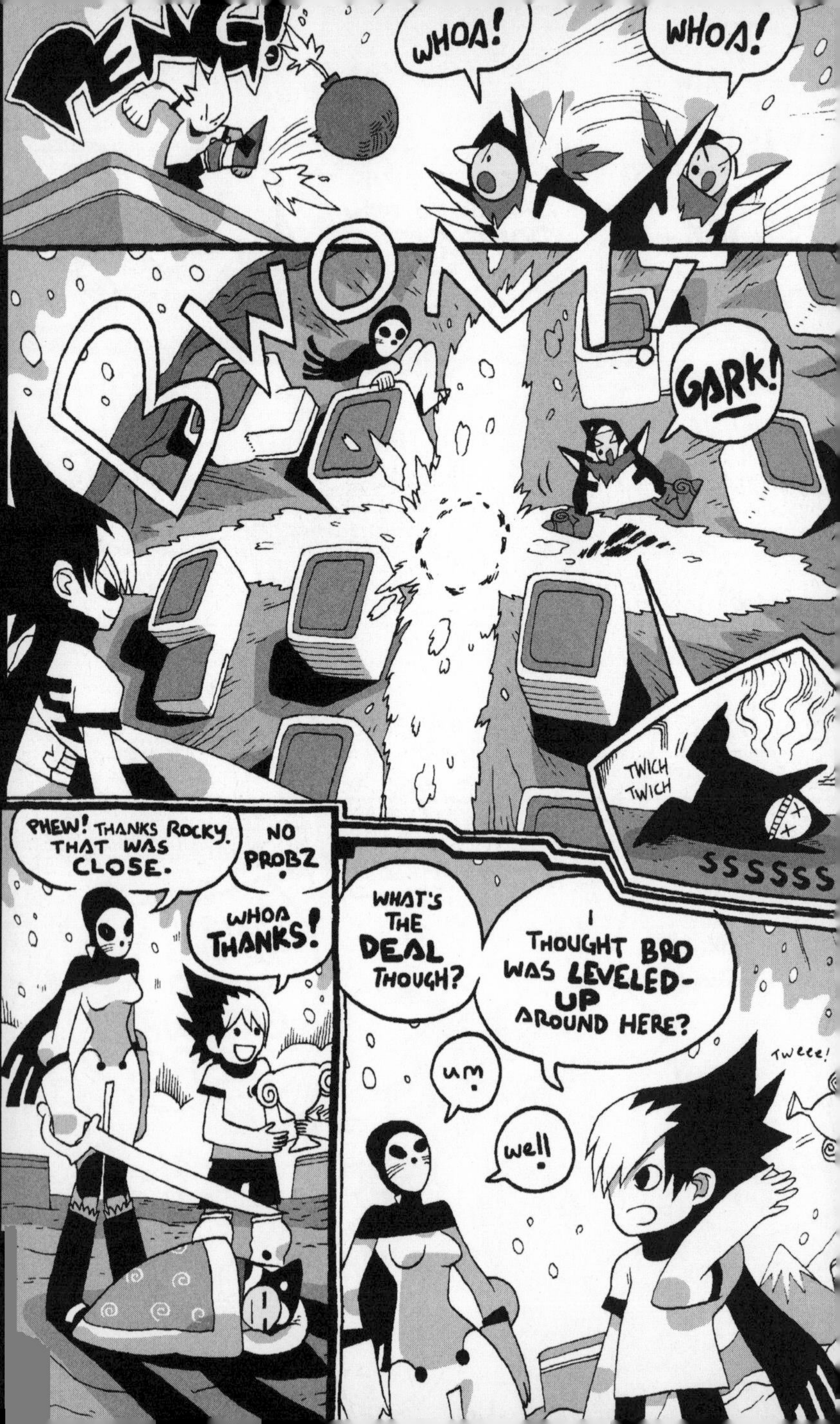

WHOA!
WHOA!
GARK!
TWICH TWICH
SSSSSS
PHEW! THANKS ROCKY. THAT WAS CLOSE.
NO PROBZ
WHOA THANKS!
WHAT'S THE DEAL THOUGH?
I THOUGHT BAD WAS LEVELED-UP AROUND HERE?
um.
well
Tweee!

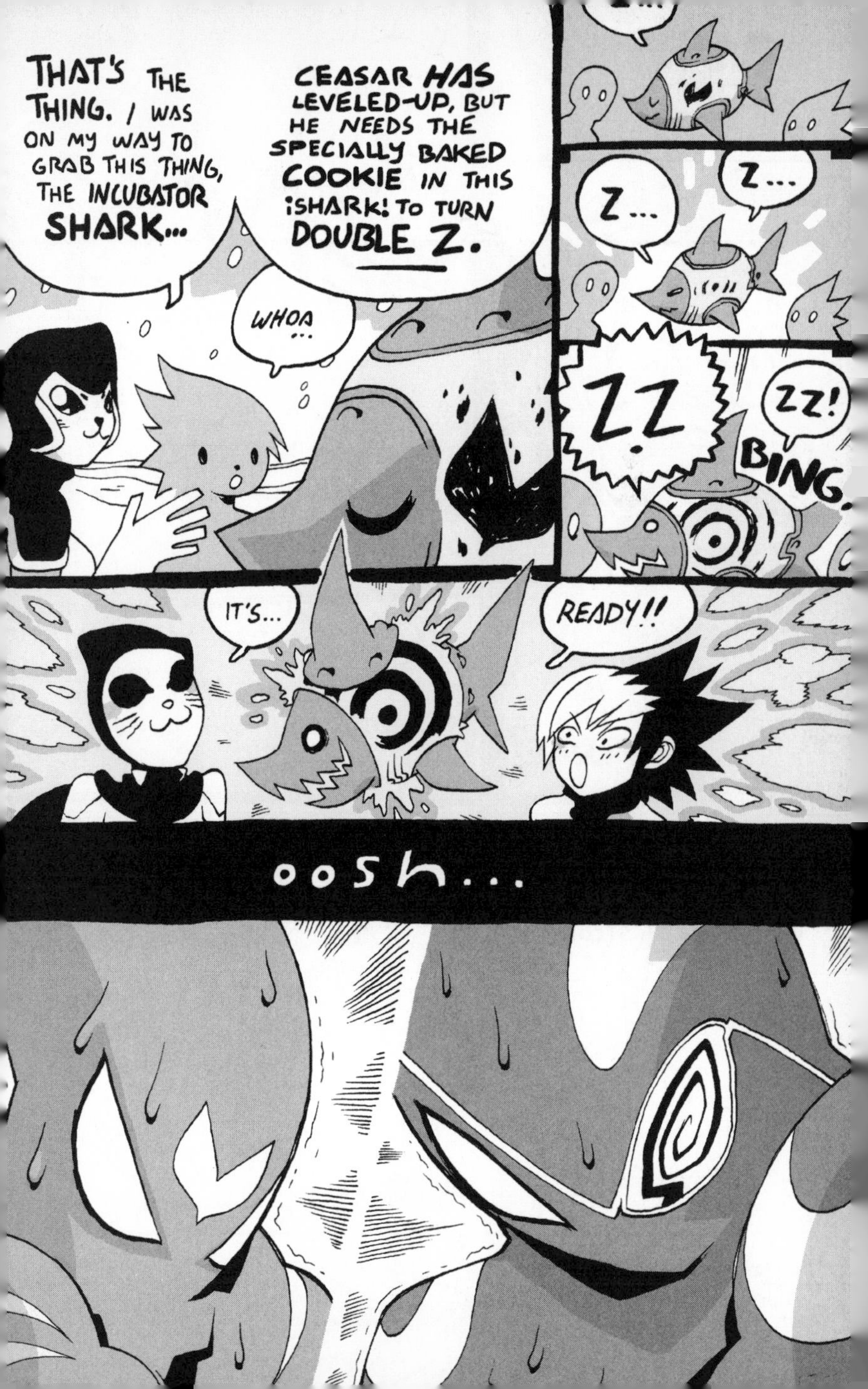
THAT'S THE THING. I WAS ON MY WAY TO GRAB THIS THING, THE INCUBATOR SHARK...
CEASAR HAS LEVELED-UP, BUT HE NEEDS THE SPECIALLY BAKED COOKIE IN THIS ¡SHARK! TO TURN DOUBLE Z.
WHOA ...
Z...
Z...
ZZ
ZZ!
BING.
IT'S...
READY!!
oosh...

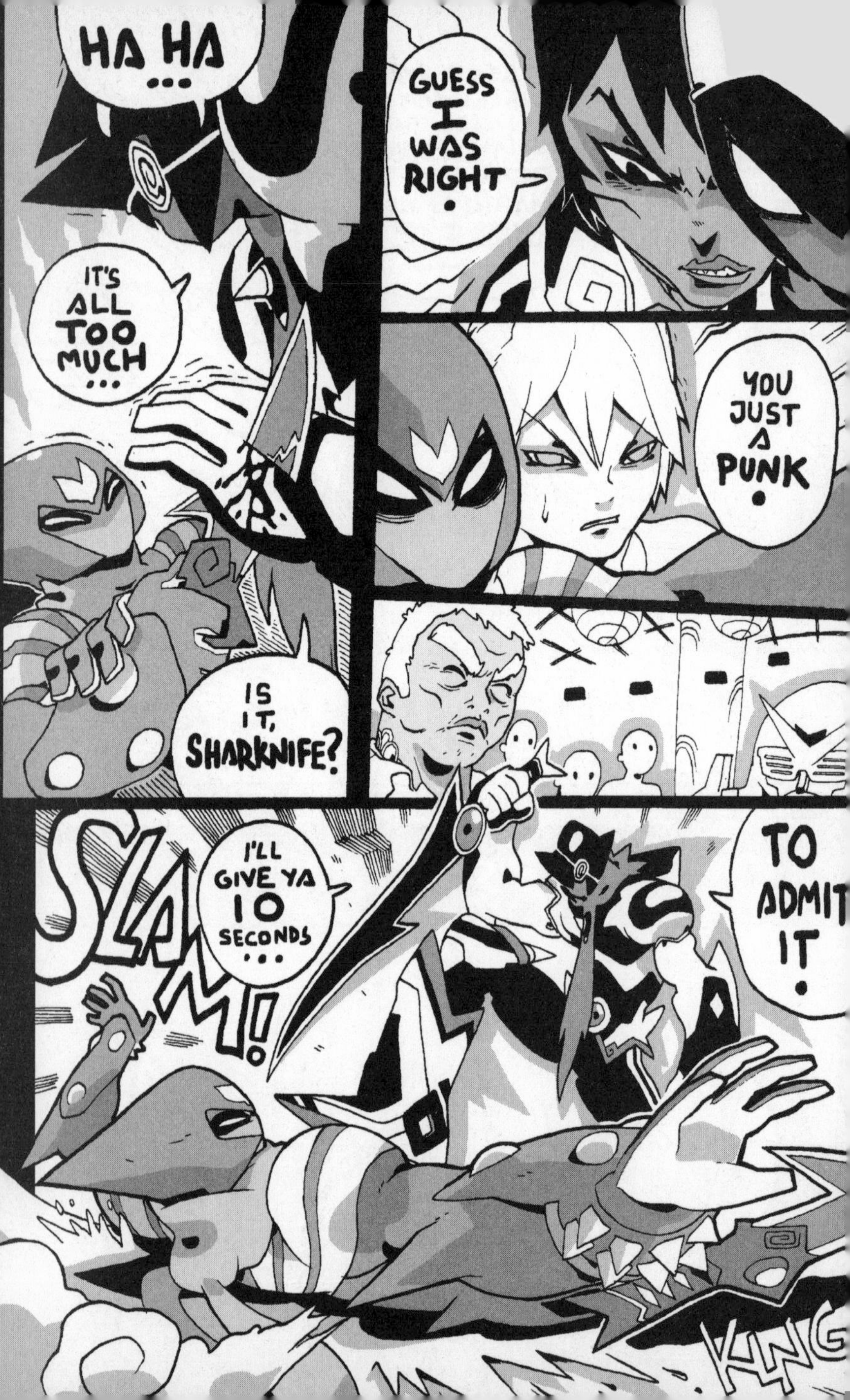
HA HA ...
GUESS I WAS RIGHT.
IT'S ALL TOO MUCH ...
YOU JUST A PUNK.
IS IT, SHARKNIFE?
SLAM!
I'LL GIVE YA 10 SECONDS ...
TO ADMIT IT.
KLNG

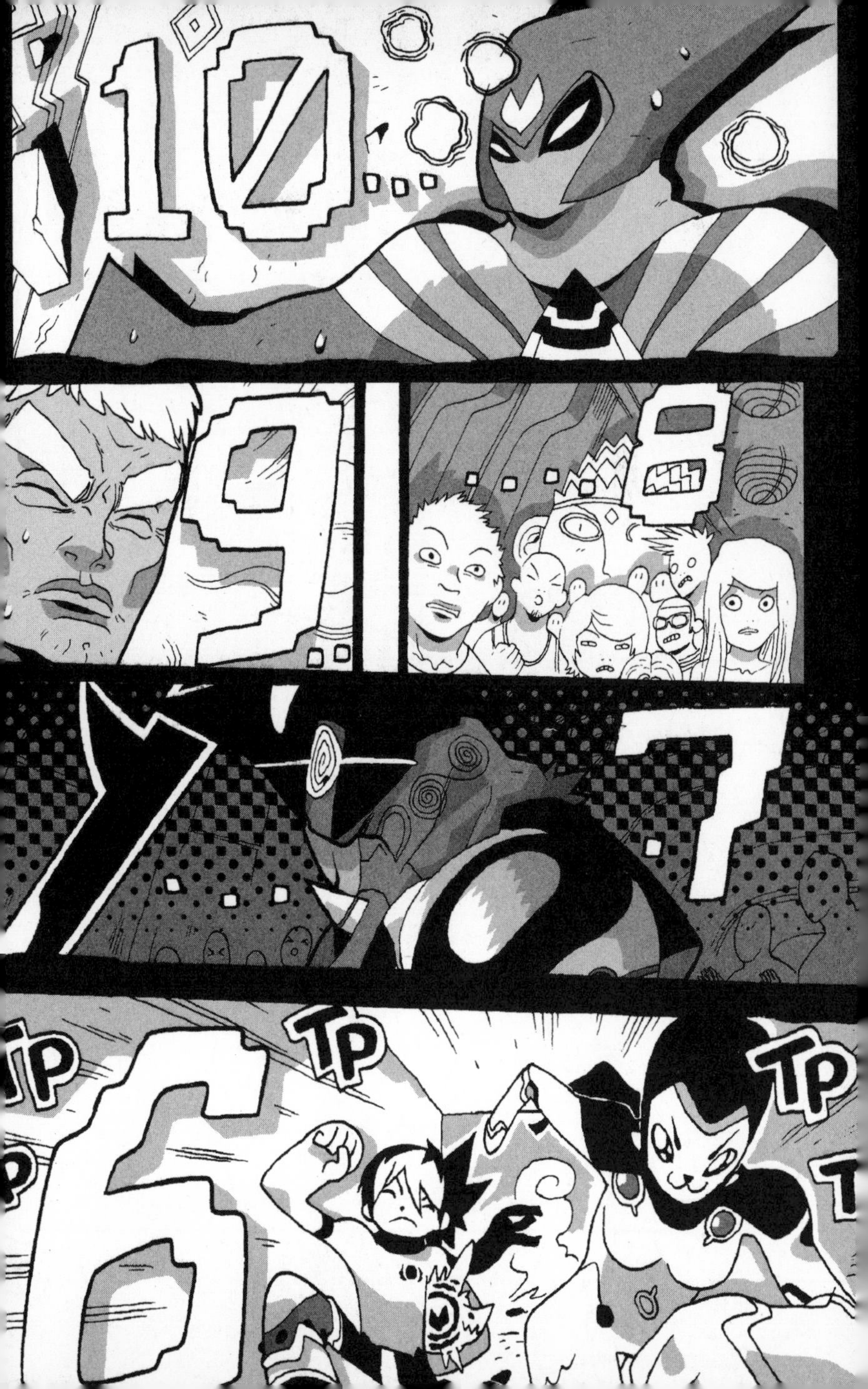

10....
9..
...8
7
6
TP
TP
TP

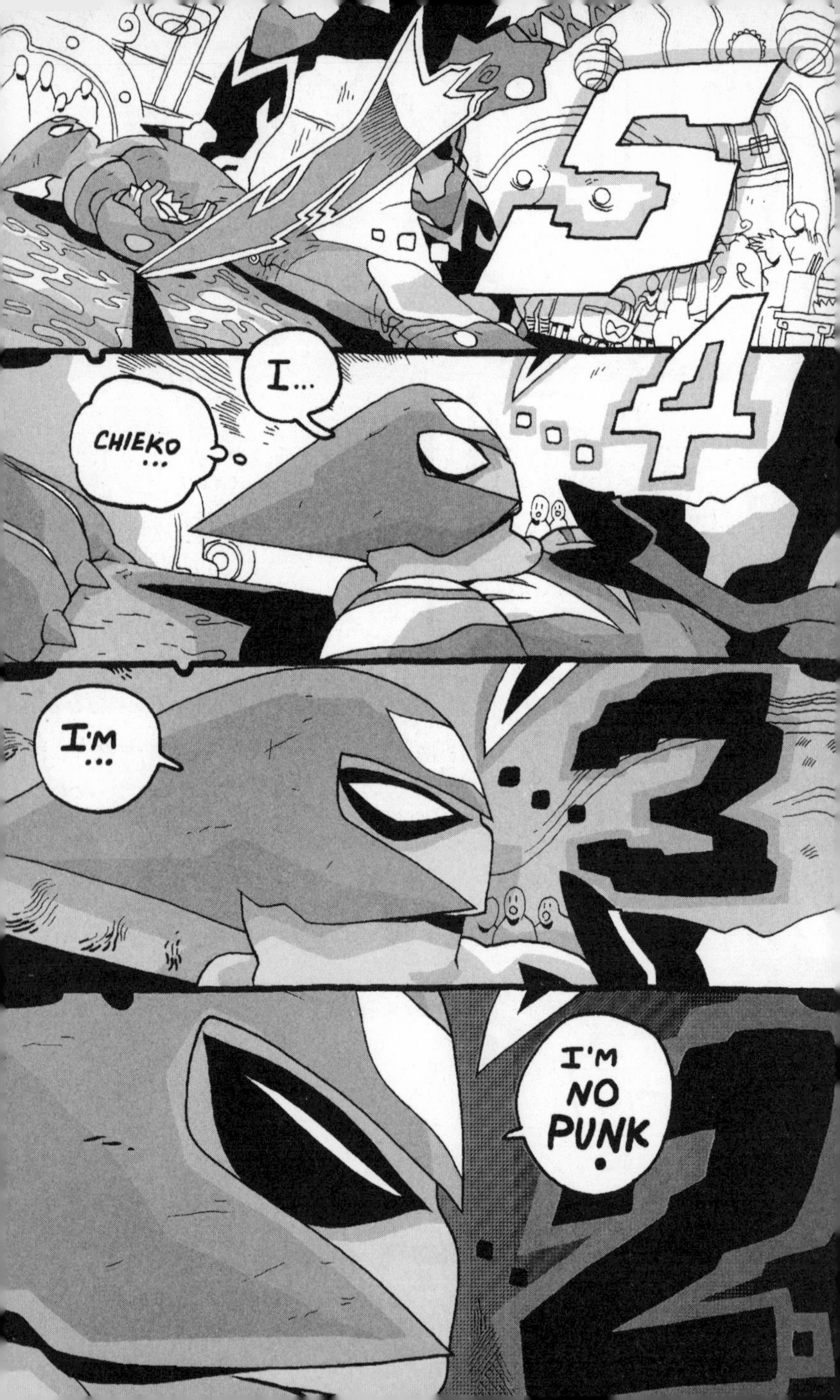
5
I...
CHIEKO...
4
I'M...
3
I'M NO PUNK.

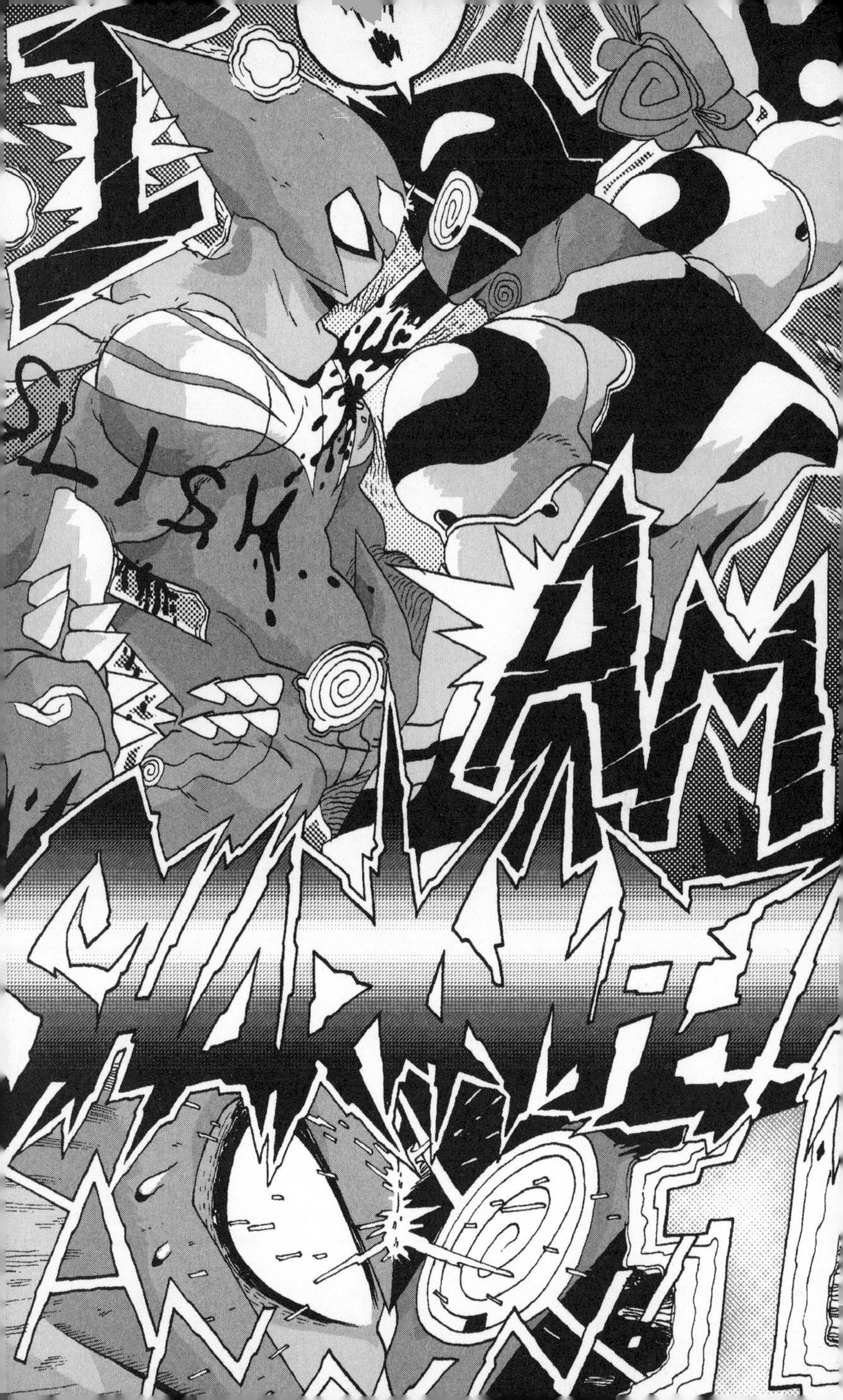
SLISH

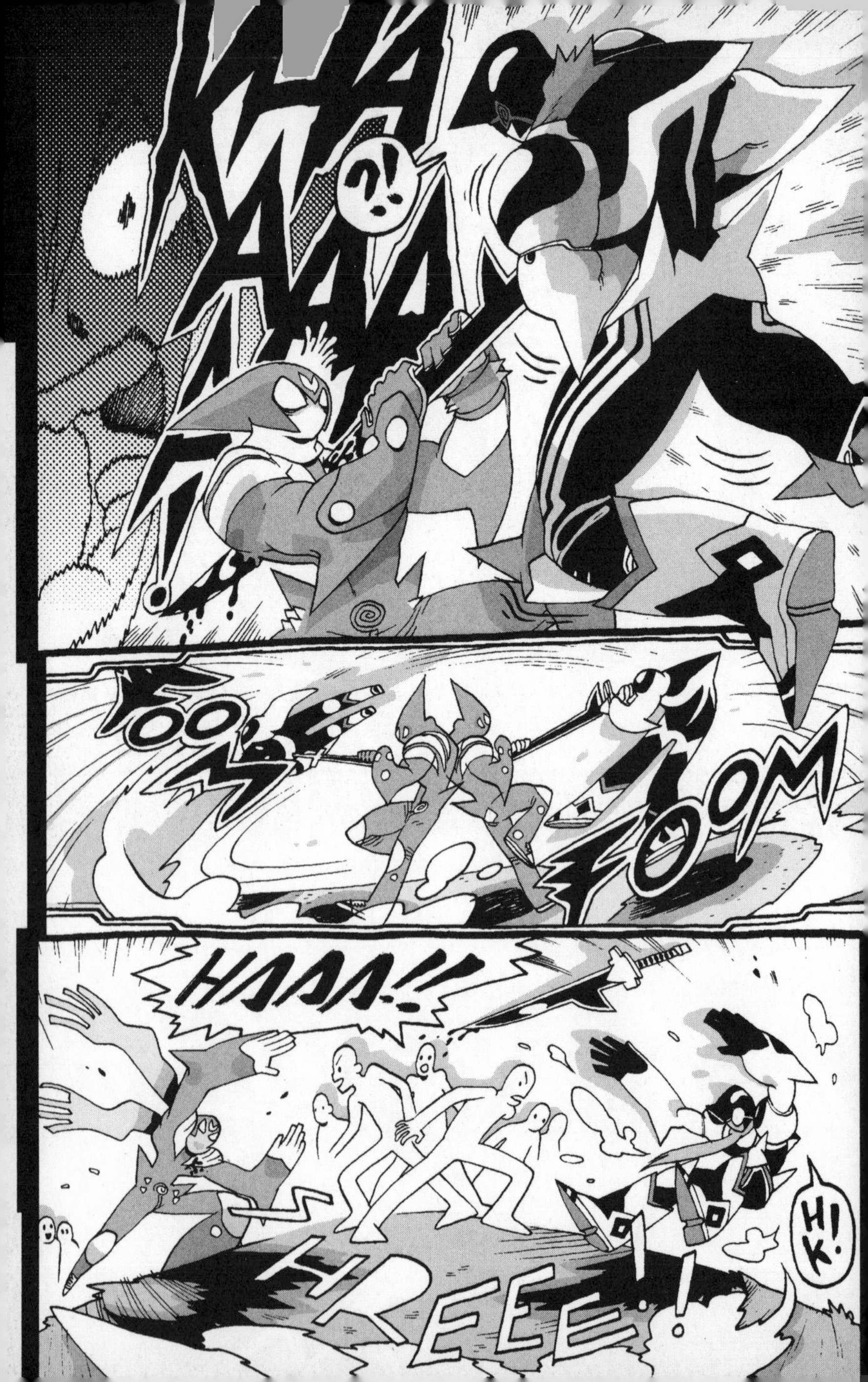
WAAAA!
?!
FOOM
FOOM
HAAA!!
HIK!
HREEE!!

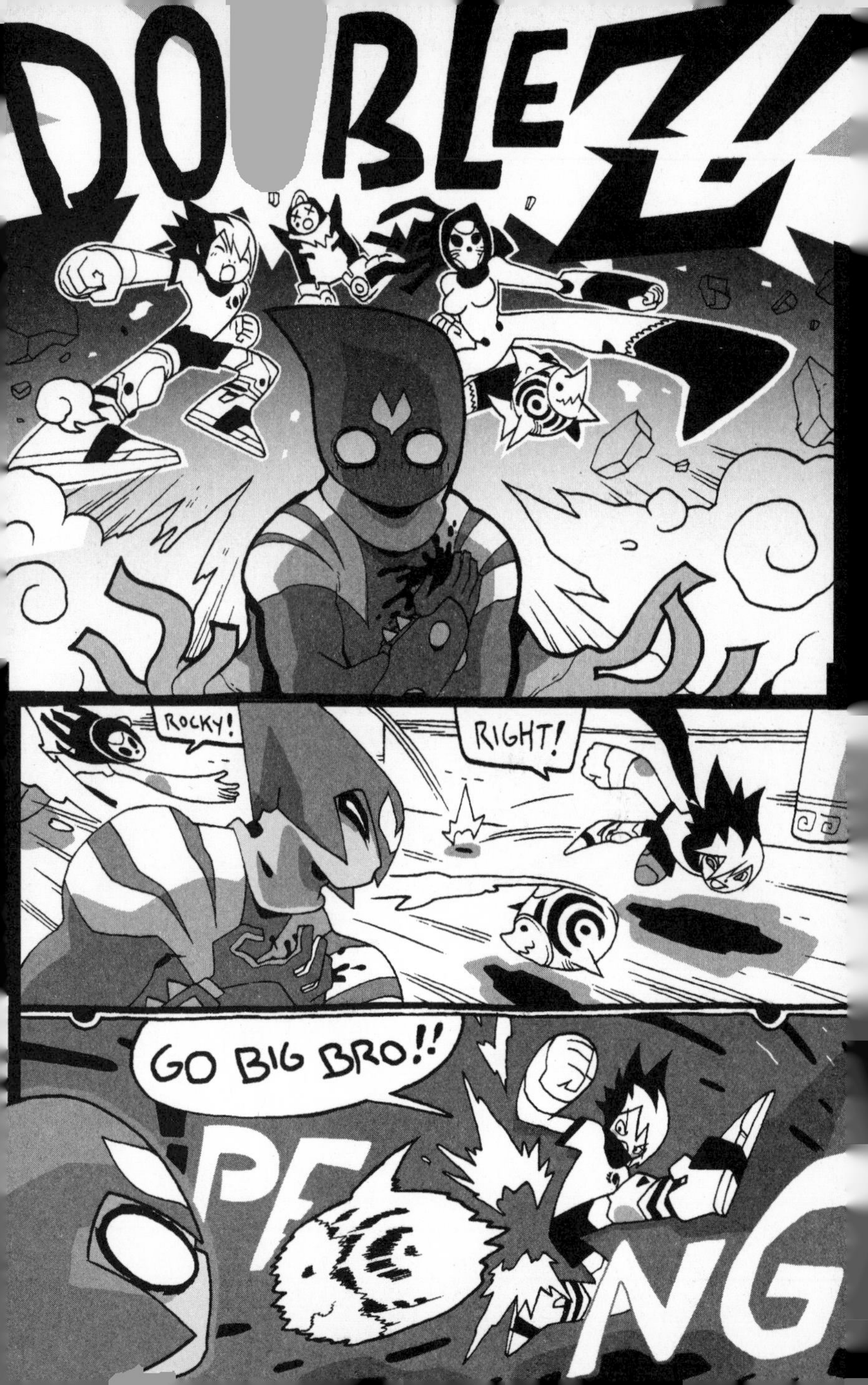
DOUBLE Z!
ROCKY!
RIGHT!
GO BIG BRO!!

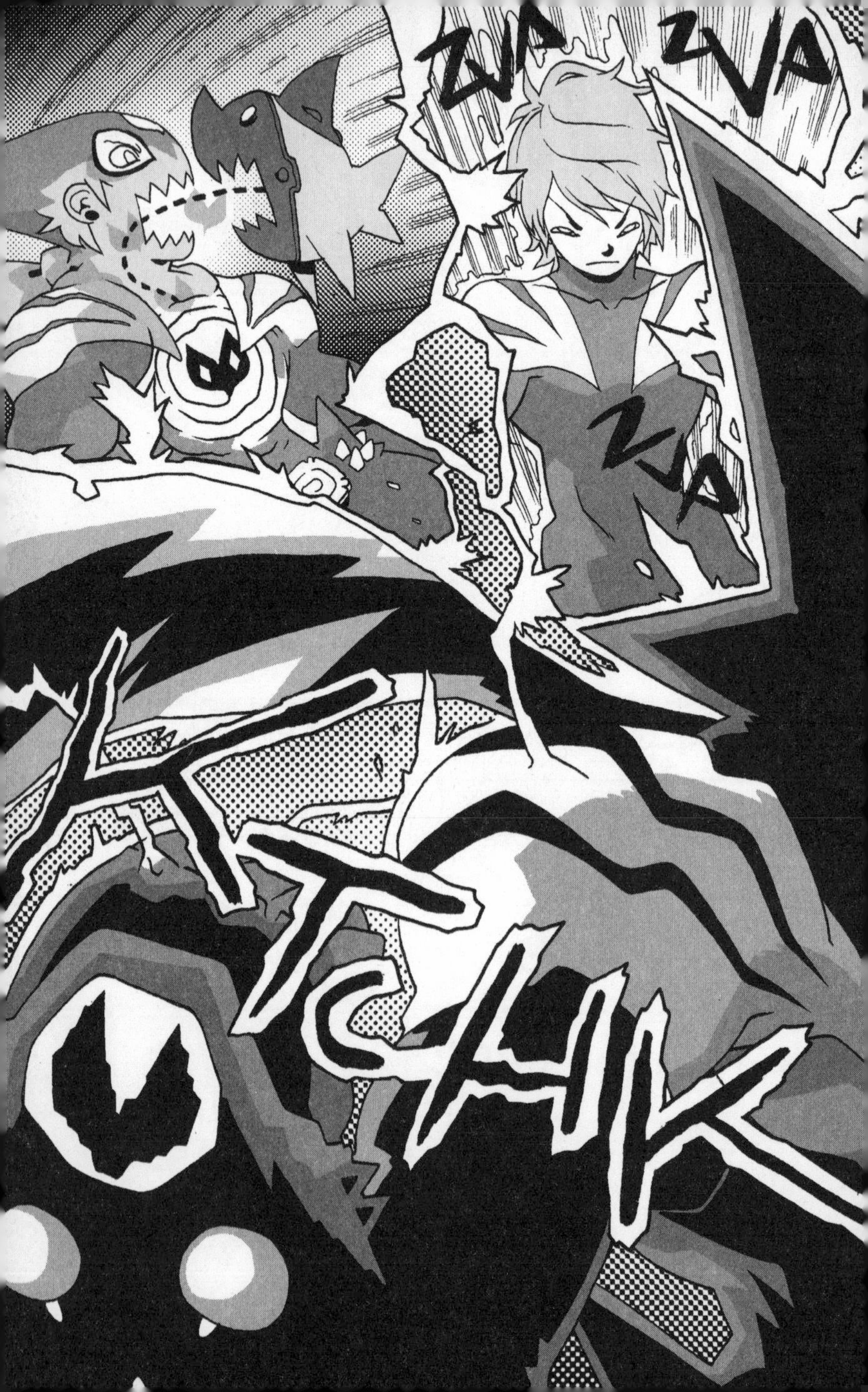
ZVA ZVA
ZVA
KATCHAK

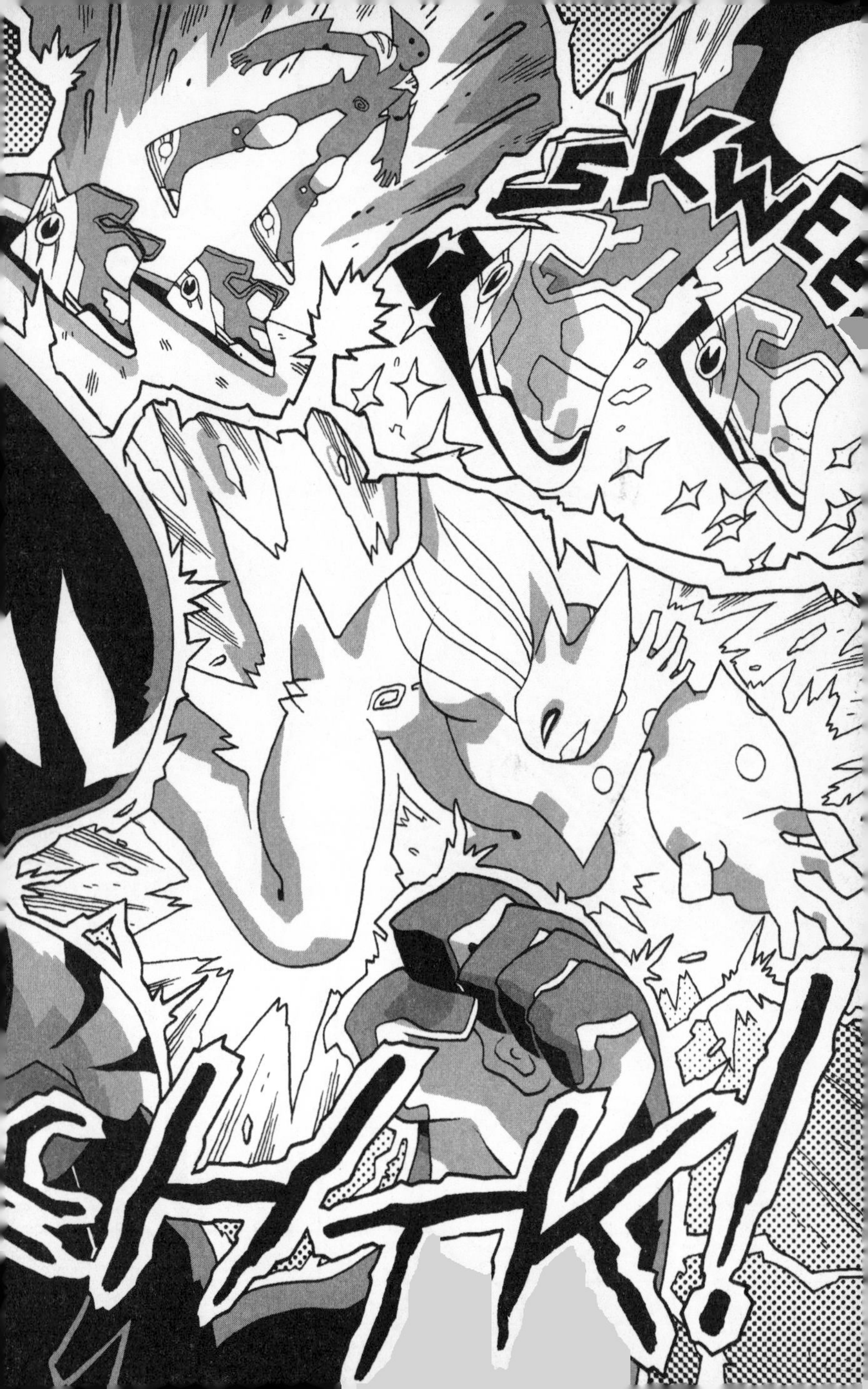
SKWEE
SHHTK!

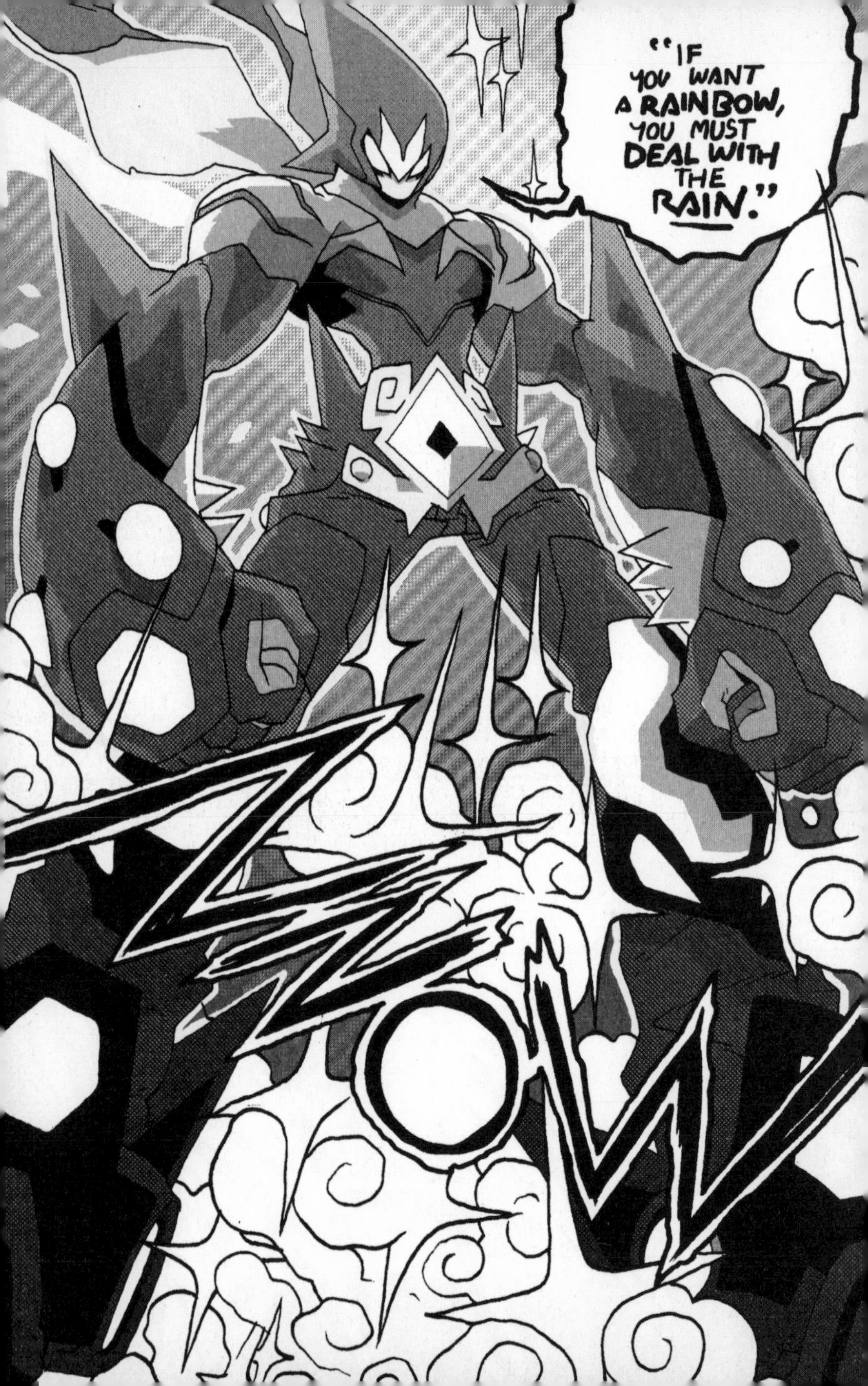
"IF YOU WANT A RAINBOW, YOU MUST DEAL WITH THE RAIN."
ZZOW

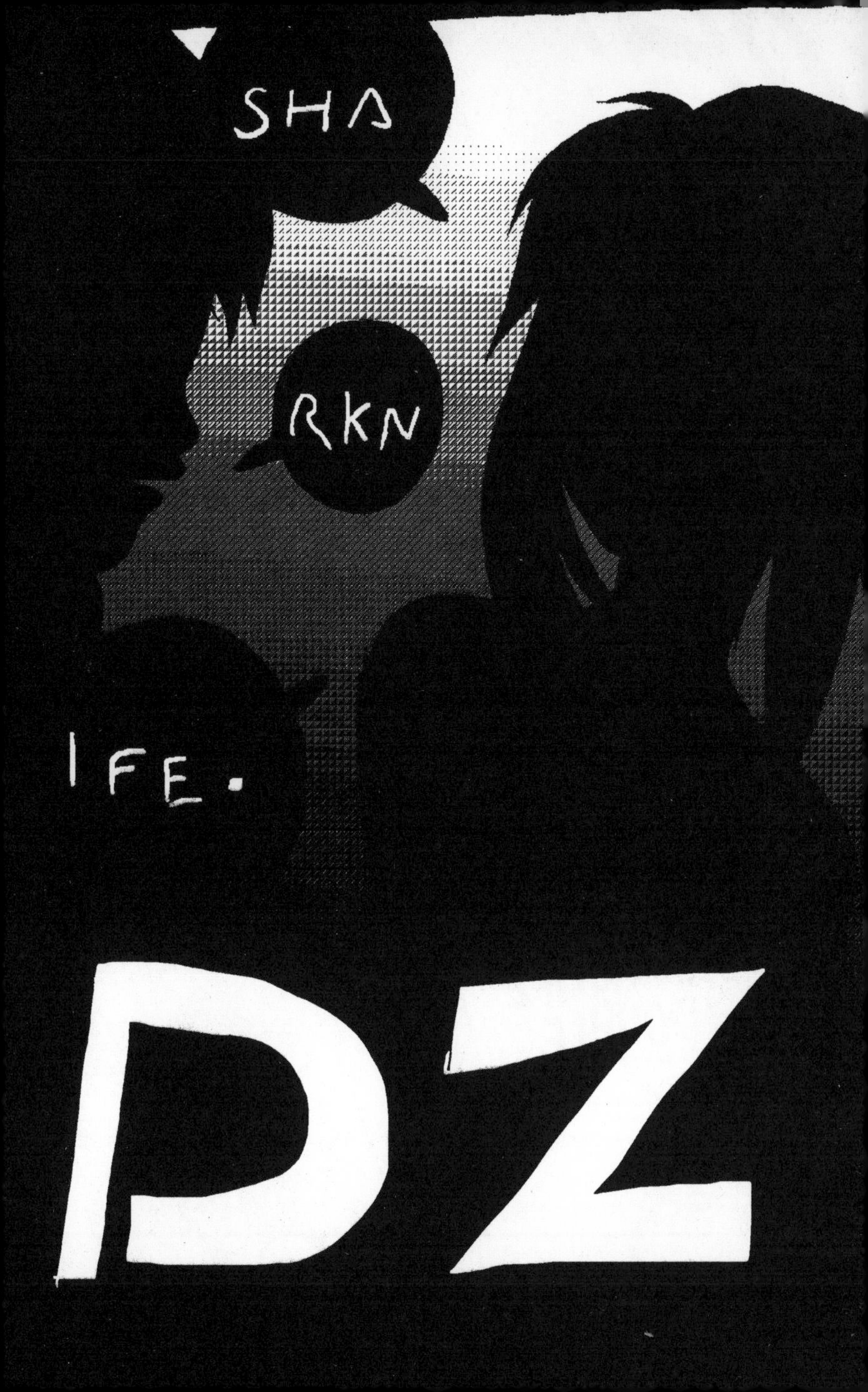
SHA
RKN
IFE.
DZ

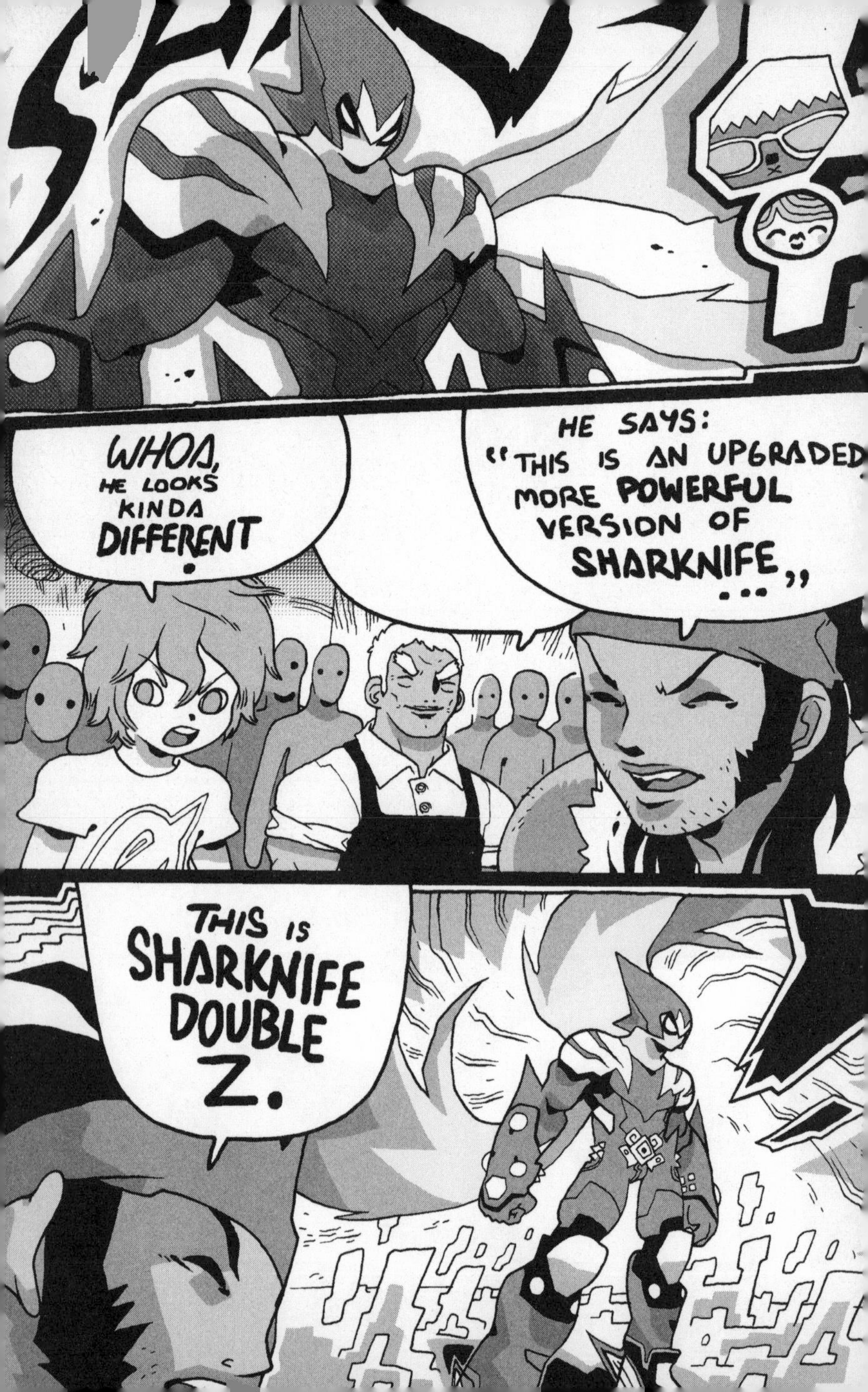
WHOA, HE LOOKS KINDA DIFFERENT.
HE SAYS: "THIS IS AN UPGRADED MORE POWERFUL VERSION OF SHARKNIFE"...
THIS IS SHARKNIFE DOUBLE Z.

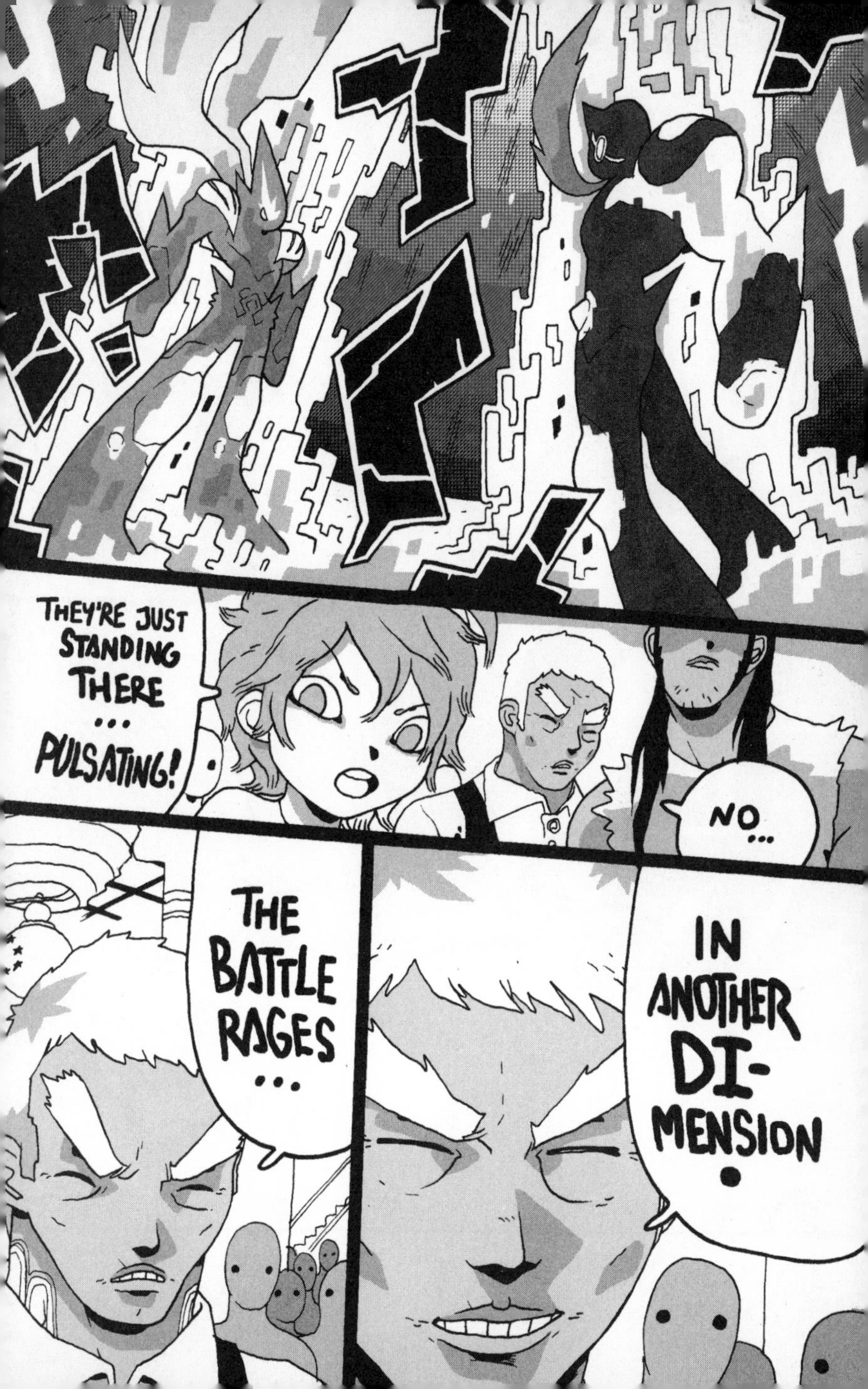
THEY'RE JUST STANDING THERE ... PULSATING!
NO...
THE BATTLE RAGES ...
IN ANOTHER DI-MENSION.

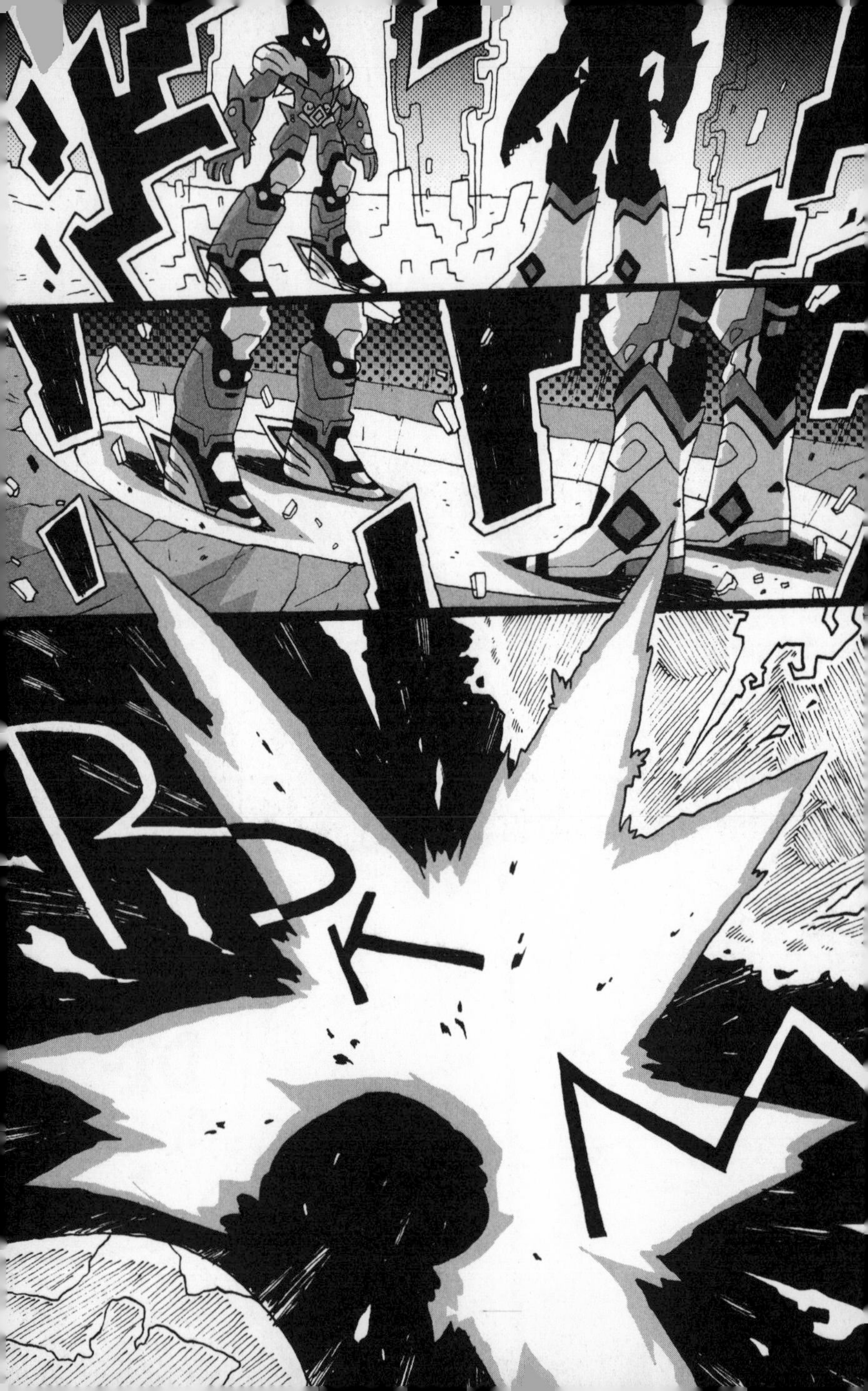

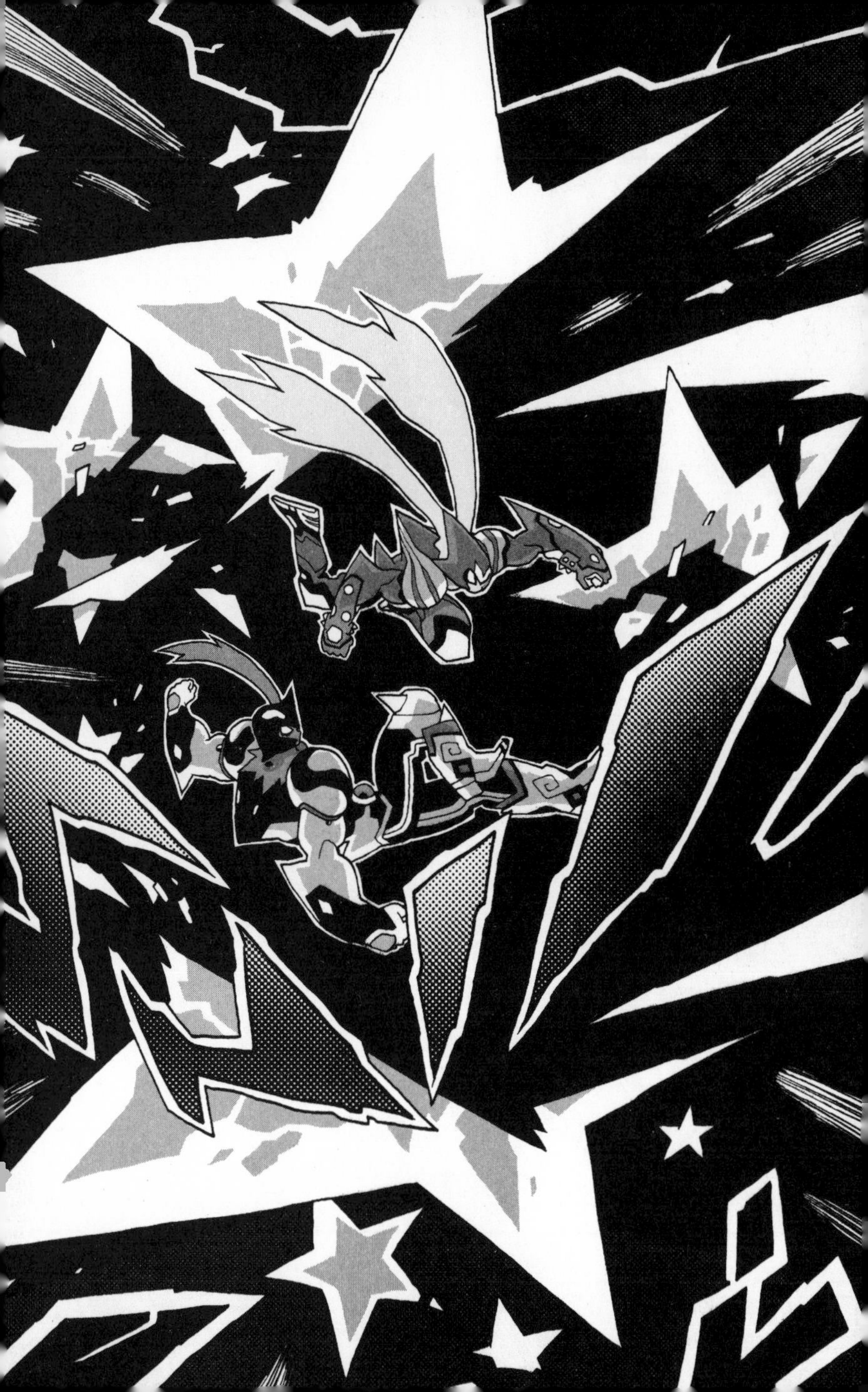

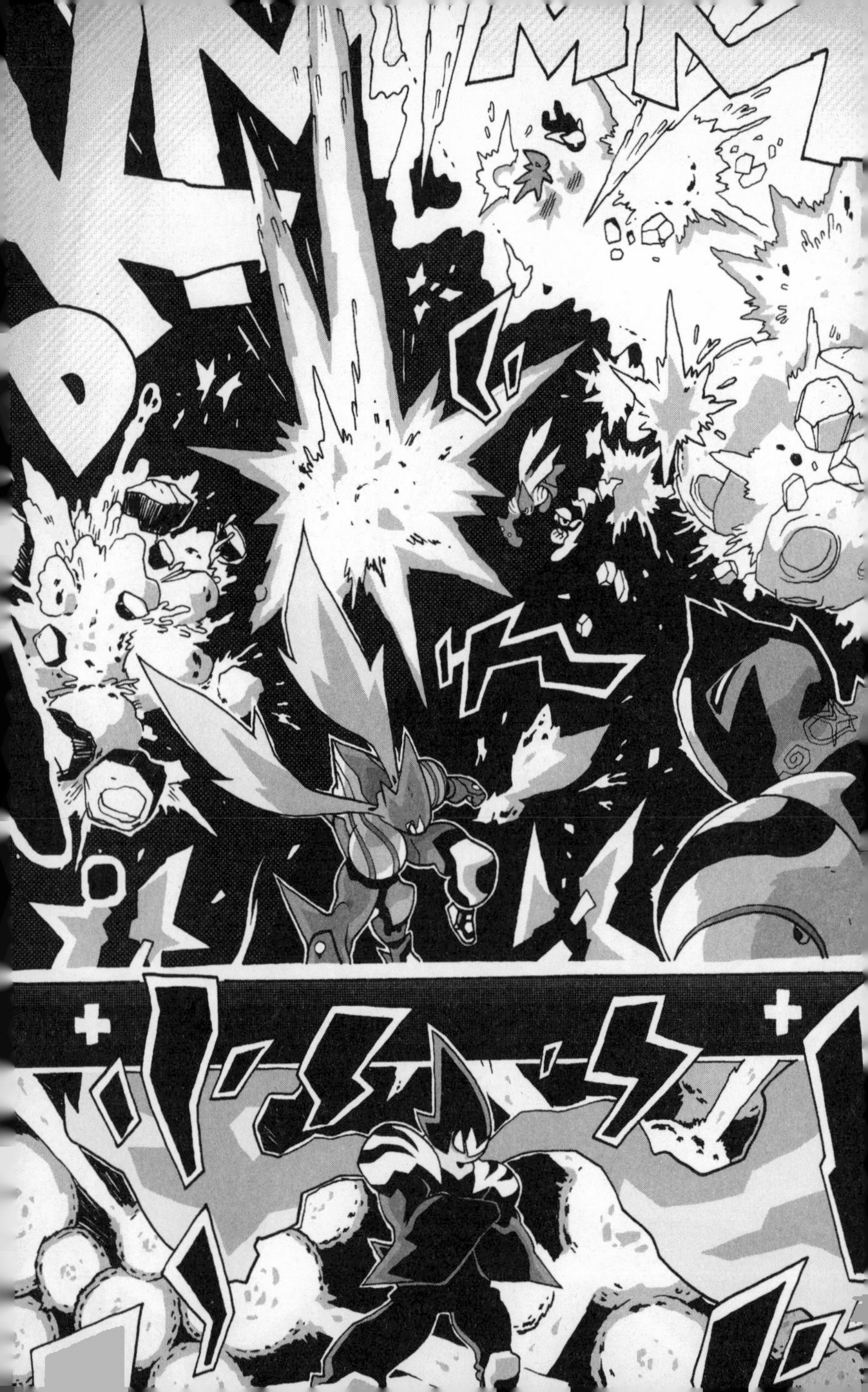

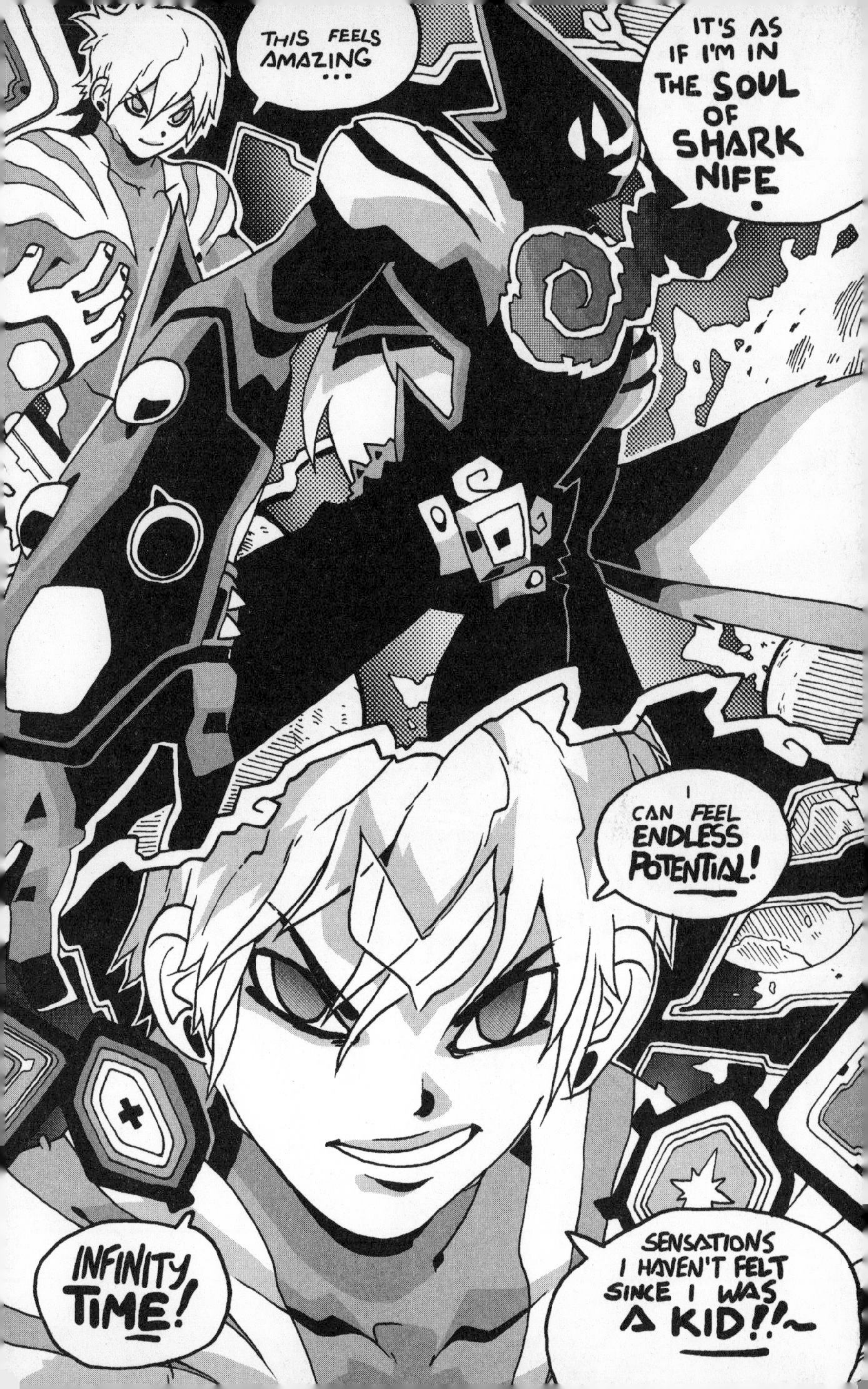
THIS FEELS AMAZING ...
IT'S AS IF I'M IN THE SOUL OF SHARK NIFE.
I CAN FEEL ENDLESS POTENTIAL!
SENSATIONS I HAVEN'T FELT SINCE I WAS A KID!!~
INFINITY TIME!

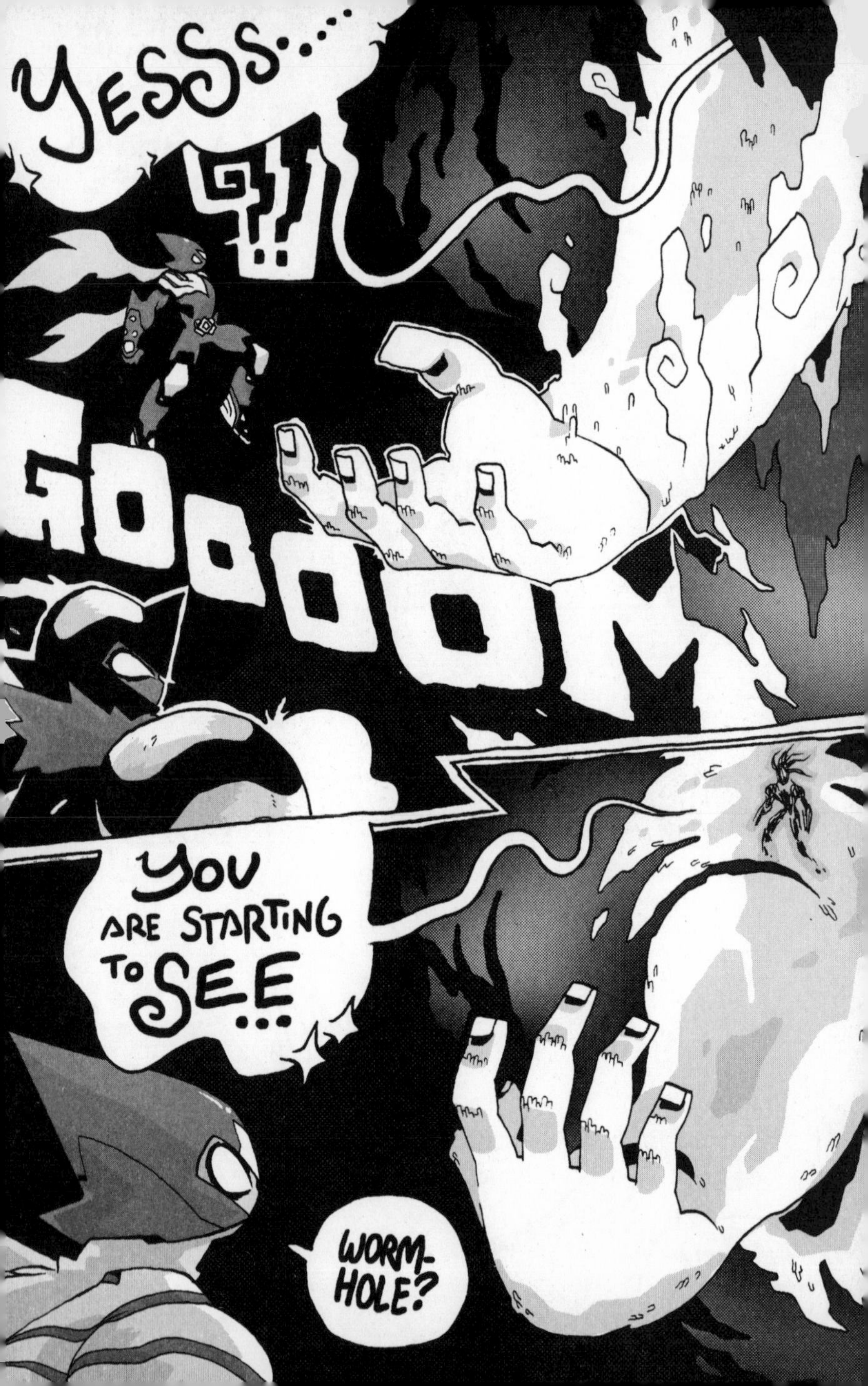
YESSS.....
G?!
BOOOOOM
YOU ARE STARTING TO SEE...
WORM-HOLE?

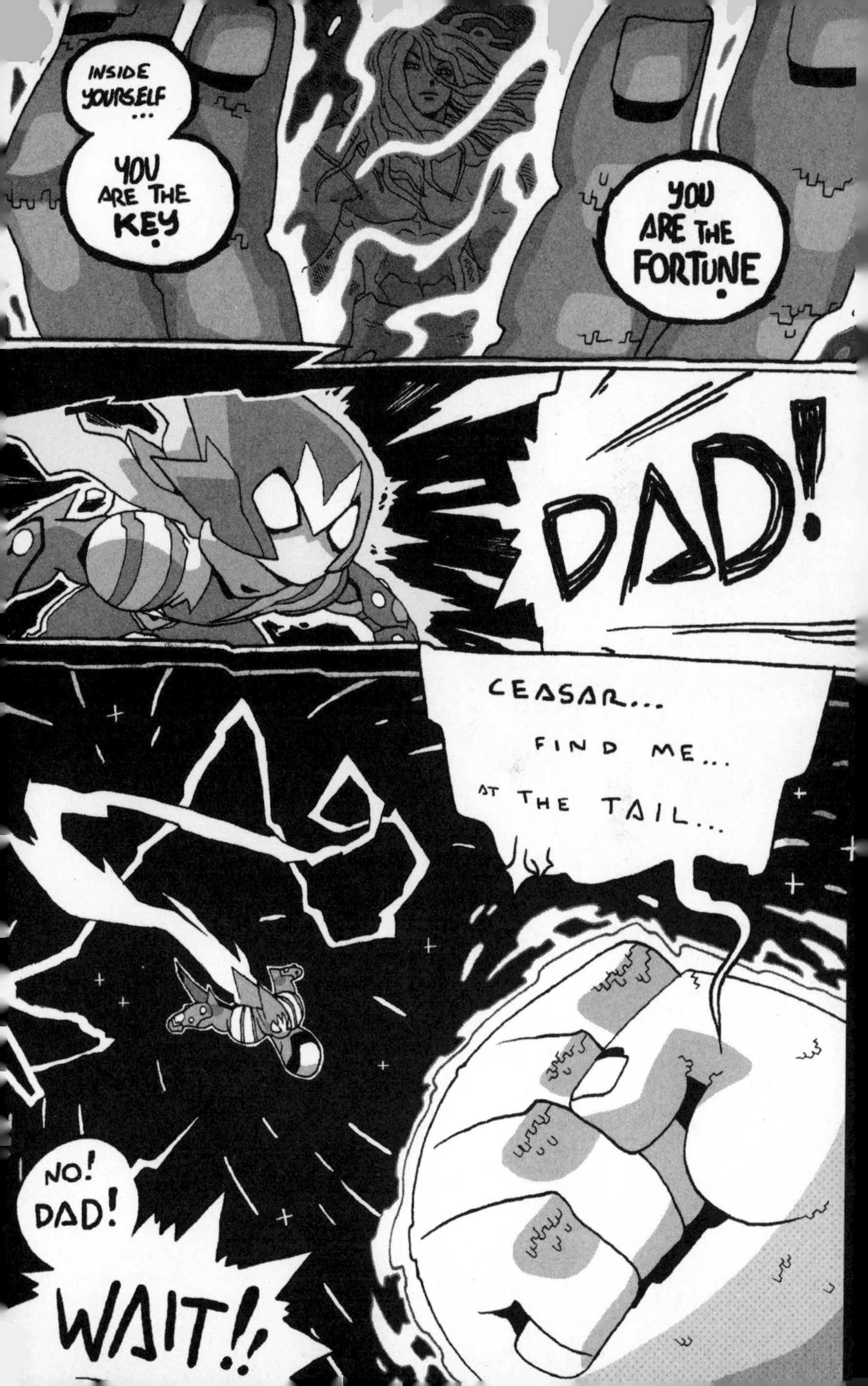
INSIDE YOURSELF...
YOU ARE THE KEY.
YOU ARE THE FORTUNE.
DAD!
CEASAR... FIND ME... AT THE TAIL...
NO! DAD!
WAIT!!

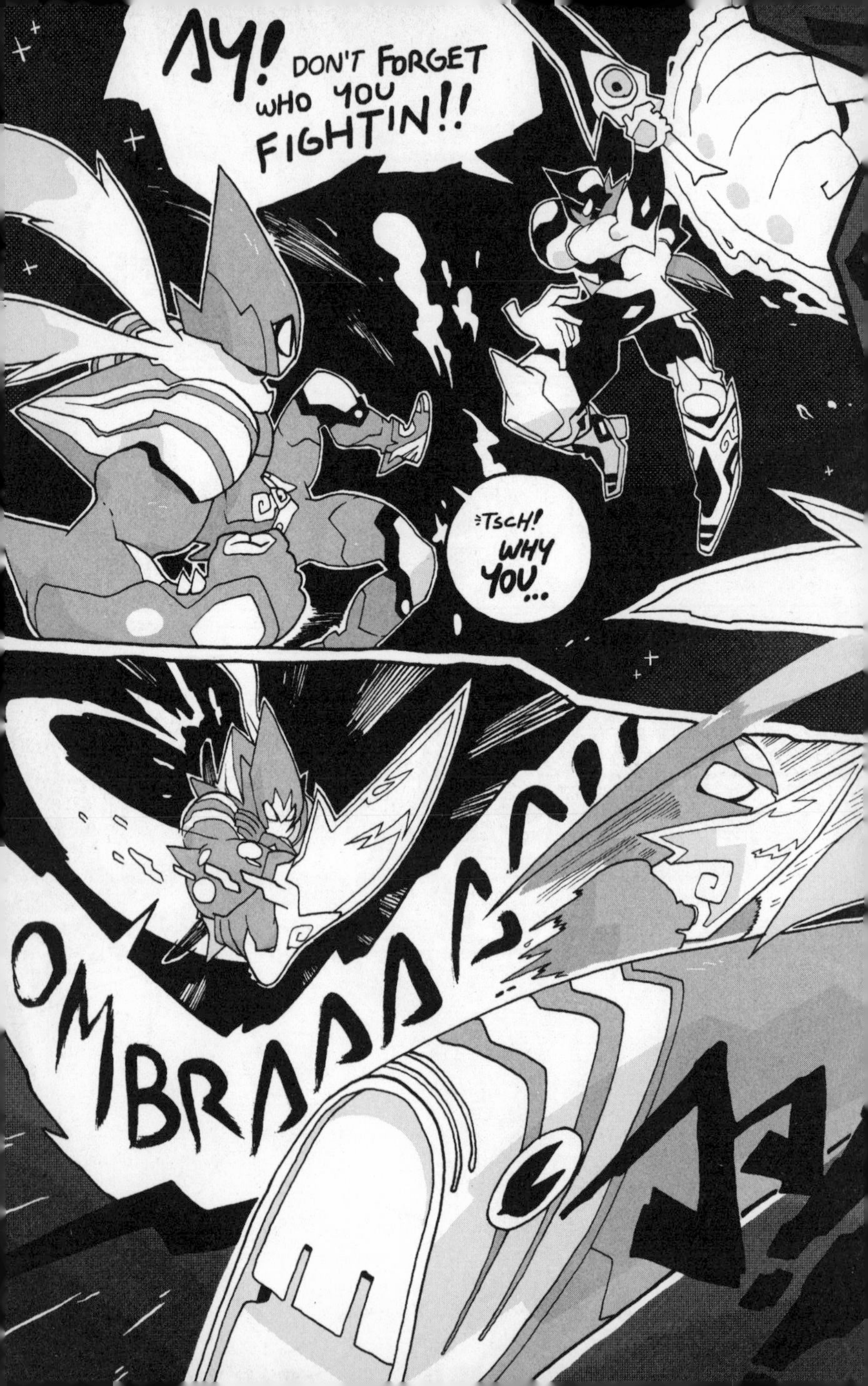
AY! DON'T FORGET WHO YOU FIGHTIN!!
TSCH! WHY YOU...
OMBRAAAAAA!!

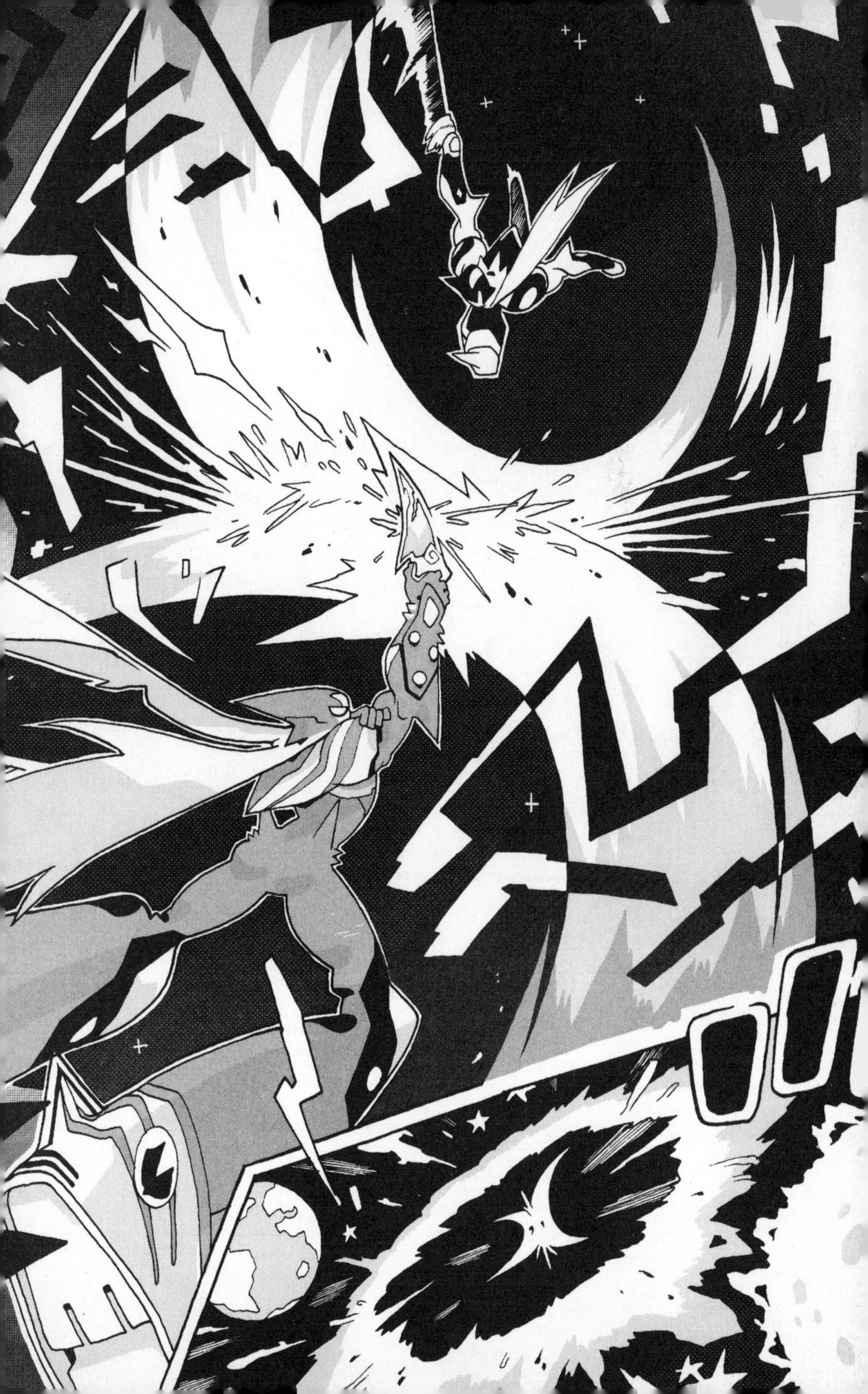

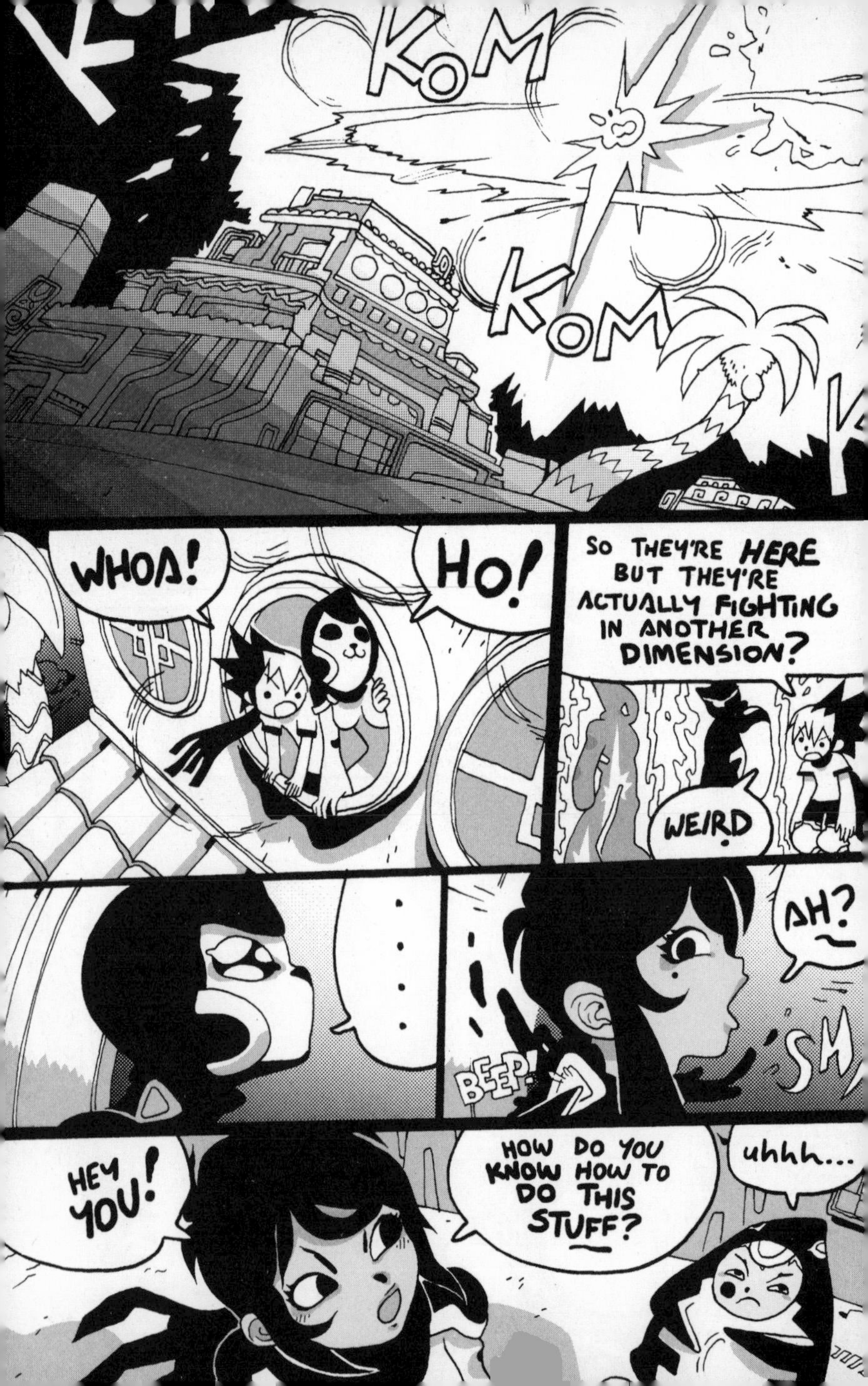
KOM
KOM
WHOA!
HO!
SO THEY'RE HERE BUT THEY'RE ACTUALLY FIGHTING IN ANOTHER DIMENSION?
WEIRD
...
AH?
BEEP!
HEY YOU!
HOW DO YOU KNOW HOW TO DO THIS STUFF?
uhhh...

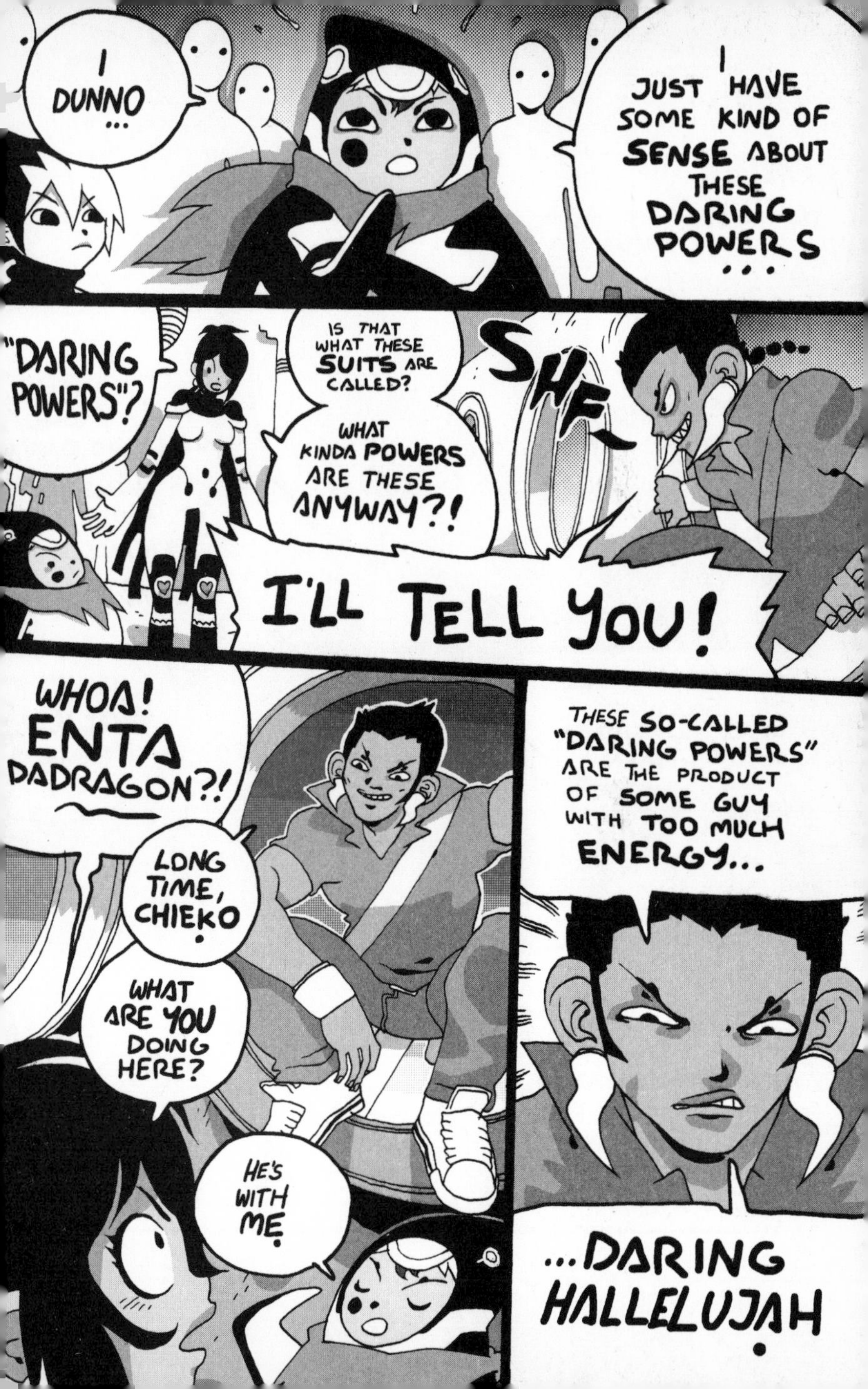
I DUNNO...
I JUST HAVE SOME KIND OF SENSE ABOUT THESE DARING POWERS...
"DARING POWERS"?
IS THAT WHAT THESE SUITS ARE CALLED?
WHAT KINDA POWERS ARE THESE ANYWAY?!
SHF
I'LL TELL YOU!
WHOA! ENTA DADRAGON?!
LONG TIME, CHIEKO.
WHAT ARE YOU DOING HERE?
HE'S WITH ME.
THESE SO-CALLED "DARING POWERS" ARE THE PRODUCT OF SOME GUY WITH TOO MUCH ENERGY...
...DARING HALLELUJAH.

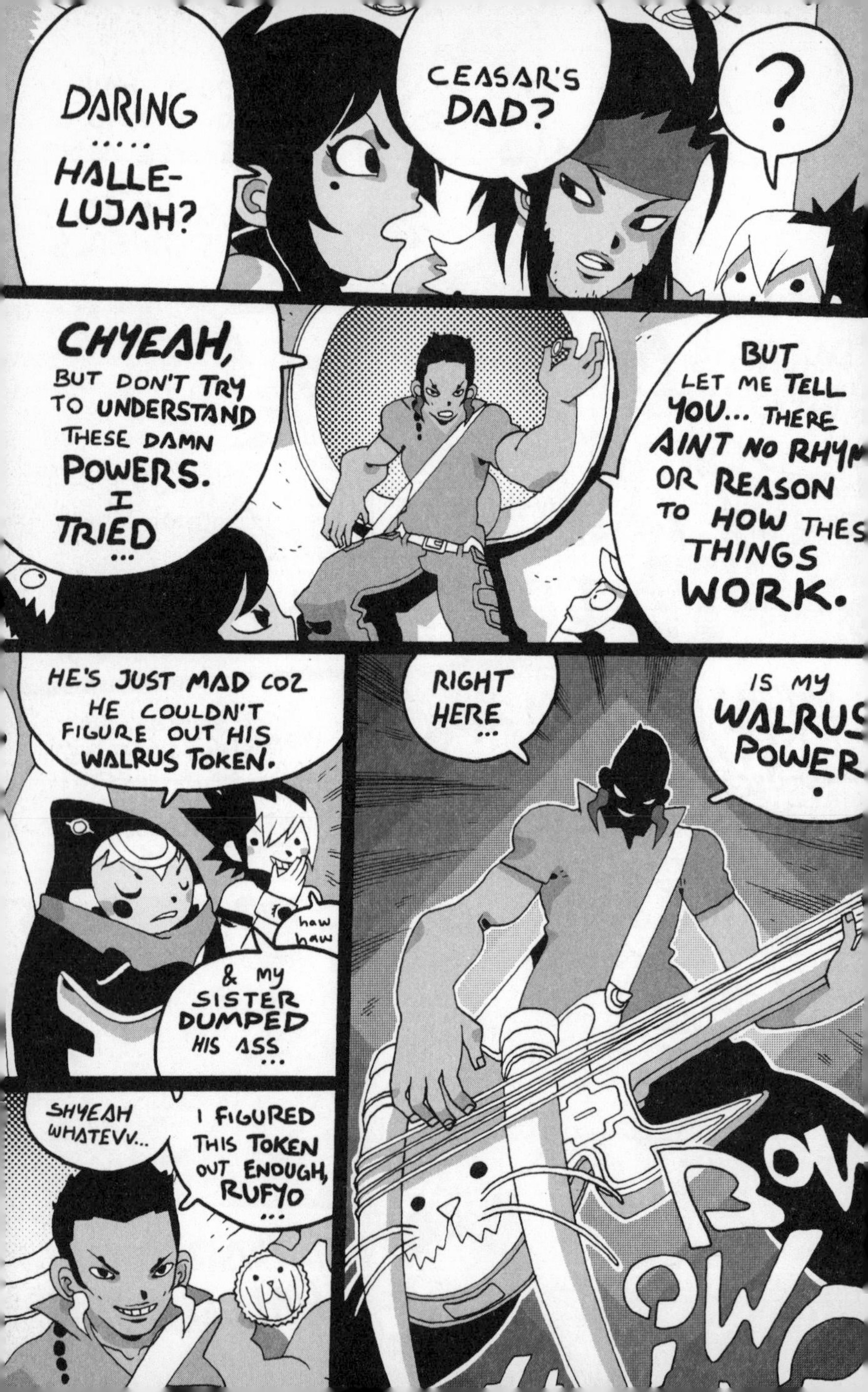
DARING ...... HALLE-LUJAH?
CEASAR'S DAD?
?
CHYEAH, BUT DON'T TRY TO UNDERSTAND THESE DAMN POWERS. I TRIED ...
BUT LET ME TELL YOU... THERE AINT NO RHYM OR REASON TO HOW THES THINGS WORK.
HE'S JUST MAD COZ HE COULDN'T FIGURE OUT HIS WALRUS TOKEN.
haw haw
& MY SISTER DUMPED HIS ASS ...
SHYEAH WHATEVV...
I FIGURED THIS TOKEN OUT ENOUGH, RUFYO ...
RIGHT HERE ...
IS MY WALRUS POWER.

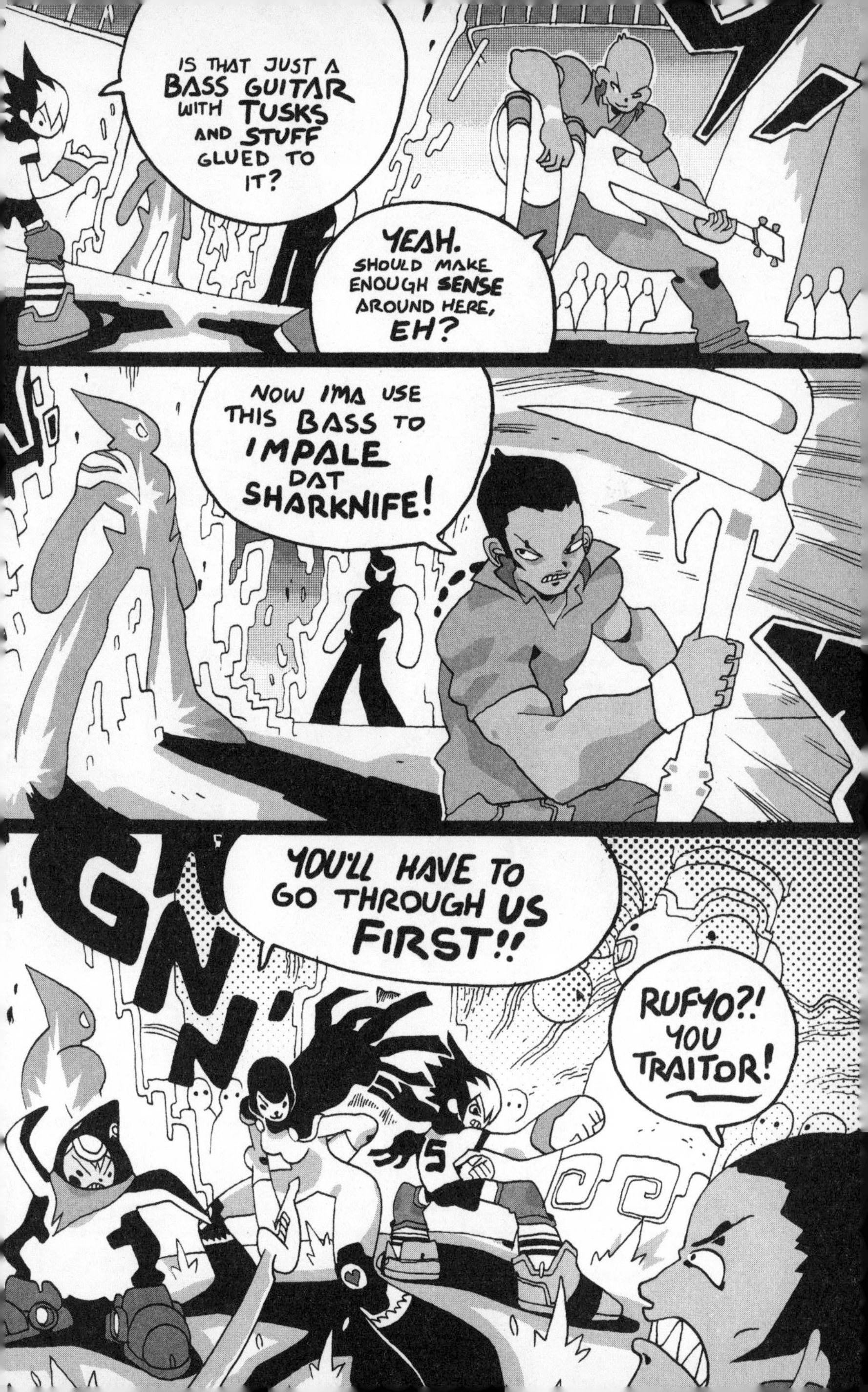
IS THAT JUST A BASS GUITAR WITH TUSKS AND STUFF GLUED TO IT?
YEAH. SHOULD MAKE ENOUGH SENSE AROUND HERE, EH?
NOW I'MA USE THIS BASS TO IMPALE DAT SHARKNIFE!
GNN
YOU'LL HAVE TO GO THROUGH US FIRST!!
RUFYO?! YOU TRAITOR!

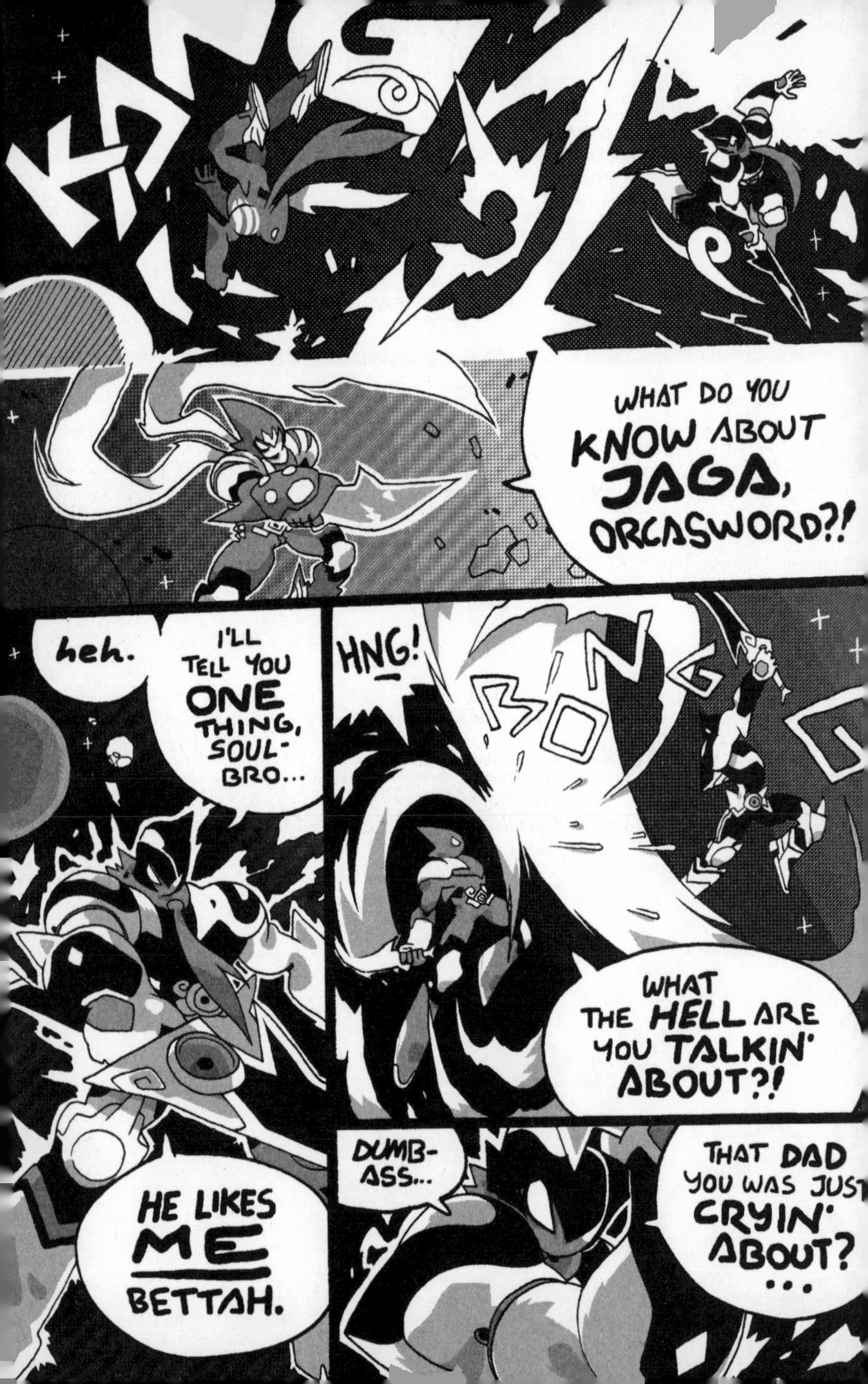
KANG
WHAT DO YOU KNOW ABOUT JAGA, ORCASWORD?!
heh.
I'LL TELL YOU ONE THING, SOUL-BRO...
HNG!
BONG
WHAT THE HELL ARE YOU TALKIN' ABOUT?!
HE LIKES ME BETTAH.
DUMB-ASS...
THAT DAD YOU WAS JUST CRYIN' ABOUT? ...

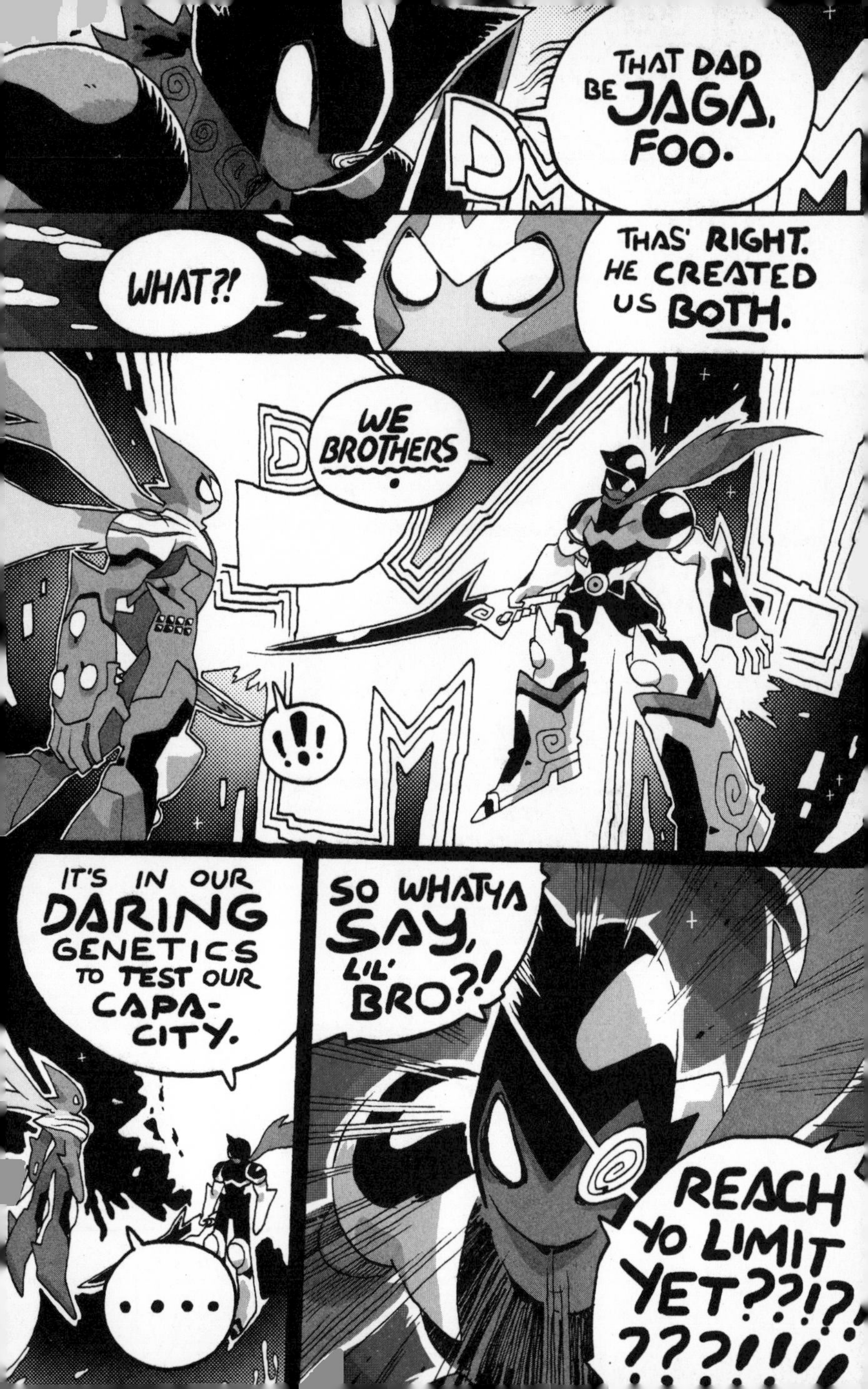
THAT DAD BE JAGA, FOO.
WHAT?!
THAS' RIGHT. HE CREATED US BOTH.
WE BROTHERS.
!!!
IT'S IN OUR DARING GENETICS TO TEST OUR CAPA-CITY.
....
SO WHATYA SAY, LIL' BRO?!
REACH YO LIMIT YET??!??????!!!!!

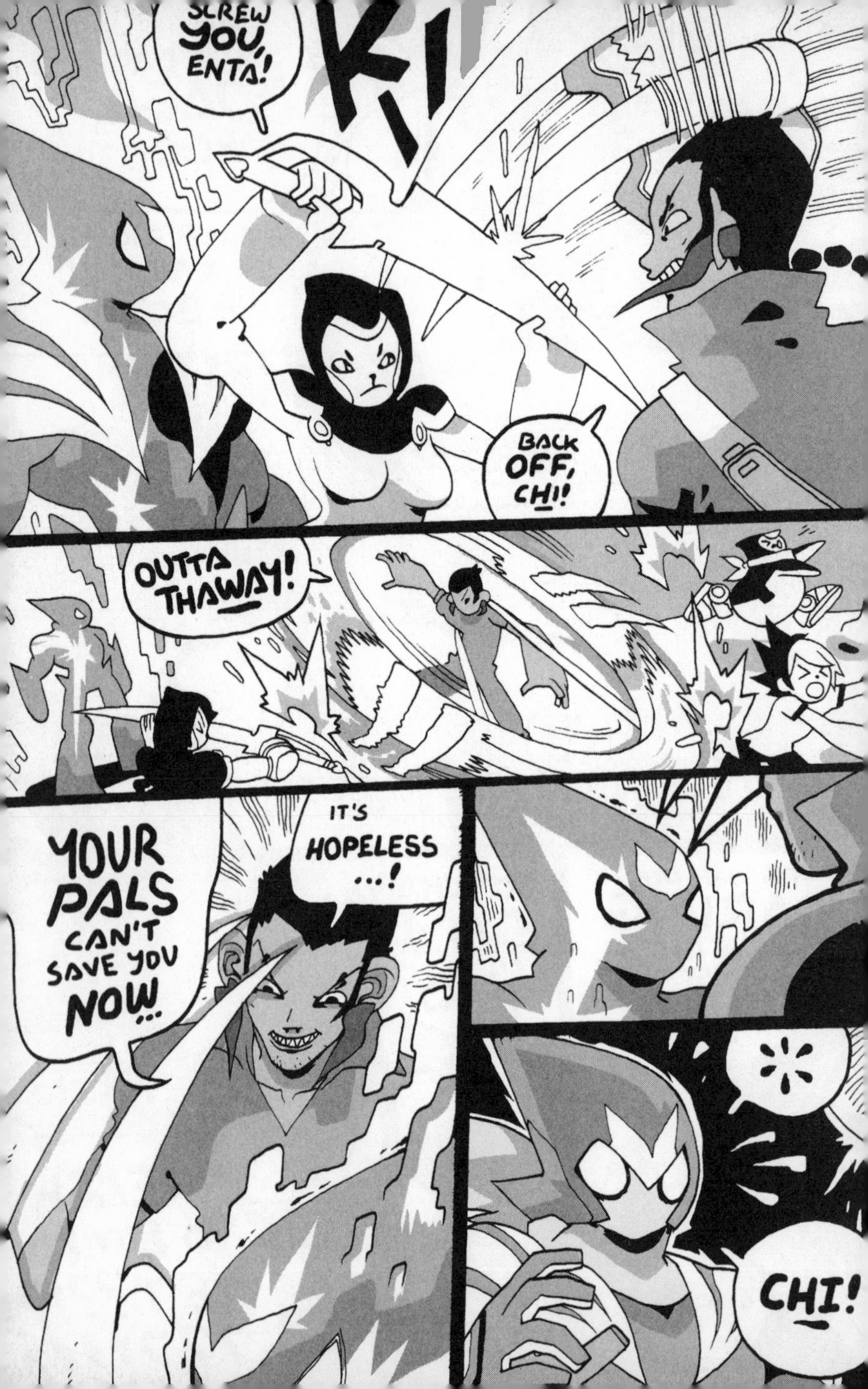
SCREW YOU, ENTA!
KI
BACK OFF, CHI!
OUTTA THAWAY!
YOUR PALS CAN'T SAVE YOU NOW...
IT'S HOPELESS ...!
!
CHI!

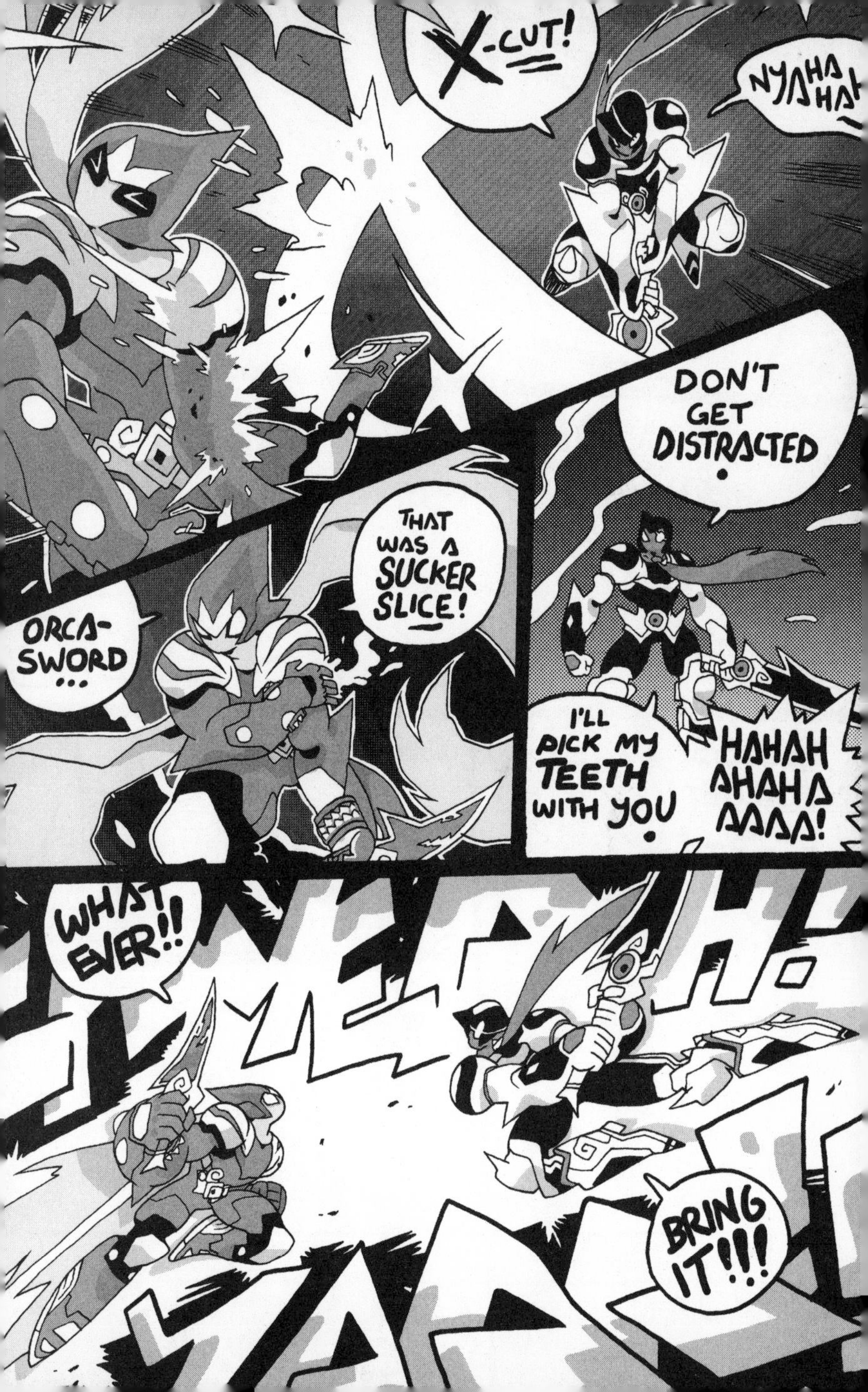
X-CUT!
NYAHA HAHA!
DON'T GET DISTRACTED.
THAT WAS A SUCKER SLICE!
ORCA-SWORD...
I'LL PICK MY TEETH WITH YOU.
HAHAH AHAHA AAAA!
WHAT EVER!!
BRING IT!!!

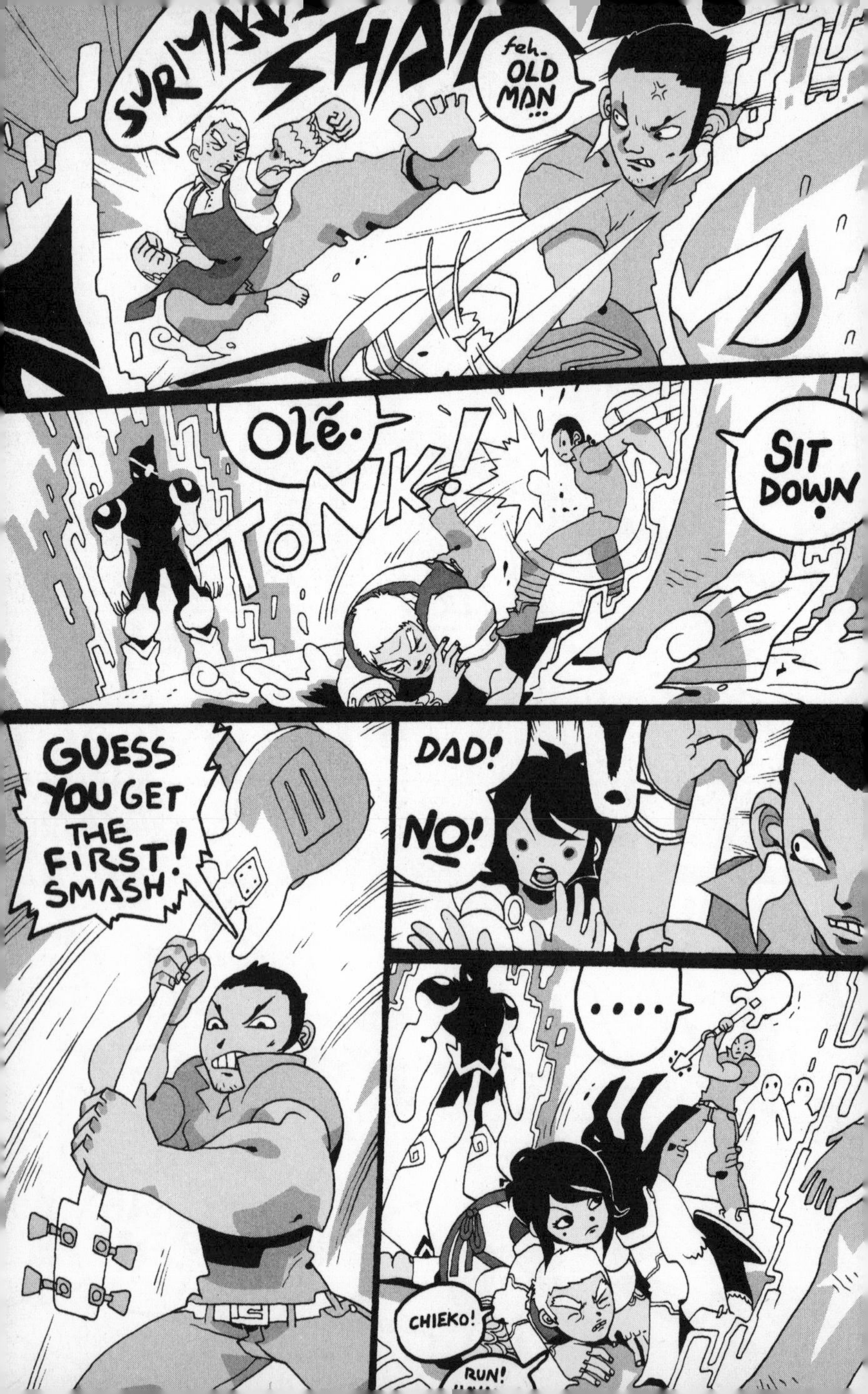

SURIYAAAAAAA
SHAK
feh. OLD MAN...
Olé.
TONK!
SIT DOWN.
GUESS YOU GET THE FIRST SMASH!
DAD!
NO!
....
CHIEKO!
RUN!

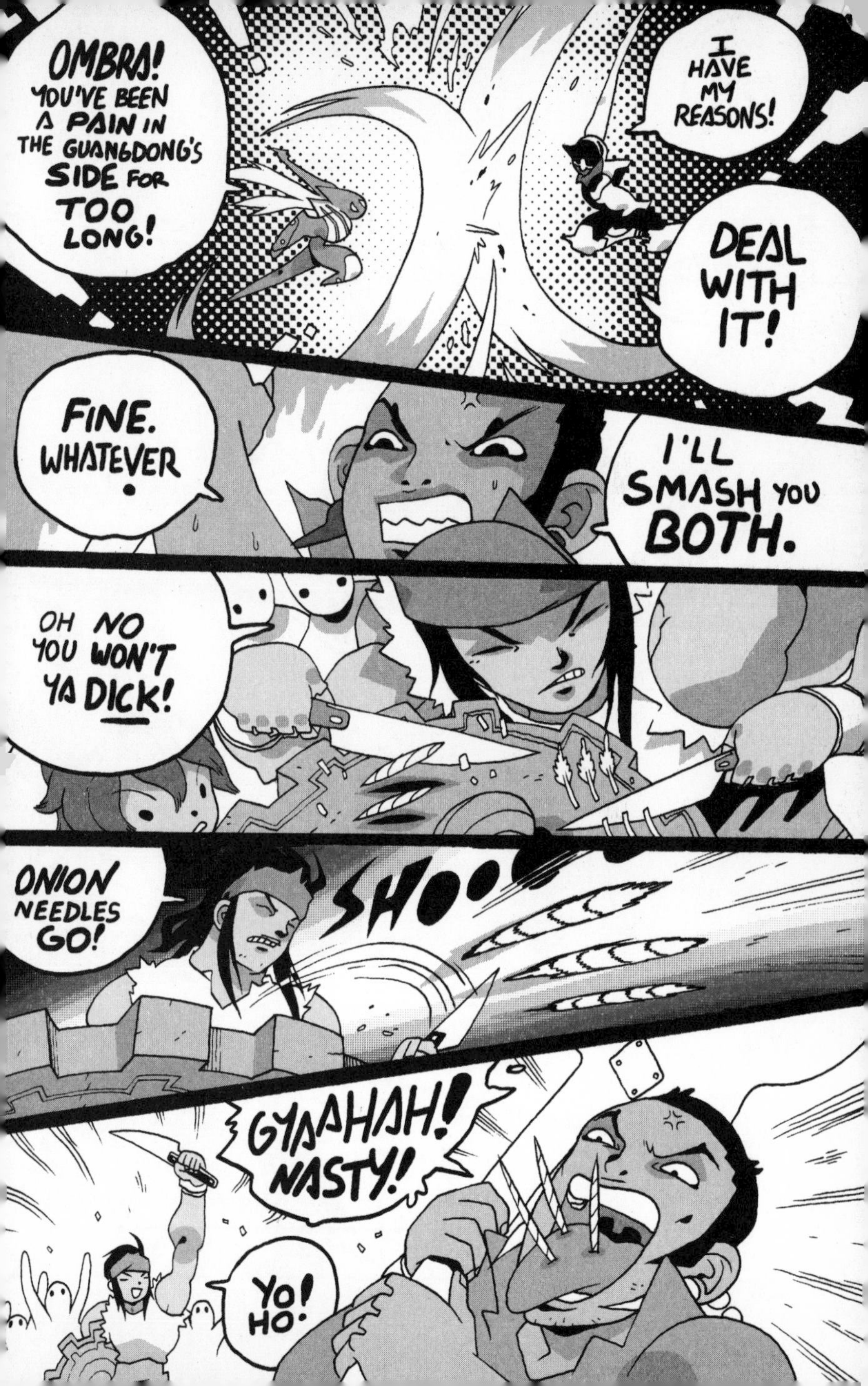
OMBRA! YOU'VE BEEN A PAIN IN THE GUANGDONG'S SIDE FOR TOO LONG!
I HAVE MY REASONS!
DEAL WITH IT!
FINE. WHATEVER.
I'LL SMASH YOU BOTH.
OH NO YOU WON'T YA DICK!
ONION NEEDLES GO!
SHOO
GYAAHAH! NASTY!
YO! HO!

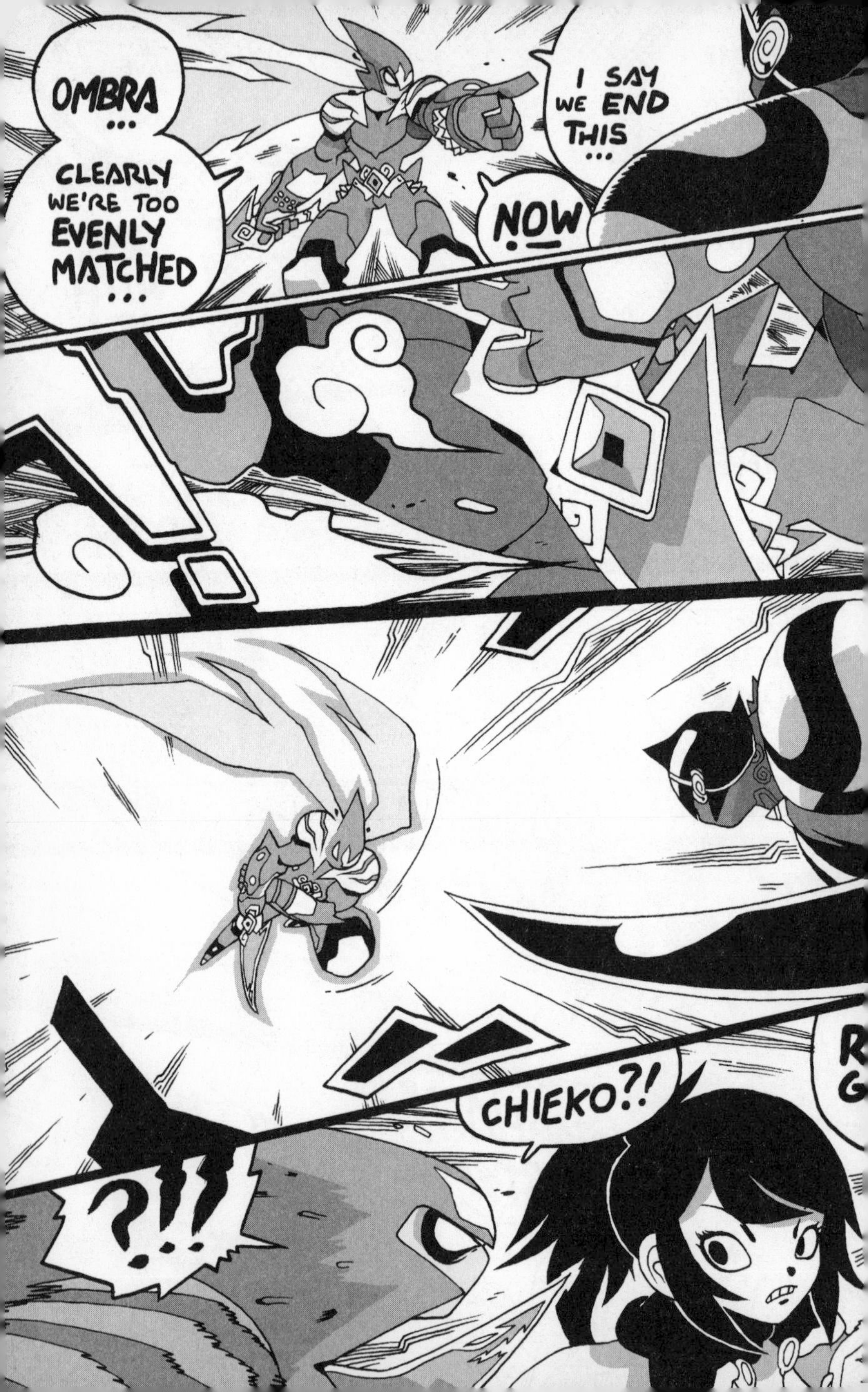
OMBRA ...
CLEARLY WE'RE TOO EVENLY MATCHED ...
I SAY WE END THIS ...
NOW
CHIEKO?!
?!!

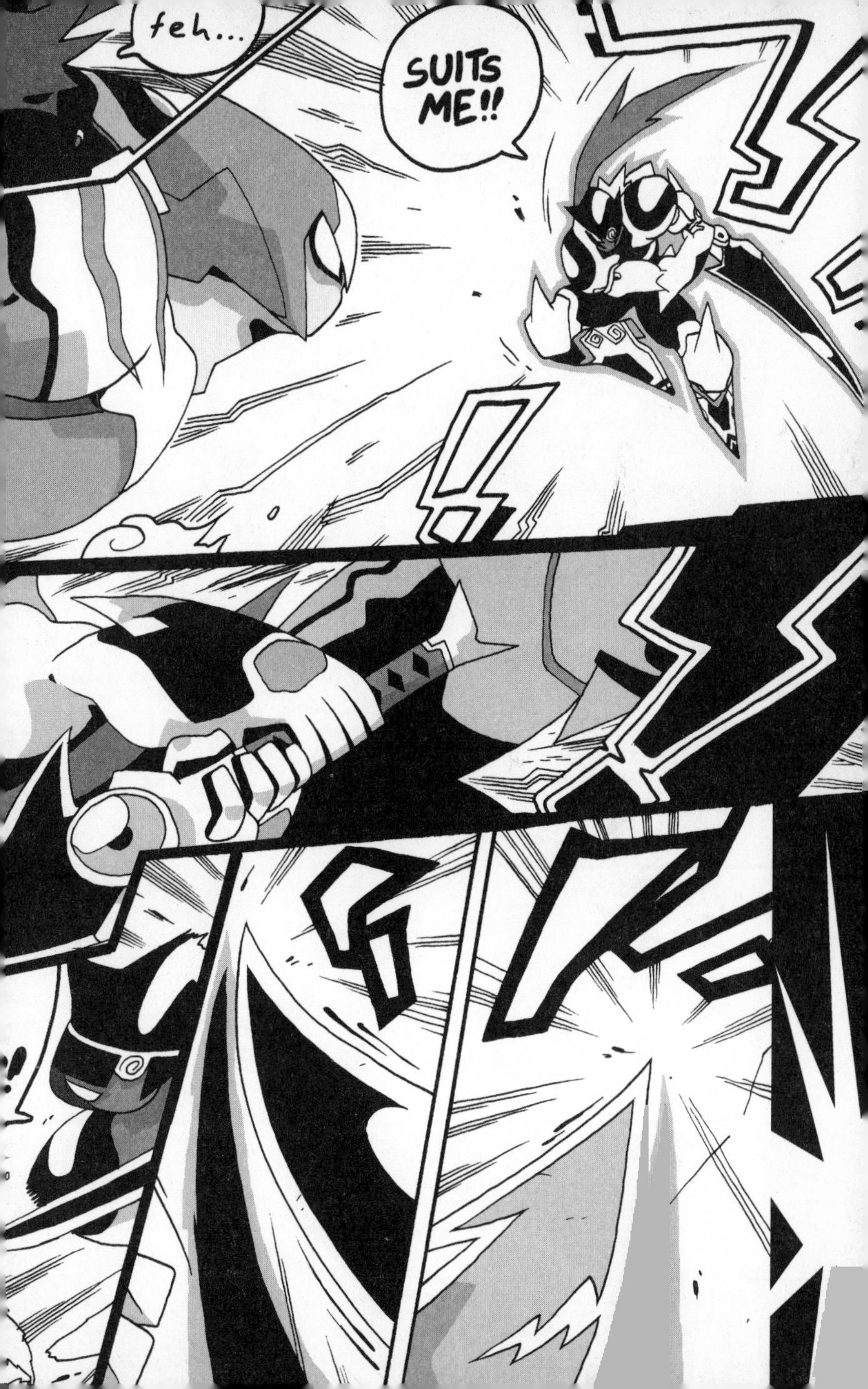
feh...
SUITS ME!!

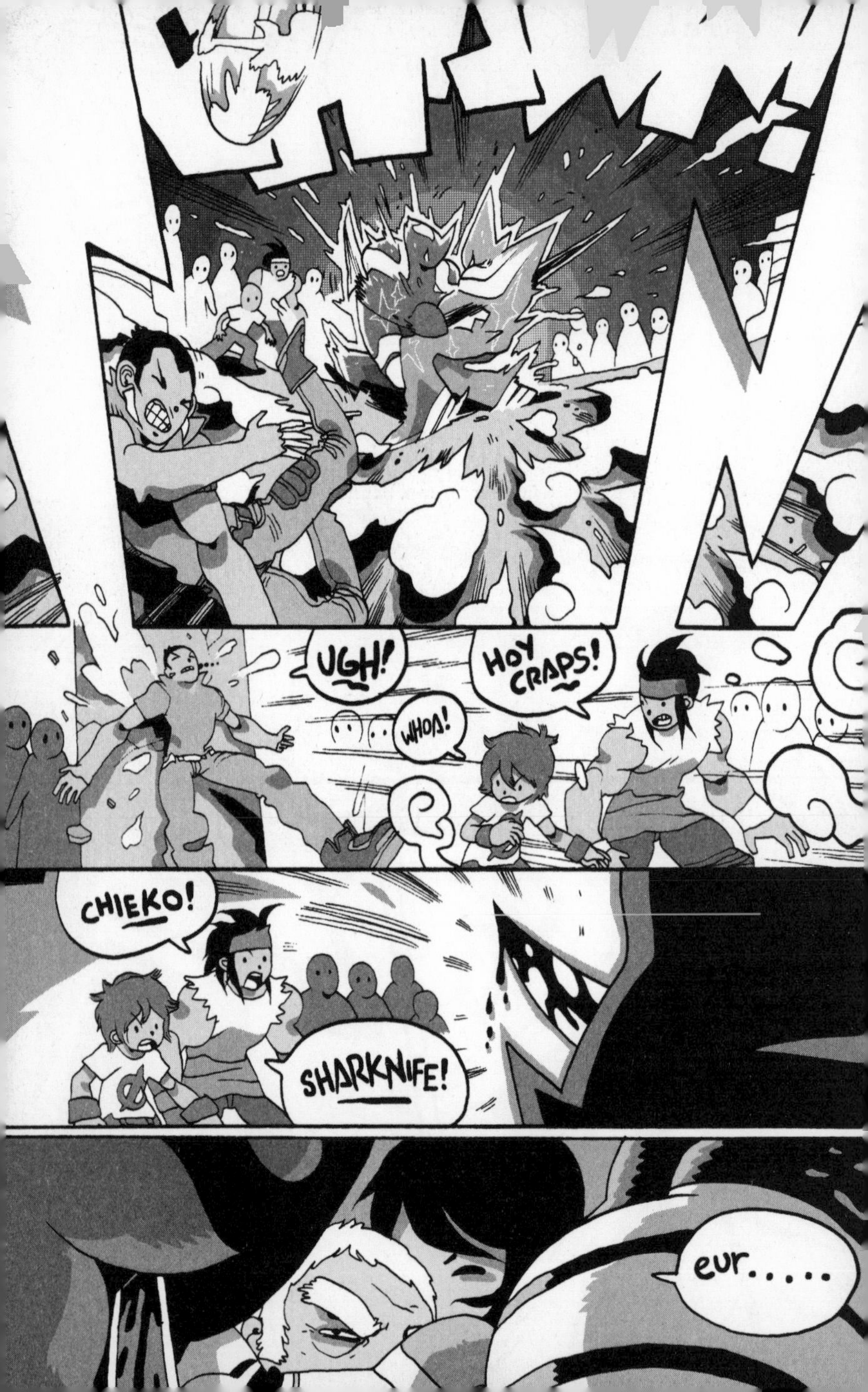
UGH!
HOY CRAPS!
WHOA!
CHIEKO!
SHARKNIFE!
eur.....

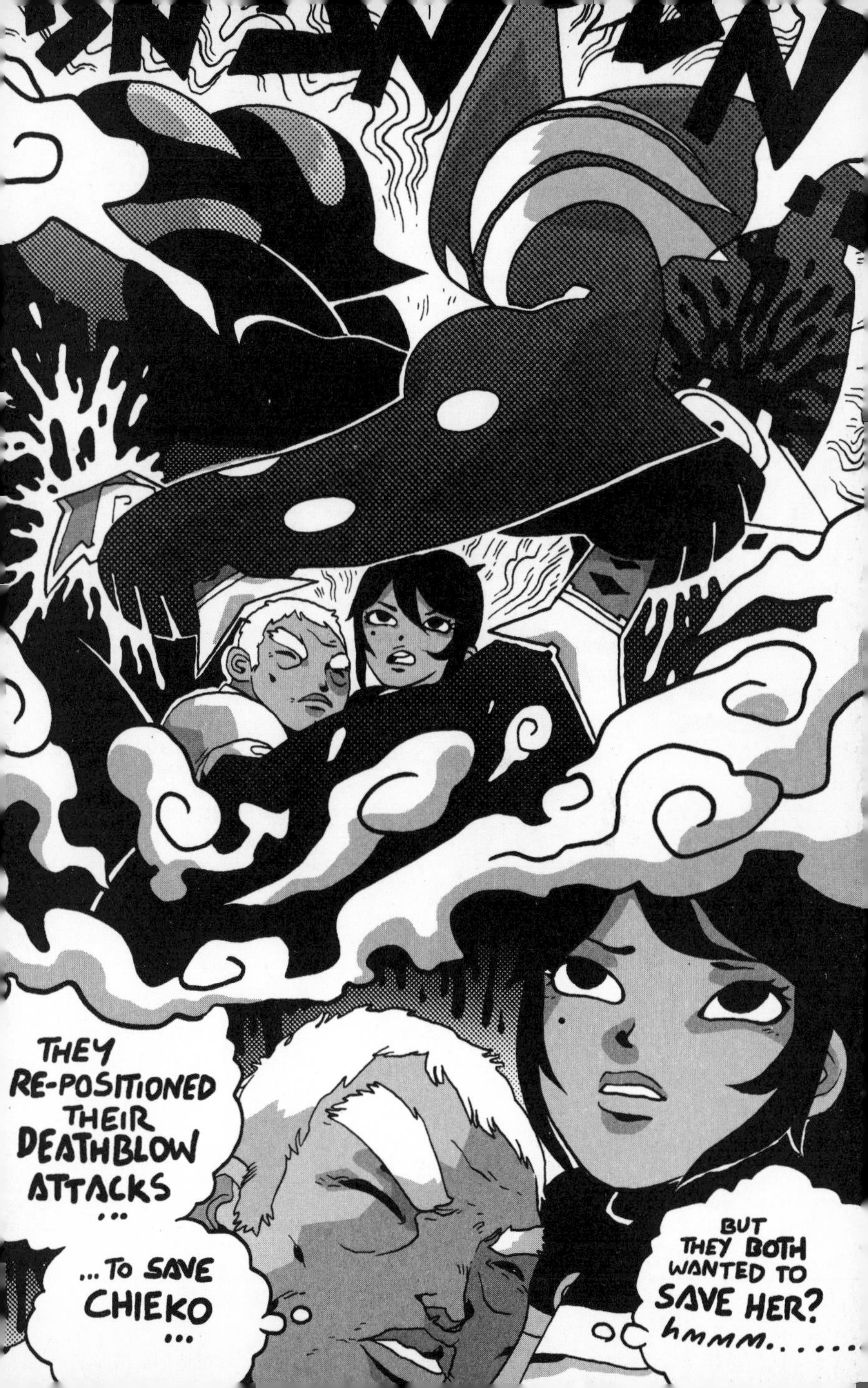
THEY RE-POSITIONED THEIR DEATHBLOW ATTACKS ...
... TO SAVE CHIEKO ...
BUT THEY BOTH WANTED TO SAVE HER? hmmm......

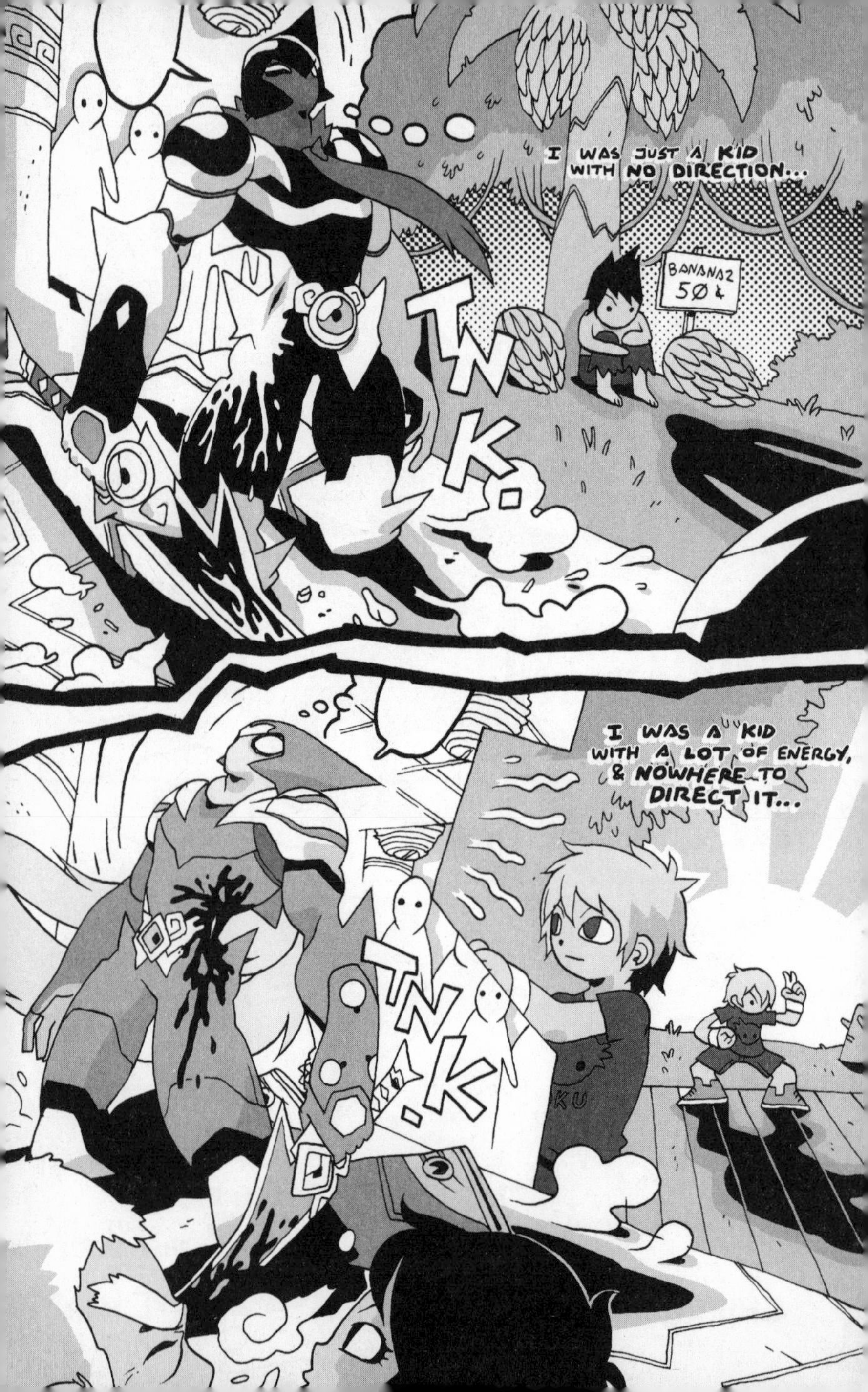
I WAS JUST A KID WITH NO DIRECTION...
BANANAZ 5Ø¢
TNK.
I WAS A KID WITH A LOT OF ENERGY, & NOWHERE TO DIRECT IT...
TNK.

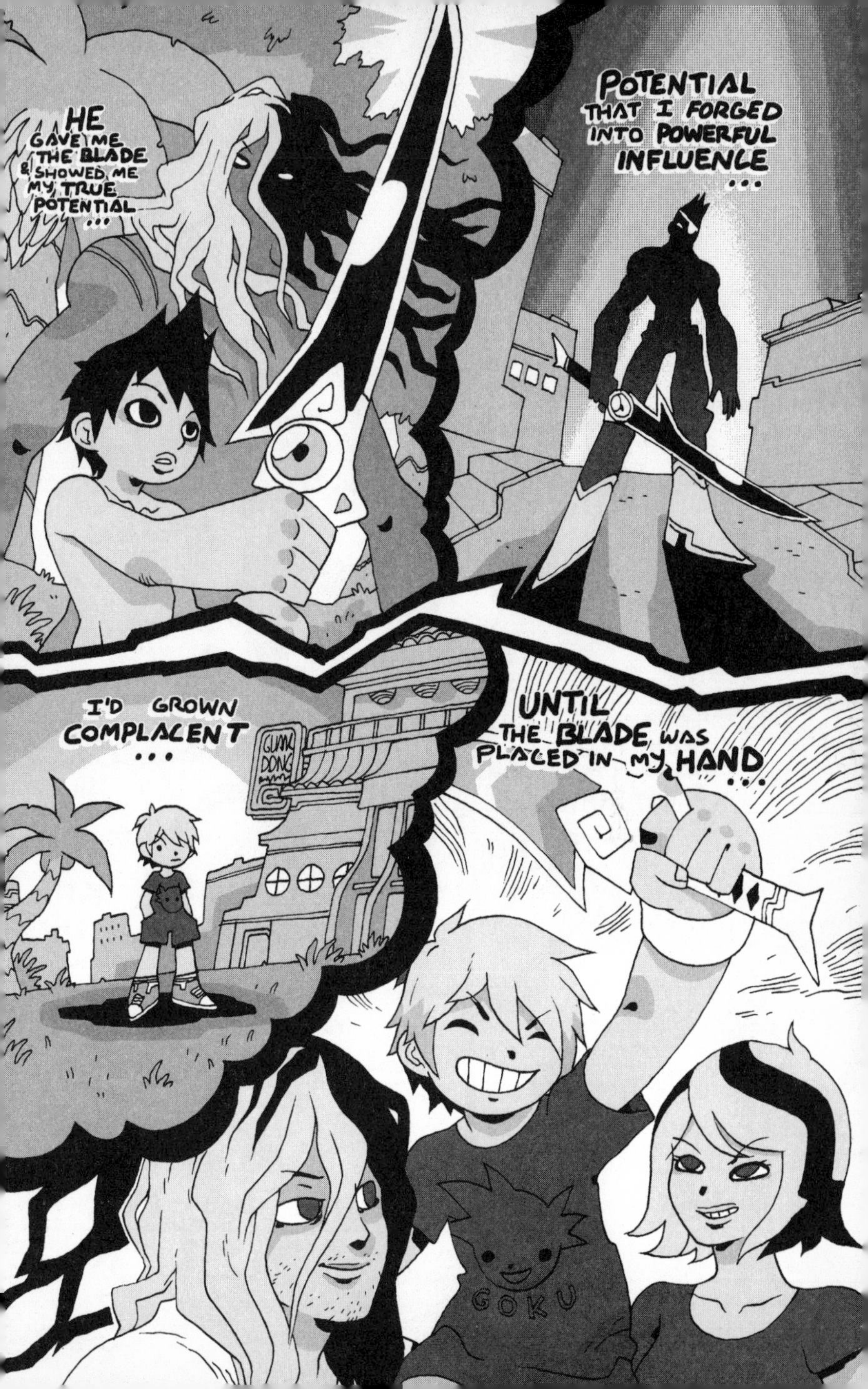
HE GAVE ME THE BLADE & SHOWED ME MY TRUE POTENTIAL ...
POTENTIAL THAT I FORGED INTO POWERFUL INFLUENCE ...
I'D GROWN COMPLACENT ...
UNTIL THE BLADE WAS PLACED IN MY HAND ...
GOKU

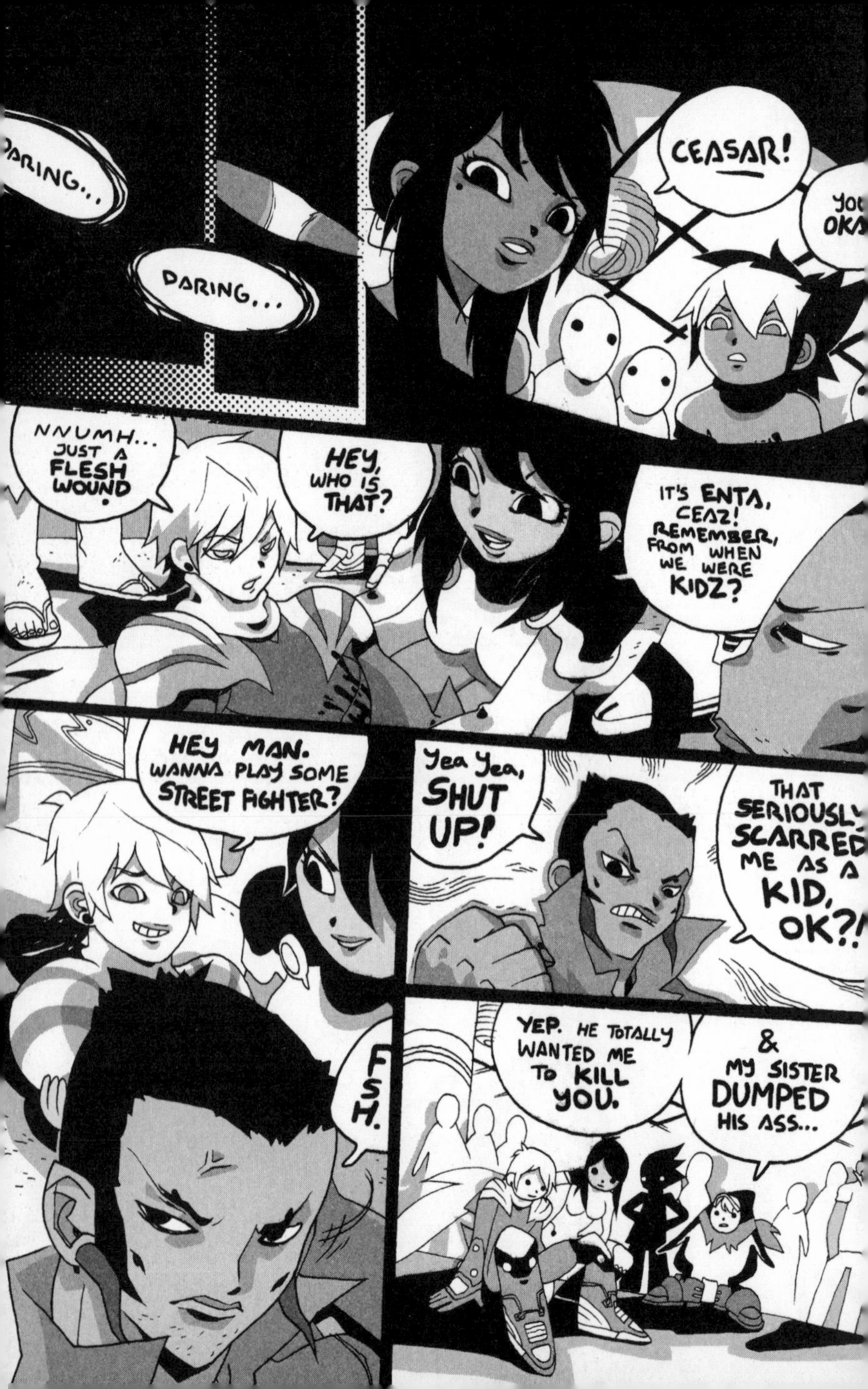
DARING...
DARING...
CEASAR!
YOU OKA
NNUMH... JUST A FLESH WOUND.
HEY, WHO IS THAT?
IT'S ENTA, CEAZ! REMEMBER, FROM WHEN WE WERE KIDZ?
HEY MAN. WANNA PLAY SOME STREET FIGHTER?
FSH.
Yea Yea, SHUT UP!
THAT SERIOUSLY SCARRED ME AS A KID, OK?!
YEP. HE TOTALLY WANTED ME TO KILL YOU.
& MY SISTER DUMPED HIS ASS...

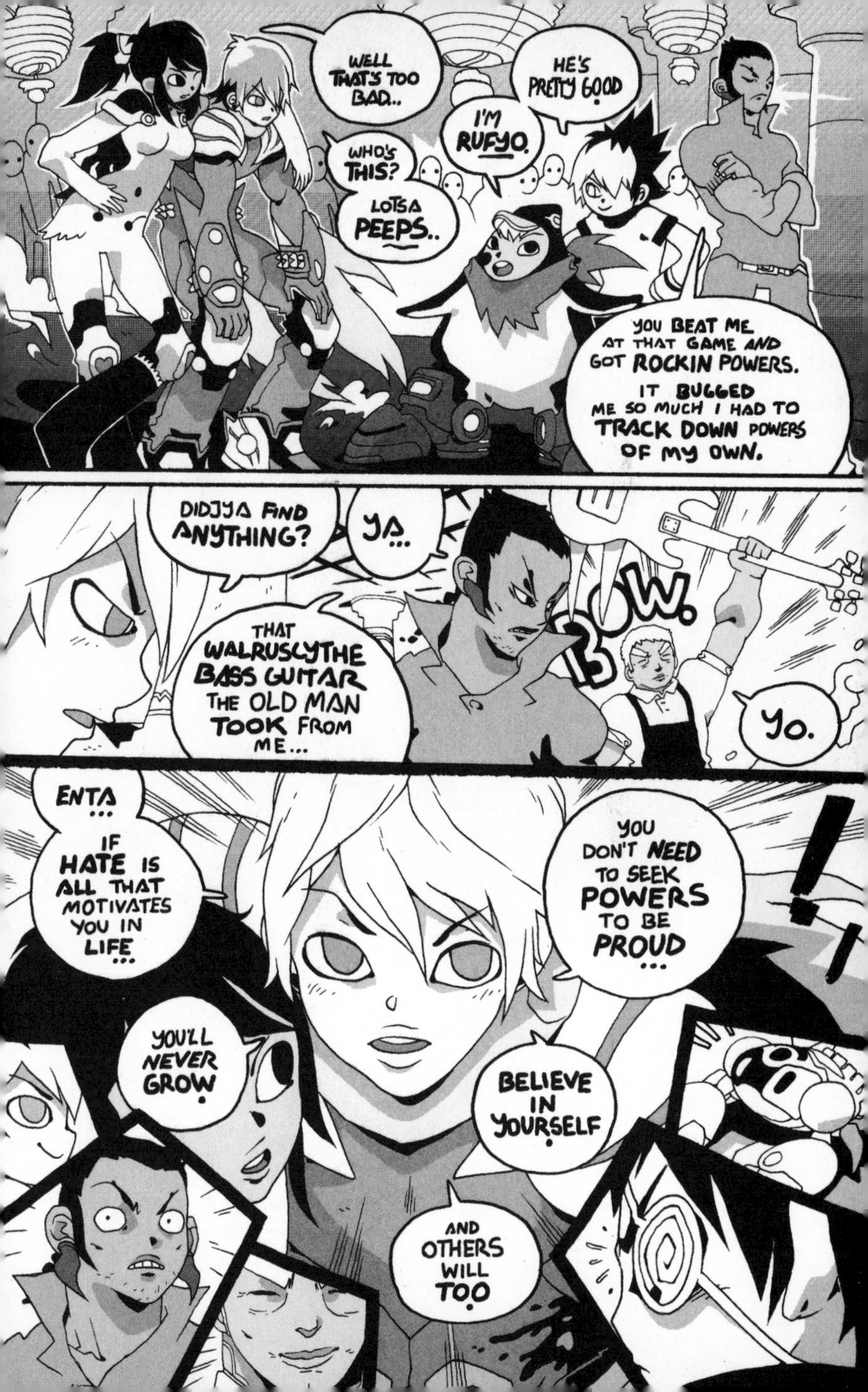
WELL THAT'S TOO BAD..
HE'S PRETTY GOOD.
I'M RUFYO.
WHO'S THIS?
LOTSA PEEPS..
YOU BEAT ME AT THAT GAME AND GOT ROCKIN POWERS.
IT BUGGED ME SO MUCH I HAD TO TRACK DOWN POWERS OF MY OWN.
DIDJYA FIND ANYTHING?
YA...
THAT WALRUSCYTHE BASS GUITAR THE OLD MAN TOOK FROM ME...
BOW.
YO.
ENTA...
IF HATE IS ALL THAT MOTIVATES YOU IN LIFE...
YOU DON'T NEED TO SEEK POWERS TO BE PROUD...
YOU'LL NEVER GROW.
BELIEVE IN YOURSELF.
AND OTHERS WILL TOO.
!!

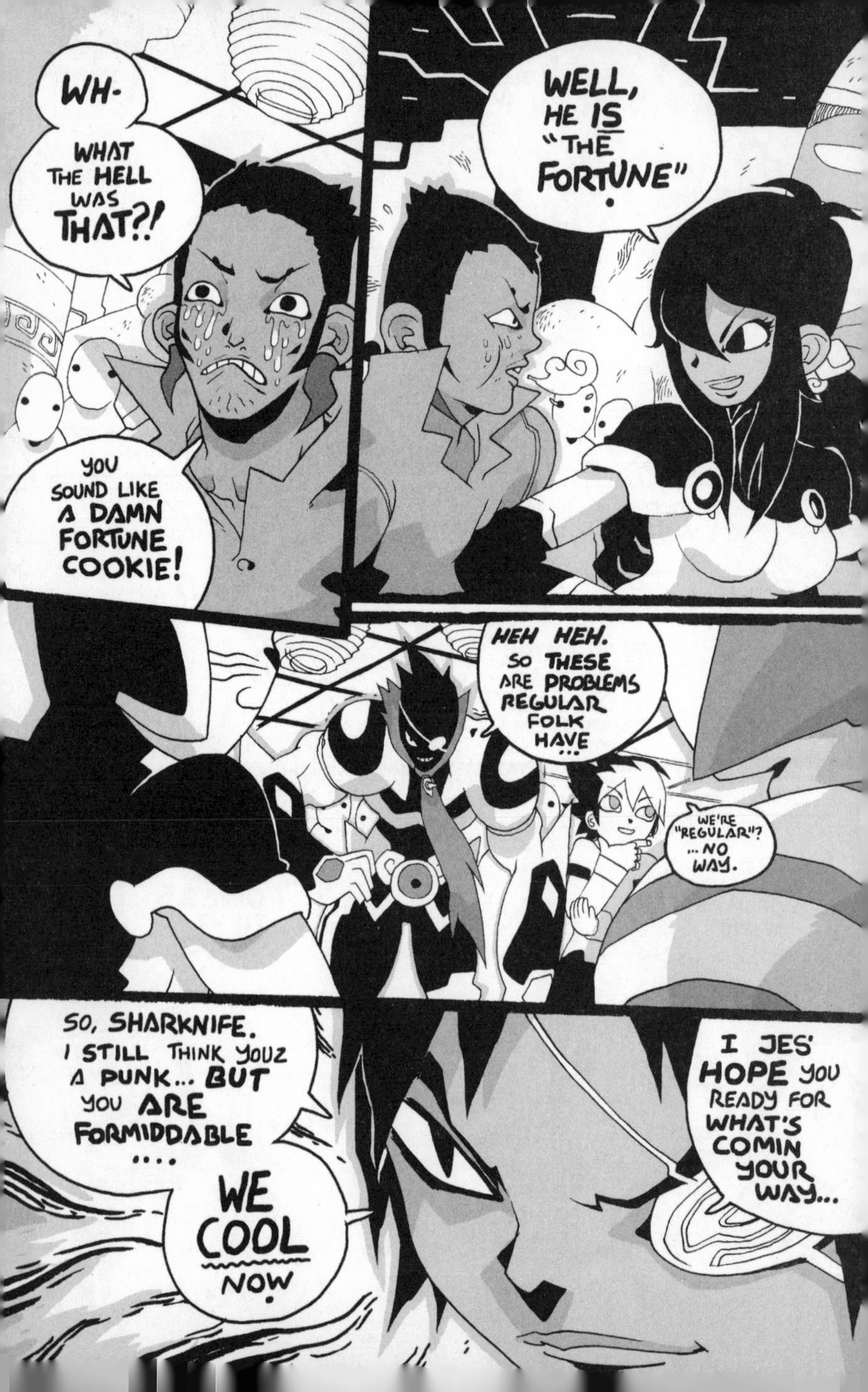
WH-
WHAT THE HELL WAS THAT?!
WELL, HE IS "THE FORTUNE".
YOU SOUND LIKE A DAMN FORTUNE COOKIE!
HEH HEH. SO THESE ARE PROBLEMS REGULAR FOLK HAVE...
WE'RE "REGULAR"? ...NO WAY.
SO, SHARKNIFE. I STILL THINK YOUZ A PUNK... BUT YOU ARE FORMIDDABLE ....
WE COOL NOW.
I JES' HOPE YOU READY FOR WHAT'S COMIN YOUR WAY...

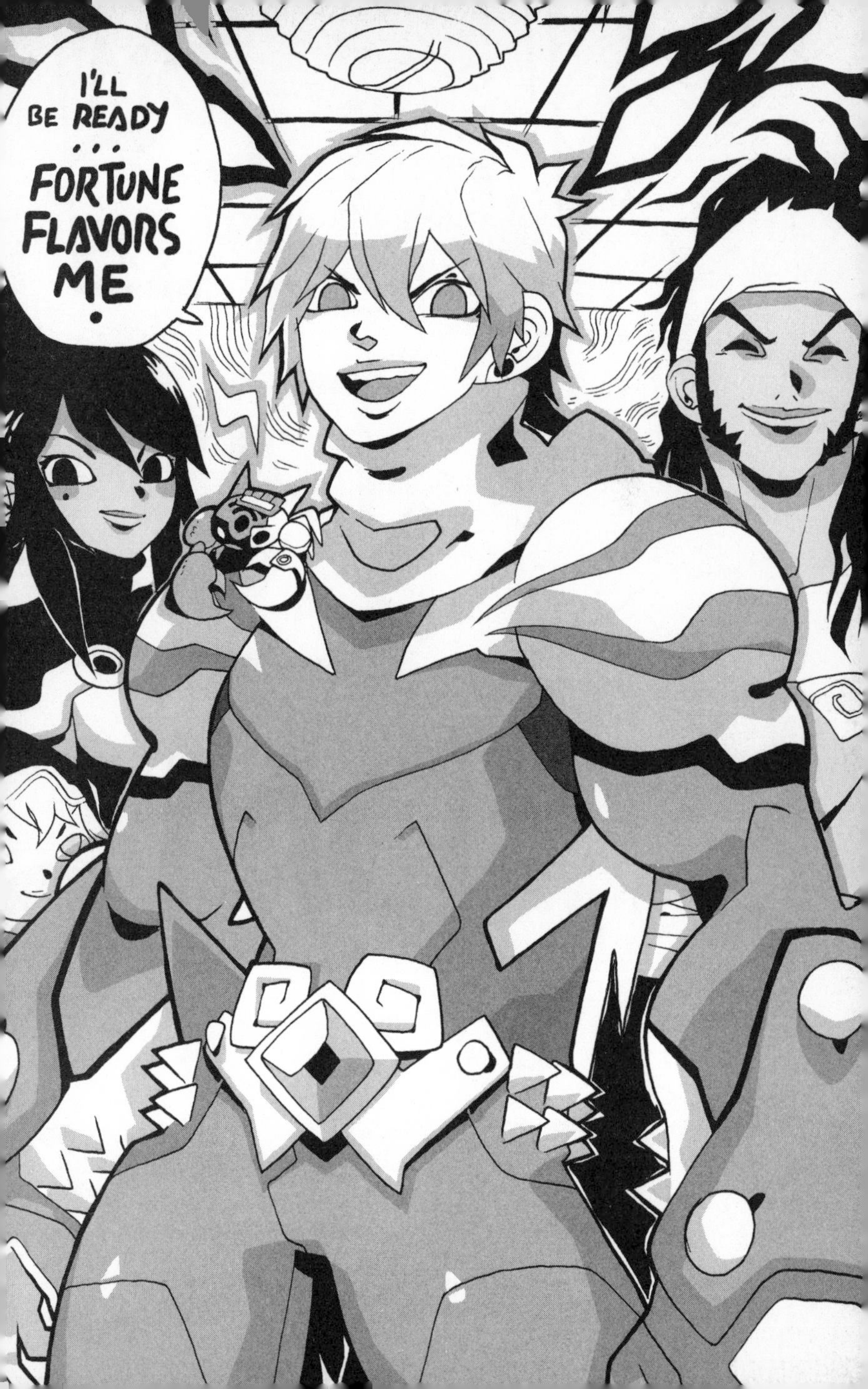
I'LL BE READY . . . FORTUNE FLAVORS ME!

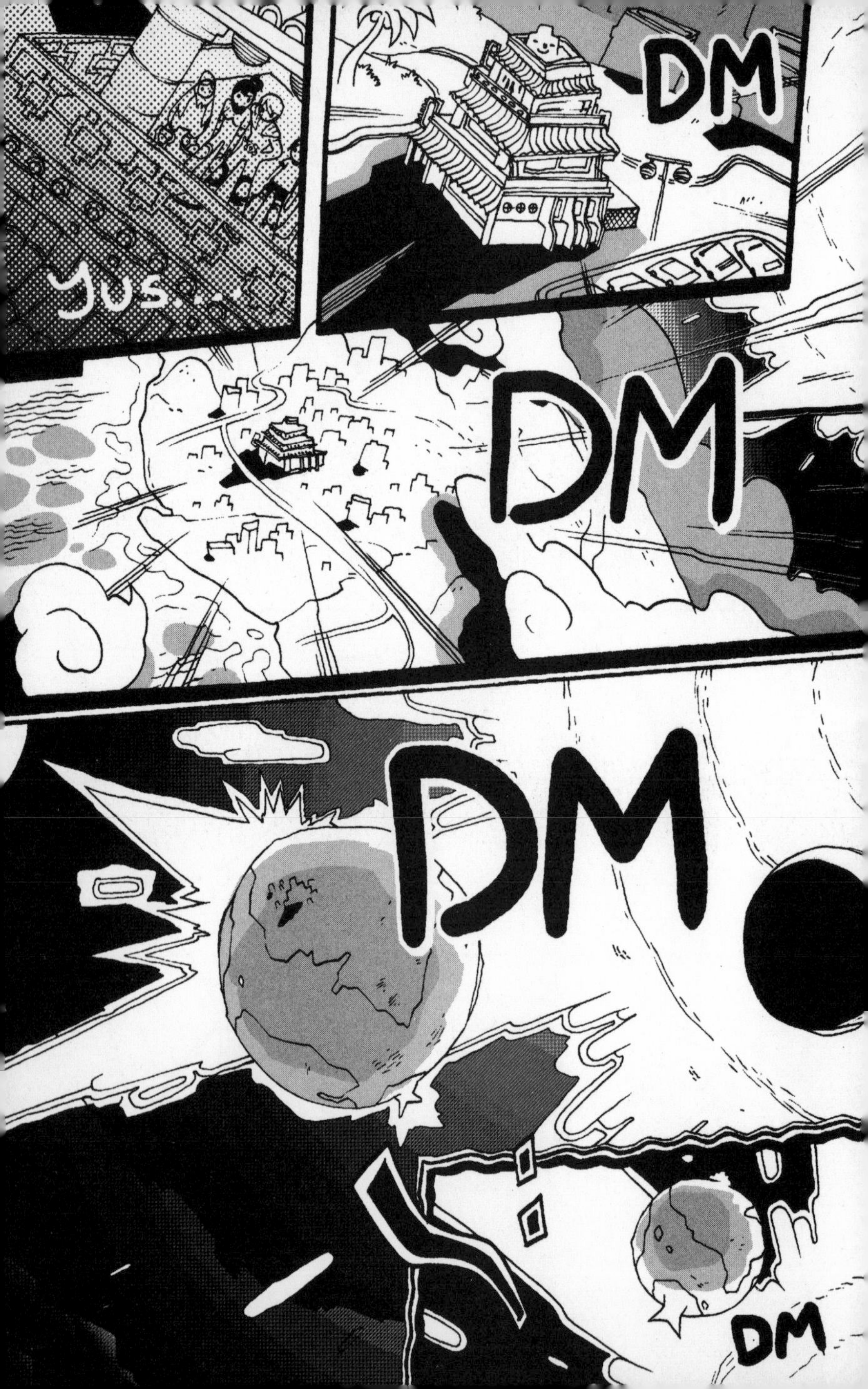
YUS...
DM
DM
DM
DM

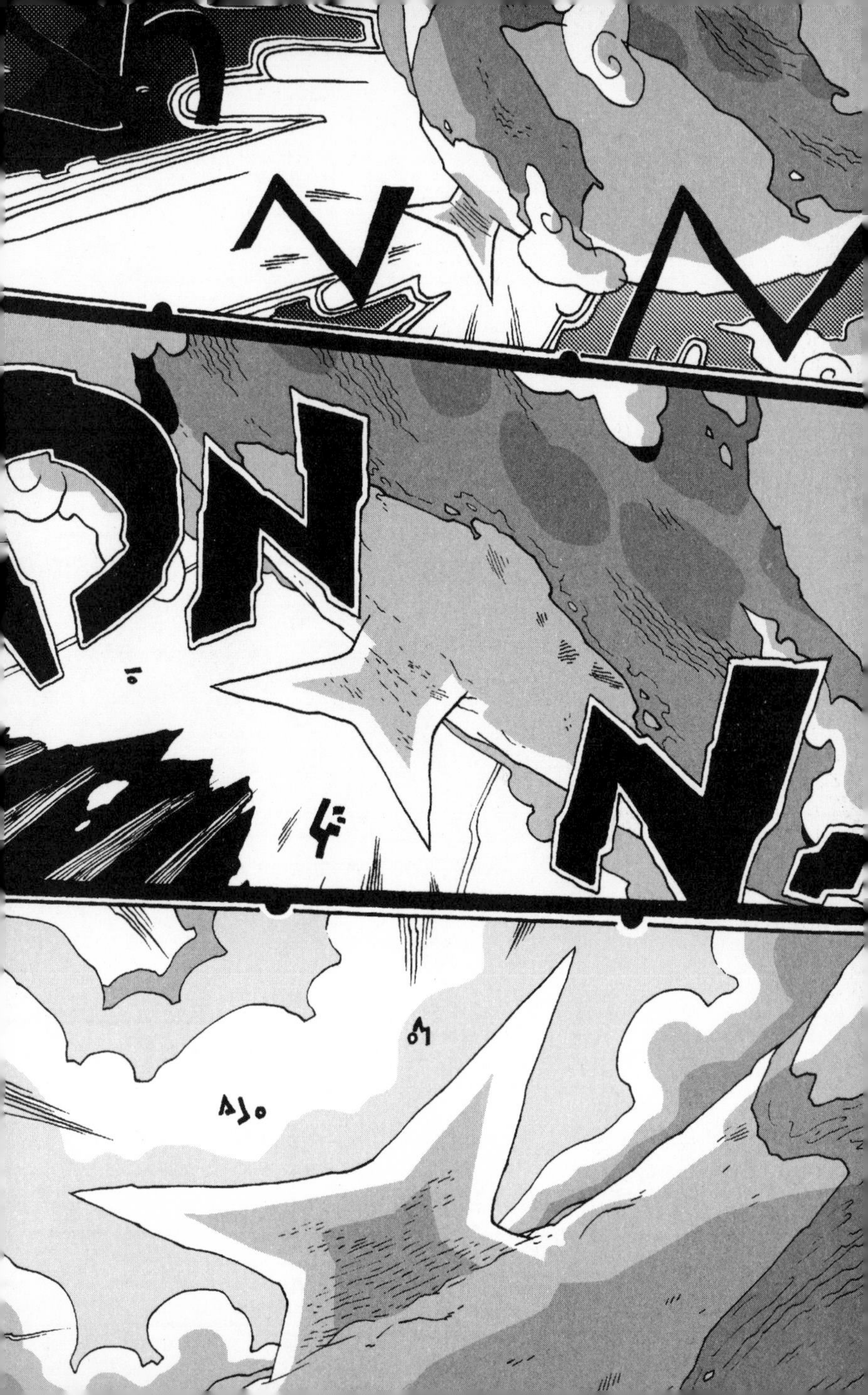

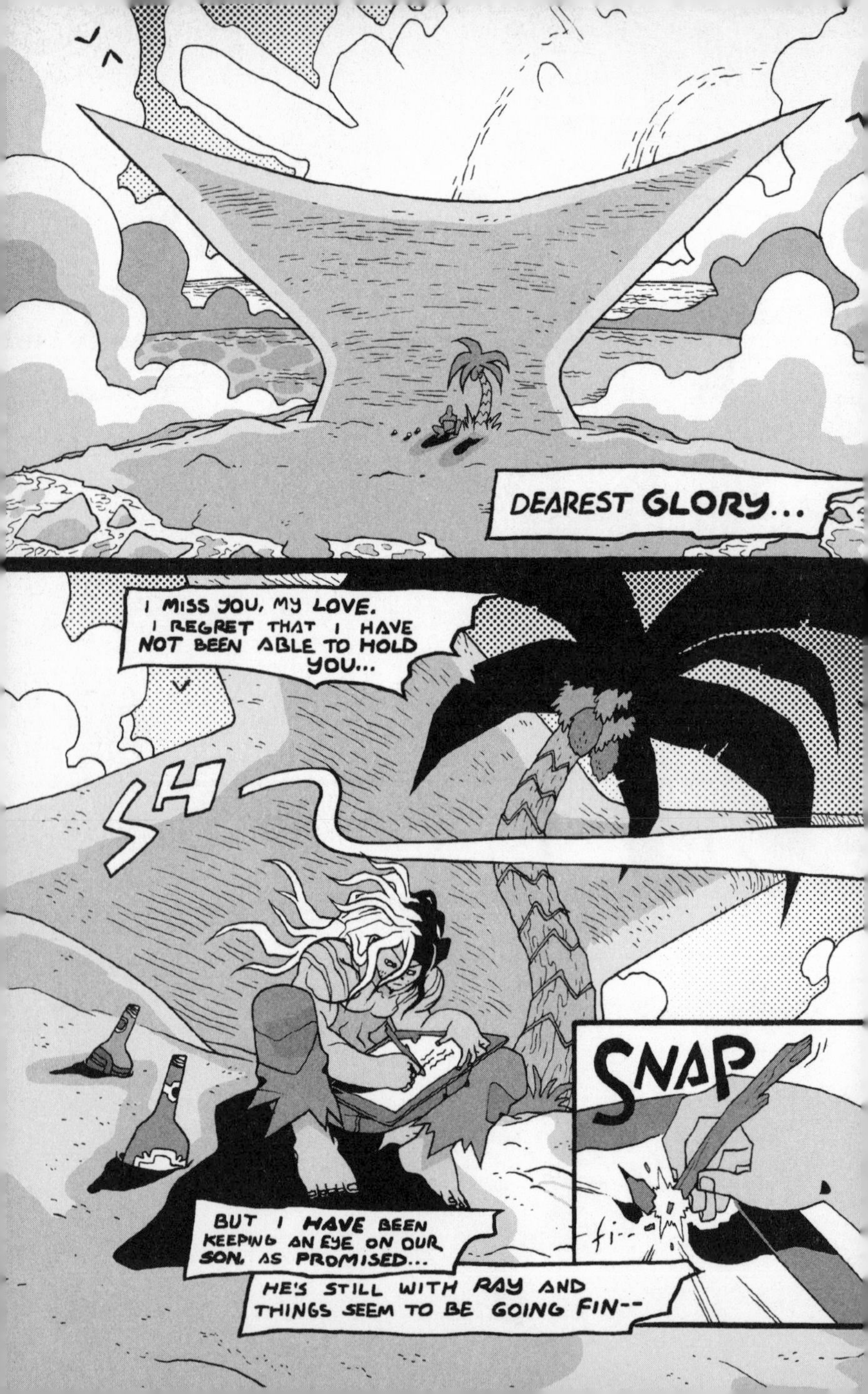
DEAREST GLORY...
I MISS YOU, MY LOVE. I REGRET THAT I HAVE NOT BEEN ABLE TO HOLD YOU...
SH
SNAP
BUT I HAVE BEEN KEEPING AN EYE ON OUR SON, AS PROMISED...
HE'S STILL WITH RAY AND THINGS SEEM TO BE GOING FIN--

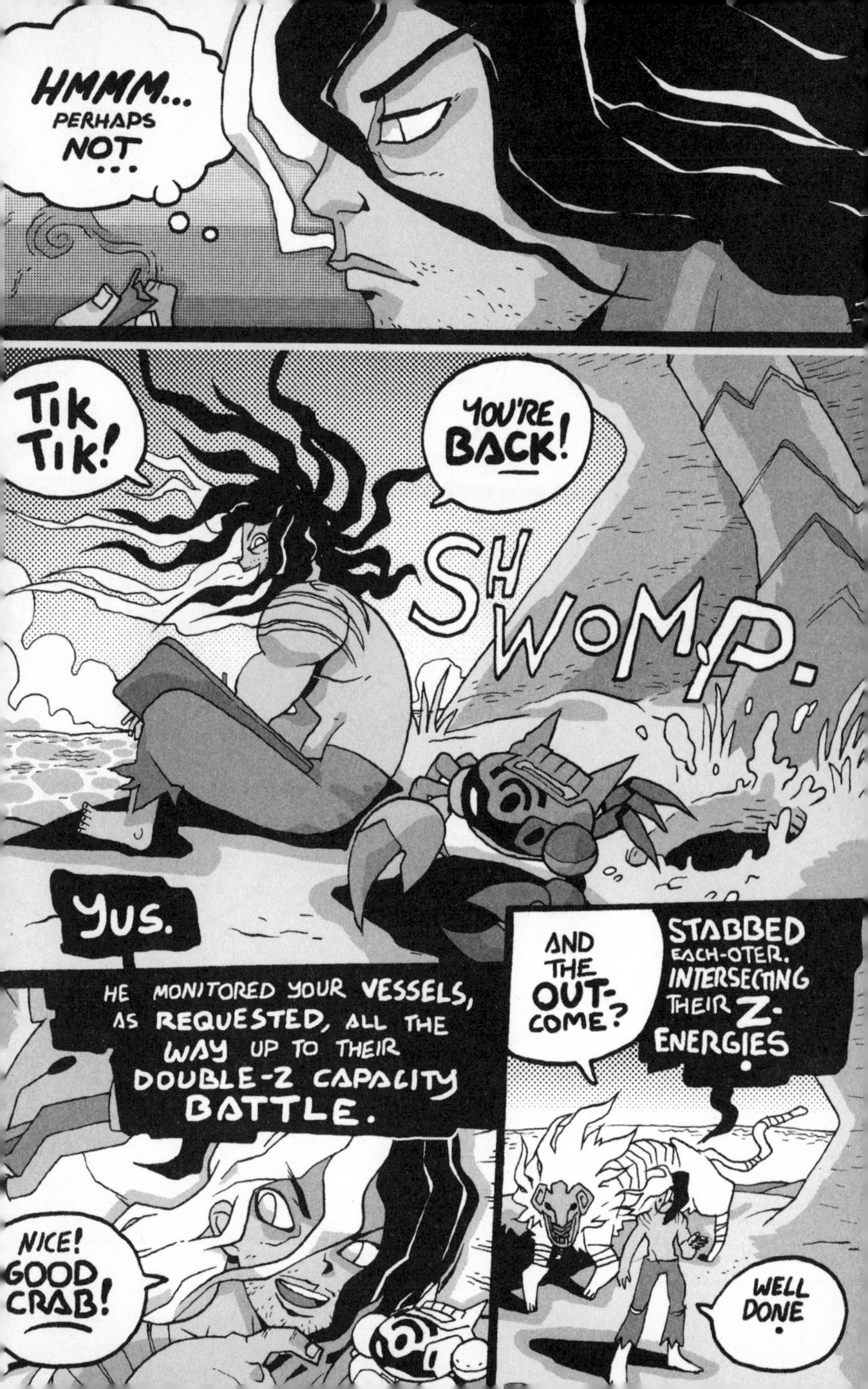
HMMM... PERHAPS NOT...
TIK TIK!
YOU'RE BACK!
SHWOMP.
YUS.
HE MONITORED YOUR VESSELS, AS REQUESTED, ALL THE WAY UP TO THEIR DOUBLE-Z CAPACITY BATTLE.
AND THE OUTCOME?
STABBED EACH-OTER. INTERSECTING THEIR Z-ENERGIES.
NICE! GOOD CRAB!
WELL DONE.

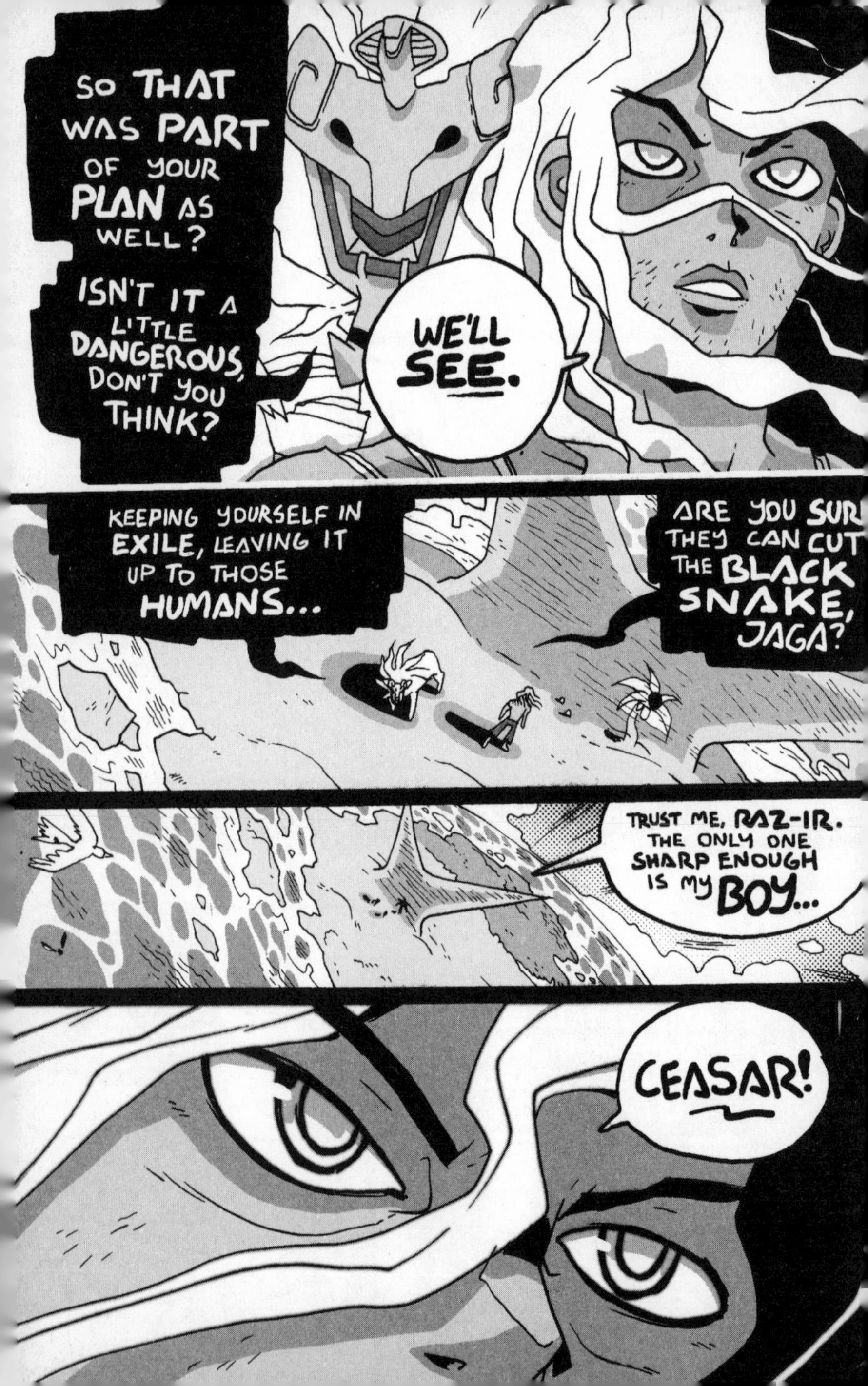
SO THAT WAS PART OF YOUR PLAN AS WELL?
ISN'T IT A LITTLE DANGEROUS, DON'T YOU THINK?
WE'LL SEE.
KEEPING YOURSELF IN EXILE, LEAVING IT UP TO THOSE HUMANS...
ARE YOU SUR THEY CAN CUT THE BLACK SNAKE, JAGA?
TRUST ME, RAZ-IR. THE ONLY ONE SHARP ENOUGH IS MY BOY...
CEASAR!

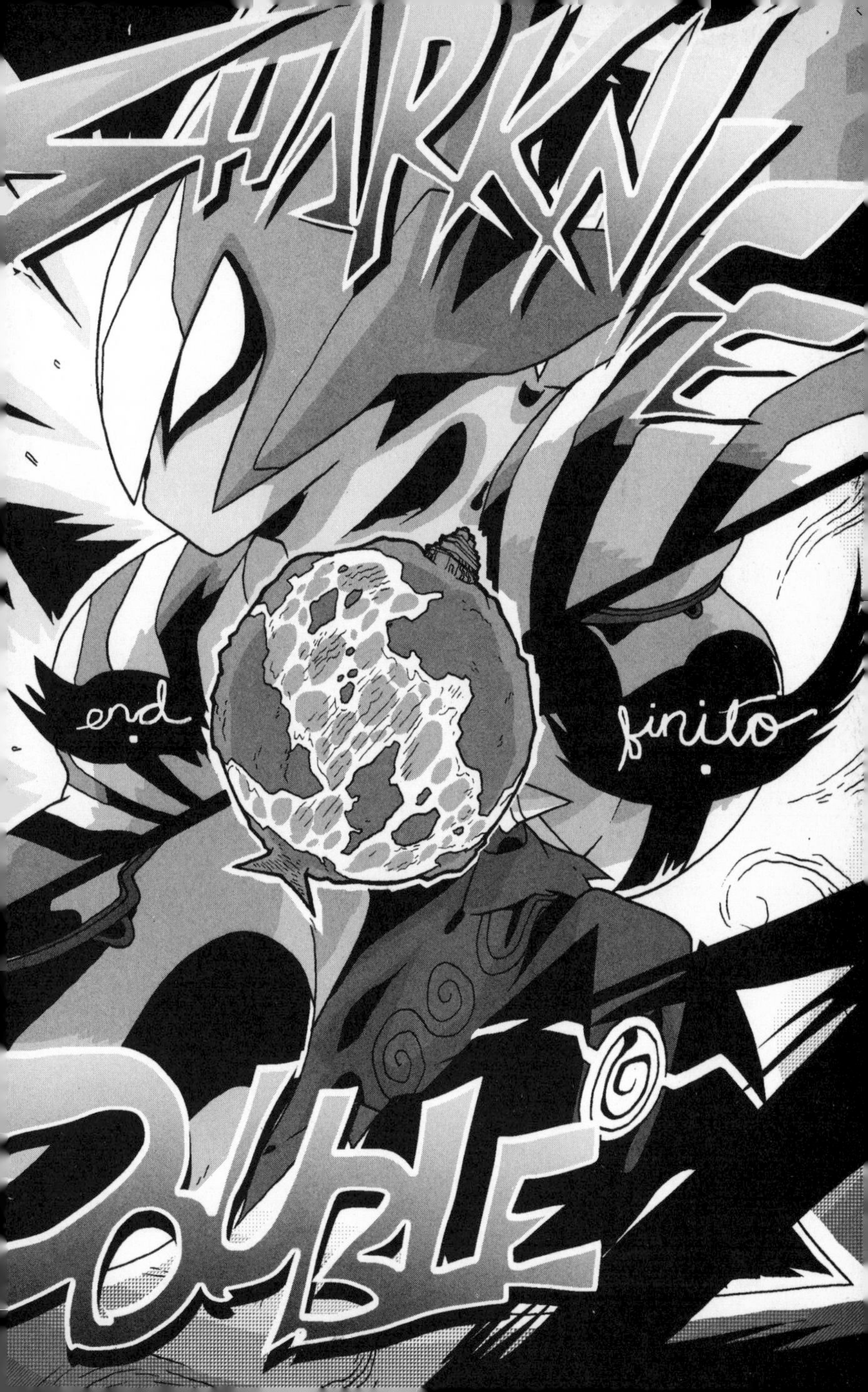
end.
finito.

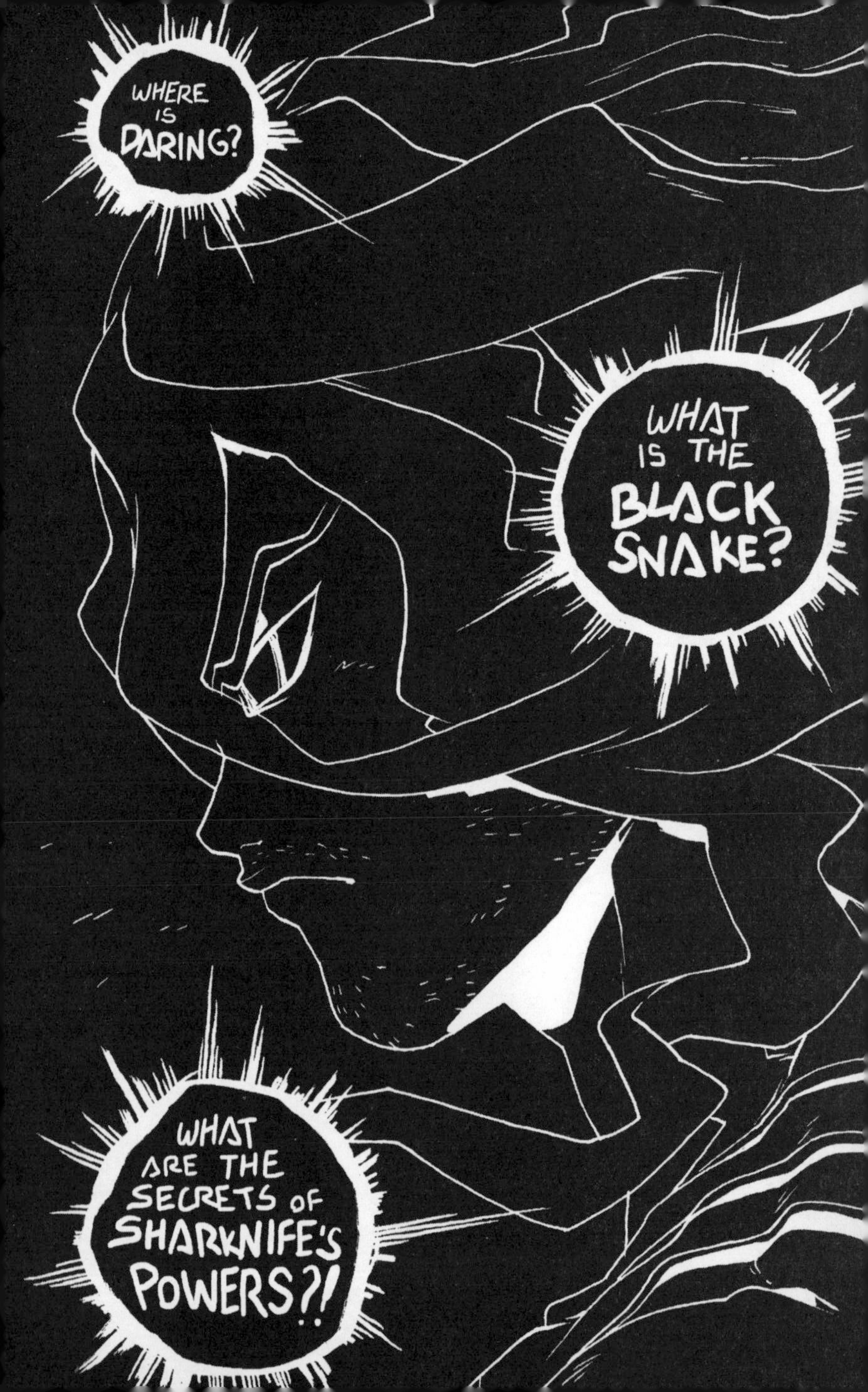
WHERE IS DARING?
WHAT IS THE BLACK SNAKE?
WHAT ARE THE SECRETS OF SHARKNIFE'S POWERS?!

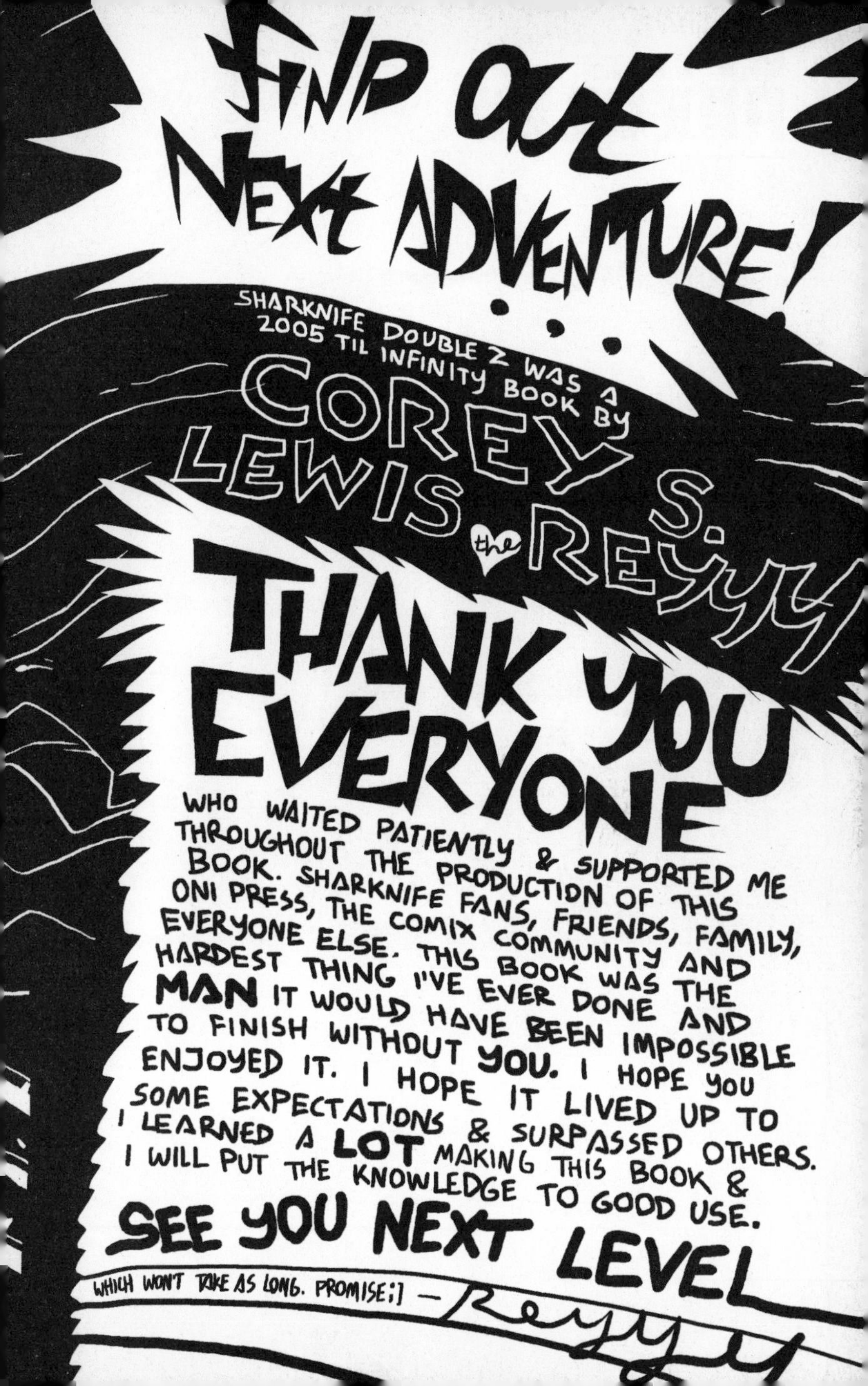
FIND OUT NEXT ADVENTURE!
...
SHARKNIFE DOUBLE Z WAS A 2005 TIL INFINITY BOOK BY
COREY S. LEWIS the REYYY
THANK YOU EVERYONE
WHO WAITED PATIENTLY & SUPPORTED ME THROUGHOUT THE PRODUCTION OF THIS BOOK. SHARKNIFE FANS, FRIENDS, FAMILY, ONI PRESS, THE COMIX COMMUNITY AND EVERYONE ELSE. THIS BOOK WAS THE HARDEST THING I'VE EVER DONE AND MAN IT WOULD HAVE BEEN IMPOSSIBLE TO FINISH WITHOUT YOU. I HOPE YOU ENJOYED IT. I HOPE IT LIVED UP TO SOME EXPECTATIONS & SURPASSED OTHERS. I LEARNED A LOT MAKING THIS BOOK & I WILL PUT THE KNOWLEDGE TO GOOD USE.
SEE YOU NEXT LEVEL
WHICH WON'T TAKE AS LONG. PROMISE ;] — Reyyy

NEW COMIX PREVIEW

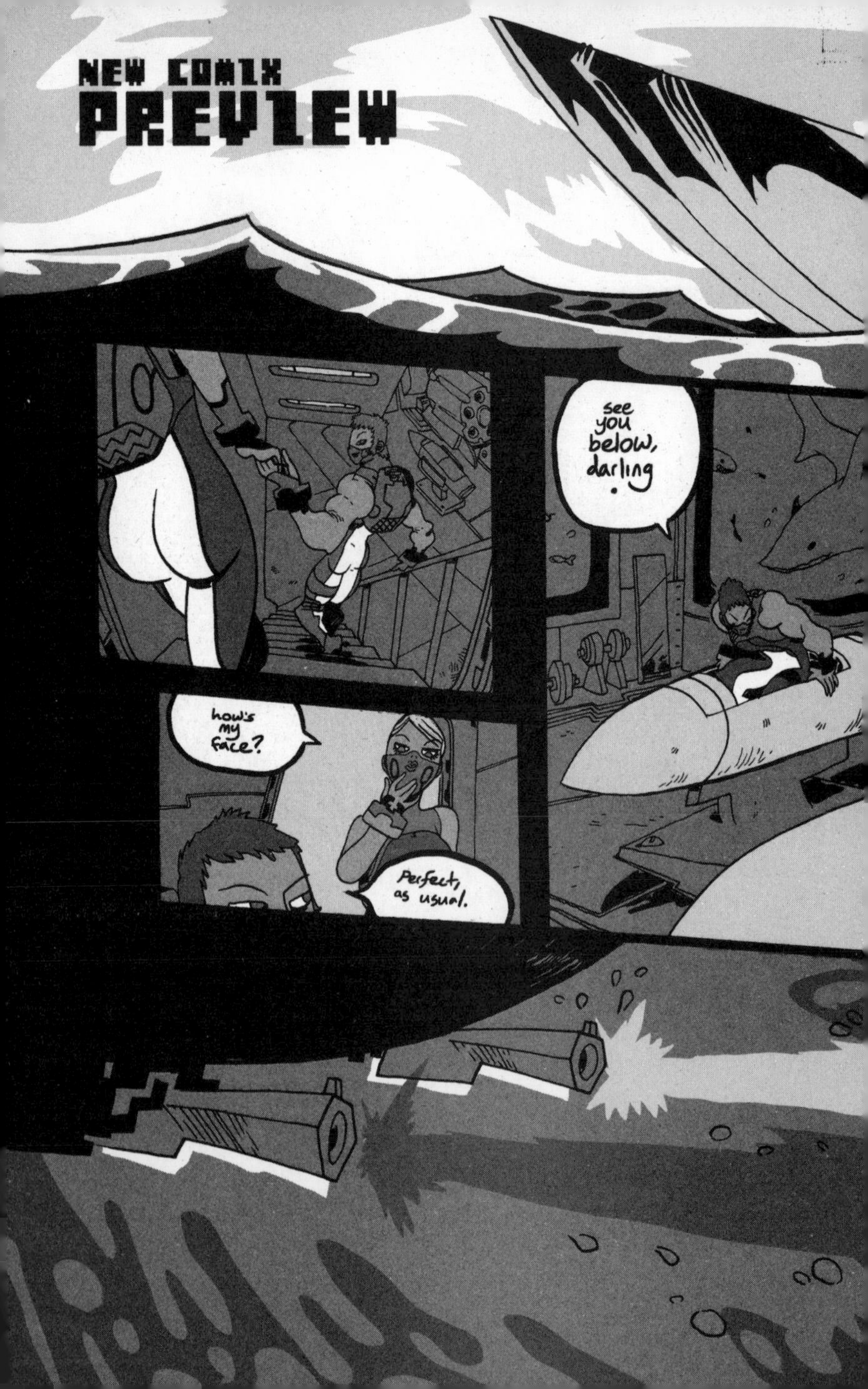

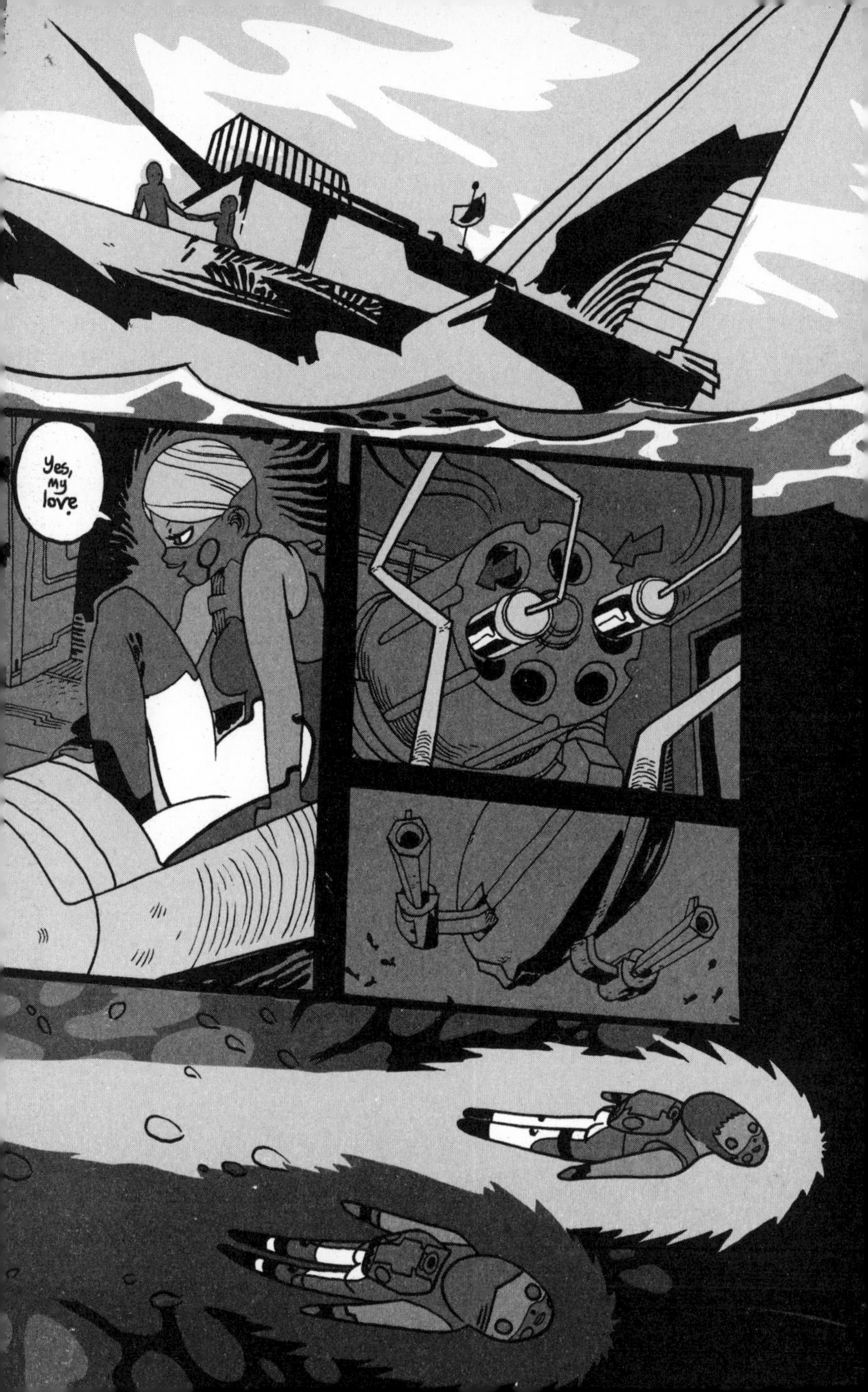
Yes, my love.

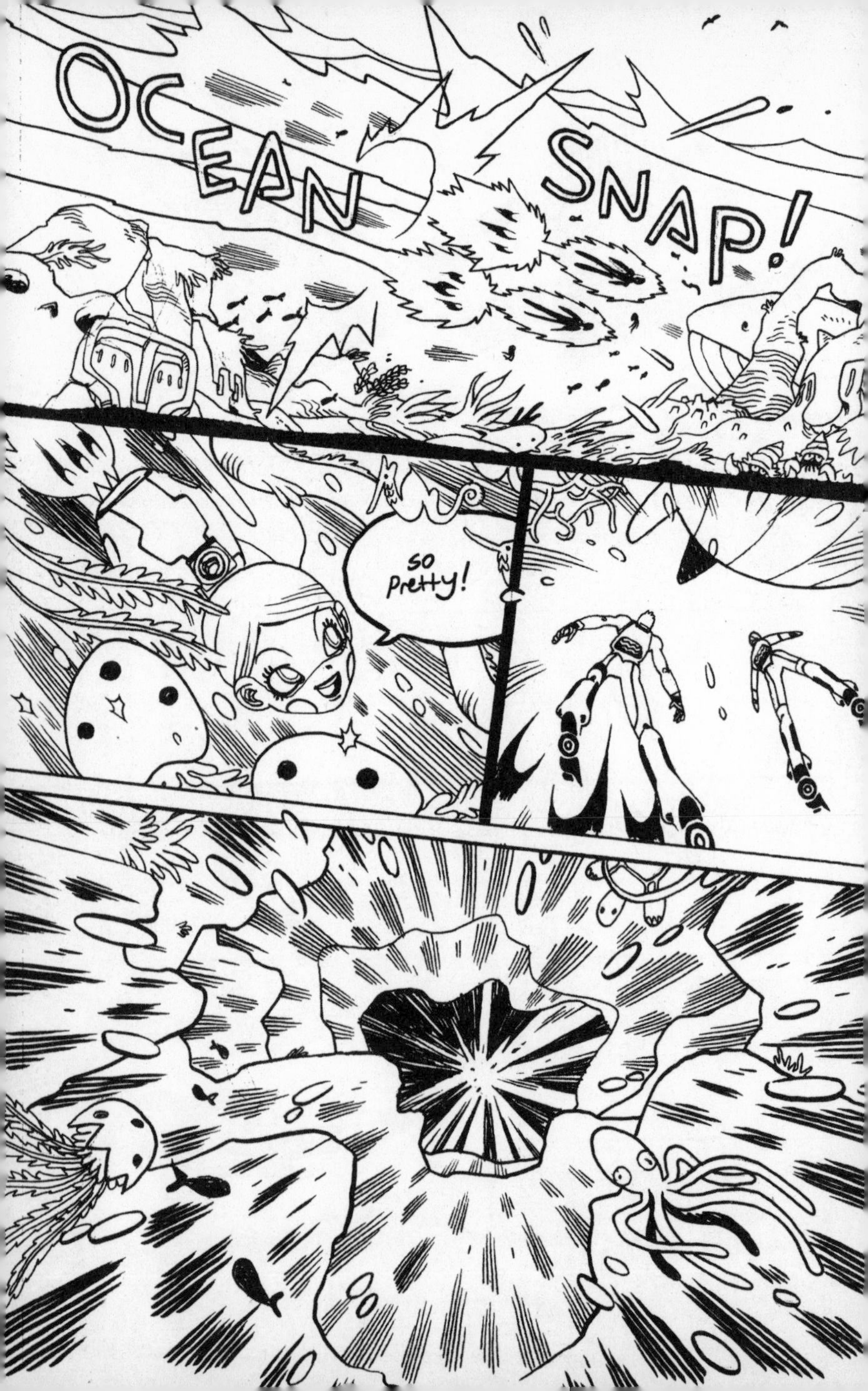
OCEAN SNAP!
so pretty!

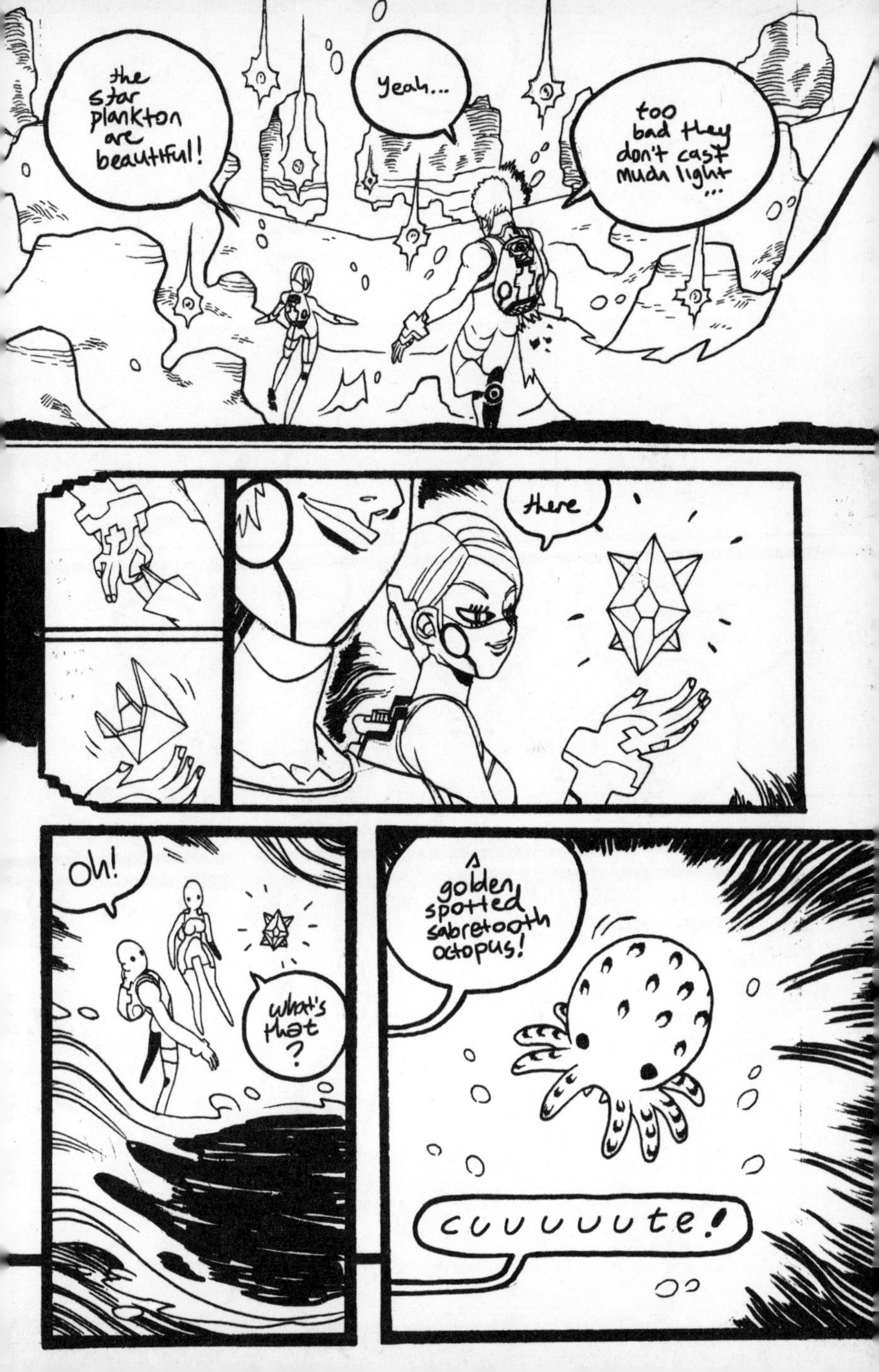

the star plankton are beautiful!
Yeah...
too bad they don't cast much light ...
there
oh!
what's that ?
a golden spotted sabretooth octopus!
cuuuuute!

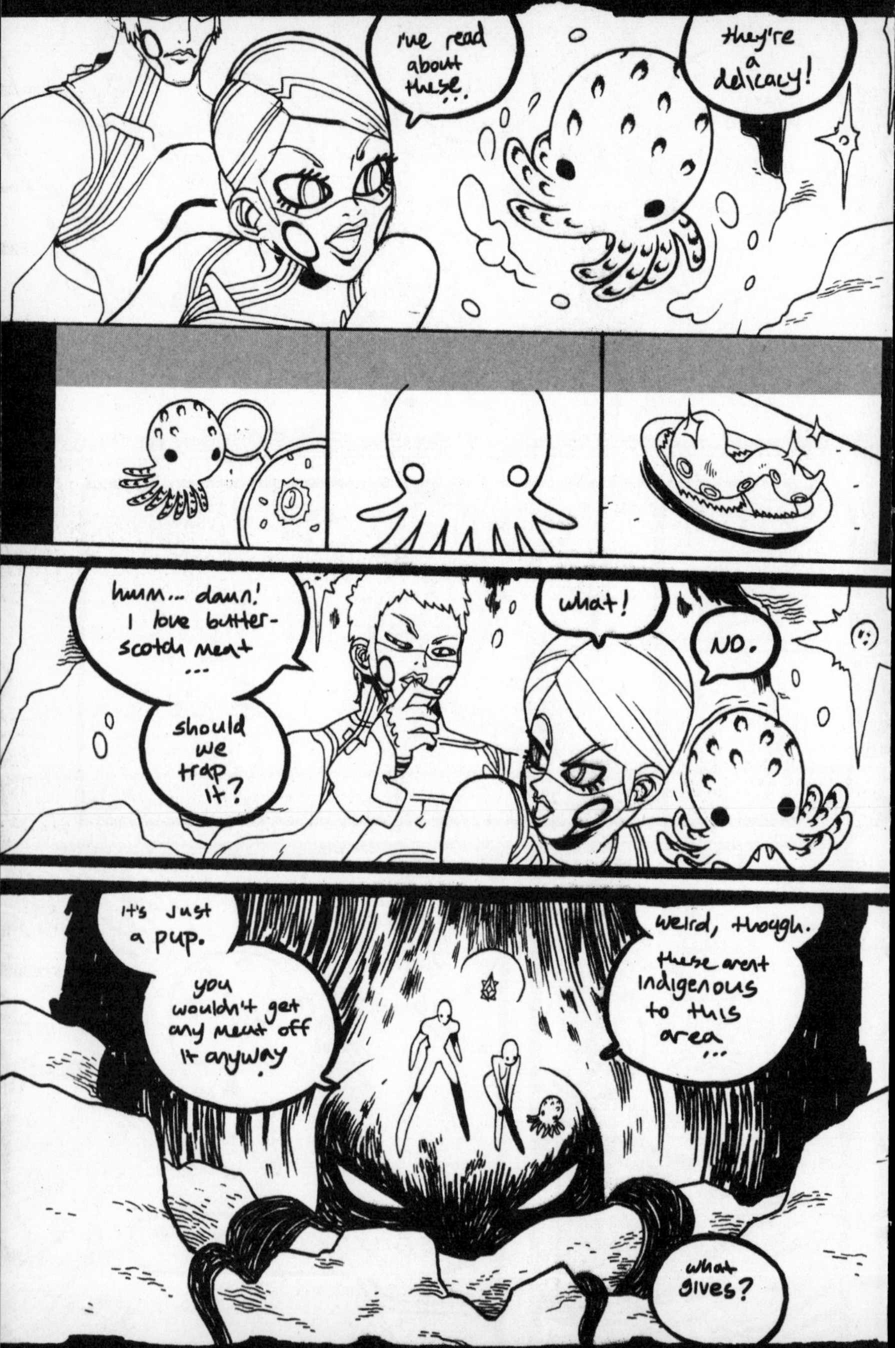
i've read about these...
they're a delicacy!
humm... damn! I love butter-scotch meat...
should we trap it?
what!
NO.
it's just a pup.
you wouldn't get any meat off it anyway.
weird, though.
these aren't indigenous to this area...
what gives?

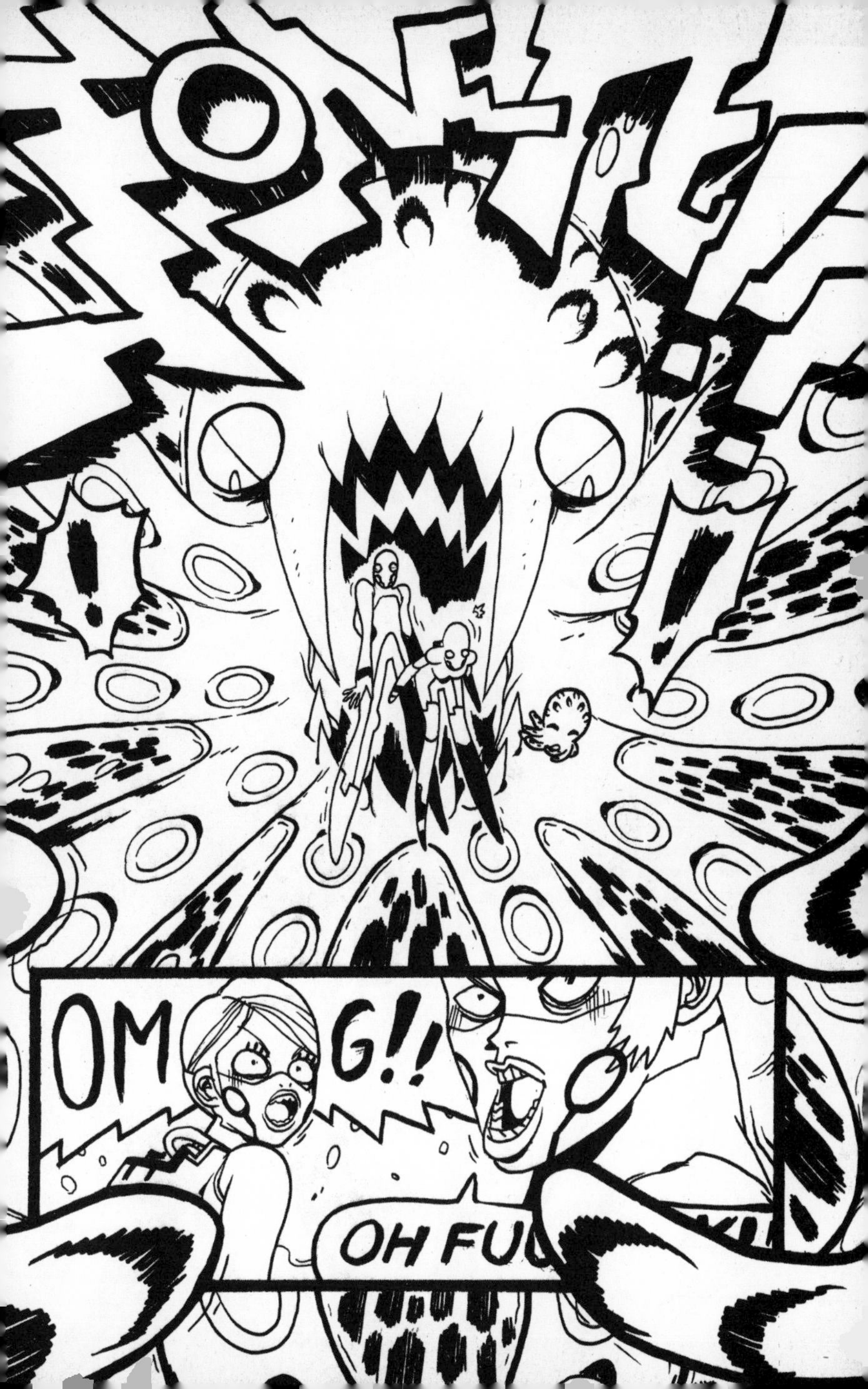
OMG!!
OH FU

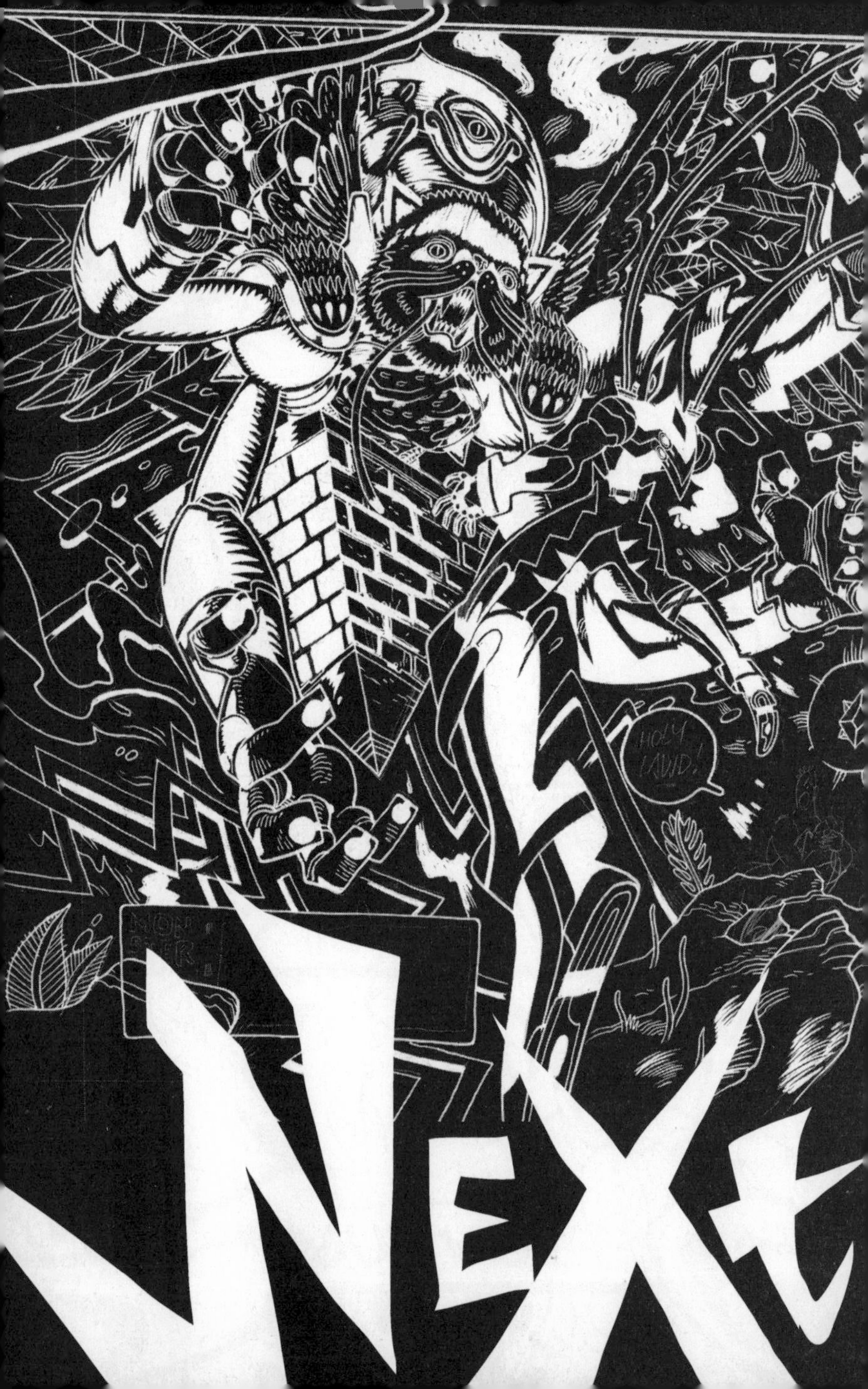

HOLY LAWD!
NEXT

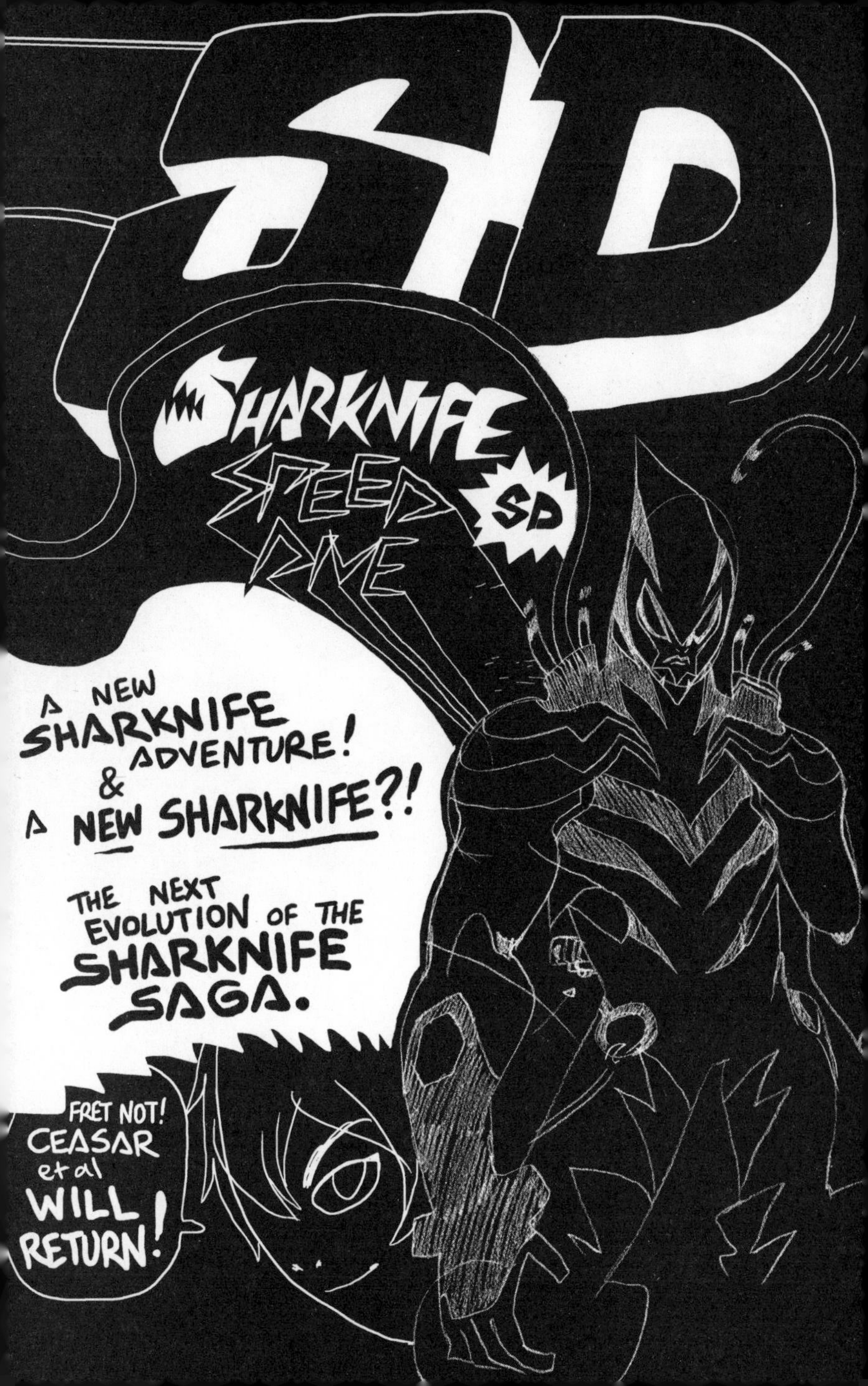
SD
SHARKNIFE
SPEED DIVE
SD
A NEW SHARKNIFE ADVENTURE!
& A NEW SHARKNIFE?!
THE NEXT EVOLUTION OF THE SHARKNIFE SAGA.
FRET NOT! CEASAR et al WILL RETURN!

NOW, SINCE YOU'VE ALL BEEN SUCH GOOD BOYS & GIRLS, A BONUS COMIC!

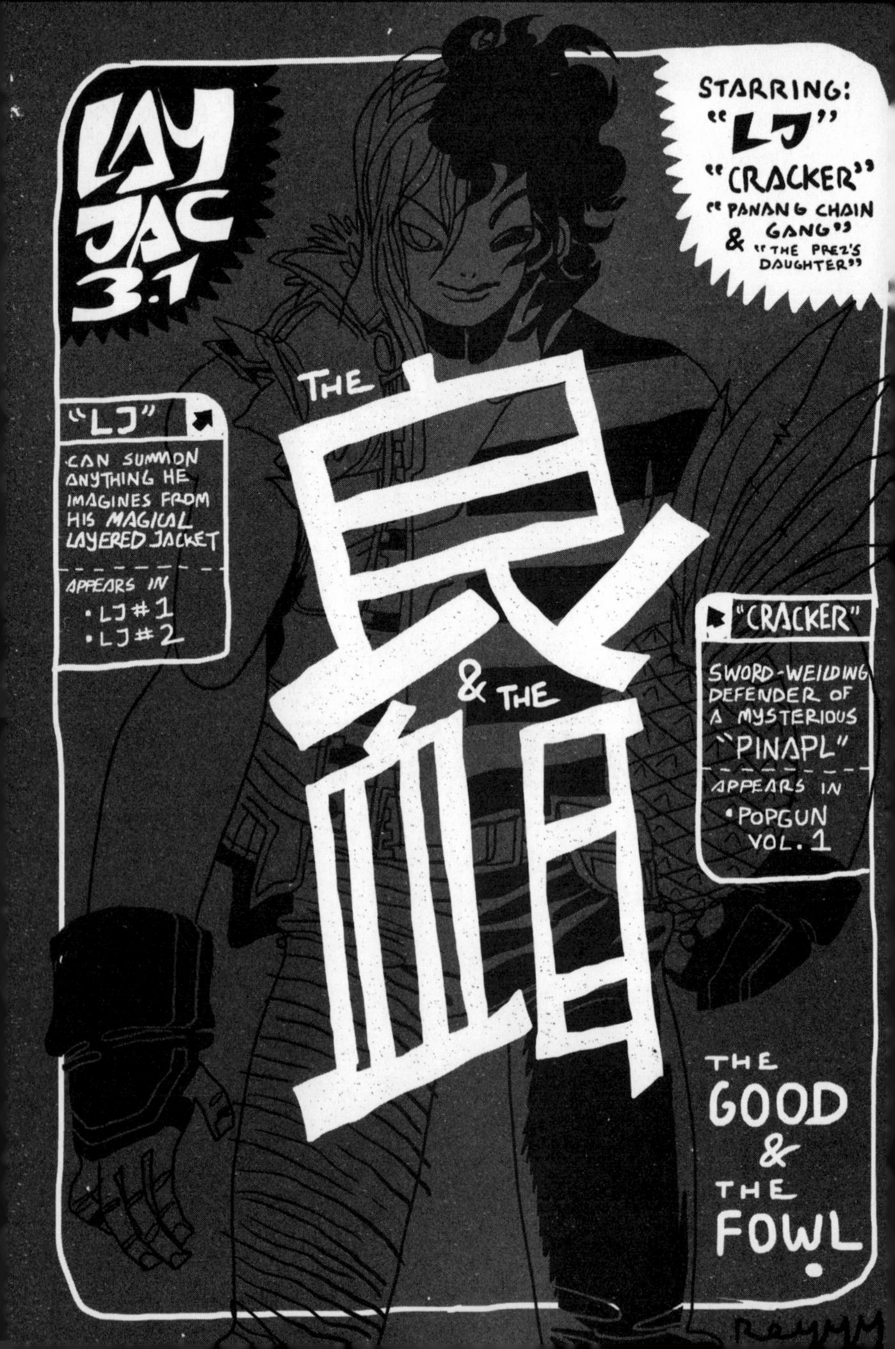

LAY JAC 3.1
STARRING: "LJ" "CRACKER" "PANANG CHAIN GANG" & "THE PREZ'S DAUGHTER"
"LJ"
CAN SUMMON ANYTHING HE IMAGINES FROM HIS MAGICAL LAYERED JACKET
APPEARS IN
• LJ #1
• LJ #2
THE 良 & THE
"CRACKER"
SWORD-WEILDING DEFENDER OF A MYSTERIOUS "PINAPL"
APPEARS IN
• POPGUN VOL. 1
THE GOOD & THE FOWL.
RAYMM

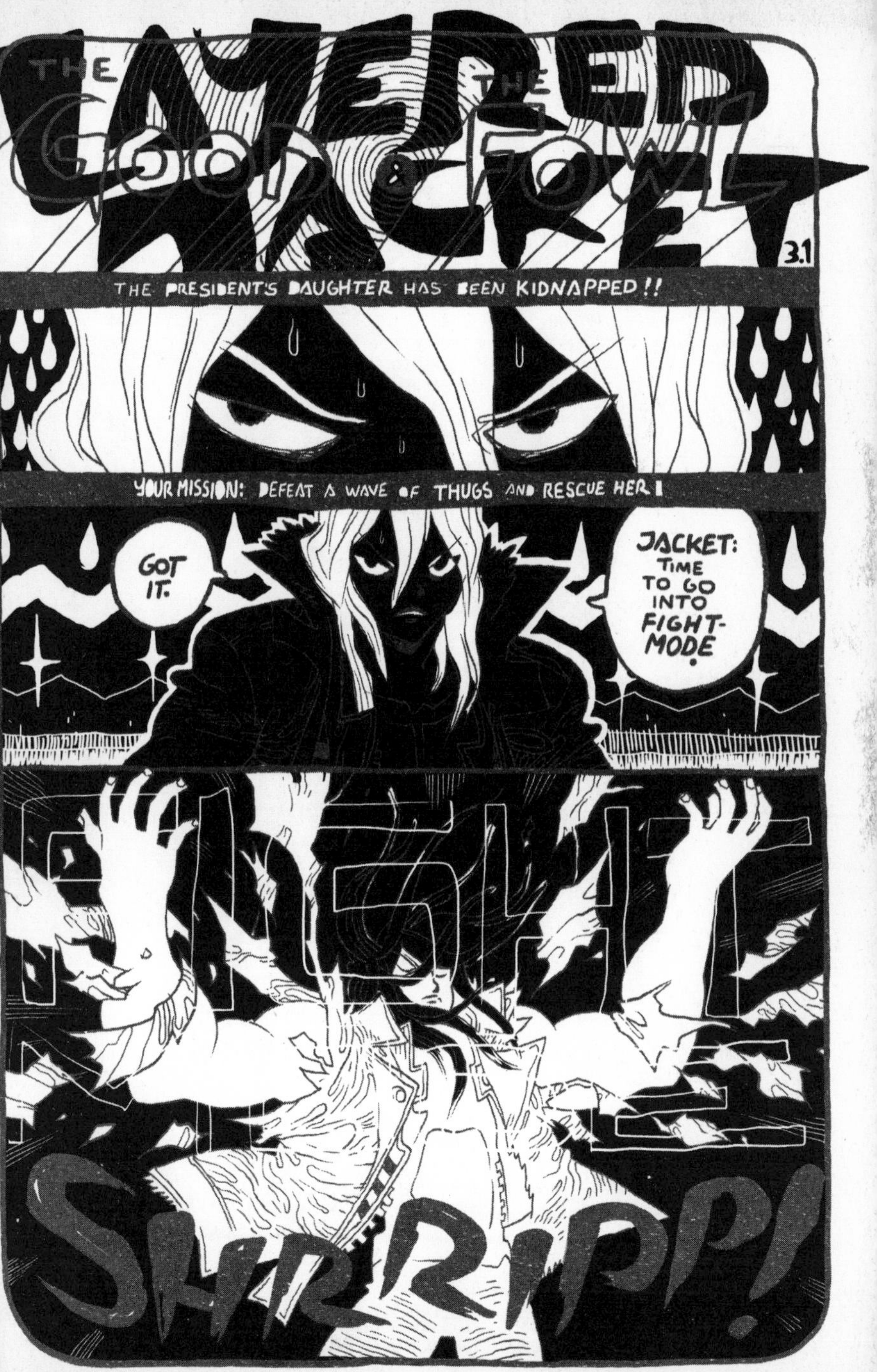
THE LAYERED JACKET
THE GOOD & THE FOWL
3.1
THE PRESIDENT'S DAUGHTER HAS BEEN KIDNAPPED!!
YOUR MISSION: DEFEAT A WAVE OF THUGS AND RESCUE HER!
GOT IT.
JACKET: TIME TO GO INTO FIGHT-MODE.
SHRRIPP!

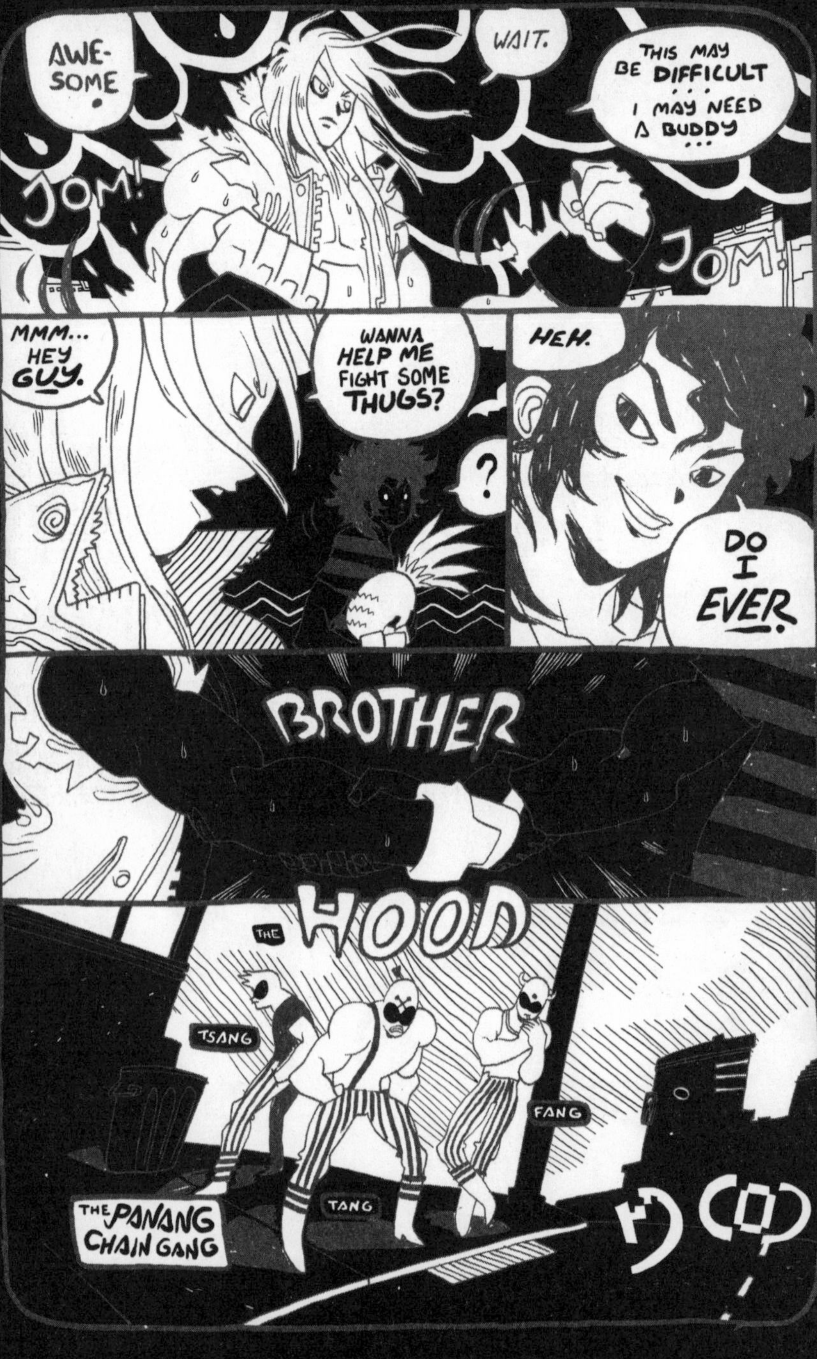
AWE-SOME.
WAIT.
THIS MAY BE DIFFICULT . . . I MAY NEED A BUDDY . . .
JOM!
JOM!
MMM... HEY GUY.
WANNA HELP ME FIGHT SOME THUGS?
?
HEH.
DO I EVER.
BROTHER
HOOD
THE
TSANG
FANG
TANG
THE PANANG CHAIN GANG

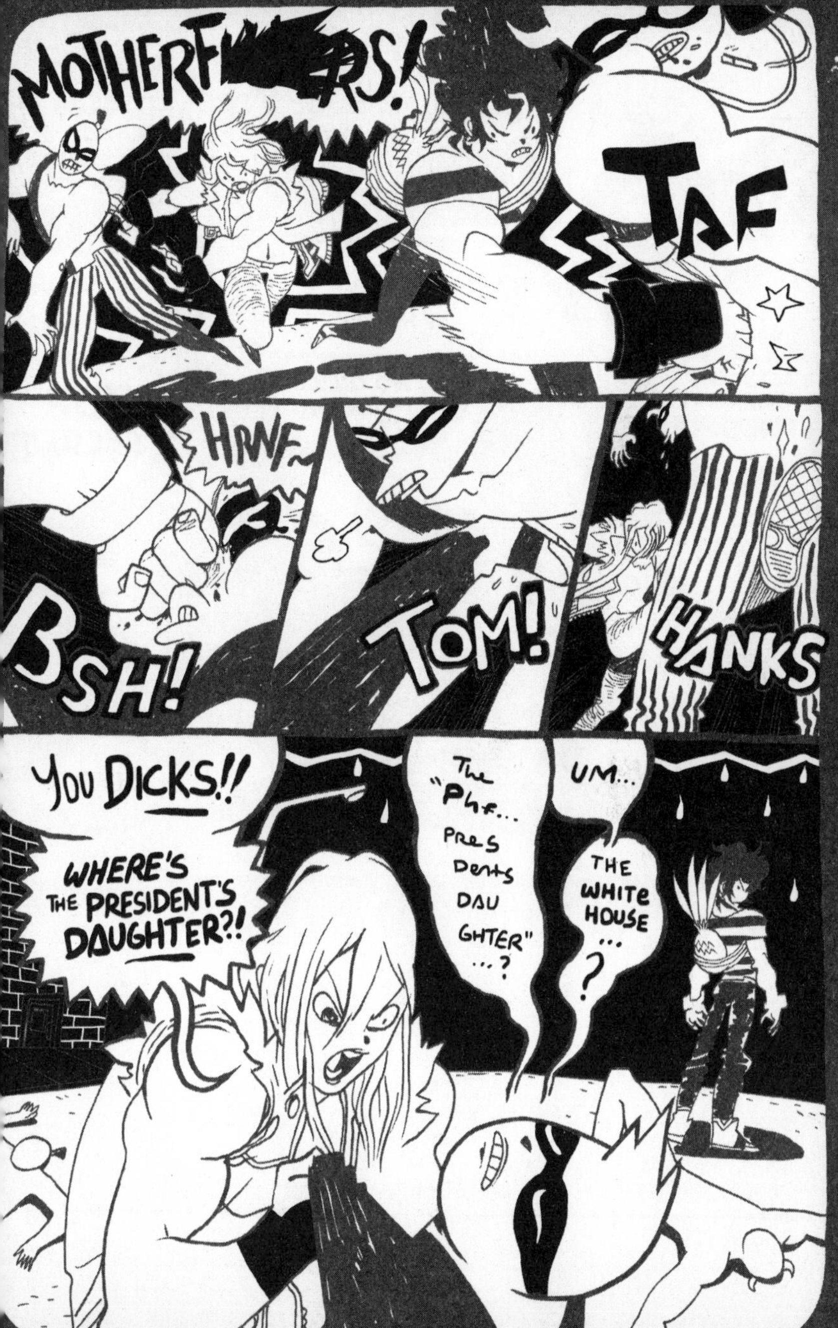

MOTHERF[redacted]RS!
TAF
HRNF~
BSH!
TOM!
HANKS
YOU DICKS!!
WHERE'S THE PRESIDENT'S DAUGHTER?!
The "Phf... PRES DENTS DAU GHTER" ...?
UM...
THE WHITE HOUSE ... ?

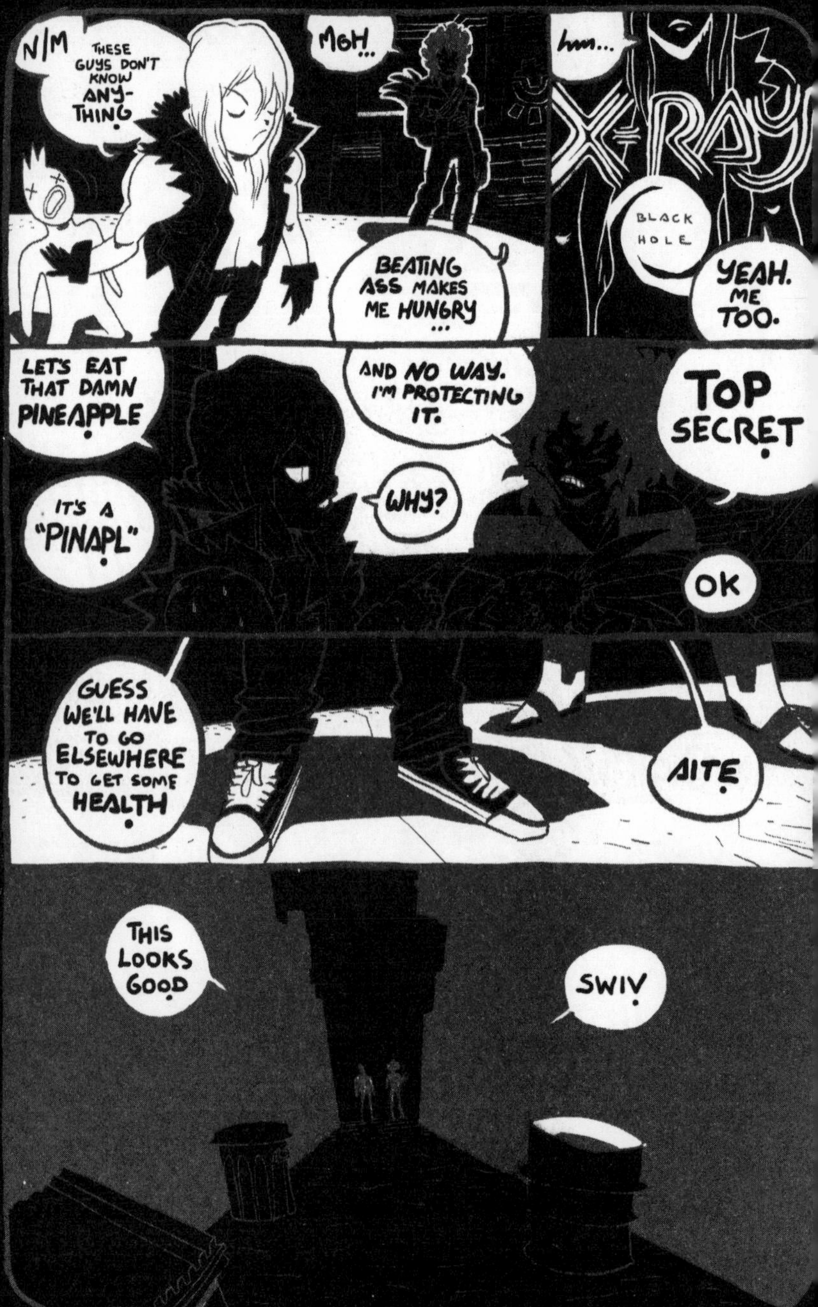
N/M THESE GUYS DON'T KNOW ANY-THING.
MoH...
BEATING ASS MAKES ME HUNGRY...
hm...
X-RAY
BLACK HOLE
YEAH. ME TOO.
LET'S EAT THAT DAMN PINEAPPLE.
AND NO WAY. I'M PROTECTING IT.
TOP SECRET.
WHY?
IT'S A "PINAPL".
OK
GUESS WE'LL HAVE TO GO ELSEWHERE TO GET SOME HEALTH.
AITE.
THIS LOOKS GOOD.
SWIV.

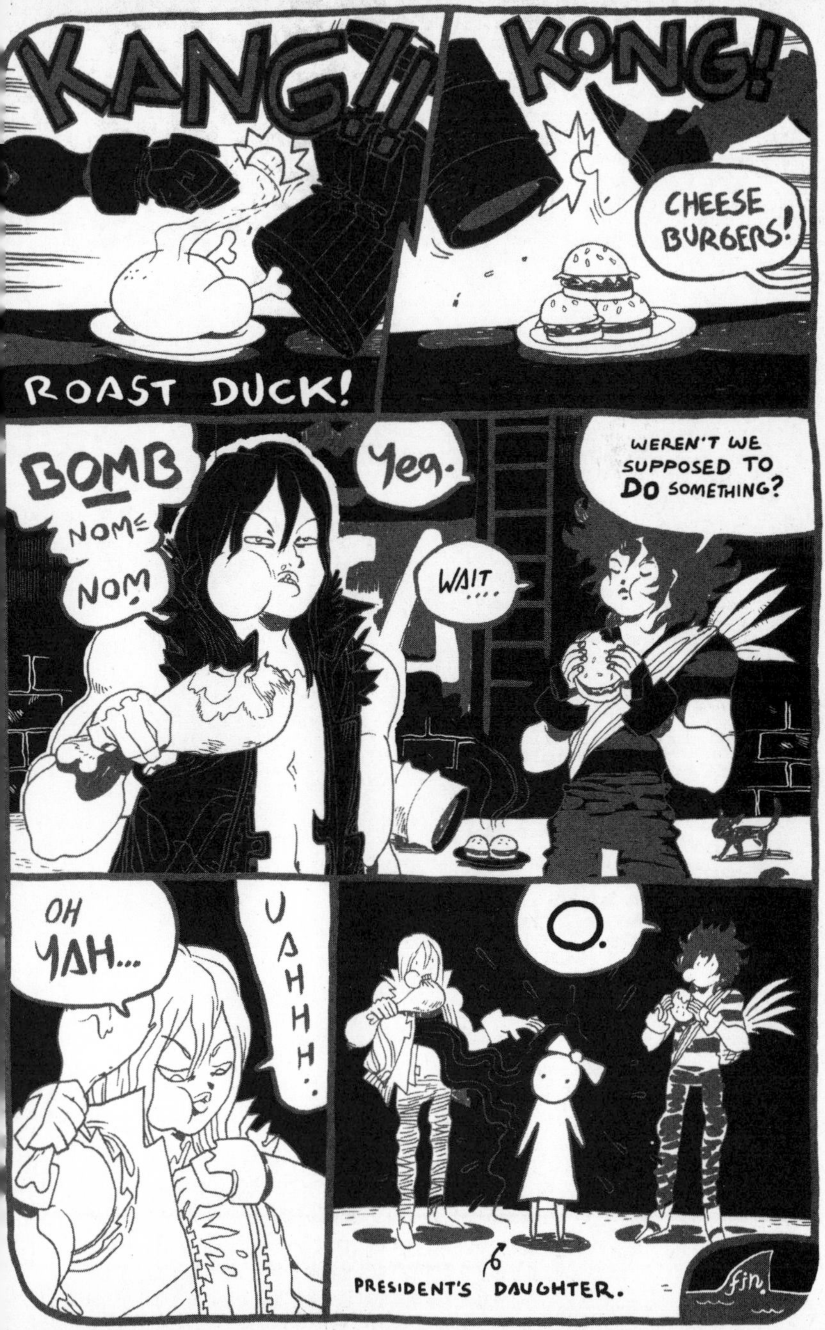
KANG!!!
KONG!
CHEESE BURGERS!
ROAST DUCK!
BOMB NOME NOM
Yeg.
WAIT....
WEREN'T WE SUPPOSED TO DO SOMETHING?
OH YAH...
UAHHHH.
O.
PRESIDENT'S DAUGHTER.
fin.

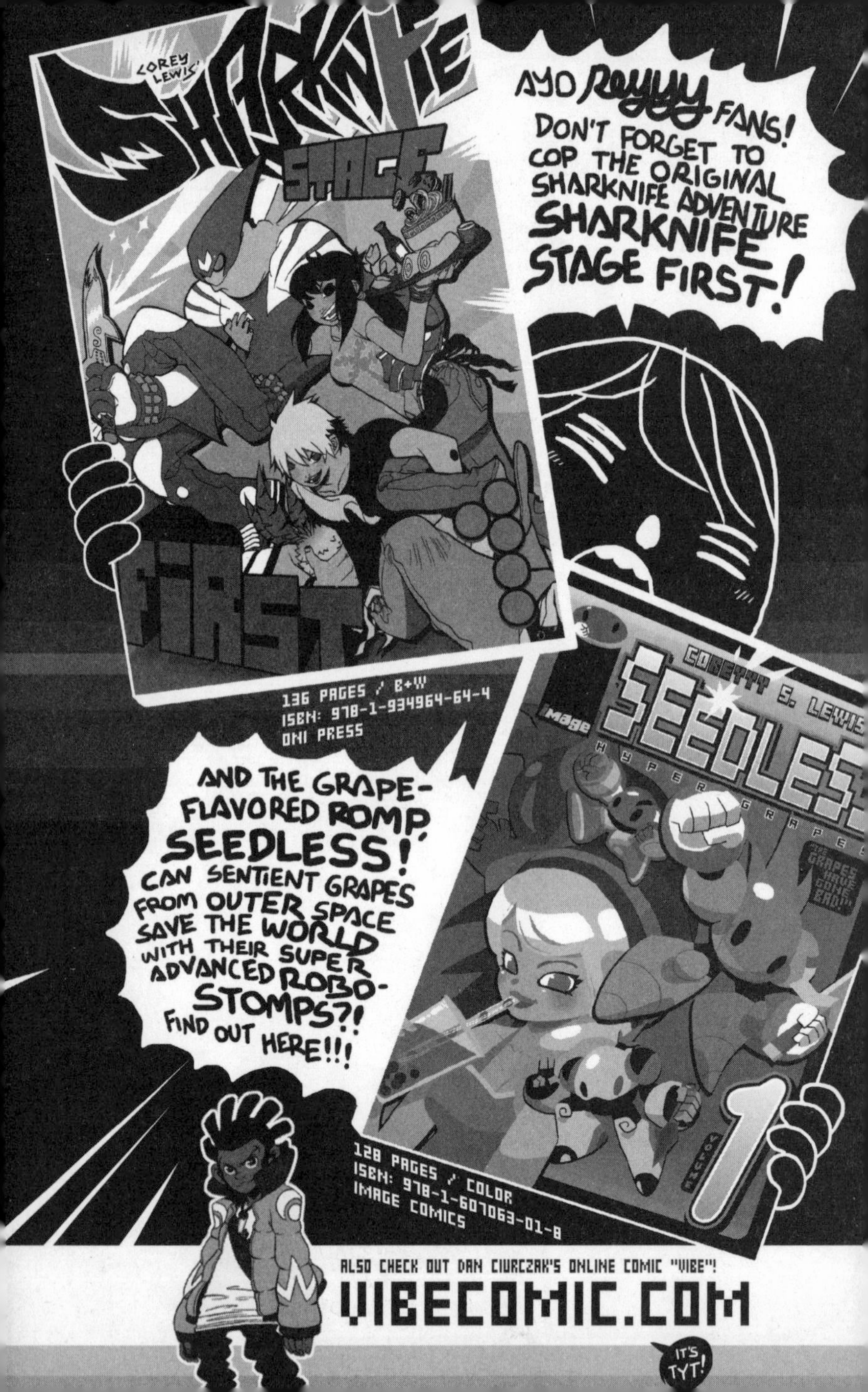

Corey Lewis'
SHARKNIFE
STAGE FIRST
AYO Reyyy FANS!
DON'T FORGET TO COP THE ORIGINAL SHARKNIFE ADVENTURE SHARKNIFE STAGE FIRST!
136 PAGES / B+W
ISBN: 978-1-934964-64-4
ONI PRESS
AND THE GRAPE-FLAVORED ROMP, SEEDLESS!
CAN SENTIENT GRAPES FROM OUTER SPACE SAVE THE WORLD WITH THEIR SUPER ADVANCED ROBO-STOMPS?! FIND OUT HERE!!!
image
COREYYY S. LEWIS
SEEDLESS
HYPER GRAPES
THE GRAPES HAVE GONE BAD!!
1
128 PAGES / COLOR
ISBN: 978-1-607063-01-8
IMAGE COMICS
ALSO CHECK OUT DAN CIURCZAK'S ONLINE COMIC "VIBE"!
VIBECOMIC.COM
IT'S TYT!

CHECK OUT THESE OTHER MIND-BENDING GRAPHIC NOVELS FROM ONI PRESS!

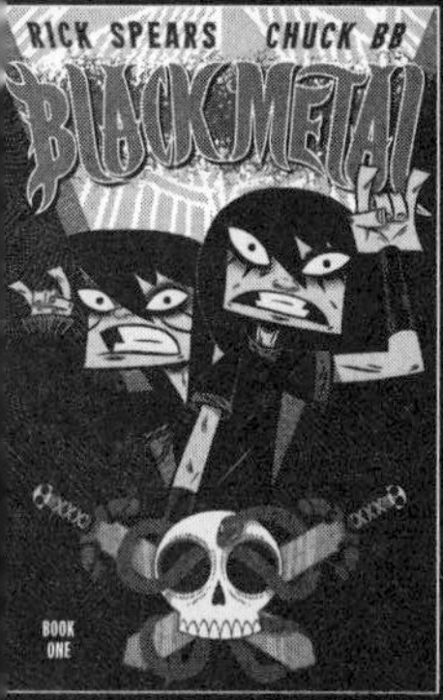
RICK SPEARS CHUCK BB
BLACK METAL
BOOK ONE

BLACK METAL, VOL. 1
Rick Spears & Chuck BB
160 pages · Digest
B&W · $11.99 US
ISBN 978-1-932664-69-0

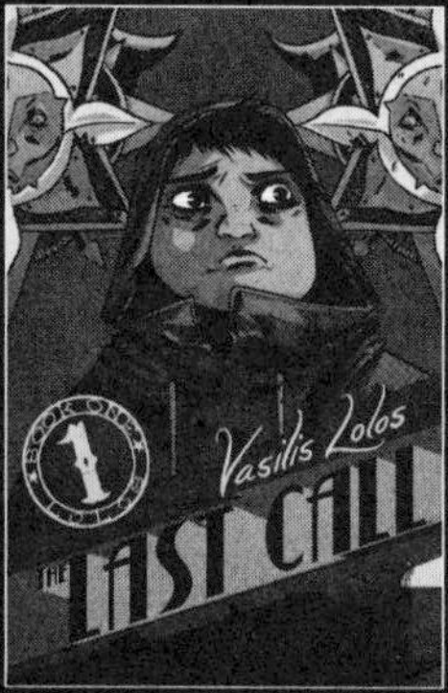
BOOK ONE
Vasilis Lolos
THE LAST CALL

LAST CALL, VOL. 1
Vasilis Lolos
136 pages · Digest
B&W · $11.95 US
ISBN 978-1-932664-69-0

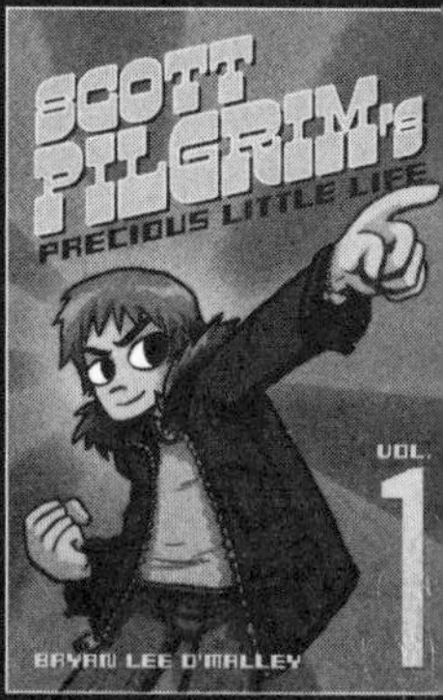
SCOTT PILGRIM'S
PRECIOUS LITTLE LIFE
VOL. 1
BRYAN LEE O'MALLEY

SCOTT PILGRIM, VOL. 1:
Bryan Lee O'Malley
168 pages · Digest
B&W · $11.99 US
ISBN 978-1-932664-08-9

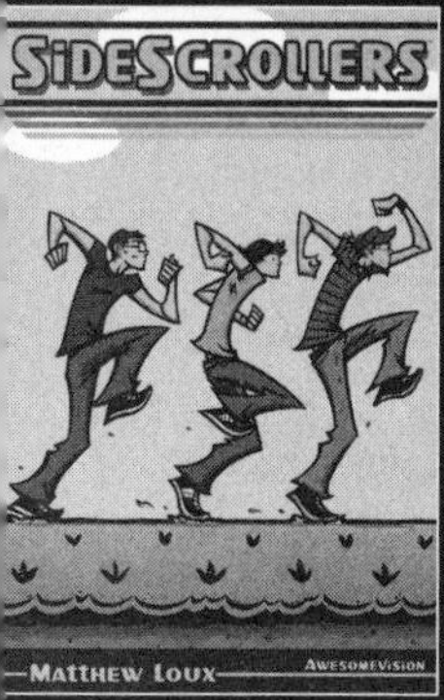
SIDESCROLLERS
MATTHEW LOUX
AWESOMEVISION

SIDESCROLLERS
Matthew Loux
216 pages · Digest
B&W · $11.99 US
ISBN 978-1-932664-50-8

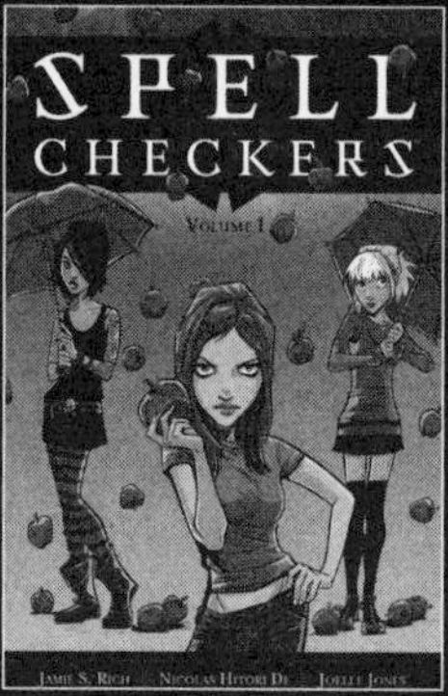
SPELL CHECKERS
VOLUME I
JAMIE S. RICH NICOLAS HITORI DE JOËLLE JONES

SPELL CHECKERS, VOL. 1
Jamie S. Rich, Nicolas Hitori De, Joëlle Jones
152 pages · Digest
B&W · $11.99 US
ISBN 978-1-934964-32-3

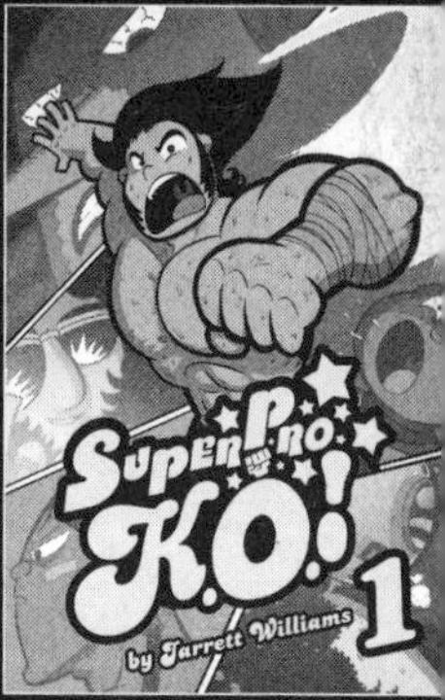
SuperPro K.O.! 1
by Jarrett Williams

SUPERPRO K.O., VOL. 1
Jarrett Williams
256 pages · Digest
B&W · $11.99 US
ISBN 978-1-934964-41-5

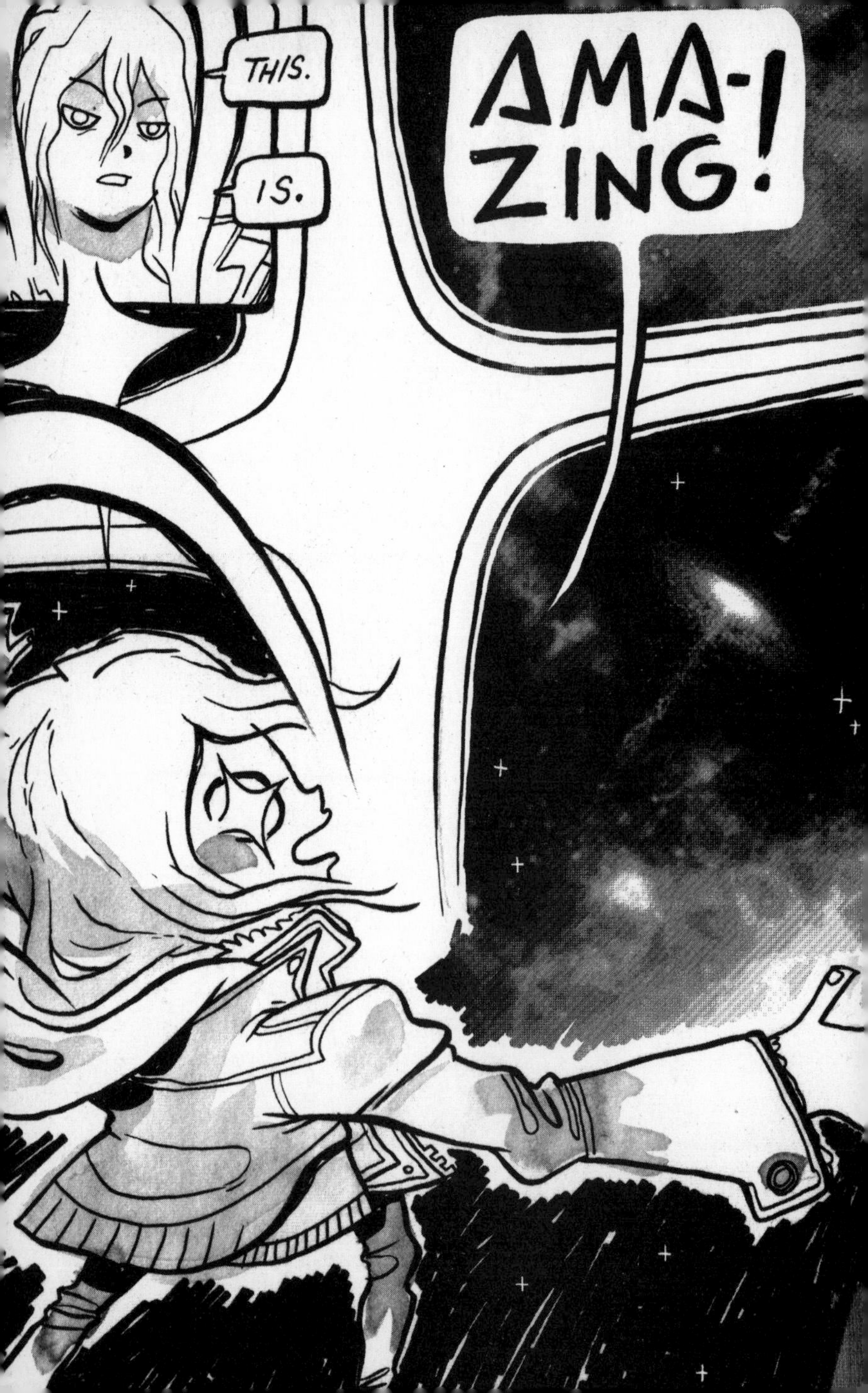
THIS.
IS.
AMA-ZING!